American Journalism and International Relations

Foreign Correspondence from the Early Republic to the Digital Era

American Journalism and International Relations argues that the American press's disengagement from world affairs has critical repercussions for American foreign policy. Giovanna Dell'Orto shows that discourses created, circulated, and maintained through the media mold opinions about the world and shape foreign policy parameters.

This book is a history of U.S. foreign correspondence from the 1840s to the present, relying on more than 2,000 news articles and twenty major world events, from the 1848 European revolutions to the Mumbai terror attacks in 2008. Americans' perceptions of other nations, combined with pervasive and enduring understandings of the United States' role in global politics, act as constraints on policies. Dell'Orto finds that reductive media discourse (as seen during the 1967 war in the Middle East or Afghanistan in the 1980s) has a negative effect on policy, whereas correspondence grounded in events (such as during the Japanese attack on Shanghai in the 1930s or the dissolution of the Soviet Union in 1991) fosters effective leadership and realistic assessments.

Giovanna Dell'Orto is assistant professor in the School of Journalism and Mass Communication at the University of Minnesota, where she received her PhD in 2004. She was a reporter for the Associated Press in three U.S. states and Italy. She is the author of *The Hidden Power of the American Dream: Why Europe's Shaken Confidence in the United States Threatens the Future of U.S. Influence* (2008) and *Giving Meanings to the World: The First U.S. Foreign Correspondents, 1838–1859* (2002) and coauthor (with Hazel Dicken-Garcia) of *Hated Ideas and the American Civil War Press* (2008).

For my family, my love, and for all the foreign correspondents who lost their lives while trying to shine a small light on world affairs

American Journalism and International Relations

Foreign Correspondence from the Early Republic to the Digital Era

GIOVANNA DELL'ORTO
University of Minnesota

CAMBRIDGE
UNIVERSITY PRESS

32 Avenue of the Americas, New York NY 10013-2473, USA

Cambridge University Press is part of the University of Cambridge.

It furthers the University's mission by disseminating knowledge in the pursuit of education, learning and research at the highest international levels of excellence.

www.cambridge.org
Information on this title: www.cambridge.org/9781107448599

First published 2013
First paperback edition 2014

A catalogue record for this publication is available from the British Library

Library of Congress Cataloguing in Publication data

Dell'Orto, Giovanna, 1977–
American journalism and international relations : foreign correspondence from the early republic to the digital era / Giovanna Dell'Orto, University of Minnesota. – First edition.
pages cm
Includes bibliographical references.
ISBN 978-1-107-03195-1 (hardback)
1. Foreign news – United States – History. 2. Journalism – Political aspects – United States. 3. Press and politics – United States – History. 4. Foreign correspondents – United States – History. I. Title.
PN4888.F69D445 2013
070.4′3320973–dc23 2012042737

ISBN 978-1-107-03195-1 Hardback
ISBN 978-1-107-44859-9 Paperback

Contents

Acknowledgments *page* vii

1. Introduction: The American Press and International Relations 1
   A Constructivist Perspective on IR, Communication, and Journalism 3
   Constructing International Affairs 3
   Constructing Communication 9
   Constructing Foreign Correspondence 19
   Studying the Construction of the World through Foreign Correspondence 25
   Conclusions 31
2. A New Country, A New Profession: America and Its Foreign Correspondents Get Ready to Take on the World 34
   Journalism's Professionalization: Nineteenth-Century Writers and Readers 35
   Getting Entangled: U.S. Foreign Relations in the Nineteenth Century 40
   America Covers the World: Nineteenth-Century Media Discourses 43
   Conclusions 64
3. America Takes Global Center Stage: The Ascent of a Political and Communication Power 67
   The Power of the Press: Taking on the World, in the Public's Interest 68
   Taking the Lead: American Policy Goes Global 74
   America Covers the World: Media Discourses in the World Wars Era 77
   Conclusions 106

4. The Media Are American in the American Century: The Apex of American Political and Communication Power 109
The Bulldog: U.S. Journalism Tackles the Cold War 110
From a Bipolar to a Unipolar World: Winning the Cold War 117
America Covers the World: Media Discourses in the Cold War 121
Conclusions 153

5. A Web of Disentanglements: American Policy and Media Struggle to Engage the Post–Cold War World 157
Clicks for All: U.S. Journalism Stumbles into the Twenty-First Century 159
Redefining Power: Global Leadership in the Twenty-First Century? 165
America Covers the World: Post–Cold War Media Discourses 170
Conclusions 201

6. The Importance of Being There and Making People Care: The Troubled Present and Possible Futures of U.S. Foreign Correspondence 204
Can the Market Save the Marketplace of Ideas? Possible Futures of Journalism 206
Staying Power: Possible Futures of Foreign Correspondence 215
It's What We're Here For: U.S. News Leaders Protect Foreign Reporting 221
"Pretty Bloody Crucial": International Correspondence Strategies Abroad 227
Conclusions 232

7. Conclusion: Reaffirming Journalism's Role in World Affairs 235
The Discursive Role of Media in International Relations 238
Evolving Media Discourses of the World 243
Evolving Foreign Policy Paradigms 248
Foreign Correspondence and World Affairs 251
Conclusion: The Irreplaceable Mediator in Danger 255

Bibliography 259
Index 279

Acknowledgments

Over a decade, three institutions have been the principal shapers and nurturers of my research in the role of the news media in global affairs: The University of Minnesota, the Associated Press, and Johns Hopkins University's School of Advanced International Studies (SAIS), Bologna Center.

No scholar could ask for better intellectual or logistical support than I have received, as both student and faculty, from the University of Minnesota's School of Journalism and Mass Communication (SJMC) under the enlightened leadership of Albert R. Tims. To Raymond D. Duvall, chair of the Department of Political Science, I am most grateful for essential guidance. My research has benefited from conversations with more colleagues and students at the university than I could list, beginning with my mentor in all things historical, Hazel Dicken-Garcia, while the unflappable staff at SJMC and university libraries made unearthing two centuries of newspaper stories a smooth process. To the newsmen and women of the Associated Press, of which I was one, I am thankful for standing for the enduring values of professional journalism – a global, not-for-profit wire service has a special responsibility to uncover news in the public interest beyond the vagaries of the public's interests. The reporters, editors, photographers, and managers I worked with in Minneapolis, Rome (Italy), Phoenix, and Atlanta deserve special mention. Without the tireless and cheerful help of Valerie Komor and Francesca Pitaro at archives in AP's New York headquarters, this book would be missing a critical mass of its historical sources. Finally, SAIS, particularly through mentors like Marco Cesa and director Kenneth Keller, provided fertile ground for bridging scholarship and foreign policy practice.

Any major research project can only become a meaningful book through enthusiastic encouragement and careful corralling by a committed editor – I am greatly indebted to Robert Dreesen at Cambridge University Press, aided by Abigail Zorbaugh and the reviewers. I am also thankful to colleagues who made suggestions at conferences of the International Studies Association, International Communication Association, American Journalism Historians Association, and International Association for Media and Communication Research, as well as the Symposium on the 19th Century Press, the Civil War, and Free Expression and the American Journalism Historians Association and Association for Education in Journalism and Mass Communication History Division joint spring meeting. In particular, Ken Rogerson and Michael Sweeney raised vital points that critically strengthened and broadened this book's arguments.

To the following journalists, I am grateful not only for graciously agreeing to lengthy interviews but also for their commitment to the future of foreign news: Heather Allan, John Bussey, Chen Weihua, John Daniszewski, Malcolm Downing, Paul Eedle, Alain Frachon, Charles Hanley, Larry Heinzerling, David E. Hoffman, Charles Hutzler, Patrick Jarreau, Peter Osnos, Dan Perry, Mark Porubcansky, Harriet Sherwood, Alvin Shuster, and Greg Winter.

While many scholars and executives wring hands over the business of new news media, a few dedicated correspondents continue to risk their lives to make some tiny addition to our collective knowledge of the world. I dedicate this book to all foreign correspondents who died for the belief that understanding should inform our actions. And, of course, I also dedicate it to my family. Most simply, without my parents, Dario Dell'Orto and Paola Casella Dell'Orto, nothing would be.

I

Introduction

The American Press and International Relations

From the time when getting foreign news meant rowing a boat to catch the packet of newspapers thrown overboard as ships were docking from their Atlantic crossing, to today's anywhere/anytime niche delivery on smartphones, one aspect of international mass communication has not changed: It remains an essential locus for the creation, definition and transformation of the power relationships that lie at the heart of international affairs. It is impossible to understand how nations interact without taking into account what images they form of one another – largely through the mass media – and what consequent expectations they bring to their relations.

This book argues that the press has been a crucial factor – an irreplaceable mediator – in international affairs, historically and currently, by functioning as the public arena where meanings for things literally foreign become understandable realities that, in turn, serve as the basis for policy and action. This new model of the nexus between news and foreign policy is needed to take us beyond traditional analyses that have the media either deviously driving or blindly following foreign policymakers. Rather, the focus here is on how the news media shape, for better or for worse, our basic understanding of what the world beyond our borders is like. This argument is tested through extensive original historical research that answers two fundamental questions: What images of the world outside the United States have American news media helped create? How have those images in news coverage interacted with U.S. foreign policy? In turn, those questions raise two more normative ones that the book also addresses: What should the American press do to better cover the world? What might the future hold for American foreign correspondence?

The very visible role of some foreign correspondents and major international news organizations in the conduct of international affairs is the most studied manifestation of the inextricable link between international mass communication and international politics. The most recent, comprehensive history of American foreign correspondence focuses on those kinds of spectacular interactions.[1] Examples abound in this research as well: Cuban rebels and Spanish leaders both addressed Americans directly in interviews reproduced verbatim in the *New York Times* before the Spanish-American War of 1898, and the Spaniards castigated the public's sway over Congress. When Mikhail Gorbachev signed his resignation in 1991, thus penning "the end" to the Cold War, he did so with a Montblanc borrowed from the president of CNN. From the same perspective and the other end of the power spectrum, studies of developing countries have often faulted Western-centric media for perpetuating dependency and imperialistic practices through distorted direction, content and sheer quantity of news flow.

But the vital importance of the press – and today's multiplatform news media – in international relations does not stop at who writes what about whom from where (and in what language and on whose behalf). Important as the flow of information is, it does not explain the essential role that communication plays in international relations at the most visceral level. Assuming that there can be no effective power unless it is buttressed by the perception of it, this book shows that the "translation" of meanings – of national identities, and intentions, across boundaries – is the inevitable and, ethically, most affecting core of international communication. The press matters in global affairs because the images of national identities it helps create and negotiate influence expectations and consequently policies.

Today, the battle for the soul of journalism is being played out just as the United States and the world are interrogating themselves about what the nation is, should do and can do globally; these are concerns that highlight the urgency of the research agenda undertaken in this book. The real way in which Americans engage the world is fundamentally shaped by the images that the U.S. press helps create and perpetuate, making it an "irreplaceable mediator" between the world and how Americans, both citizens and policymakers, act in it. In order to begin to get at that mediator essence, this book proposes a new theoretical framework that integrates mass communication with international relations as a particularly useful way to conceptualize and, ultimately, to call for restoring the power and responsibility of the media in international affairs.

It then tests the model through an extensive discourse analysis, based on more than 2,000 news articles, of how the American press has covered the world and what images it has brought back to its readers. Do the same general understandings of the world, specific countries and regions and the United States' global role inform both media coverage and actual policies? This book is the first to provide a narrative of the evolution of America's understandings of the world, analyzing coverage of twenty defining international events from 1848 to 2008 and including both a production perspective (such as the profession of foreign correspondent and journalism education) and an

[1] John Maxwell Hamilton, *Journalism's Roving Eye: A History of American Foreign Reporting* (Baton Rouge: Louisiana State University Press, 2009).

audience perspective (such as the appetite for foreign news among U.S. readers and political engagement in foreign affairs).

Those discourses of the world, and of the United States' role in it, are found to have shaped the box within which foreign policy options were debated – and to have occasionally provided the means to think outside of it. Either by succeeding in enriching the public's understanding of foreign nations, or by tragically failing to do so, the news media have had a pivotal role in shaping national identities and therefore setting constraints for foreign policies at particular historical times. The contribution of such a constructivist approach – focused on exploring the ecology of discourses within which policymakers act – implies that dwindling foreign news coverage must entail less room for understanding, with catastrophic consequences for action. Therefore, this history of American journalism's engagement with world affairs also provides the launching pad for a discussion of what the future of foreign correspondence might be in the twenty-first century, amid a revolutionized communication and policy environment.

A Constructivist Perspective on IR, Communication, and Journalism

Three crucial conceptual assumptions about international politics, communication and journalism underlie this new model of the effects of the news media on foreign policy, and they are first defined briefly before delving into a discussion of their merits as well as the questions they leave unanswered through the existing literature. First, identities and interests are not essentialist but socially, collectively constructed. Thus, both macrolevel explanations of international systems and analyses of individual policies need to take into account discourses – or the collective frameworks that give meaning to material factors (e.g., that define what people understand as the national interest or power) – and provide boundaries of interpretation for decision makers above and beyond their individual psychological and cognitive schemas. Second, communication is not the transparent transmission of a fixed meaning; rather, it serves as a necessary locus for the negotiation of meaning within historically, culturally specific broad understandings. Language, therefore, does not simply reflect a material reality but constitutes it insofar as it provides the only way we can know any social fact. Third, the news media, despite numerous and glaring failings, can and do provide a unique, valuable space for public debate that is not simply a replica of political discourse; if one believed, as many critics increasingly do, that all the mainstream media do is lap up manipulation by political and business actors, then defending their role in international affairs would be a priori a meaningless exercise.

Constructing International Affairs

Exploring international affairs first, then, this perspective is greatly indebted to constructivism and discourse theories, especially the works of Alexander Wendt (at the systemic level) and Henrik Larsen (at the foreign policy level).[2] Neither interprets constructivism as a denial of the great importance of power, interests and institutions, the traditional explicative tools of realism and liberalism. Rather, they convincingly argue that the meanings we give to the material environment – and therefore the effects it ends up having – should not be taken for granted, because an object does not force a representation of it on our minds but rather is relationally constructed. Interests themselves are but ideas, collectively held in a specific culture at a specific historical time – an insight recently shared by strategic culture analysts.[3] In a classic example, according to Wendt's famous pronouncement, "anarchy is what states make of it," not because anarchy exists only as a mental construct, but because how states configure their position within it is inevitably influenced by the ideas they share about what anarchy means to them. To paraphrase Larsen and to bring analysis from the first to the third level, nuclear weapons certainly have an intrinsic, easily quantifiable essence, but Washington in 2012 can confidently be expected to react very differently to one such weapon in North Korea or fifty in the United Kingdom, on the basis of a series of existing understandings about regimes, alliances, interests, representations of the past, and other factors.

Distribution of Power and Ideas

Wendt's focus is on the systemic level, the level of culture defined as shared knowledge and constituted of narratives that "are not merely the shared beliefs held by individuals at any given moment... but inherently historical phenomena which are kept alive through the generations by an on-going process of socialization and ritual enactment."[4] The basic tenet of his theory, accepted here, is that human associations (including states) are held together by shared ideas more than by material forces – some of those ideas being, this book argues, images of one's own nation and foreign ones. Therefore, international relations are not governed only by the distribution of power – measured in capabilities, as it is for the realist school – but by the "distribution of ideas" (to which we should add power measured in influence).[5]

The major preoccupation of foreign policy becomes "managing the casting and recasting of socially constructed identities" – an assumption that begs for better study of just what those identities are, how they emerge and how they are transformed, something that this book argues happens through mass communication, too. Interests and identities, then, are ideas "endogenous" to interaction, and they lie at the core of interactions because, as Katzenstein puts it, they are constructed through them.[6] According to Wendt, states interact in

[2] Alexander Wendt, *Social Theory of International Politics* (Cambridge: Cambridge University Press, 1999); Henrik Larsen, *Foreign Policy and Discourse Analysis* (London: Routledge, 1997).

[3] John Glenn, "Realism versus Strategic Culture: Competition and Collaboration?" *International Studies Review* 11–3 (September 2009): 523.

[4] Wendt, 1999, 163.

[5] Wendt, 1999, 1, 96.

[6] Alexander Wendt, "Anarchy Is What States Make of It: The Social Construction of Power Politics," *International Organization* 46–2 (1992): 394; Peter J. Katzenstein, *The Culture of*

part to try to sustain their conceptions of "self" and "other,"[7] because ideas held by a state are given meaning by ideas shared with other states – another affirmation of the importance of images and the relevance of discourses among nations. Thus, the construction of identity is itself a form of power, as in Wendt's example about the identity of the United States as "hegemon," which is constructed by a "generalized other" rather than by the United States.[8] This casts international communication and its role in image formation and meaning construction as a crucial player in the international arena, recalling Michel Foucault's statement that "discourse is the power . . . to be seized."[9]

The assumption that the meaning and consequently the effect of hard and soft power and interests depend on actors' collectively held ideas raises the two gravest objections to such a constructivist perspective: How do those ideas emerge, and how do they change? More drastically, from a methodological standpoint, how can we even provide evidence that those ideas exist and that they are causal or constitutive of any discrete action? On the question of change, a systemic constructivist perspective seems to imply that change is inhibited because states are interested in maintaining a stable identity, especially when other states have come to perceive such identity as an objective fact and are further disposed to do so by the structure created in the interaction.[10] Some students of newer, suprastate identities like the European Union's have even argued that they are purposefully constructed as timeless.[11] Wendt ultimately appears ambiguous on both questions of change and causality, arguing that culture is a "self-fulfilling prophecy," while not denying the role of agents in "carrying" it, and that constructivism is more of a constitutive than a causal theory seeking to account for, not to explain, effects. In other words, early constructivist work appears to be content with suggesting that social construction matters. But the challenge remains, as noted in a 1998 article about "the constructivist turn in international relations theory," to address "when, how, and why it occurs, clearly specifying the actors and mechanisms bringing about change, the scope conditions under which they operate, and how they vary across countries."[12] The biggest catch-22 is the question of agency – if agents and structures, material and discursive arrangements, are mutually constitutive, how can that constitution be operationalized?

National Security: Norms and Identity in World Politics (New York: Columbia University Press, 1996). Also Richard Price and Christian Reus-Smit, "Dangerous Liaisons? Critical International Theory and Constructivism," *European Journal of International Relations* 4–3 (1998): 267.

7 Wendt, 1999, 316.

8 Wendt, 1999, 177.

9 Michel Foucault, "The Order of Discourse," in *Untying the Text*, ed. Robert Young (Boston: Routledge & Kegan Paul, 1981), 53.

10 Wendt, 1992, 411.

11 Ian Manners and Richard G. Whitman, "The 'Difference Engine': Constructing and Representing the International Identity of the European Union," *Journal of European Public Policy* 10–3 (2003): 396.

12 Jeffrey T. Checkel, "The Constructivist Turn in International Relations Theory," *World Politics* 50–2 (1998): 325.

Discourses and Foreign Policy Choices

This book highlights the actor role of the news media in constituting a crucial part of the discursive environment that delimits policy choices, with the caveat that this constructivist perspective cannot account for causality in isolation and it cannot predict specific foreign policy actions or their support by the public. What this analysis can reveal, however, is the range of actions that are likely and of others that are literally unthinkable for policymakers and citizens alike. A similar inquiry, bringing constructivism to the finite and causal level of foreign policy, was Larsen's discourse analysis of France's and Britain's politics vis-à-vis Europe in the 1980s. While careful to note that an analysis of political discourse cannot account for, let alone predict, every short-term policy decision, Larsen argues that discourse provides "a kind of framework within which the foreign policy of a particular country *can* take place."[13] In other words, once established, historically situated discourses – about foreign realities, about one's own country, and about the very nature of international politics and statehood – cannot help influencing foreign policies because they provide the only frame within which decision makers can make sense of material data. Therefore, constructivist analysis can avoid some of the pitfalls of more traditional approaches to foreign policy, which Larsen criticizes for being too centered on individual decision makers, for treating beliefs only in terms of perceptions of the real, and for considering language transparent.

The first two points highlight the essential distinctions between a constructivist approach to foreign policy and the cognitive, psychological treatment of images in foreign policymaking established by Robert Jervis, even though on the surface they may sound similar enough to be confused. A precursor to the study of international images was the UNESCO-sponsored opinion poll in the late 1940s dealing with the "maps of the world" in the mind of citizens of nine nations (including the United States).[14] In the 1950s and 1960s, K.E. Boulding, Ole R. Holsti and others argued that actors on the international stage base their decisions on their "image" of a reality, and they tend to perceive even new information according to existing belief systems predicated on "stereotyped national images."[15] More recently, Martha Cottam argued that images of foreign nations are based on perceptions of hostility and that they influence every stage of foreign policymaking.[16] Other studies suggest that even

[13] Larsen, 21; emphasis added.

[14] William Buchanan and Hadley Cantril, *How Nations See Each Other* (Urbana: University of Illinois Press, 1953), 1.

[15] K.E. Boulding, "National Images and International Systems," *The Journal of Conflict Resolution* 3–2 (June 1959): 120–131; Ole R. Holsti, "The Belief System and National Images: A Case Study," *The Journal of Conflict Resolution* 6–3 (September 1962): 244–252.

[16] Martha L. Cottam, *Images and Intervention: U.S. Policies in Latin America* (Pittsburgh, PA: University of Pittsburgh Press, 1994), 19.

"spectacular" events have little power to change images,[17] and that people's "world views" have the largest impact on their actions.[18]

In his 1970 classic text, Jervis defined a decision maker's image of another actor as "those of his beliefs about the other that affect his predictions of how the other will behave," further influenced by the actor's own goals and estimates of the international environment.[19] Jervis argued that the mechanisms of image making are not innocent mental workings; they are linked to precise power and very concrete interests. States often use images of other states and of their own nation's role to justify action;[20] according to Jervis, states also try to influence others states' images of themselves in order to avoid making real changes in policies. Jervis focused on how a state can project a desired image cheaply, arguing that such a strategically positioned image – often independent of actual behavior – could prove more effective than military or economic power. There are points of convergence with this book's theoretical premises: the importance of images and perceptions, their effects in the real(ist) world, and their relative perceptual independence from actions. But Jervis and, as discussed later in this chapter, many scholars of media and foreign policy focus on specific actors' framing of reality intended as manipulation, deception and misrepresentation both of capabilities and intentions. Even some post-structuralist and critical discourse analysts of foreign policy, who go so far as arguing that identity and policy are ontologically inseparable and there are no objective identities outside of discourse, still appear to conceive of discourses or representations as conscious ways of presenting and legitimizing policies.[21]

The constructivist framework here, on the other hand, focuses on larger, socially constructed discourses – "collectively held or 'intersubjective' ideas and understandings"[22] – that are beyond direct, individual manipulation, or rather that constrain any attempt to rational manipulation because even that can only be comprehended within the parameters of accepted discursive formations

[17] Karl W. Deutsch and Richard L. Merritt, "Effects of Events on National and International Images," in *International Behavior: A Social-Psychological Analysis*, ed. Herbert C. Kelman (New York: Holt, Rinehart and Winston, 1985), 132–184.

[18] Judith Goldstein and Robert O. Keohane, eds. *Ideas and Foreign Policy: Beliefs, Institutions, and Political Change* (Ithaca, NY: Cornell University Press, 1993), 8. Also, Mark Laffey and Jutta Weldes, "Beyond Belief: Ideas and Symbolic Technologies in the Study of International Relations," *European Journal of International Relations* 3–2 (June 1997): 193–237.

[19] Robert Jervis, *The Logic of Images in International Relations* (New York: Columbia University Press, 1970), 5.

[20] K.J. Holsti, "National Role Conceptions in the Study of Foreign Policy," *International Studies Quarterly* 14–3 (1970): 233–309.

[21] Lene Hansen, *Security as Practice: Discourse Analysis and the Bosnian War* (London: Routledge, 2006); Dirk Nabers, "Filling the Void of Meaning: Identity Construction in U.S. Foreign Policy after September 11, 2001," *Foreign Policy Analysis* 5–2 (2009): 191–214.

[22] Martha Finnemore and Kathryn Sikkink, "Taking Stock: The Constructivist Research Program in International Relations and Comparative Politics," *Annual Review of Political Science* 4 (2001): 392.

and terminologies. This conceptualization returns us to Larsen's third point, derived from Foucault, about the constitutive power of language, which should be studied insofar as it mediates meaning and it is the means through which social meaning is communicated. Language, in other words, is never neutral but rather is the expression and the reification of specific, historically situated discourses. As such, language, the statements it composes, and the discourses those statements in turn constitute take us one step beyond pure ideology and in fact can transcend it, precisely as they transcend individual or national goals. Therefore, studying national texts – political, as Larsen does, or media, as done here – for discourses about macro concepts (e.g., national identity and global role) can give us insight into how each state makes sense of the world and, by implication, what kind and range of policies its decision makers can adopt.

The focus on national discourses spotlights another central assumption shared here – that even in today's age of global cultural, economic and to some extent political interdependence, the state remains a key actor, precisely because it defines its own relational identity. Whereas some have argued that twenty-first-century global communication technology transformations are ushering in changes to the world order and substantially weakening the nation-state, the vast majority of literature in international relations, as well as international communication, rests – as the very term "international" implies – on use of the state as a unit of analysis, albeit from different ontologies, as pointed out by Stephen Crofts Wiley's article on nationality in the era of globalization.[23] Sociologist Michael Schudson argued that using the state as a unit of analysis is not problematic as long as the nation is also examined as a historical, not an essentialist, construct.[24] Indeed, since the late nineteenth century, the nation has been defined not so much by race, language (meaning idiom and not discourse), religion, geography and interests but by memories, culture and consent – a common identity creating an "imagined community," to use Benedict Anderson's words.[25] There has been a recent surge in studies of national or ethnic identities, socially constructed and based on selected memories and histories, as fundamental explicative tools in recurring conflicts.[26] But most of those

[23] Stephen B. Crofts Wiley, "Rethinking Nationality in the Context of Globalization," *Communication Theory* 14:1 (2004): 78–96; Wendt, 1992, 424. Also, Larsen, 198; Daya Kishan Thussu, ed. *Internationalizing Media Studies* (New York: Routledge, 2009); Robert A. Pastor, ed. *A Century's Journey: How the Great Powers Shape the World* (New York: Basic Books, 1999), 5. For the perspective that the world order is being transformed by communication technologies, see Ronald J. Deibert, *Parchment, Printing, and Hypermedia: Communication in World Order Transformation* (New York: Columbia University Press, 1997).

[24] Michael Schudson, "Culture and the Integration of National Societies," in *The Sociology of Culture*, ed. Diana Crane (Cambridge: Blackwell Publishers, 1994).

[25] Ernest Renan, "What Is a Nation?" in *Nation and Narration*, ed. Homi Bhabha (London: Routledge, 1990), 19; Benedict Anderson, *Imagined Communities* (London: Verso, 1991).

[26] Eiki Berg and Piret Ehin, eds. *Identity and Foreign Policy: Baltic-Russian Relations and European Integration* (Farnham: Ashgate, 2009); Pål Kolstø, ed. *Media Discourse and the Yugoslav Conflicts: Representations of Self and Other* (Farnham: Ashgate, 2009).

studies are based on analysis of political statements, whereas one country's construction of another's identity through international mass communication is one of the central concerns of this book.

One last contribution from Larsen's conceptualization is the acknowledgment that such a discourse analysis, despite its inherently high level of abstraction and consequently low falsification, does not necessarily contradict but rather can complement more power-based explanations of policy. Whereas national interests are necessary to explain most policies, it is difficult to see interests "independently of the values of the individual states as they are embedded and constructed in the language."[27] As another proponent of the study of "powerful discourses" in international relations put it, discourses render a real thing "meaningful to us in particular ways" and therefore "delimit the possibilities for action in relation to it" above and beyond material interests.[28]

Therefore, conducting discourse analysis to better understand the nexus between news media and foreign policy does not mean to deny the importance of interests, power and geopolitical factors at the systemic level nor does it mean to exclude the possibility or even likelihood of manipulation, misrepresentation and misperception at the individual decision-making level. Rather, it is to argue for the added value of looking at the socially constructed, historically situated, non-essentialist discourses or ways of understanding and taking for granted certain phenomena, which form the inevitable ecology within which meanings are formulated, communicated and become the basis for actions. We are bound, further, to ask, what else constitutes that ecology? To return to an earlier question, how do certain discourses take hold in certain cultures at certain historical times?

Constructing Communication

This book attempts to provide a part of the answer to that question, although admittedly by no means the complete answer. The suggestion put forth here is that researchers go look for insight beyond political communication into mass media communication – not so much for coverage of specific policies or activist editorials but for the construction of foreign realities per se through history – on the basis of the premise that mass communication is an essential site for the formation of meaning around foreign realities. Once such discursive formations are identified, we can then look for correspondence in foreign policy trends and decisions, which are formulated within the same universe of values and perceptions created and reflected in discourse. Whereas competing frameworks of understanding might exist in other spheres (such as political communication or popular culture) and further explicative factors in geopolitical, economic

[27] Larsen, 197.

[28] Charlotte Epstein, *The Power of Words in International Relations: Birth of an Anti-whaling Discourse* (Cambridge, MA: MIT Press, 2008), 6, 2.

and other terms need to be considered, what we look for as evidence of the importance of media discourse for foreign policy is consonance between those other factors and the discursive values about self and other.

Such a research program is inherently partial, because it seeks to find mediated discourses as they exist, might be transformed through time, and have an influence on material arrangements, but it does not address how discursive formations originated at their inception beyond refuting the suggestion that they be simple, top-down manipulations by elites. Despite that shortcoming, it remains valuable because it can illuminate the formation and the germs for change in the macro concepts about foreign realities that ultimately drive and frame policies beyond systemic pressures and individual mechanisms. Indeed, some students of international relations have argued that the field's lack of media understanding makes it "fail to grasp the new shape of world politics."[29] Even if we do not know exactly where certain discursive formations came from, just showing what they are and how they are maintained or transformed in the public sphere is crucial because they delimit ways of thinking and therefore, by default, of acting. For example, the finding that every anti-authoritarian movement abroad has been constructed, at best, as a little 1776, cements the understanding of the United States as the global paragon of democracy, an essential discourse for U.S. intervention around the world.

Creating Meaning through Mass Communication

Such a constructivist perspective, drawing on the works of Foucault again as well as James Carey and Stuart Hall, rests on the definition of mass communication as the creation and negotiation of meaning rather than the transmission of a fixed, agreed-upon meaning.[30] Thus, the focus is not on the media – U.S. correspondents abroad, in this case – as capable of objectively and fairly conveying information about the rest of the world, or as serving as legitimization for official positions; rather the focus is on how those written accounts create a meaning for foreign realities for American audiences, including policymakers. This does not imply that there is no reality – rather that any reality, and particularly a foreign one that does not come within most people's purview except through media, is only understandable through some translation and negotiation of meaning. The principal research agenda, then, is to uncover the role the news media have played in negotiating international meaning construction and in serving as essential means whereby "*any* body of 'knowledge' comes to

[29] Brigitte L. Nacos, Robert Y. Shapiro and Pierangelo Isernia, eds. *Decisionmaking in a Glass House: Mass Media, Public Opinion, and American and European Foreign Policy in the 21st Century* (Lanham, MD: Rowman & Littlefield, 2000), 27.

[30] James W. Carey, *Communication as Culture: Essays on Media and Society* (New York: Routledge, 1992); Stuart Hall, "The Rediscovery of 'Ideology': Return of the Repressed in Media Studies," in *Culture, Society and the Media*, ed. Michael Gurevitch et al. (London: Methuen, 1982), 56–90.

be socially established *as* 'reality,'" to quote the foundational theory of social construction of reality as outlined by Peter Berger and Thomas Luckmann.[31]

Although Berger and Luckmann's focus was on institutions, not on the media, their conceptualizations belong to the paradigm shift in sociological study from the positivistic, behavioral approach to the critical, ideological perspective. It is the same approach that is broadening the tradition of media effects studies, as discussed in this chapter, and, in a way, it parallels the turn from realism to alternative explanations in international relations. Most communication discourse analysts are indebted to Foucault,[32] whose definition of discourse went from the broadly theoretical domain of all statements to particular practices accounting for a few texts.[33] Discourse as used in this book – as a collective framework of understanding – falls in the middle, focusing on a group of statements belonging to the same conceptualization, which, Foucault argued, is always historically situated.[34]

Media Discourses and Power

The most important distinction to be made here is that discourse theory allows a less political approach to power than analyses using ideology; in other words, it is not assumed that dominating elites come up with discursive constructions that they then force, through the press, on the public. This clarification is necessary to distinguish the present study from those following *critical* discourse theory, which is defined as the study of how discourse reproduces "social domination" and therefore is based on the premise that "language is not powerful on its own – it gains power by the use powerful people make of it."[35] Rather, language is assumed here to indeed have its own power and discourse to function in a much more interactive way between culture and media, with decision makers, the press and the public engaged in the struggle for the construction of meaning. The focus of this kind of research is on how discourses create identities and establish them as "real," not on how such constructed reality benefits any particular social or national group.[36] Even just becoming aware of the existence of discourses is a valuable research project, because discursive practices

[31] Peter L. Berger and Thomas Luckmann, *The Social Construction of Reality: A Treatise in the Sociology of Knowledge* (New York: Doubleday, 1966), 1–18.

[32] See the extensive review in Sara Mills, *Discourse* (London: Routledge, 2004). For a similar book, focusing not on Foucault's study of discourse but on that of Ernesto Laclau and Chantal Mouffe, see Marianne W. Jørgensen and Louise Phillips, *Discourse Analysis as Theory and Method* (London: SAGE, 2002).

[33] Michel Foucault, *The Archaeology of Knowledge* (New York: Pantheon Books, 1972), 80.

[34] Foucault, 1972, 99, 117.

[35] Ruth Wodak and Michael Meyer, eds. *Methods of Critical Discourse Analysis* 2nd ed. (Los Angeles: Sage, 2009), 9; Gilbert Weiss and Ruth Wodak, eds. *Critical Discourse Analysis: Theory and Interdisciplinarity* (New York: Palgrave Macmillan, 2003), 14.

[36] For this crucial distinction between critical and constructivist approaches to discourse, see Nelson Phillips and Cynthia Hardy, *Discourse Analysis: Investigating Processes of Social Construction* (Thousand Oaks, CA: SAGE, 2002), 19–21.

make it virtually impossible to think outside of them, thereby eliminating other possible meanings,[37] and they give the aura of common sense to constructed meanings. This constitutes their power, with inevitable consequences for their effects and with the implication that any change in discursive formations will still emerge from within existing configurations.

The focus on power and discourse is the identifying characteristic in the shift in media studies from what Hall called the "brutal, hard-headed" effects tradition to the "critical" approach influenced by cultural studies.[38] The theorizing of a social construction of reality helped shift the concept of consensus to a process defined as the movement "towards the winning of a universal validity and legitimacy for accounts of the world which are partial and particular, and towards the grounding of these particular constructions in the taken-for-grantedness of the 'real.'"[39] The appropriation of any reality through discourse is crucial for public understanding of it, and that appropriation usually happens through references to a society's collective knowledge – a concept parallel to the use of analogies in foreign policy decision making. Norman Fairclough and Teun van Dijk – who study discourse in the media, focusing on language in the news – also discuss discourse as a force of social control through language use. Whereas their work tends to highlight the nefarious effects of ideology and oppression through the media, this book focuses on the negotiation of meanings through communication.

Even though discourses distill and generate a common sense, they are embedded with both dominating and competing constructions that can signal paradigm shifts – they are "a space of multiple dissensions," in Foucault's words.[40] They both reflect and are constitutive of social, political, and cultural practices, because events and reality rarely have intrinsic meanings that can be deciphered outside of discursive frameworks that shape language and media content. As Gunther Kress argued, "Discourse finds its expression in text." However, this is never a straightforward relation; any one text may be the expression or realization of a number of sometimes competing and contradictory discourses.[41] Therefore, no text can be meaningful in isolation – interplay with other texts (what Fairclough calls intertextuality) gives researchers clues as to the discourse it belongs to.[42] In the second half of the twentieth century, for example, correspondents started referring regularly to "media management" by governments, so that their stories became reflections not just of foreign realities but of the various efforts to color those news narratives in specific ways.

[37] Epstein, 9.

[38] Hall, 59–61.

[39] Hall, 65.

[40] Foucault, 1972, 155.

[41] Gunther Kress, "Ideological Structures in Discourse," ch. 3 in Teun A. van Dijk, *Handbook of Discourse Analysis: Discourse Analysis in Society* vol. 4 (London: Academic Press, 1985), 27.

[42] Phillips and Hardy, 4–5.

Media Discourses, Media Effects

Again it is essential to note that speaking of frameworks of understanding does not mean strictly textual frames in the sense of manipulation of words for a purpose – because even manipulation and strategic positioning still need to occur within more broadly social discourses in order to be understood. Robert Entman, who has long studied the effect of media framing in foreign policy decisions, argued recently that the most influential media frames, whether pushed by the administration or journalistic "counterframing," are those that use "culturally resonant terms"[43]– discourse is precisely what gives any term such resonance. This constructivist conceptualization of communication allows us to move a step beyond the existing research on the effects of media on public opinion and foreign policy, in the direction of a less deterministic approach to just what consequences media can have. Some communication researchers have begun to argue that a strictly positivistic effects model – twenty minutes of exposure to TV reports of famine in Africa will make voters twice more likely to support foreign aid, to use an imaginary example – can inadvertently obscure the just-as-real, but subtler and more powerful influence that media have on how people interact with their environment. Several effects theorists argue that research should move from a "powerful and negative" effects model to one that focuses on process – looking for cumulative and contextual effects – instead of fixing on predicting outcomes. The focus on processes without the explicit prediction of specific political outcomes is also a key feature of constructivism in international relations.[44] The contribution that this book seeks to make to the study of the role of news media in international affairs by looking at mediated discourses about foreign realities is exactly in that line.

As such, it differs from the existing studies of the role of communication in systemic analysis of world politics as well as studies of media and foreign policy.[45] In the first camp, two recent, notable works have sought to explain how the international system has changed, historically and presently, because of dramatic changes in communication technologies.[46] Their theoretical premise is a useful version of the much-maligned McLuhanesque medium theory, although they add a simil-constructivist argument that elements of international politics assumed to be essential and unchanging, such as national

[43] Robert M. Entman, *Projections of Power: Framing News, Public Opinion, and U.S. Foreign Policy* (Chicago: University of Chicago Press, 2004).

[44] Finnemore and Sikkink, 393.

[45] For a summary of the contemporary debate on the effects of the media on foreign policies, see Derek B. Miller, *Media Pressure on Foreign Policy: The Evolving Theoretical Framework* (New York: Palgrave Macmillan, 2007).

[46] Deibert; Elizabeth Hanson, *The Information Revolution and World Politics* (Lanham, MD: Rowman and Littlefield, 2008). For a similar use of communication technologies as a lens to understand early logics of globalization, see Dwayne R. Winseck and Robert M. Pike, *Communication and Empire: Media, Markets, and Globalization, 1860–1930* (Durham: Duke University Press, 2007).

interests and nations, are products of historical contingencies and subject to change over time. Both studies find that social needs drive technological change, which inherently creates disparities between haves and have-nots, which in turn change the relative power of social forces – with the current effect, for example, of what Deibert calls a "postmodern world order" characterized by uniquely fragmented communities of understanding.

News Media and Foreign Policy Interactions

To move the level of analysis from systems to policy means to refocus on communication as a political institution – as a distinct actor on the political stage or even a "discrete strategic actor."[47] In the United States, the media have been conceptualized either in a watchdog role, essential to the functioning of a democratic government, or as a tool of the government, which uses them to legitimate its hegemony. The same dichotomous model has been applied to the relationship between the media and foreign policymaking, with scholars debating the directionality of influence between foreign policy, public opinion and international news coverage. Many media scholars postulate that, either through institutional constraints (e.g., the use of governmental or legitimate "alternative" sources),[48] hegemonic control,[49] or a natural inclination to protect one's own national identity,[50] the media follow the government, tilting public discussion toward the official line of foreign policy.

Another school of thought holds that the media can drive foreign policy, with empirical studies ranging from concern with the "CNN effect" to the warmongering "yellow press" in the late nineteenth century, to the effects of the end of the Cold War and the role of journalists in directly mediating

47 Timothy E. Cook, "The News Media as a Political Institution: Backward and Looking Forward," *Political Communication* 23 (2006): 160; Matthew A. Baum and Philip B.K. Potter, "The Relationships between Mass Media, Public Opinion, and Foreign Policy: Toward a Theoretical Synthesis," *Annual Review of Political Science* 11 (2008): 40.

48 See the indexing thesis by W. Lance Bennett, "Toward a Theory of Press-State Relations in the United States," *Journal of Communication* 40–2 (Spring 1990): 103–125. For the use of sources, see Edward S. Herman, "The Media's Role in U.S. Foreign Policy," *Journal of International Affairs* 47–1 (Summer 1993): 23–45. For the "propaganda model," see Edward S. Herman and Noam Chomsky, *Manufacturing Consent: The Political Economy of the Mass Media* (New York: Pantheon Books, 1988). For a study seeking to show that the press has no independent role in foreign policy, see Nicholas O. Berry, *Foreign Policy and the Press: An Analysis of* The New York Times' *Coverage of U.S. Foreign Policy* (New York: Greenwood Press, 1990).

49 Hong-Won Park, "The Press, the State and Hegemony: A Theoretical Exploration" (PhD diss., University of Minnesota, 1999); and Daniel C. Hallin, "Hegemony: The American News Media from Vietnam to El Salvador, A Study of Ideological Change and Its Limits," in *Political Communication Research*, ed. David Paletz (Norwood, NJ: Ablex, 1987), 3–25.

50 Catherine A. Luther, *Press Images, National Identity, and Foreign Policy: A Case Study of U.S.-Japan Relations from 1955–1995* (New York: Routledge, 2001), 32–33. She argued that national identity is such a strong influence on the press that journalists might oppose governmental policies they perceive as running counter to their interpretation of national identity (37–45).

conflicts.[51] A 1991 collection of studies succinctly titled *The Media and Foreign Policy* argued that "an important and powerful international communications network capable of circumventing the control of any national government and supported by its own working ideology" was "a novel influence in international politics."[52] Several, more recent studies have looked at the relationship between media coverage – a broader "CNN effect" that includes other prominent media outlets – and U.S. military intervention, especially in humanitarian crises, and concluded that the media can indeed influence policy outcomes when governmental elite consensus is absent, but they are subservient where consensus is strong.[53]

The same oppositional approach underlies the studies that examine the role of media in developing countries, emerging power blocs and dominating nations within the context of globalization. The majority of those inquiries look for the ways in which the media – national and foreign – help or hinder development, democracy, and even war and peace. Different authors find that mass communication, through new media technologies, is helping to turn public opinion in support of democratization, or terrorism, or everything in between, just as global communication is helping to either centralize or disperse traditional sources of political power and cultural identity.[54] One study warned that the predominance of corporate interests behind global media consolidation

[51] On the 1898 war, see especially Joseph E. Wisan, *The Cuban Crisis as Reflected in the New York Press (1895–1898)* (New York: Columbia University Press, 1934); and Philip Seib, *Headline Diplomacy: How News Coverage Affects Foreign Policy* (Westport, CT: Praeger, 1997). For the "CNN effect," see Warren P. Strobel, *Late-Breaking Foreign Policy: The News Media's Influence on Peace Operations* (Washington: United States Institute of Peace Press, 1997). For journalists as diplomats, Eytan Gilboa, "Media-Broker Diplomacy: When Journalists Become Mediators," *Critical Studies in Media Communication* 22–2 (June 2005): 99–120; Maurice Walsh, *The News from Ireland: Foreign Correspondents and the Irish Revolution* (London: I.B. Tauris, 2008). For a single collection of articles supporting or disproving the influence of the media on policymaking, see Nacos, Shapiro and Isernia, eds., and Eytan Gilboa, ed. *Media and Conflict* (Ardsley: Transnational Publishers, 2002).

[52] Simon Serfaty, ed. *The Media and Foreign Policy* (New York: St. Martin's Press, 1991), 2.

[53] Piers Robinson, *The CNN Effect: The Myth of News, Foreign Policy and Intervention* (London: Routledge, 2002); Alexander G. Nikolaev and Ernest A. Hakanen, eds. *Leading to the 2003 Iraq War: The Global Media Debate* (New York: Palgrave Macmillan, 2006).

[54] Deibert; Philip Seib, *The Al Jazeera Effect: How the Global Media Are Reshaping World Politics* (Washington: Potomac Books, 2008); Isaac A. Blankson and Patrick D. Murphy, eds. *Negotiating Democracy: Media Transformations in Emerging Democracies* (Albany: State University of New York Press, 2007); Philip Seib, ed. *New Media and the New Middle East* (New York: Palgrave Macmillan, 2007); Majid Tehranian, *Global Communication and World Politics: Domination, Development, and Discourse* (Boulder, CO: Lynne Rienner, 1999); Edward S. Herman and Robert W. McChesney, *The Global Media: The New Missionaries of Global Capitalism* (London: Cassell, 1997); Howard H. Frederick, *Global Communication & International Relations* (Belmont, CA: Wadsworth Publishing, 1993); Krishna Kumar, *Promoting Independent Media: Strategies for Democracy Assistance* (Boulder, CO: Lynne Rienner, 2006); Greg McLaughlin and Stephen Baker, *The Propaganda of Peace: The Role of Media and Culture in the Northern Ireland Peace Process* (Chicago: Intellect, 2010). For a summary review,

is eroding an essential public sphere, whereas others more convincingly argued that "core beliefs embedded within national cultures are far more impervious" to globalization than much literature suggests.[55]

Public Opinion's Role

Such viewpoints, of course, are essentially an extension of the argument that the media either directly shape policies and politics or are meek vehicles of American or Western hegemony and control (the updated "manufacturing consent" model). Most of these perspectives rest on the assumption that the media greatly influence public opinion. Several studies seek to prove empirically how news media images of foreign nations affect readers' perceptions through framing, exposure or cultivation.[56] As pithily put by Albert Gunther, in a thesis shared at least implicitly by most media scholars, people and policymakers "assume that what mass media are saying today must be what the public will be thinking tomorrow" – or, whatever the direction of influence might be, people perceive the media to have an effect on public opinion, and that indeed grants the media influence.[57] In turn, most scholarship agrees that public opinion "influences policy most of the time, often strongly," thus looping back to the relationship between media, the public and elite decision makers.[58]

Since public opinion polling started in the 1930s, a practical and inherently normative question has driven research into this relationship – does, and should, public opinion matter in conducting foreign affairs?[59] More realistically, what kind of public ("opinion leaders," including the news media, or random Gallup respondents) matters to what kind of policymakers (elected

see Simon Cottle, "Journalism and Globalization," in *The Handbook of Journalism Studies*, ed. Karin Wahl-Jorgensen and Thomas Hanitzsch (New York: Routledge, 2009), 342.

55 Angela M. Crack, *Global Communication and Transnational Public Spheres* (New York: Palgrave Macmillan, 2008); Pippa Norris and Ronald Inglehart, *Cosmopolitan Communications: Cultural Diversity in a Globalized World* (Cambridge: Cambridge University Press, 2009).

56 Robert M. Entman, "Framing U.S. Coverage of International News," *Journal of Communication* 41–4 (1991): 6–27; David K. Perry, "The Image Gap: How International News Affects Perceptions of Nations," *Journalism Quarterly* 64 (1987): 416–433; Yahya R. Kamalipour, ed. *Images of the U.S. around the World* (Albany: State University of New York Press, 1999).

57 Albert C. Gunther, "The Persuasive Press Inference: Effects of Mass Media on Perceived Public Opinion," *Communication Research* 25–5 (October 1998): 487; Gunther and J. Douglas Storey, "The Influence of Presumed Influence," *Journal of Communication* 53–2 (June 2003): 199–215. See also William A. Gamson and Andre Modigliani, "Media Discourse and Public Opinion on Nuclear Power: A Constructionist Approach," *American Journal of Sociology* 95–1 (July 1989): 1–37.

58 Paul Burstein, "The Impact of Public Opinion on Public Policy: A Review and an Agenda," *Political Research Quarterly*, 56–1 (March 2003): 29.

59 A succinct review of the topic is Ole R. Holsti, *Public Opinion and American Foreign Policy* (Ann Arbor: University of Michigan Press, revised edition 2004). A recent edited volume broadens the query beyond the United States: Richard Sobel, Peter Furia and Bethany Barratt, eds. *Public Opinion and International Intervention: Lessons from the Iraq War* (Dulles, VA: Potomac Books, 2012).

officials in Congress and the White House, or more insulated State Department professionals) on what kind of policies (trade, war, or aid)? In an exhaustive review of American public opinion on foreign affairs, Holsti found that, between Pearl Harbor and the post-9/11 Afghanistan war, the general public and, even more strongly, opinion elites have supported an "active role" for the United States in the world – although of course consensus breaks down in articulating what that means.[60] Party lines, ideological preferences, levels of education, and exposure to global affairs information in the news media all have some effect on public opinion, although "even a poorly informed and inattentive public is not necessarily isolationist or unilateralist," as Holsti put it.[61]

Unsurprisingly given the dramatic stakes involved, numerous studies, as well as governmental debates since at least the turn of the twentieth century and most starkly since the Vietnam War, have focused exclusively on wartime media, engaging the question of whether and when they slavishly support the government or pursue their own antiwar agenda, especially as flag-draped caskets start coming home. Put another way, there has always been a "continuing contest" between journalists and the military, "in which one side waves the banner of freedom of speech and the other trumpets the security of the state."[62] Findings usually mirror those noted earlier in this section. Given that public attention is scant even in the early stages of military conflict, and that it tends to fall in line with existing partisan alignments anyway, only in rare circumstances can journalists turn public opinion against a war, but most often, rallying around the flag, awash in patriotism, and, increasingly, in the relentless PR machine, journalists follow the government's cues.[63] Wartime journalism has been found to be uniquely "deferential and uncritical of elites" and powerful only in shaping public opinion as consensus around armed intervention is

60 Holsti, 2004, 103.

61 Holsti, 2004, 286.

62 Paul L. Moorcraft and Philip M. Taylor, *Shooting the Messenger: The Political Impact of War Reporting* (Washington: Potomac Books, 2008), ix.

63 For succinct summaries of these debates over wartime journalism and as well as twenty-first-century research examples, see Sean Aday, "Chasing the Bad News: An Analysis of 2005 Iraq and Afghanistan War Coverage on NBC and Fox News Channel," *Journal of Communication*, 60–1 (March 2010): 144–164; Sean Aday, "Leading the Charge: Media, Elites, and the Use of Emotion in Stimulating Rally Effects in Wartime," *Journal of Communication* 60–3 (September 2010): 440–465; Piers Robinson, Peter Goddard, Katy Parry and Craig Murray, "Testing Models of Media Performance in Wartime: U.K. TV News and the 2003 Invasion of Iraq," *Journal of Communication* 59–3 (September 2009): 534–563; Susan L. Carruthers, *The Media at War: Communication and Conflict in the Twentieth Century* (New York: St. Martin's Press, 2000); Kenneth Osgood and Andrew K. Frank, eds. *Selling War in a Media Age: The Presidency and Public Opinion in the American Century* (Gainesville: University Press of Florida, 2010). On public attention, see Baum and Potter, 43, and Adam J. Berinsky, *In Time of War: Understanding Public Opinion from World War II to Iraq* (Chicago: University of Chicago Press, 2009).

widespread at the beginning of a conflict, when the public's political predispositions are momentarily overcome and the government maintains tight control over the news agenda.[64]

As Derek Miller pointed out in a recent review of literature on media effects (via public opinion) over foreign policy decisions, most scholarship in this field fails to find direct ways to measure influence, regardless of its direction.[65] Miller himself goes back to how the earliest writers on press freedom argued that the press was related to governance, and he defines media pressure as "threats to the reputation of the executive" in the act of publication per se, irrespective of the influence on public opinion.[66] The perspective outlined in this book seeks to shed an altogether different kind of light on the question of the role of journalism in public attitudes toward international affairs. It does not attempt to weigh all sources that the public draws on to form its worldviews. Rather, it argues that a discursive analysis of media images of foreign nations (and, reflexively, America's role toward them) can reveal the "box" within which the domestic public – both ordinary citizens and decision makers such as the U.S. president or Congress – thinks about the world beyond the United States. It aims to show how culture- and time-specific interpretations become commonsensical, or "real" objects, as opposed to subjective meanings open to different understandings, so that any conscious, issue-specific framing done by political elites will only resonate with the public if it fits such discourses.

The assumption is that the press has a large influence on policies and how they are received, not because of intentional frames and/or relationships with political actors – as valid as those concerns are – but because it is largely through the ecology of discourses created, circulated and maintained through the press that foreign realities are understood and acted on. To quote Walter Lippmann's celebrated insight, "The only feeling that anyone can have about an event he does not experience is the feeling aroused by his mental image of that event. That is why until we know what others think they know, we cannot truly understand their acts."[67] Lippmann's focus on the untrustworthiness of "the pictures in our heads" led him to advocate for the "organization" of public opinion by experts for press consumption. Mass communication, on the contrary, should be a profoundly democratic "marketplace of ideas" – not only in the sense that the media are "a middleman or trader of information, simultaneously beholden to two actors whose interests often conflict: leaders

[64] Aday, September 2010, 445.

[65] For a similar review, see Brenda M. Seaver, "The Public Dimension of Foreign Policy," *The International Journal of Press Politics* 3–1 (1998): 65–91. For a more general review encompassing all kinds of policies, see Sigrid Koch-Baumgarten and Katrin Voltmer, eds. *Public Policy and Mass Media: The Interplay of Mass Communication and Political Decision Making* (London: Routledge, 2010).

[66] Miller, 16, 37.

[67] Walter Lippmann, *Public Opinion* (New York: Free Press, 1922), 9.

and the public,"[68] but rather that they can be a crucial site of struggles over which definitions of reality become socially accepted as real.

Constructing Foreign Correspondence

In international mass communication, the media are a part of the negotiation of power across national and cultural borders because they serve to integrate discourses that convey and help fix identities of other nations, thereby delimiting policy options.[69] From the constructivist perspective of international affairs and communication outlined so far, foreign correspondence texts emerge not only as constitutive reflections of American discourses about foreign realities, but also as active mediators between different national discourses. The news media, then, have great power, which leads us to the third assumption that underlies this book, namely that they also have an increasing, and increasingly threatened, responsibility to provide more information about foreign realities so that they can truly serve as the public space for meaningful construction of identities. As international relations expert and newspaper commentator Timothy Garton Ash put it in a recent column:

> In today's interconnected world, it matters more than ever that countries understand each other. Such understanding depends on knowing the social facts and individual human stories that are the meat and drink of foreign corresponding. If we have less of this global public good at a time when we need more of it, the results will not merely be depressing. They could be downright dangerous.[70]

Mediating between National Discourses

An article by an American correspondent in a foreign country exists within U.S. discursive formations (about the United States, the foreign country, their relations, etc.), or it would not be intelligible to its American writer and readers. It also has, however, the potential to enlarge and complicate those formations by introducing new ways of talking about that country, apprehended on the ground there, without which much of that reality would be meaningless. Without at least some perception and appropriation of foreign discourses, international exchange of meaning would be literally lost in translation. A striking example from my own professional journalism career: In 2006, I interviewed Andre, a 14-year-old Russian boy from a St. Petersburg orphanage, for an Associated Press article about adoption. To break the ice, I asked what I thought was the most innocuous question one can ask a child, "What do you

[68] Baum and Potter, 50.

[69] On the role of communication in limiting policy options, see Emanuel Adler, "Constructivism and International Relations," in *Handbook of International Relations*, ed. Walter Carlsnaes et al. (London: SAGE, 2002), 95–118.

[70] Timothy Garton Ash, "We Are Getting Less Foreign News at the Very Moment When We Need More," *Guardian*, April 16, 2009, 29.

want to do when you grow up?" The boy replied with a single word, to which the translator smiled and repeated the question. Andre, somewhat taken aback, repeated the same word: "Work."

Not a soccer star, a doctor, a diplomat, or a firefighter – he wanted to be someone who works. Indeed, statistics from advocacy groups show that of Russian boys who age out of orphanages at 18 years old, 10 percent commit suicide, 30 percent commit a crime, and 40 percent become vagrants within the first year.[71] For someone in Andre's circumstances, my question about career choices was literally incomprehensible. My query about career and his answer about work were not a problem of semantic miscommunication; those simple words implied general conceptual frameworks – about working, perhaps even more broadly about adulthood and opportunity – that we each took for granted and felt no need to explain, but which we did not share, and therefore they threatened to make nonsensical our exchange. That single word, "work," was the expression of an entire discourse foreign, presumably, to most of my readers – and our small window into it.

It is by opening that window that international mass communication can best fulfill its fundamental role in international affairs. This view can generate two immediate concerns – one from professional journalists, who might argue they should be nothing but empty vessels for objective information, and the opposite from media critics who argue that journalism is but the puppet of elite interests. To the first objection, I say, precisely so; the biggest problem with today's foreign correspondence is simply that there is not enough of it. Perhaps even more so than other forms of journalism, international newsgathering is today lamentably endangered by shifting business models, new technologies and the rise of nonprofessional journalists. As the editor of a recent textbook for international journalists put it, "no website, however worthy and informative, or no packaged report, slickly produced in London or New York, will ever be able to surpass the impact of original journalism, the discoveries of a single reporter or documentary maker or photojournalist on assignment somewhere in the world."[72]

Foreign Correspondence under Threat

This is not a nostalgic paean for some misty good old times. It is, rather, a sober realization that the whole system of producing substantial news is in grave danger, and that, in turn, imperils the very existence of an essential site for public discourse. The simplest chance for the mainstream press to stay relevant and fulfill its mission as a forum for democracy is to "do what [it does]

[71] Giovanna Dell'Orto, "Overseas Orphans Get Summer Vacation in U.S. and Sometimes Chances at New Lives," published on the Associated Press international wire on September 5, 2006.

[72] John Owen and Heather Purdey, eds. *International News Reporting: Frontlines and Deadlines* (Chichester: Wiley-Blackwell, 2009), 2.

best – deep reporting backed by institutional process," as the *Columbia Journalism Review* succinctly put it in a recent editorial.[73] The problem with the "vanishing newspaper," according to one study, is not so much with the paper part but with the news – what will make the news industry survive if it cannot generate enough revenue online and nobody buys papers? The Project for Excellence in Journalism's 2009 State of the News Media Report highlighted the urgency of the problem. Since 2001, U.S. newsrooms have bled one out of every five journalists – especially in overseas bureaus – as people increasingly turn to online news sources, but the news industry has not managed to stay in the black on online ad revenue. "Fewer people and less space," the report argued, "equates to significant erosion of the serious, accountability reporting that newspapers do more than any other medium." In mid-2009, the acting chair of the Federal Communications Commission, Michael Copps, similarly said that the media's struggle to "keep investors happy" is gravely endangering the vital public service that news media perform in a democracy.[74]

Some have suggested that when it comes to foreign news reporting, it might be a positive development that media consumers no longer have to rely on mainstream media or professional correspondents because bloggers, average citizens, and "parachute drop-in" journalists might be able to bring more varied and more relevant perspectives to home audiences.[75] Others, however, including all editors interviewed for this research, are instead seeking to validate journalistic credibility and social responsibility as part of a sustainable business plan, to reinvigorate youth interest in the news, and to highlight how the turn to blending community activist with journalist could set a very dangerous precedent for defending theories of press freedom.[76] Even more essentially, whereas there might be a wealth of information available to those who willingly seek it, "what is under threat is the broad, serendipitous daily exposure to news of the world that comes from turning the pages of a newspaper over your morning tea (so long as that newspaper is not the News of the World)," to quote Garton Ash's column again. Threats to that mass exposure are

73 "Escape the Silos," *Columbia Journalism Review* (November/December 2010): 4.

74 Copps's speech at the opening plenary session of the International Communication Association's 2009 annual convention, May 21, 2009, in Chicago.

75 David D. Perlmutter and John Maxwell Hamilton, eds. *From Pigeons to News Portals: Foreign Reporting and the Challenge of New Technology* (Baton Rouge: Louisiana State University Press, 2007).

76 Philip Meyer, *The Vanishing Newspaper: Saving Journalism in the Information Age* (Columbia: University of Missouri Press, 2004): 33; John C. Merrill, Peter J. Gade and Frederick R. Blevens, *Twilight of Press Freedom: The Rise of People's Journalism* (Mahwah, NJ: Lawrence Erlbaum Associates, 2001); Robert G. Picard, "The Challenges of Public Functions and Commercialized Media," in *The Politics of News, the News of Politics* 2nd ed., ed. Doris A. Graber et al. (Washington: CQ Press, 2008), 211–229; David T.Z. Mindich, *Tuned Out: Why Americans Under 40 Don't Follow the News* (New York: Oxford University Press, 2005).

ultimately threats to the ability of citizens worldwide to understand an ever-more interconnected globe.[77]

This book shares the latter view, arguing that professional journalists with enough background knowledge, interest and language fluency are best positioned to serve as mediators between an easily distracted public and a vast mass of realities out there in the world that it is imperative to make sense of. Already, a host of studies has suggested that the American public has little attention for, and knowledge of, foreign policy issues, especially if they concern countries far from the U.S. military and dominant cultures.[78] Some even argue that if media coverage were to suddenly bloom, people would remain uninterested, harming the "demand" side in the marketplace of foreign public affairs.[79] If news is only an information good like any other on the market, then, a critic speculated, "social sciences currently do not provide good answers on how much news is enough to make democracy's delegated decision making work well."[80]

The ideal of an informed citizenry capable of safeguarding freedom and making wise voting choices, however, has been an essential, though variously interpreted, staple of U.S. public life since the revolutionary era.[81] As two students of Americans' political knowledge convincingly demonstrated, "there is no way around the necessity of a broadly informed public in a democracy," and systemic factors, particularly the nature of the information environment, determine how informed the public can be.[82] Their conclusion is that, even though today's environment is unequalled in the quantity of information provided, the quality of accessible information needs to be raised for political knowledge to rise. A more recent study of news recall suggests a relevant snowball effect – whereas the amount of media coverage is a major predictor of audience recall, levels of prior knowledge also influence it, and those levels are presumably triggered by the media environment to begin with. In other words, the more news the media provide, the more people are likely to recall that information as well as to pay attention to future news.[83]

The greatest harm that foreign correspondence can do, then, is not through distorted coverage but through the lack of coverage, which allows discourses

77 Cottle, 347.

78 Thomas Knecht, "A Pragmatic Response to an Unexpected Constraint: Problem Representation in a Complex Humanitarian Emergency," *Foreign Policy Analysis* 5–2 (2009): 141.

79 Seaver, 66; Baum and Potter, 50.

80 James T. Hamilton, *All the News That's Fit to Sell: How the Market Transforms Information into News* (Princeton, NJ: Princeton University Press, 2004), 5.

81 Richard D. Brown, *The Strength of a People: The Idea of an Informed Citizenry in America, 1650–1870* (Chapel Hill: University of North Carolina Press, 1996).

82 Michael X. Delli Carpini and Scott Keeter, *What Americans Know about Politics and Why It Matters* (New Haven: Yale University Press, 1996), 17, 272.

83 Vincent Price and Edward J. Czilli, "Modeling Patterns of News Recognition and Recall," *Journal of Communication* 46–2 (Spring 1996): 56.

to become so impoverished that manipulation inevitably triumphs. The danger with the cacophony of unreliable accounts of the world is that, to paraphrase Jean Baudrillard, "there is more and more information, and less and less meaning."[84] It is this book's premise that meaningful information – or enough information with enough context to enable us to assign it meanings – is precisely what we should expect the press to provide when it deals with foreign affairs.

Evaluating Foreign News Coverage

There is ample evidence, of course, that journalism has repeatedly and glaringly failed to provide informative or even accurate renderings of the world well before the current challenges to the profession. Many of the prevailing approaches to international mass communication follow that line of criticism by studying the inadequacies and power abuses of news flow and news coverage, ranging from the imperial gaze to the inability to question the factual bases of policy choices.[85] There has been a "landslide" of international communication inquiries in the past decades about the inequities of international news flow[86] – and very little attention to the process of construction of meaning.[87] As classic textbooks like Arnold de Beer and John Merrill's *Global Journalism* suggest, the central focus of theoretical and research inquiries is systemic, centered on "global news and the way it flows within countries and intercontinentally," with much emphasis on economics and technologies.[88]

The study of news flow has its roots in modernization and the U.S. public diplomacy efforts of the 1950s and especially in the reaction they provoked from the "Third World," culminating in the dependency and world-system

[84] Quoted in Philip M. Taylor, *Global Communication, International Affairs and the Media since 1945* (London: Routledge, 1997), 3.

[85] To cite but two of numerous examples: Lance W. Bennett, Regina G. Lawrence and Steven Livingston, *When the Press Fails: Political Power and the News Media from Iraq to Katrina* (Chicago: University of Chicago Press, 2007), which however focused on Washington, not foreign, correspondents; and the classic Edward W. Said, *Covering Islam: How the Media and the Experts Determine How We See the Rest of the World* (New York: Pantheon Books, 1981).

[86] Tsan-Kuo Chang, "All Countries Not Created Equal to Be News," *Communication Research* 25–5 (1998): 528.

[87] Despite the title, this is no exception: Philo C. Wasburn, *The Social Construction of International News: We're Talking about Them, They're Talking about Us* (Westport, CT: Praeger, 2002).

[88] Arnold S. de Beer and John C. Merrill, *Global Journalism: Topical Issues and Media Systems* 4th ed. (Boston: Pearson, 2004), xvii. For very similar approaches to global or international communication, see also Thomas L. McPhail. *Global Communication: Theories, Stakeholders, and Trends* (Boston: Allyn and Bacon, 2002); Art Silverblatt and Mikolai Zlobin, *International Communications: A Media Literacy Approach* (Armonk, NY: 2004); Daya Kishan Thussu, *International Communication: Continuity and Change* 2nd ed. (New York: Oxford University Press, 2008); Howard Frederick, *Global Communication and International Relations* (Belmont, CA: Wadsworth, 1993); Robert Fortner, *International Communication: History, Conflict, and Control of the Global Metropolis* (Belmont, CA: Wadsworth, 1993).

theories.[89] To quote T.K. Chang, the message behind the latter two theories is that "all countries [are] not created equal to be news."[90] Both theories rest on the concept that where a country stands in the economic/political structure of the world system largely determines how much and how well it is covered in international news and what its chances are in the international "marketplace of ideas" as a news producer and distributor. Given their intellectual ethos in reform movements (like the New World Information and Communication Order), studies informed by dependency and world-system theories usually conclude that non-core countries (i.e., outside the United States and Western Europe) fare badly as to the direction, content and sheer quantity of news flow, with disastrous consequences for the chances of development and democracy. Other analyses seeking a longer historical perspective on the global media system argue that hegemonic practices and imperial policies established in the nineteenth century continue to shape global media today.[91] Skeptics have argued that accounts of media globalization are exaggerated when it comes to news, because in many countries the dominant medium is still television, which "domesticates" the international news it provides.[92] A recent study of the global communications system argued that its structuring and its regulation are a matter of foreign policy that states ignore at their peril.[93] A compendium of studies of journalism in different regions of the world seeks to bypass the concern entirely, by arguing that journalism is becoming a global phenomenon itself that can no longer be studied within national borders.[94]

Much of the rest of international communication literature focuses on professional journalism, usually either to blame or praise correspondents for their work, an approach that also tends to restrict to individuals what is a broader systemic role. Some standard works take the historical approach (such as the aptly named *Foreign Correspondence: The Great Reporters and Their Times* and Hamilton's aforementioned study); others offer a census-like, survey and interview take (such as Stephen Hess' *International News & Foreign Correspondents*); still another studied foreign correspondents covering war in El

89 See Bella Mody, *The Geopolitics of Representation in Foreign News: Explaining Darfur* (Lanham, MD: Lexington Books, 2010); Sujatha Sosale, *Communication, Development and Democracy: Mapping a Discourse* (Cresskill, NJ: Hampton Press, 2008); Jill Hills, *Telecommunications and Empire* (Urbana: University of Illinois Press, 2007); Alvin So, *Social Change and Development* (Newbury Park, CA: SAGE, 1990); Anthony Smith, *The Geopolitics of Information: How Western Culture Dominates the World* (New York: Oxford University Press, 1980).

90 Chang, 528–563.

91 Winseck and Pike.

92 James Curran, unpublished panel presentation to the International Communication Association, Chicago, May 2009.

93 Monroe E. Price, *Media and Sovereignty: The Global Information Revolution and Its Challenge to State Power* (Cambridge, MA: MIT Press, 2002).

94 Martin Löffelholz and David Weaver, eds. *Global Journalism Research: Theories, Methods, Findings, Future* (Malden, MA: Blackwell, 2008).

Salvador as the ethnography of a culture (indeed, all too often foreign correspondent comes to mean war correspondent, both in reality and in academic studies).[95] For many researchers, the basic assumptions are that Western (especially U.S.) media dominate the world and that their coverage of non-Western realities is grossly distorted.[96] The premise of these critiques is that, because of economic, political and historical (especially colonial) reasons, there are many traps for Western newsmakers who try to comprehend the non-Western realm, but these studies look for images, bias and distortion and not for what gives images meaning and how they are constructed.

If, on the other hand, we assume that identities are social and that historical constructions are "always 'in process,'"[97] then our research focus inevitably shifts to study how national identities have been negotiated through international mass communication and what impact they likely had on relations between countries. After all, viewed as a process of constructing meanings, international communication and international relations, at the most basic level, are about the same issue – power, or the creation, maintenance and transformation of power relationships. The press is a crucial player, because it has both the power and the responsibility of functioning as a "marketplace of ideas," with a pivotal role in shaping national identities through its stories. Those stories are at the heart of this book – the stories the American press has told about the rest of the world, how those stories have become part of the United States' interaction with the world, and how much it matters that they continue to be written.

Studying the Construction of the World through Foreign Correspondence

To discover the meaning and the effects of those stories means to study discourses, defined again as the way a subject is talked about – in this case how foreign nations are talked about – and the constructed societal meanings that make terms and themes understandable and commonsensical at a particular historical time. The following four chapters will provide a chronological analysis, sustained by extensive original discourse analysis of more than 2,000 news

[95] Mark Pedelty, *War Stories: The Culture of Foreign Correspondents* (New York: Routledge, 1995).

[96] See Jeremy Tunstall, *The Media Are American* (New York: Columbia University Press, 1977) and "Are the Media Still American?" *Media Studies Journal* 9–4 (Fall 1995): 7–16; Jonathan Fenby, *The International News Services* (New York: Schocken Books, 1986); Mort Rosenblum, *Who Stole the News?* (New York: J. Wiley, 1993); Jaap van Ginneken, *Understanding Global News* (London: SAGE, 1998); William A. Hachten and James F. Scotton, *The World News Prism: Global Media in an Era of Terrorism* 6th ed. (Ames: Iowa State Press, 2002).

[97] Stuart Hall and Paul du Gay, eds. *Questions of Cultural Identity* (London: SAGE, 1996), 2–4. Hazel Dicken-Garcia and K. Viswanath, "An Idea Whose Time Has Come: International Communication History," *Mass Communication & Society* 5–1 (2002): 3.

articles, of how the American press has covered the world and what images it has brought back to its readers. From the mid-nineteenth century to today, what foreign news has been covered and what discourses of the world have emerged in the American press? How do those images compare with U.S. foreign policies contemporary to them? Crucially, do the same frameworks of understanding of the world shape both media coverage and actual policies?

The point is not whether the American press has been manipulated or manipulative in its coverage of foreign countries, their intentions and U.S. policies. Whereas government, business and audience constraints cannot be dismissed, the focus in the following chapters is on what discourses in news media tell us about sociocultural meanings about the rest of the world, with the assumption that mass communication is crucial to the development, maintenance and eventual transformation of social reality.[98] Such a view does not imply a diminished importance of reporting foreign news – on the contrary, as noted earlier, the ability of the American press to provide a locus for enriching and shifting discourses about the world makes it essential that more journalists cover more stories so that it better embraces that responsibility.

The evolution, through the press, of a commonsensical, widely shared, self-sustaining understanding of foreign countries is assumed to have influenced Washington's foreign policies and their reception domestically at critical historical junctures. It is only within those accepted meanings that decisions and even manipulations can be made, and that elements of discursive change can be introduced. What, then, have been the discourses about foreign realities in the American press throughout its history? Accepting Wendt's argument that the inscription of subjective meanings over material realities is one of the strongest forms of power, how have states' identities been created and negotiated through mediated interactions?

A Note on Method: Finding Discourses of National Identity and Role

Images of nations in the press are representations of one "nation's sense of identity in relation to other nations," as one scholar of national identity in the media put it.[99] The very idea of national identity is constructed through discourses, disseminated via mass communication, and it always comprises "the construction of difference/distinctiveness and uniqueness."[100] An image, in other words, is the "joint product" of the characteristics of both the object and the observer.[101] Similarly, the assumption here is that discourses about foreign realities in the American press belong to three essential formations: A

98 See Larsen, 25–27.

99 Catherine Luther, "National Identities, Structure, and Press Images of Nations: The Case of Japan and the United States," *Mass Communication & Society* 5–1 (2002): 58.

100 Rudolf De Cillia, Martin Reisigl and Ruth Wodak, "The Discursive Construction of National Identities," *Discourse & Society* 10–2 (1999): 153.

101 Herbert Kelman, ed. *International Behavior* (New York: Holt, Rinehart and Winston, 1966): 26.

generalized construction of the "other," accompanied by a discourse of the self (i.e., another country is unlike America, which implies a definition of what the United States is), and a discourse about the specific identity of a particular country or region. The analytical methodology to discover and describe those discourses follows a modification of the three-step approach outlined by Fairclough: Examination of texts, discursive practices (text production, reception and distribution), sociocultural practices (situational, institutional and societal), and the links between those three components.[102] The primary research focuses on media texts, studying terms and themes in U.S. foreign correspondence. Discursive and sociocultural practices are addressed principally through existing literature and, in Chapter 6, interviews with editors.

The first goal in discourse analysis of the primary sources is to identify the major themes, implicit or explicit, and prevalent linguistic choices (e.g., vocabulary, metaphors,[103] descriptions and images) in the selected foreign correspondence texts. The second purpose of analysis is to identify intertextuality – defined here as the taken-for-granted, familiar "scripts" (meaning repertoires of general knowledge) in a given culture that were incorporated in the texts studied.[104] Intertextuality is assumed to be one of the crucial ways language is linked to sociocultural practices and change within them. Intertextuality includes the presuppositions taken for granted in texts, those implicit assumptions referring to ways things are talked about in a particular culture – "traces of the discourse practice in the text," in Fairclough's words.[105]

Some such traces are implicit, because they are so well known that they do not necessarily need to be mentioned specifically in order to affect construction of meaning. Lack of representation in text becomes as important as presence and ways of representation when we assume that commonsensical constructions are often left unsaid precisely because they are so common that there is no need to articulate them, and yet they make all the difference in international communication. A *New York Times* article on South Africa's first post-apartheid election, for example, described the vote "like South Africa itself, a hybrid of high-tech and make-do, of anxiety and expectation, of Europe and Africa"[106] – with "Europe" and "Africa" standing in, without further explanation, for civilization and its antithesis.

[102] Norman Fairclough, *Media Discourse* (New York: Edward Arnold, 1995), 16–17.

[103] Some studies of political communication are merging discourse analysis with critical metaphor analysis (see Bryan Meadows, "Distancing and Showing Solidarity via Metaphor and Metonymy in Political Discourse: A Critical Study of American Statements on Iraq during the Years 2004–2005," *Critical Approaches to Discourse Analysis across Disciplines* 1–2 [2007]: 1–17), but, in this book, metaphors are noted only as rhetorical tools indicative of particular discursive strategies.

[104] Fairclough, 30.

[105] Fairclough, 61.

[106] Bill Keller, "As All Go to the Polls: Who, How, Where, When," *New York Times*, April 5, 1994, A7.

Discourses about foreign realities and, by default, about the United States' own position, are therefore herein uncovered and analyzed in the foreign correspondence of the U.S. newspapers and wire service considered most influential in four different eras: the nineteenth century (starting after the establishment of the first foreign bureaus in 1838); the World Wars era; the Cold War era; and the post–Cold War, 9/11 era. Five significant foreign events per era were selected, without claiming that they were the most important top-twenty events in world history, but to ensure geographical and political diversity and to capture significant areas of interest for U.S. policymaking. They range from revolutions (e.g., in 1848 France and 1910 Mexico) to economic transformations (e.g., the 1853 opening of trade in Japan and the 2002 debut of the euro) and social changes (e.g., the 1994 end of apartheid and disintegration of the Soviet Union in 1991).

The justification for studying discourses over such a broad period of time is not in the expectation of an unbroken continuity of discourse. Although we cannot assume that discourses about foreign realities at one point in time signal some benchmark in a linear progression of discourse, comparing them across time is valid because they are bound to be related and referential. Furthermore, the history of American foreign correspondence uncovered in this book serves as fundamental theory testing for the argument about the effects of news media on foreign policymaking, in line with the recent rapprochement between international relations and historical scholarship.[107] Given that the study of power and change is essential to both disciplines, tracing both through time is crucial for deeper understanding.

Contrary to most treatments of foreign news reporting, this research avoided correspondence about wars the United States fought – if one's country is involved, war correspondence is essentially domestic news and it is best analyzed as a separate phenomenon.[108] For this research, interest is in broader foreign coverage, before U.S. troops are committed and where they are not, because the perception of what kind of world is out there cannot but have influenced Washington's decision making in how to interact with it. Visual and broadcast journalism are not studied, for historical and methodological analytical consistency. In addition, many studies show that television focuses on "superficial treatment of the more spectacular aspects of the news," which does not correlate with higher levels of comprehension on the part of viewers; whereas newspapers (in print or online) continue to this day to offer a wider

[107] Steve Yetiv, "History, International Relations, and Integrated Approaches: Thinking about Greater Interdisciplinarity," *International Studies Perspectives* 12–2 (May 2011): 94–118; Colin Elman and Miriam Fendius Elman, "The Role of History in International Relations," *Millennium – Journal of International Studies* 37–2 (2008): 357–364.

[108] For recent, noteworthy studies of war correspondence, see Michael S. Sweeney, *The Military and the Press: An Uneasy Truce* (Evanston, IL: Northwestern University Press, 2006) and Phillip Knightley's series, most recently *The First Casualty: The War Correspondent as Hero and Myth-Maker from the Crimea to Iraq* (Baltimore: Johns Hopkins University Press, 2004).

variety of in-depth, contextualized stories than other platforms, which might help some readers learn more about the world.[109]

For the second and third steps, in order to provide necessary context about discursive and sociocultural practices, both a production perspective (the profession of foreign correspondent, journalism education, institutional practices, etc.) and an audience perspective (the appetite for foreign news from U.S. readers, political engagement in foreign affairs, rituals of news consumption, etc.) are included. A particular focus is on news values as defined by changing professional and institutional practices; "values" such as feelings of affinity for particular countries, distance, scale, domestic relevance, source legitimacy and the very notions of objectivity and neutrality in journalism have all influenced what foreign occurrences become news and appear to have held steady in recent decades.[110] As a former journalist myself, I am keenly aware that no academic analysis of news stories can be complete without an understanding of the practices that constrain news reports, and their effect will be noted in the study of language and discourses.[111] Describing the importance of journalism's institutional and professional practices, however, does not mean reducing what journalists do to the mindless actions of puppets whose strings are pulled by corporate interests – such a limited perspective, popular in some media critics circles, needlessly vitiates journalism as both an object of study and a vital democratic sphere.[112]

Finally, major trends in U.S. foreign policy for the periods and events examined are reviewed and compared to the discourses found in foreign correspondence. Obviously, there are many different interpretations of the history of American foreign policy, ranging from realism and its emphasis on national interests to revisionism and its blame on aggressive expansion. This research does not seek to solve those disputes, but rather looks for an expected correspondence in the general frameworks of understanding of foreign realities

[109] Douglas A. Van Belle, "Bureaucratic Responsiveness to the News Media: Comparing the Influence of *The New York Times* and Network Television News Coverage on US Foreign Aid Allocations," *Political Communication* 20–3 (2003): 268; John Robinson and Mark Levy, *The Main Source: Learning from Television News* (Beverly Hills: Sage Publications, 1986), 232–233.

[110] Carruthers; Tsan-Kuo Chang, Brian Southwell, Hyung-Min Lee and Yejin Hong, "A Changing World, Unchanging Perspectives: American Newspaper Editors and Enduring Values in Foreign News Reporting," *International Communication Gazette* 74–4 (June 2012): 367–384. For a global look at news values, see Pamela J. Shoemaker and Akiba A. Cohen, *News around the World: Content, Practitioners, and the Public* (New York: Routledge, 2006).

[111] For an excellent introduction to news from a journalist's viewpoint, see Colleen Cotter, *News Talk: Investigating the Language of Journalism* (Cambridge: Cambridge University Press, 2010). The classic study of journalists' routines is Gaye Tuchman, *Making News: A Study in the Construction of Reality* (New York: Macmillan, 1978).

[112] Bartholomew H. Sparrow, *Uncertain Guardians: The News Media as a Political Institution* (Baltimore: Johns Hopkins University Press, 1999), 5; David Edwards and David Cromwell, *Newspeak in the 21st Century* (London: Pluto Press, 2009), 14.

shared by the U.S. press and policymakers as well as for any differences that suggest the distinctive importance of professional foreign correspondence as a locus of meaning. Those findings reflect the value of discourse analysis of news media texts in the context of international affairs, even though this research does not claim to uncover either the truth or the ultimate origin of the statements that belong to any particular discourse.

The ability to make causal inferences in historical qualitative research is limited, as King, Keohane and Verba put it, by the impossibility of rerunning "history with everything constant save for one investigator-controlled explanatory variable."[113] Constructivist approaches such as this book's, however, unlike postmodern ones, find causality in the constitution of discourses: The way a particular social fact is constructed (a foreign identity, in this case) is not mere description but a causal link, because "how things are put together makes possible, or even probable, certain kinds of political behaviors and effects."[114] Discourses in foreign news, supported by a secondary analysis of social, political, and institutional practices, are indicative of the range of possible, as well as implicitly excluded, outcomes. Actual correspondence of media discourses with foreign policy trends will be the evidentiary test of the theoretical formulation that underpins this book. Even though it cannot predict every action in every circumstance, foreign correspondence does provide a significant, distinct site for the formation of understandings of national identities, and that is why it matters. Again, the essential theoretical premise is that "state identity fundamentally shapes state preferences and actions"[115] – and so, this book argues, does the identity of another state, constructed in part through mass communication and deciphered through discourse analysis.

This model is offered as an additional theoretical and evidentiary causal link about the range of impacts, not as a substitute for analysis of political, social, institutional and psychological mechanisms that must also be accounted for in any foreign policy analysis. Clearly, such analysis, with a broader interpretation of causality than other social scientific approaches, has lower falsification and inter-reader reliability than other methodologies, such as more quantitative content analyses that capture words rather than concepts. But I believe that it is a fair trade for its higher ability to point to essential discursive and nondiscursive contexts as well as for its better grasp of a subtler model of media influence on the social and political environments. One additional disclaimer: A history of the discourses about the world in the American press cannot treat any specific case in the depth it would deserve, and certainly does not claim to cover every journalistic opus, every country reported on, and every policy decision. It would be extremely interesting, for example, to examine in depth each of the

113 Gary King, Robert O. Keohane and Sidney Verba, *Designing Social Inquiry: Scientific Inference in Qualitative Research* (Princeton, NJ: Princeton University Press, 1994), 82.

114 Finnemore and Sikkink, 394.

115 Finnemore and Sikkink, 398.

twenty cases presented in the next four chapters and, adding primary analysis of governmental documents, to study the interplay of press and politics in the case of Cuba in the 1890s or the Middle East in the 1960s or the European Union in the 2000s. That kind of detailed case study is not attempted here; rather, the selected examples provided are supposed to lend support to the general argument, and the reader is asked to judge its persuasiveness on the overall approach, with the hope that narrower, more detailed studies will follow.

Conclusions

In essence, then, to conduct discourse analysis of American press images of the world and to look for their correspondence to policy trends means examining taken-for-granted knowledge critically, recognizing the cultural and historical situatedness of discourse, and following the links between knowledge and social processes/actions.[116] It means discovering ways of knowing and talking about – discourses of – foreign realities because they ultimately shape actions regarding foreign countries. Chapters 2 through 5 present the findings of such analysis for four distinct eras: the establishment of American foreign correspondence and the beginning of U.S. global power, 1838–1900; the confirmation of the United States as a dominating global presence, 1901–1945; the Cold War era, 1946–1991; the post–Cold War, new media era, 1992 to the present. Before a final chapter with theoretical, historical and normative conclusions, Chapter 6 examines the endangered status of foreign news in the American press today, in the second decade of the twenty-first century, and possible scenarios for the future of the foreign correspondent profession through interviews with news leaders both in the United States and abroad. This review of the history of American journalism's engagement with the world, in fact, does not attempt only to illuminate how the American press portrayed the world outside the United States and how that coverage interacted with U.S. foreign policy. It is also intended to provide the launching pad for a discussion of what the future of foreign correspondence and international news might be as the twenty-first century progresses.

The last chapter offers reflections on the consequences for U.S. power globally and for the relations between the Unites States and the rest of the world. Such an approach has become increasingly relevant within circles debating the relative decline of American power linked to rising anti-Americanism abroad, although historians of international relations have long argued that both scholars and policymakers would be better off if they examined "the cultural infrastructures of the nations and political systems they are dealing with," or, put another way, if they tried to understand how foreign "others" think.[117]

[116] Jørgensen and Phillips, 5–9.

[117] Adda B. Bozeman, *Politics & Culture in International History: From the Ancient Near East to the Opening of the Modern Age* 2nd ed. (New Brunswick, NJ: Transaction Publishers, 1994), 6.

Nothing can hinder power, as measured in capabilities, as can a failure to project power as influence. And if indeed politics in the twenty-first-century world rely more on soft- than hard-power balancing, as some are suggesting, the importance of international understanding becomes all the more critical.[118] "In the information age, success is not only whose army wins, but whose story wins," as soft-power theorist Joseph Nye has repeatedly argued.[119]

This book suggests that the importance of constructing and reporting complex stories about the world to Americans is integral to, and transcends, preserving American power. The call for the American press's continued involvement in the coverage of foreign news does not rest on the assumption that the press can either uncritically transmit better stories about American policies or somehow always get right an objective truth about foreign places. Rather, it rests on the assumption that the press, by providing more and more insightful coverage of foreign realities and American realities, can best serve its function as locus for negotiation of meaning, which lies at the center of the hope for a more equitable international system.

Two major concerns drive the entire effort: the vital role that the press has in translating nations for one another and the responsibility that such a role entails for journalism, particularly the influential American press. The time to ask ourselves what role the press plays in international relations is, critically, now. Now that U.S. managers mobilize more correspondents to Westminster Abbey than Afghanistan because royal weddings generate more "most-clicked" stories than war. Now that, according to one count, only five U.S. newspapers have multiple bureaus abroad, and one of those publishes only online.[120] Now that budget cuts and niche delivery are making it more difficult to get substantive foreign news in the United States – precisely when urgent global problems require the kinds of solution that come from nations working together because they know one another more, not less.

Since 2000, despite such newsworthy events as two wars abroad, a global economic meltdown, and seismic changes in immigration, American newspaper reporters based in foreign countries have declined by at least 25 percent.[121] It is useless to wax nostalgic about some largely mythical great correspondent – but it is just as dangerous to think that bloggers, occasional visitors and advocates can provide the vast basis of information necessary for substantive meanings to be extrapolated and challenged. The assumption that meanings for social realities are negotiated and not found highlights the urgency of keeping the gathering of foreign news vigorous and painstaking. Momentous foreign

[118] T.V. Paul, James J. Wirtz and Michel Fortmann, eds. *Balance of Power: Theory and Practice in the 21st Century* (Stanford, CA: Stanford University Press, 2004).

[119] The concept is explored in Joseph S. Nye Jr., *The Future of Power* (New York: Public Affairs Books, 2011).

[120] Michael Anft, "The World, in Eight Weeks," *Johns Hopkins Magazine* (February 2009): 33.

[121] Anft, 32.

policy decisions can only be made within ecologies of discourse that emerge through, and are reflected by, news media content. An impoverished discursive environment will certainly lead to less democratic debate and possibly an unnecessarily restricted policy range.

The contribution of such a constructivist approach is to explore "the social creation of the environment in which decision makers act"[122] – therefore assuming that dwindling coverage must entail less room for understanding, with catastrophic consequences for action. Even though this book argues that professional foreign correspondence is essential for better-informed policies, ill-executed journalism can have disastrous effects. Many have criticized journalists, for example, for not countering the Bush administration's claims of weapons of mass destruction in Iraq in 2003. Such major failures reinforce the critical point made here: The media have a great responsibility not only factually but also discursively to shine some light on world events that can enrich understanding beyond existing stereotypes. Hence, it is not "oxymoronic" to use constructivist research such as this book for a normative prescription – indeed, the necessity of "substantive coverage" provided by the media to a mass public is a key tenet of democratic theory.[123] Given the pivotal place of the news media as idea mediators in international affairs, it is vital to the public interest of the United States – and the rest of the world – that the American press further embraces its role of providing better informed and more complete stories about the world to America.

[122] A. Cooper Drury et al., "Note from the Editors," *Foreign Policy Analysis* 3–3 (July 2010): 189.

[123] Matthew J. Hoffmann, "Is Constructivist Ethics an Oxymoron?" *International Studies Review*, 11–2 (June 2009): 231–252; Seaver, 65.

2

A New Country, A New Profession

America and Its Foreign Correspondents Get Ready to Take on the World

> I hear from all sides exclamations of amazement at the enterprise, and, as it is called, audacity of the United States press. Its representatives are pushing farther than any. Go in what direction you will, on the left bank of the Rhine, or on the right; at Berlin, Frankfort and Mayence, or in the tiny little villages which are suddenly becoming invested with the attributes of important and historical spots, "There are those (to use the strong expressions of jealous and worsted rivals) d – d Yankees."[1]

In August 1870, as the war between France and Prussia was raging along the Rhine, the London correspondent of the *Chicago Tribune* wrote the characteristically tongue-in-cheek, self-congratulatory note in the previous paragraph to its editors, who bluntly subtitled the article "Advantages of American Correspondents Over European." Barely more than thirty years after an enterprising New York editor had started the first formal U.S. foreign correspondence, American reporters were jostling one another and European journalists to cover the world. Throughout the nineteenth century, the American press steadily increased the supply of eyewitness news of the world it offered to readers across the country. As U.S. journalism was growing into a profession – a social institution separate from the partisan politics where it had originated – American diplomats were beginning to explore the global reaches of what had been a strictly continental power.

Foreign news – a staple of colonial and early nineteenth-century U.S. newspapers – changed drastically in the mid-1800s with the introduction of the

[1] "Europe," *Chicago Tribune*, August 18, 1870, 2. Throughout the nineteenth century, newspaper articles hardly ever had bylines. In direct quotation, this book retains the original spelling; e.g., Frankfort instead of Frankfurt.

first professional corps of foreign correspondents. James Gordon Bennett, editor of the *New York Herald* – the most successful early proponent of a new kind of journalism that broke away from promoting political parties and went into the business of selling news to the masses – sailed to Europe in 1838 on the return trip of the first Atlantic-crossing steamboat to set up his news "bureaus."[2] News gathering and reporting were replacing political advocacy and disquisition in the antebellum press, and foreign news became one of the most heated arenas for competition among U.S. newspapers. The development of foreign correspondence went together with the emergence of news agencies that specialized in the fastest delivery of news digests. One such agency – the Associated Press, run as a cooperative of U.S. newspapers – would become by the turn of the century the major purveyor of foreign news to Americans. Then as now, the correspondents' dispatches told a more nuanced, personal story of the world in which the United States was taking its first steps.

This chapter engages America's, and its foreign correspondents', first forays into world affairs to begin to answer the fundamental questions that guide this book: What discourses of the world have emerged in the American press? Do they belong to the same general frameworks of understanding of the world as major foreign policy trends contemporary to them? What can the images of the world created in the media tell us about the role of the press in international affairs? The focus is on how newspapers in New York, Chicago and New Orleans covered five events with enduring consequences: The European revolutions of 1848; the opening of Japan to international trade in 1853; the Franco-Prussian War of 1870–1871; the Cuban Revolution in 1895; and the Boxer Uprising in China in 1900. Linking each event are burgeoning journalistic standards and practices that parallel Washington's growing involvement in world affairs, culminating in the 1898 war and the establishment of the United States as a global power. Before delving into the discourses about foreign nations (and the United States) that emerge from the coverage of each event, the next two sections highlight the era's social, political and cultural practices within which discourses existed by briefly exploring major developments in journalism, especially foreign news, and American foreign relations.

Journalism's Professionalization: Nineteenth-Century Writers and Readers

By as early as 1750, most colonial Americans who could read had access to a newspaper, and the news industry grew immensely through the Revolutionary Era to assume a social importance that has led many media historians to argue

[2] On Bennett's crucial contributions to early American journalism, see James L. Crouthamel, *Bennett's New York Herald and the Rise of the Popular Press* (Syracuse, NY: Syracuse University Press, 1989), 48 ff.

that there would not have been an American Revolution without newspapers.[3] Political tracts – original or reprinted from other newspapers – together with commercial notices constituted the basic fare, and political propaganda was the explicit raison d'être of most publications in the late eighteenth and early nineteenth centuries. Foreign items, usually reprinted from European and other newspapers, dominated the relatively little news content there was; before as well as after independence, short news bulletins came nearly exclusively from western European countries – Great Britain foremost among them – and dealt with politics, conflicts and foreign relations. It was hardly breaking news – most of it consisted of reprints from British newspapers and historians have concluded that it took between six and eleven weeks for the account of a foreign event to appear in American newspapers in the colonial era. As late as in 1815, nearly 2,000 soldiers were killed in the Battle of New Orleans, fought two weeks after the signing of a peace treaty with Britain in Belgium, news of which reached the northeastern United States a month after the battle.[4] In addition to being late, the news content reprinted from overseas presses was written for a very different domestic audience, and American readers could but guess at the culturally specific references that overseas editors had included.

As the new country turned to building its own nationhood and statehood in the first decades of the nineteenth century, journalism also turned its attention to domestic matters and, most importantly, to actual newsgathering that implied more than waiting for someone else to do the reporting. The practice reflected in the following 1814 notice in the Philadelphia *Democratic Press* was waning: "The editor of this paper will sincerely thank any of his friends, who will favor him with loan of foreign papers, particularly French or English."[5] While reprinting of content from other newspapers continued to be a part of the foreign news menu – the vast majority of news from the 1900 Boxer Rebellion came via the London dailies – enterprise and competition figured prominently starting in the 1810s and 1820s. At first, American editors bought boats – and in some cases had slaves row them – to be the first to reach the incoming ships carrying foreign newspapers.[6] From the 1830s to the end of the century, the emergence of foreign correspondents and the technological progress in the speed of newsgathering and distributing fit the radical transformation of the

3 For American journalism in colonial times, see Michael Emery, Edwin Emery and Nancy Roberts, *The Press and America: An Interpretive History of the Mass Media* 9th ed. (Boston: Allyn and Bacon, 2000); Al Hester, Susan Parker Humes and Christopher Bickers, "Foreign News in Colonial North American Newspapers, 1764–1775," *Journalism Quarterly* 57–1 (Spring 1980): 18–22, 44; Paul Langford, "British Correspondence in the Colonial Press, 1763–1775: A Study in Anglo-American Misunderstanding before the American Revolution," in *The Press and the American Revolution*, ed. Bernard Bailyn and John B. Hench (Boston: Northeastern University Press, 1980), 273–313; Arthur M. Schlesinger, *Prelude to Independence: The Newspaper War on Britain, 1764–1776* (New York: Alfred Knopf, 1958).

4 Mitchell Stephens, *A History of News* 3rd ed. (New York: Oxford University Press, 2007), 210.

5 Quoted in Stephens, 213.

6 Michael Schudson, *Discovering the News* (New York: Basic Books, 1978), 26; T.H. Giddings, "Rushing the Transatlantic News in the 1830s and 1840s," *The New York Historical Society*

American news media, from an elite service in the hands of parties to a mass-marketed product run by irreverent editors who professed themselves men of the people, although they also openly sought the political limelight.[7]

The beginning of a modern conceptualization of journalism dates from the emergence of the penny press in the 1830s and the dramatic upheavals of the Civil War in the 1860s. The latter institutionalized the changes inaugurated by the first: The American newspaper went from a tool of party politics – with a staff often of one, who rarely left the office, putting together opinion pieces for a minuscule circulation – to a professionally produced, advertising-supported compilation of up-to-the-minute news that reflected a developing interest in standards of objectivity and accuracy.[8] The era of the editor made way for the era of the reporter, including the foreign correspondent, an occupation that increasingly took on the specialization, training and uniqueness of a profession. Opinions and facts were beginning to go their separate ways, although news content was far from dispassionate. By the end of the century, large news organizations dominated the market and vied for supremacy in influence over public opinion as well as political leadership – the sensationalist excesses and strident political commentaries of the Hearst versus Pulitzer battle for U.S. involvement in the Cuban Revolution of the 1890s are perhaps the most notorious examples.

For the mainstream press at least, the legacy of the American Revolution, especially the rights enshrined by the First Amendment, meant a guaranteed role in the process of American democracy, as purveyors of information and facilitators in the public sphere. The U.S. system of republican governance made the mass diffusion of information central to its very existence – as evident not only in freedom of expression protections but in the severe crackdowns on information perceived as a threat to existing values, such as abolitionist literature. More pragmatically, through subsidies for public education, postal services and newspaper exchange systems, the U.S. government set the foundation for the widespread availability and centrality of the press to the American people – so much so that French observer Alexis de Tocqueville remarked the American man was "plunging into the wildernesses of the New World with his Bible,

Quarterly 42–1 (1958): 50–51; Victor Rosewater, *History of Cooperative News-Gathering in the United States* (New York: D. Appleton and Co., 1930).

7 For American journalism in the first half of the nineteenth century, see: Donald R. Avery, "American Over European Community? Newspaper Content Changes, 1808–1812," *Journalism Quarterly* 63–2 (Summer 1986): 311–314; Gerald J. Baldasty, *The Commercialization of News in the Nineteenth Century* (Madison: University of Wisconsin Press, 1992); Willard G. Bleyer, *Main Currents in the History of American Journalism* (Boston: Houghton Mifflin, 1927); Robert Desmond, *The Press and World Affairs* (New York: D. Appleton-Century Co., 1937); Hazel Dicken-Garcia, *Journalistic Standards in Nineteenth-Century America* (Madison: University of Wisconsin Press, 1989); Donald L. Shaw, "At the Crossroads: Change and Continuity in American Press News, 1820–1860," *Journalism History* 8–2 (1981): 38–50.

8 David T.Z. Mindich, *Just the Facts* (New York: New York University Press, 1998); Dan Schiller, "An Historical Approach to Objectivity and Professionalism in American News Reporting," *Journal of Communication* 29 (1979): 46–51.

ax, and *newspapers*."[9] The press had helped Americans conceptualize themselves as such, as opposed to British subjects, during the Revolutionary Era. Throughout the nineteenth century, it brought issues to the national agenda that redefined what America was and what its role in the world should become, and the Associated Press, as noted in the next section, helped solidify the country's self-definition.[10]

The century, however, witnessed a major shift in how the press fulfilled its social role: It increasingly focused on event-based stories rather than ideas, and, in line with the imperatives of a mass-product industry, it sought the lowest common denominator for the broadest variety of content.[11] In so doing, the press did manage to establish itself as a unique social institution of tremendous capabilities and reach. For both information and entertainment, it became a daily necessity for the vast majority of Americans – the century witnessed a major expansion in both the number of newspapers and their circulation, which grew significantly faster than the increasingly urban population.[12] As one historian put it, the challenge for most readers changed throughout the nineteenth century from one of getting scarce information to making sense of an overabundance of it.[13]

From Pigeons to Eyewitnesses: Nineteenth-Century Foreign News

Those changes also affected the way the press covered the world. For much of the nineteenth century, the vast majority of foreign news was either taken from European newspapers – especially the London dailies – or provided by the Associated Press (AP), a cooperative formed in 1846 as an association of New York newspapers that wanted to pool resources for a pony express route that would bring news faster from the Mexican War front.[14] That war, incidentally, was also the first to be covered by professional U.S. war correspondents, who would become a specialized kind of journalist later in the century with the Civil War.[15] The AP posted its first "foreign correspondent" in Halifax, Nova Scotia, in the late 1840s. His job was to master relays of

9 Quoted in Paul Starr, *The Creation of the Media: Political Origins of Modern Communications* (New York: Basic Books, 2004), 48; emphasis added.

10 Menahem Blondheim, *News over the Wires: The Telegraph and the Flow of Public Information in America, 1844–1897* (Cambridge, MA: Harvard University Press, 1994), 191, 195.

11 Dicken-Garcia, 228–232.

12 David W. Bulla and Gregory A. Borchard, *Journalism in the Civil War Era* (New York: Peter Lang, 2010), 212; Thomas C. Leonard, *News for All: America's Coming-of-Age with the Press* (New York: Oxford University Press, 1995).

13 Richard D. Brown, *Knowledge Is Power: The Diffusion of Information in Early America, 1700–1865* (New York: Oxford University Press, 1989), 271.

14 Reporters of the Associated Press, *Breaking News: How the Associated Press Has Covered War, Peace, and Everything Else* (New York: Princeton Architectural Press, 2007); Bleyer, 296.

15 Michael S. Sweeney, *The Military and the Press: An Uneasy Truce* (Evanston, IL: Northwestern University Press, 2006), 17; Phillip Knightley, *The First Casualty: The War Correspondent as Hero and Myth-Maker from the Crimea to Iraq* (Baltimore: Johns Hopkins University Press,

pigeons, horses, trains and wire cables so that AP members could get European news within the shortest time from when transatlantic steamships touched the first North American harbor. In 1866, after the successful establishment of the transatlantic telegraphic connection, the AP opened its first overseas bureau, in London. However, until the early twentieth century, the organization got most of its news through an arrangement with other wire services. Reuters, first alone and then in a cartel with Havas and Wolff – all reliable providers of their respective governments' views – gave AP news from Europe and its overseas spheres of influence, and the AP reciprocated with U.S. news.[16] By reprint or telegraph, then, the vast majority of foreign news in the United States passed through London's filter and then through what one study has called the AP's "monopoly of knowledge."[17]

From the 1850s to 1900, a typical foreign news digest in American newspapers looked like this: War, business and celebrity news was prominently displayed across several columns of the front pages and written in what came to be called a "straight" news style – just the facts, or what passed for them, without too much embellishment. The layering of details was stunning, but one wonders how readers made out with hardly any background or analysis that might have helped them follow the dense lines of tiny print. In 1859, a prominent New York editor warned his colleagues not to rely on "a single electrician at a seaport town" – a telegraph operator transmitting news bulletins from overseas – for accurate international coverage.[18] Corps of foreign correspondents were charged with making sense of the growing avalanche of information. In the United States, five newspapers dominated various phases of nineteenth-century foreign correspondence, and they are selected for this chapter's analysis: The earliest organizer, James G. Bennett, made his *New York Herald* the world's largest daily by 1860, and the paper eventually published a widely followed international edition in Europe. George Wilkins Kendall, founder of the *New Orleans Picayune* and himself a correspondent in the war with Mexico in 1846 and later in Europe, earned prominence in the South for foreign service. Horace Greeley of the *New York Tribune*, widely considered the most influential editorialist of the century, hired as foreign specials not the ink-strained wretches who toiled under no bylines or pen names, but figures still recognizable today – Margaret Fuller, one of the first women to work for mainstream American newspapers; Bayard Taylor, arguably the most famous

2004), 41; James Melvin Lee, *History of American Journalism* (Boston: Houghton Mifflin, 1923), 260.

16 Reporters of the Associated Press, 262; John Hohenberg, *Foreign Correspondence: The Great Reporters and Their Times* 2nd ed. (Syracuse, NY: Syracuse University Press, 1995), 12–13; Starr, 180.

17 Blondheim, 1, 96.

18 "The New British Minister," *New York Times*, January 6, 1859, 4. For a history of antebellum foreign correspondence, see Giovanna Dell'Orto, *Giving Meanings to the World: The First U.S. Foreign Correspondents, 1838–1859* (Westport, CT: Greenwood, 2002).

travel writer of his time; and even Karl Marx. The *New York Times*, founded in 1851 by Henry J. Raymond, also chased excellence in foreign reporting, managing a major scoop for American journalism when Raymond found himself covering the decisive battle in the French-Sardinian push of the Austrians out of Italy in 1859. Through a complicated relay that included Raymond's wife rushing to meet a ship about to leave port in France, the editor and his Paris-based correspondent managed to get their accounts of the Battle of Solferino into the *Times* in New York before the British newspapers with accounts by the London *Times* correspondent arrived in America – a drastic contrast to the reliance of U.S. newspapers on their overseas counterparts just a generation before. Finally, Joseph Medill took over the *Chicago Tribune* in 1855, turning it into the most influential Western newspaper of the time.

Their efforts to bring American readers the news from as far as Japan challenge the scholarly wisdom that the U.S. press truly started to cover the world only in the twentieth century.[19] On the contrary, these five newspapers tried to provide the context, feeling and nuance missing from the AP's early cables. Their interest parallels the broadening global focus of America's politicians.

Getting Entangled: U.S. Foreign Relations in the Nineteenth Century

American foreign policy through the nineteenth century was dominated by two somewhat paradoxically related themes: a desire to remain neutral from Great Power empire building and related conflicts, and expansion, first territorial and, after 1865, economic.[20] For the newly independent, still vulnerable country, a dominant preoccupation remained to avert or minimize conflict with the great colonial powers, especially Great Britain, France and Spain. It is not surprising that in its first years, the new nation's leaders would think foremost in defensive terms and, to quote Thomas Jefferson, try to avoid all manners of "entangling alliances." Parallel to that, however, were the urge and the need to expand – in landmass, in economic power, and in global stature. Even as U.S. presidents and secretaries of state sought insulation from European and colonial conflicts, they actively courted trade agreements and territorial annexation (in North America) that repeatedly brought the country into and on the brink of wars.

19 Michael Emery, *On the Front Lines: Following America's Foreign Correspondents across the Twentieth Century* (Washington: American University Press, 1995), xii.

20 For a review of American foreign policy, see Jerald A. Combs, *The History of American Foreign Policy*: Volume I, to 1920, 3rd ed. (Armonk, NY: M.E. Sharpe, 2008); Ernest May, *American Imperialism* (New York: Atheneum, 1968); Bradford Perkins, *The Cambridge History of American Foreign Relations: Volume I, The Creation of a Republican Empire, 1776–1865* (Cambridge: Cambridge University Press, 1993); Charles Vevier, "American Continentalism: An Idea of Expansion, 1845–1910," *American Historical Review* 65–2 (1960): 323–335; Rush Welter, *The Mind of America: 1820–1860* (New York: Columbia University Press, 1975); Roger S. Whitcomb, *The American Approach to Foreign Affairs* (Westport, CT: Praeger, 1998); Michael Cox and Doug Stokes, eds. *US Foreign Policy* (Oxford: Oxford University Press, 2008), 46–62.

The War of 1812 with Great Britain reinforced the American perception that the new country could take on the world stage on par with the old world – some argued largely because of the aforementioned communication delay that made General Andrew Jackson's victory look like a decisive battle even though it was in fact fought after peace had been negotiated.[21]

Between that war and the outbreak of the Civil War, the issue of territorial expansion took over as Washington's main preoccupation in foreign policy, and indeed in domestic policy, because it was so closely related to sectional conflicts over the expansion of slavery. In 1823, President James Monroe issued a statement of principle that would become known as the Monroe Doctrine. It essentially enshrined the principles of noninterference, manifested in the promise to stay away from European affairs, and of expansion, making the Americas a U.S. domain off-limits to Europe's reach. America's westward march was speeded along by new transportation and communication technologies, including railways, steamboats and, at midcentury, the telegraph. Florida, Texas, the Southwest and the Northwest all became American in the space of about thirty years. Standing in the way had been a few British and Spanish colonists, plus Mexicans and Native Americans, sparsely populating vast expanses of land that, Washington reasoned, would only benefit from its oversight and Americans' industrious efforts. Indeed, some have argued that a sense of mission stemming from self-righteousness guided U.S. foreign policymakers, who appeared to believe that planting the American flag all over the continent benefited all concerned and spared the new world the dreadful war-ridden fate of the old one. According to one historian, Manifest Destiny, one of the guiding principles in the 1840s and 1850s, "was the ultimate expression of the Americans' most vigorous hopes for raising the rest of the world to their own level."[22]

Two different sorts of constraints stopped expansion from growing north and south of the current borders of the United States – reaching over for too much of Canada meant yet another, hardly affordable direct confrontation with Britain, and taking too much of Mexico meant somehow integrating vast populations of Mexicans. After all, the Northwest Ordinance of 1787, agreed on by Congress, clearly established that all U.S. territory would ultimately be "on equal footing with the original States in all respects whatever."[23] The choice was either to admit people of a different race as citizens or rule Central America as a colony – the fact that Washington chose neither is indicative of how different Americans believed their kind of expansionism to be from European-style imperialism and colonialism.

Whereas the economic and population booms of the midcentury years were certainly leading factors in the drive to expand, so was the shared sense of

[21] Combs, 53.

[22] Welter, 66.

[23] Quoted in Perkins, 172.

mission, which rested on the assumption that American intervention would by default be beneficial to those reached by it. Penny press and then yellow press editors, through their editorials, helped turn Manifest Destiny into a popular ideology that stood virtually unchallenged at the time as its expression ranged from a desire for annexation to the ideal of the United States as a beacon to the world, according to Frederick Merk.[24] One major conceptualization underlies the parallel trends of neutrality and expansion – a firmly rooted belief in American exceptionalism. Nayak and Malone, who have called exceptionalism "America's foundational narrative," argue that the concept helped position the United States, at least in its leaders' minds, in a role destined to dominate not only non-Western realms, but (Western) Europe as well, and as such it was uniquely American.[25] As they targeted expansion and conflict management to avoid dirtying America's hands with colonial conflicts, while bringing the benefits of civilization to its Providence-ordained territory, U.S. leaders seem to have followed the guiding principle of American uniqueness.

Before ambitions of global power became the overarching concern at the end of the century, Washington's goal was to create a model society, one founded on republicanism and individualism – missionary expansionism, peace and prosperity would somehow follow. In fact, once it had managed to survive the mortal threat of the Civil War – a threat that heightened fears Great Britain would again intervene in U.S. affairs – the United States emerged in 1865 as a historical oddity: a "republican empire," in the happy oxymoron by one historian.[26] The war's end solidified the position of the United States as the world's foremost agricultural and industrial power, a combination that eventually pushed it to pursue new markets overseas, where the major world powers were already fighting over them.

In the immediate postwar years, when the domestic politics of Reconstruction dominated the agenda, Congress and the American people in general had little interest in aggressive expansion, as evidenced by neglect of the main tools for it – armed forces, particularly the navy, and diplomatic activity. What little international activity there was focused on protecting existing American interests abroad, particularly commercial. It is only in the 1880s and 1890s that the rising social, manufacturing and commercial power of the United States tilted the scale toward expansion, although it continued to be more in search of markets than land and cautiously attempted to stay aloof from the free-for-all that was exacerbating rivalries among European and Asian powers. The end of the century saw two parallel manifestations of America's global ambitions after a

[24] Frederick Merk, *Manifest Destiny and Mission in American History* (Cambridge, MA: Harvard University Press, 1995).

[25] Meghana V. Nayak and Christopher Malone, "American Orientalism and American Exceptionalism: A Critical Rethinking of US Hegemony," *International Studies Review* 11–2 (2009): 253–276.

[26] Perkins, 233.

heated national debate: the 1898 war against Spain to free Cuba – which under the guise of a nation-building effort gave the United States its first overseas possessions, with fleet ports at strategic locations like Guantánamo and the Philippines – and the open door notes with China.

Much controversy still surrounds the Spanish-American War, including the role of feverishly pro-war public opinion and the inevitability of the acquisition of an empire, an uncomfortable proposition for most Americans in the late nineteenth century, especially after Filipinos fought back against the U.S. "liberators." President McKinley, keenly aware of the importance of the press and public support, tried hard to sell a new world power role to the American people, thus becoming to some historians the first "modern" president.[27] In fact, since the eighteenth century, constitutional ambiguities over executive versus legislative power in the formulation of American foreign policy made policymaking significantly more sensitive to public opinion than in most other countries.[28] The policy toward China is perhaps more characteristic of the diplomatic principles that would endure in the twentieth century: intervention abroad, not for colonial purposes, but to check European imperialism and to preserve the interests of American business.[29] This very attitude also brought a final and enduring rapprochement with Great Britain, which recognized in an alliance with the United States a check against more aggressive Great Powers.

The inherent contradiction between policies favoring isolation or a peculiarly business-like missionary form of interventionism stemmed at a philosophical level from the widely shared belief, both among policymaking elites and the public, that the U.S. republican form of government was uniquely conforming to the ideals of freedom and individual dignity. The fact that its constitution was grander in every aspect meant that its way of life and consequent global role were both intrinsically different from anything that happened before or elsewhere. The inherent faith in the United States and disdain for foreign countries was a natural condition for a nascent republic, perhaps, but one fraught with danger for a future world power. To a large extent, American superiority and condescension framed the picture of the world portrayed by the first foreign correspondents.

America Covers the World: Nineteenth-Century Media Discourses

Throughout the nineteenth century, as the country found and then started flexing its global muscle, new technologies sped increasing amounts of foreign

27 George C. Herring, "Imperial Tutor," in *Selling War in a Media Age: The Presidency and Public Opinion in the American Century*, ed. Kenneth Osgood and Andrew K. Frank (Gainesville: University Press of Florida, 2010), 18–47.

28 George C. Herring, *From Colony to Superpower: U.S. Foreign Relations since 1776* (Oxford: Oxford University Press, 2008), 92.

29 Cox and Stokes, eds., 51.

news – including dispatches from new professionals – to newly industrialized newspapers read by the widest masses ever. This book's principal argument is that the press, starting then, has functioned as the public arena where meanings for things literally foreign become understood within general frameworks that in turn inform political actions. What, then, were the images of the world and, by reflex, of the United States that were created and negotiated in the earliest American foreign correspondence? In the coverage of five significant events from 1848 to 1900, what discursive formations emerge about a generalized "other," the non-American; the construction of America that that implies; and the specific identity of covered countries and regions? The findings reflect analysis of more than 300 articles and editorials from the *New York Herald*, *New York Tribune*, *New York Times*, *New Orleans Picayune*, and *Chicago Tribune*.[30]

Revolutions of 1848: Can Europe Handle Republicanism?

In a long letter detailing the start of the February 1848 revolution in France, the Paris correspondent of the *New York Herald* admonished readers: "Trust one who is on the spot, and whose business it is to learn the real sentiments of the people.... You may reckon upon a series of these letters to arrive weekly by the steamers, giving you such comments on the current events of this most momentous epoch as you are not likely to gather from the journals either of London or Paris which may reach you, and which none but an eye witness or ear witness on the spot can supply."[31]

The unidentified writer laid out the basic principle that all future U.S. foreign correspondents would follow in their reporting from across the world: They would be where news happened, eyewitnesses to it, making it their business to know not just events but what foreign peoples thought. As revolutions spread across Europe in the spring of 1848, American reporters rushed to the scene, convinced that they were witnessing the birth of European republicanism. In excruciating blow-by-blow accounts accompanied by sweeping generalizations, they told American readers that charming old Europe was finally following the

[30] The dates selected for study are: February 1 to June 30, 1848, for the revolution in France; July 1, 1853, to December 31, 1855, for the trade mission to Japan; July 19 to August 31, 1870, and May 10 to May 30, 1871, for the beginning and the end of the war between France and Prussia; October 1, 1895, to January 31, 1896, for the revolution in Cuba; June 20 to August 14, 1900, for the Boxer Uprising. The *New York Times* and *Chicago Tribune* were not studied for the 1848 event; the first was founded in 1851, and fire destroyed the early files of the latter, founded in 1847, so that only a few scattered issues remain prior to 1852. When available, online databases were used (e.g., for the *New York Times*) and the search terms were as follows: France; Japan and Perry; France and Prussia; Cuba and correspondent; Boxer. In all other cases, microfilm was used; every newspaper issue for the dates listed at the beginning of this note was then examined. Some of the oldest copy, especially for the *New York Tribune*, was at times illegible.

[31] "Additional Intelligence of Importance from Europe," *New York Herald*, March 30, 1848, 1.

new world's lead, even though they disagreed on whether it would succeed or succumb to lawlessness.

The revolutions of 1848, although ultimately unsuccessful in achieving regime changes, have been considered "the largest, the most widespread, and the most violent political movement of nineteenth-century Europe."[32] The roots of the revolutionary movements that took to the streets from France and Germany to Italy and the Austrian Empire were in the contrast between the political ideals of the French Revolution of 1789 and the continuing monarchic regimes supported by peasants living in virtual serfdom. The economic crisis and the increased activism of the 1840s provided the spark that ignited Europe's unrest. In Paris, violent street demonstrations between protesters and soldiers led to the king's abdication and the proclamation of the republic in February 1848, followed by massive celebrations and continued class conflict. The creation of parliamentary governments and the spread of civil liberties went along with enduring political and social struggles, as socialist ideas clashed with liberal republican ones. Ultimately, events in France again set the trend for European developments: Radical revolutionary arrangements were overwhelmed by a restoration to order by old-regime monarchical forces, even though modern French politics would be greatly influenced by the polarization of the political awakening affected by the revolution.

When the revolution broke out in France, Americans strongly sympathized with its republican ideals and the press expressed near-unanimous support.[33] When the movement took clearly socialist leanings, however, appearing to aim for an overthrow not just of the monarchy but also of the labor and property systems, its only stalwart supporter in the U.S. press was the *New York Tribune*, whose correspondents were steadfast in insisting that the French were behaving "most nobly – most generously toward property and indeed all private rights."[34] The paper's editor, Greeley, had long questioned the free-market and labor systems, and he saw in the revolution the first sign of inevitable change, "proceeding to the full experiment of democracy."[35] The other editors studied here compared the movement unfavorably to U.S. republicanism, taking the occasion to extol American virtues as unique. The "special correspondent" of the *New Orleans Picayune*, for example, wrote from London: "Let us hope that the glorious example we have set mankind in the New World may be successfully carried out in the Old."[36]

That correspondent was none other than Editor George Wilkins Kendall himself. Just returned from covering the Mexican War, he had sailed to Europe

[32] Jonathan Sperber, *The European Revolutions, 1848–1851* 2nd ed. (Cambridge: Cambridge University Press, 2005), 2.

[33] Adam Tuchinsky, *Horace Greeley's New-York Tribune: Civil War-Era Socialism and the Crisis of Free Labor* (Ithaca, NY: Cornell University Press, 2009), 84.

[34] "The French Revolution," *New York Tribune*, March 31, 1848.

[35] "The Foreign News," *New York Tribune*, March 28, 1848.

[36] "European Correspondence," *New Orleans Picayune*, May 14, 1848.

in March for a vacation but found himself covering uprisings across the continent.[37] The *New York Tribune* also had an extraordinary observer in place by April: Henry Börnstein, a German intellectual who offered readers (in German and English translation by *Tribune* staff) a much more sympathetic approach to the radical vision of the revolutions than other European writers at the time, liberally sprinkling his copy with the 1789 cry, "Vive la Republique!"[38] Different as they were, the correspondents for the three newspapers studied all prided themselves in firsthand observation, as noted at the beginning of this section. In characteristic self-deprecating style, for example, Kendall told readers that, after some shoe-leather reporting of the protests in London ("for six long hours I have been on my feet"), he would rush to Paris to provide "speculations that may be reliable as regards the future, as well as a correct account of events as they pass."[39] Once in the French capital, he tried his best to find his way to where news might break, "although I knew as little of Paris as of Hindostan."[40] The Paris correspondent of the *New York Herald* signed articles as "An Observer," whereas the regular Paris correspondent of the *New York Tribune* signed his letters, "A Looker-on" and, evidently referencing the painstakingly detailed articles of the time, quipped, "I am really making this letter longer than the Revolution was."[41]

In addition to such insistence on eyewitness newsgathering from abroad, there are also hints at the correspondents' independence from their papers' editorial line, a thorny issue that continues to plague the relationship between reporters in the field and desk editors today. An editorial note in the *New York Tribune*, after bragging that the paper would be "unsurpassed" in foreign news, said about Börnstein's column: "While *we do not always adopt his views* we are confident that his letters must excite in this country a degree of attention paid to those of no other regular European correspondent of the American press."[42]

One dominant way in which these correspondents framed the revolution was guaranteed to attract domestic interest – constant reference to the United States. Kendall's first letter stated, "Let me tell you one thing that will be gratifying to all my countrymen, and that is that American stock – I mean the estimation in which we are all held – has wonderfully improved of late."[43] Börnstein argued that, "Now or never the time comes for North America to take her place in the great Council of Nations, and to put her word into the

37 Fayette Copeland, *Kendall of the Picayune* (Norman: University of Oklahoma Press, 1943), 240.

38 Tuchinsky, 88–95; "The Great Movements of Europe," *New York Tribune*, May 1, 1848.

39 "European Correspondence," *New Orleans Picayune*, May 10, 1848.

40 "European Correspondence," *New Orleans Picayune*, May 25, 1848.

41 "France," *New York Herald*, February 21, 1848; "The French Revolution," *New York Tribune*, March 31, 1848.

42 "The Foreign News," *New York Tribune*, May 1, 1848; emphasis added.

43 "European Correspondence," *New Orleans Picayune*, May 4, 1848.

deciding scale."[44] It might be fitting for a new country and a new profession that these correspondents significantly wrote more of the United States than they did of Europe – their discourses of the "self" are almost to the exclusion of discourses of the "other."

Furthermore, they repeatedly constructed the United States as the exemplary republic. The cause of the "disturbances," according to the *New York Herald*, was "the determination of the people to establish a Republican Government *on the model* of that of the United States."[45] The question remained whether Europe, now immersed in "rivers of blood," would be capable of holding on to newfound freedoms. Or, as Kendall put it, "In Europe they may fight as hard for equality and freedom as the best, but will they know how to use those blessings when attained?" Where would France find "some one man with all the virtues and abilities of Washington?" "*We can*," the New Orleans editor wrote as many other Americans would proclaim exactly 160 years later, but could the Europeans?[46]

After all, this was a set of countries bedeviled by a "system of corrupt influence," "less in area than the present limits of the United States" but still plagued by some "forty-nine kings, emperors,&c. . . . maintaining the most costly establishments for themselves, their households, and their mistresses" while those who bore the burden were kept "in the most indigent circumstances."[47] Even giving that Europe was more refined, Kendall reported, "I have slept just as soundly, while rolled up in a blanket on the prairie, as in the downiest couch French ingenuity has invented."[48] The French understood so little of the United States and, by inference, true republican government that many opposed creating in Paris an institution like the U.S. Senate, Kendall added.[49] Nevertheless, the correspondents studied all implied or stated that Europeans, albeit "an inexperienced people in a republican form of government," would eventually ride the violence out and establish self-government – "the inauguration of republicanism in Europe."[50] Börnstein even suggested that out of the "deep chaos" a "European Republican Union" would emerge – easily 100 years ahead of the times.[51]

Proudly observing as eyewitnesses the convulsions of 1848, American journalists saw a reflection of U.S. democratic ideals possibly taking hold in the Old

44 "The Great Movements of Europe," *New York Tribune*, May 1, 1848.

45 "State of the Markets," *New York Herald*, March 19, 1848; emphasis added.

46 "European Correspondence," *New Orleans Picayune*, May 4, 1848; emphasis original. For more on Kendall's doubts, see Copeland, 246–247.

47 "France," *New York Herald*, February 21, 1848.

48 "European Correspondence," *New Orleans Picayune*, June 7, 1848.

49 "European Correspondence," *New Orleans Picayune*, June 2, 1848.

50 "The Old World," *New York Herald*, June 30, 1848; "Additional Intelligence of Importance from Europe," *New York Herald*, March 30, 1848. See also "European Correspondence," *New Orleans Picayune*, May 25, 1848, and June 13, 1848.

51 "The French Republic," *New York Tribune*, May 23, 1848, and May 9, 1848.

World, although they left open to question whether the latter could measure up. An early editorial by Bennett sums up all the themes discussed thus far.[52] In it, the press was described as a new player in world affairs: "Journalism has brought about the recent event. It is really and truly a newspaper revolution." The cradle of "the great intellectual movement of the human mind" behind the revolution had its seeds in 1776. That revolution, the editorial continued, had made the United States "'the model republic,' which is now imitated in Europe, and which has established its power and independence, almost equal to the greatest nation of the old world." Finally, the time had about come for "this vast country – united, animated, powerful, belligerent and rich" to show Europe what it could do. There might only be twenty-five million Americans, Bennett concluded, but with "wealth, capacity and intelligence sufficient" to intervene on the side of democracy in France. The dominant journalistic image of revolutionary France in 1848, then, was of a model and powerful United States.

The 1853 Expedition: Opening Up Japan to America's Trade and News

"A letter from this part of the world may not be uninteresting, though there may be nothing in it," a correspondent from Hong Kong wrote to the *New York Herald* in 1853.[53] The first bit of "nothing" that the writer reported was about the Japan expedition, Commodore Matthew Perry's naval mission to persuade Japan to guarantee the rights of U.S. sailors and, most consequentially, to open trade. This is about as far as American diplomacy went in the antebellum era – protecting Americans and seeking avenues for trade – but it generated a tremendous amount of interest and discussion among the American public. Indeed, the five newspapers studied spared no effort in bringing their readers news of the expedition in every way they could – from correspondents on the Asian mainland, from private letters by military personnel, from reporters in Washington and, most famously, from the expedition itself in the case of Bayard Taylor of the *New York Tribune*, who joined the squadron as a master's mate.[54]

Perry's trade mission, peaceful as it was, marks one of the first times that Washington took the lead in opening relations with the non-Western world, and it started Japan's defensive race to commercial and military industrialization.[55] It also gave both Japan and the United States a historical memory of each other that would last well into the twentieth century. For more than a century

52 "The New Revolution in France–The Position of the United States," *New York Herald*, March 20, 1848.

53 "Our China Correspondence," *New York Herald*, July 20, 1853.

54 Hohenberg, 21.

55 George Feifer, *Breaking Open Japan: Commodore Perry, Lord Abe, and American Imperialism in 1853* (New York: HarperCollins, 2006).

before the treaty was signed, Japan's doors had only been open to Chinese and Dutch traders, and Americans had little interest in East Asia.[56] The 1848 annexation of California, opening up Pacific ports, as well as the increase in Western trade with China and more capacious steamships, led to efforts to trade with the Japanese empire, often suffused with missionary tendencies to bring Western enlightenment to the supposedly barbarous and dictatorial realm. Perry's expedition was the first significant step in the U.S. effort to become a Pacific power.[57]

Perry sailed in late 1852, carrying both threats – a remarkably well-armed squadron – and inducements, including a model railway and equipment for the newly discovered telegraph. His opening gesture was to set up a naval base on Okinawa; in July, he sailed into Tokyo Bay and delivered President Fillmore's message to Japanese representatives before returning to Okinawa to give Japan time to respond.[58] In February 1854, Perry sailed again to Tokyo, and a treaty opening two ports was signed in March.[59] The *New York Times* published the full text of the treaty, marking it "confidential," and drawing the administration's ire for revealing secret diplomatic processes.[60] Trade missions by both Americans and Europeans started in earnest, to almost universally negative public reaction in Japan, a resentment that some have argued directly related to Pearl Harbor.[61]

On the contrary, the treaty was met with jubilation in the United States, including in the vast majority of the newspapers, except for the generally anti-imperialist *New York Tribune*.[62] The *New York Herald* had aggressively embraced the expedition from the beginning, arguing, "We must carry our point, should it cost another opium war."[63] The *New York Times*, which had proudly stated, "We are a step in advance of every other nation in our relations with this exclusive government," found Perry's results "in the highest degree gratifying."[64]

Newspapers tried hard to get news about the mission, noting, as the *Chicago Tribune* did, that the "public generally have taken a very lively interest in the matter, and no item of foreign news has been looked for with more eagerness

[56] William L. Neumann, *America Encounters Japan: From Perry to MacArthur* (Baltimore: Johns Hopkins University Press, 1963), 6.

[57] Herring, 2008, 177.

[58] Neumann, 34. The islands are referred to in 1850s newspapers as Loo Choo islands.

[59] Neumann, 45.

[60] "The Treaty between the United States and the Empire of Japan," *New York Times*, July 17, 1854. Feifer, 263.

[61] Feifer, passim.

[62] Tuchinsky, 183.

[63] "Net Prospects for the Japan Expedition," *New York Herald*, November 1, 1853. The same editorial, and much content, was reprinted in the weekly edition of the *Herald*.

[64] "Highly Interesting from the Japan Expedition," *New York Times*, October 31, 1853; "The Japan Expedition," *New York Times*, June 13, 1854.

than the result of the mission to Jeddo [Tokyo]."[65] The *New Orleans Picayune* commented on the difficulty of getting news from Asia, because it had to either come across the Pacific and then the western United States or via "overland express through India," through Europe, and eventually the Atlantic: "The currents of news from east and west round the world frequently meet each other at this longitude," the editor remarked.[66] The *New York Times* used letters from members of the squadron, reports from the Navy Department in Washington, and even "a private letter from an American gentleman in China."[67] The *New York Herald* had regular letters from Hong Kong signed "Samqua" – who broke the news of the treaty in an article headlined, "Opening the Japanese Empire" – and an occasional "correspondent," apparently a member of the squadron rather than a journalist, writing from Okinawa.[68]

The vast majority of the articles described Perry's squadron rather than the foreign lands it encountered, praising the "American enterprise and American ingenuity" that had "penetrated" the "mystery which for so many centuries has hung over these fabled realms."[69] When the Japanese were described, it was almost invariably as primitive ("their manners, their customs, their dress – all appear to remain precisely the same as described two hundred years ago"), "semi-barbarians," or at best, "industrious, ingenious, but exceedingly benighted inside barbarians of the imperial islands of Japan."[70] The scorn of the *Herald*'s correspondent in Hong Kong ranged from the political – the "excessively revolting, to say the least" "obsequiousness of the lower orders to their superiors" – to the culinary – "cooked worms, fried snakes, and a variety of indigestible compounds."[71] Whenever praise was lavished, it was for features that would be of use to an imperialist policy, as in this letter for the *New-Bedford Mercury* reprinted in the *New York Times*: "[Shimoda's] is one of the most magnificent bays and harbors in the world, and capable of holding all the fleets of the Pacific in security."[72]

65 "What the Japan Expedition Has Accomplished," *Chicago Tribune*, November 4, 1853.

66 "American Interference in the China War," *New Orleans Picayune*, July 19, 1853. In 1853–1854, New Orleans battled two epidemics of yellow fever that killed more than 10,000 people, so it is not surprising that the *Picayune* would devote its attention mostly to local matters; Thomas Ewing Dabney, *One Hundred Great Years: The Story of the Times-Picayune from its Founding to 1940* (Baton Rouge: Louisiana State University Press, 1944).

67 For letters from military officers, see "The Japanese Squadron," August 6, 1853; "The Japan Expedition," October 20, 1853; "From Japan," June 26, 1854; "The Japanese Treaty," August 11, 1854. From Washington, see "Latest Intelligence by Telegraph to the New-York Daily Times," August 22, 1853. For private correspondence, see "Japan," December 8, 1853.

68 "Opening the Japanese Empire," *The Weekly Herald*, June 17, 1853. Among many others, see references to "Our Loo Choo Correspondence" on April 27, 1854.

69 "The Opening of Japan," *The Weekly Herald*, July 1, 1854.

70 "Highly Interesting from the Japan Expedition," *New York Times*, October 31, 1853; "The Japanese Expedition – What Is It," *Chicago Tribune*, December 6, 1853; "The Treaty with Japan," *Chicago Tribune*, June 15, 1854.

71 "The Opening of Japan," *New York Herald*, July 1, 1854.

72 "Later from China," *New York Times*, October 21, 1854.

The only foreign correspondent with the expedition was Taylor, who toured the country to speak about his experiences and whose articles were reprinted in many newspapers.[73] Taylor sailed with Perry's squadron into Okinawa and then Tokyo's bay in July 1853, gushed at the apparent American success, and sailed back home without awaiting the Japanese response.[74] His articles started appearing in the *New York Tribune* on November 5, 1853, and were published as a book in 1855.[75] In the book's preface, Taylor warned readers to expect a "less full and detailed" account of the visit to Japan because of his status there as an embedded journalist, to use twenty-first century parlance. He had to give all his notes to the Navy Department to be used in the official report on the expedition, he wrote, without even being able to make a copy, even though he protested that the most important accounts had already been published.

Taylor's literary narrative of the expedition reflects the typical Western colonial gaze of the time, where the natives are quaint in their "semi-civilized" state, and the landscape is "exceedingly picturesque and beautiful."[76] There are abundant historical studies on this kind of "imperialist gaze," so one example will suffice here, from Taylor's first arrival at Okinawa:

> When the next morning dawned, bright and clear, I thought I had never seen a *more lovely landscape* than the island presented. The bay was clasped by an amphitheatre of gently undulating hills, in some places terraced with waving rice-fields, in others covered with the *greenest turf*, or dotted with *picturesque groups of trees*. Bowers of the feathery bamboo – next to the palm, the most graceful of trees – almost concealed the dwellings which nestled together in the little dells opening into the bay, and which, with their stone enclosures and roofs of red tiles, hinted of *a much higher civilization than we had expected*.[77]

Americans exposed to the writings of the lone professional correspondent with Perry's expedition did get a much more detailed perspective on Japan than was available elsewhere in the press. Condescending as they were, the discourses of picturesque Japan at least were not mere reflections of the United States and its interests, and Taylor sometimes admitted that he found "a much higher civilization" than expected. Such "surprise" suggests a hint of that opening toward understanding foreign cultures that, this book argues, is an essential and unique contribution provided by foreign correspondents.

[73] "Bayard Taylor's Second Lecture before the Young Men's Association," *Chicago Tribune*, March 20, 1854; "The Japan Expedition," *Chicago Tribune*, October 31, 1853.

[74] Hohenberg, 21–22.

[75] "The Japan Expedition," *New York Tribune*, November 5, 1853; Bayard Taylor, *A Visit to India, China, and Japan, in the Year 1853* (New York: G.P. Putnam, 1855).

[76] "The Japan Expedition," *New York Tribune*, November 5, 1853.

[77] Taylor, 366; emphasis added. For more on the colonial gaze, see David Spurr, *The Rhetoric of Empire: Colonial Discourse in Journalism, Travel Writing, and Imperial Administration* (Durham, NC: Duke University Press, 1993).

The Franco-Prussian War: America's Interest in Europe's Conflicts

On the front page of its edition for July 29, 1870, less than two weeks after the start of the Franco-Prussian War, the *New York Tribune* carried this announcement: "THE TRIBUNE is the only newspaper in the United States fully represented by Special Correspondents with both Prussian and French armies and at the leading capitals; and is the only paper receiving full special dispatches. Yesterday the TRIBUNE dispatches were used, in an imperfect form, by The New York World and Sun." Changing only the papers mentioned in the last sentence, the *Tribune* kept up this self-congratulation on every front page until August 27. In that edition, and for several more days to follow, the note changed to: "THE TRIBUNE *was long* the only newspaper.... "

As noted at the beginning of this chapter, American foreign correspondents fought one another and military censors for scoops almost as ferociously as the two great European powers battled in this seminal war. A representative single page of the *New York Times* in August 1870, for example, contained letters by correspondents in Berlin, Mainz, Neustadt and Paris.[78] The newspapers studied are full of praise for their foreign service, reflecting both a growing appreciation for professional foreign correspondents as well as the great interest that American readers had in the conflict.[79] Several newspapers, including the *New York Tribune* and the *New York Times*, had established "control" bureaus in Europe in the late 1860s, which allowed them to coordinate "covering every point likely to be involved in the war" and sending special correspondents "to all the chief points at which news was likely to be obtained."[80] The correspondence in the *Times* was coordinated by the "Times News Bureau" in Paris, "to which our several correspondents with the armies, and near the points to which the attention of the world is just now directed, promptly report," and it was full of "trustworthy statements" and "fresh, important, interesting facts and reports."[81] George W. Smalley, a veteran of war reporting from the American Civil War in London for the *Tribune* from 1867 to 1895, not only reported from there but also organized a well-oiled machine of reporters providing both stories and dispatches, which is considered a landmark in war correspondence.[82] In addition to such active newsgathering, the papers also spent a fortune in using the newly operational transatlantic cable – the *Tribune* outspent all others in cable tolls, paying about $125,000, and the paper's

[78] "War Letters," *New York Times*, August 26, 1870.

[79] See, for example, the note about "able and intelligent correspondents at every point of interest" in the *New York Times*, "War Letters," August 10, 1870. Readers even wrote letters to the editors to comment on war coverage; see "The War in Europe," *Chicago Tribune*, July 30, 1870.

[80] "The War and Our Correspondence," *New York Times*, August 3, 1870.

[81] "War Mail News," *New York Times*, August 3, 1870.

[82] Knightley, 48; Joseph J. Mathews, *George W. Smalley: Forty Years a Foreign Correspondent* (Chapel Hill: University of North Carolina Press, 1973), 3, 57–65. The *Tribune* carried many telegrams signed G.W.S.; for example, see the edition of July 26, 1870.

coverage, with its emphasis on bits of news transmitted by the fastest possible means instead of grand narratives, helped set the terms for war correspondents for decades.[83] American journalists were correctly investing their enterprise – the war signaled the rise of German power, which would dominate transatlantic relations for the next seventy years.

The war united the disparate German states in a single cause championed by Prussia's Chancellor Otto von Bismarck and led to Germany's unification and its establishment as a Great Power.[84] It also led to lingering bad blood between it and France; as "Lupus" of the *New York Times* put it, "Two powerful nations which might have been of infinite use to one another have been alienated in feelings."[85] In mid-July 1870, the French and German armies mobilized toward the Rhine River, where high-casualty battles soon turned the tide against the French, so that by September Napoleon III's empire had fallen. France's new republican government tried to hold the Germans back; but despite heroic resistance in the siege of Paris, it signed an armistice in January 1871 and a full peace treaty in May, giving to Germany the regions of Alsace and Lorraine. Parisians rebelled and formed a Commune, leading to a second attack on Paris, this time by the French army. Elites across Europe condemned the Commune as a violent and radical workers' conspiracy, and so did the majority of American newspapers, including the *New York Tribune*, in stark contrast to its 1848 coverage.[86] The *New York Times*, for example, argued despondently that "if Frenchmen are to keep on indefinitely cutting each other's throats, most of us might gradually become reconciled to whatever can terminate the effusion of blood, and bring protection to industry and safety to property."[87] On a larger scale, Europeans found themselves faced with a new reality – Germany had suddenly become the great continental power, unsurpassed militarily and on the way to major industrial competition with Great Britain,[88] locking those two countries in a rivalry that would lead to John Bull's rapprochement to Uncle Sam as well as to two world wars. Washington, singularly ill-informed by its ministers in Paris and Berlin at the beginning of the war, remained insistently neutral – even though the view from Berlin was highly sympathetic to Bismarck – and refused to get involved as mediator, despite having the ability to speak "with a voice of giant power."[89]

83 Hohenberg, 36–38; Frank Luther Mott, *American Journalism: A History of Newspapers in the United States through 260 Years: 1690 to 1950* (New York: Macmillan, 1950), 380.

84 J.A.S. Grenville, *Europe Reshaped: 1848–1878* 2nd ed. (Oxford: Blackwell, 2000), 309.

85 "From Cologne to Berlin," *New York Times*, August 16, 1870.

86 Tuchinsky, 199–201.

87 "The Purple behind the Red," *New York Times*, May 19, 1871.

88 Grenville, 324.

89 Patricia Dougherty, *American Diplomats and the Franco-Prussian War: Perceptions from Paris and Berlin* (Washington: Georgetown University, 1980), 7. The quote is from "Cannot the United States Now Act as Mediator Between France and Prussia?" *New York Times*, August 21, 1870.

The newspapers studied commented on Americans' pro-German attitudes and official neutrality. An editorial in the *Chicago Tribune*, headlined "Why America Is Prussian," argued that "there is very general sympathy, on the part of the American people, with Prussia. It is not merely that we have more Germans among us than French, but that, in our national character, we have more sympathy with Prussian institutions than with French. We believe in universal education, and not in irresponsible despotism."[90] Despite those sympathies and in line with the long policy of noninterference in Europe's affairs, the *New York Herald* echoed widely shared sentiments in an editorial stating, "It is for us to be grateful that we are happily out of the conflict."[91]

Furthermore, it appears that editors and correspondents strove for some concept of objectivity in their coverage. An editorial in the French-leaning *New Orleans Picayune* stated, "We desire to see justice done to both sides, and deem it, therefore, our duty as journalists to point out prejudiced and partisan statements, no matter whether they are intended to injure the French or Prussian armies."[92] That paper, as well as the *New York Times*, attacked and ridiculed Greeley for partisan coverage and "narrow-minded malevolence," calling him "Horace von Greeley, Crown Prince of Manhattan and Grand Duke of the New York Tribune, at present in command of all the non-combatant troops which favor the Prussian cause."[93] In contrast, the *New York Herald* assured readers that its "long established" network of correspondents would provide the public with "the fullest, the most reliable, and the most authentic *record of facts* as they occur in the grand operations of the contending armies" – very modern definitions for a time that had barely seen the passing of partisan journalism.[94] Just a few days earlier, another editorial had expressed the *Herald*'s goal: "Our special written exhibit from the seat of war becomes thus of great interest to all classes of our cosmopolitan population – Germans, French and French sympathizers, and *the mighty American neutrals who wish for peace.*"[95]

The correspondents wrote at length about their job, the difficulties they faced with military censors, particularly from the French side, and how they managed to get around them.[96] The *New York Times* worried publicly for a while about the fate of one of its battlefield correspondents who had gone missing, and

90 "Why America Is Prussian," *Chicago Tribune*, July 20, 1870.

91 "The War Panic in Europe," *New York Herald*, July 19, 1870.

92 *New Orleans Picayune*, July 22, 1870.

93 "The 'Tribune' in War Paint," *New York Times*, August 24, 1870; "Gen. Von Greeley," *New Orleans Picayune*, August 28, 1870.

94 "The Herald Corps of European War Correspondents," *New York Herald*, August 24, 1870; emphasis added. For a nearly identical description of what the newspaper wanted to provide its readers, see "Special War Despatches from Europe," *New York Herald*, August 14, 1870.

95 "Our Special History of the War," *New York Herald*, August 18, 1870; emphasis added.

96 Among many, see "War Topics," *New York Tribune*, July 22, 1870; "England," *New York Herald*, August 7, 1870; "War News by Mail," *New York Times*, August 9, 1870.

a correspondent from Paris complained about "a system of terrorism which effectually paralyzes [the writers'] efforts to obtain authentic intelligence."[97] One of the *Times*' correspondents wrote about his brief detention by French police just as he was penning his article.[98] A correspondent for the *New York Herald*, who let his readers know that he spoke "French quite as well as I do English" and therefore could be particularly trusted, wrote that he would manage to follow MacMahon's army despite explicit orders to the contrary: "For go I must and go I will. But how I go is a question which I would rather not publish just at present."[99] A correspondent for the *Chicago Tribune* might not have been far off the truth when he bragged, "The American public are kept as well informed as, if they are not even better than, either the French or the English," and went on to praise the help received from U.S. diplomats, who were "true friends in need to their newspapers."[100]

The vast majority of the correspondence, rarely off the front pages, and provided either by the papers' own journalists or by the Associated Press via cable, was a blow-by-blow account of battles and movements with almost no contextualization.[101] But a few of the correspondents were longtime European observers and provided, in longer articles sent by mail, some analysis not just of the military events but the political and social repercussions.[102] "Gamma," for example, had been writing from Paris for the *New Orleans Picayune* since at least the 1840s – one of this articles references traveling to Neuilly in 1848 – and he offered this poignant commentary on civilian life in Paris at the end of the war: "There is one sight which cannot find our eyes seared – the exodus of families flying [*sic*] from war.... Can you wonder if in sight of all this havock, this ruin, this distress, we are depressed, apathetic, indifferent to everything."[103] Sometimes, the correspondents still referenced the travel literature from earlier in the century, with picturesque descriptions of "those many fine old towns of Europe which thousands of travellers have passed through, but which very few indeed have seen" and the penchant of the French for embellishing their towns

97 "The War," *New York Times*, August 20, 1870; "War Correspondence," August 16, 1870.

98 "About Metz," *New York Times*, August 24, 1870.

99 "Europe," *New York Herald*, August 9, 1870.

100 "Europe," *Chicago Tribune*, August 18, 1870. American war correspondence dominated news reports as far away as in Australia; see Peter Putnis, "Overseas News in the Australian Press in 1870 and the Colonial Experience of the Franco-Prussian War," *History Australia* 4/1 (2007): 1–18.

101 See, among many other examples, "Foreign," *Chicago Tribune*, August 1, 1870. The Paris correspondent of the *New York Times* wrote that "the agent of the Associated Press" must have already sent the paper the latest news; "War News by Mail," July 21, 1870.

102 For an example of the difference, the Paris correspondent for the *New York Herald* sent one-paragraph daily telegrams as well as a long letter about the fighting over the Commune in May 1871; "The Latest from France," May 18, 1871, and "Europe," May 14, 1871.

103 "Paris Pencilings," *New Orleans Picayune*, May 28, 1871.

with "pleasant promenades, and flowers, and music."[104] Other correspondents also resorted to stereotypes – for example, about the "light-hearted, pleasure-loving Parisians" and the "idiotic, thick-headed, presumptuous donkey" of a French provincial – and lamented Europe's technological backwardness compared to the United States.[105] Nevertheless, as editors at the *Times* argued, the intended value of long correspondence was to "throw much light on events imperfectly described by telegraphic outlines."[106]

One of the most striking aspects of the vast mobilization of American journalists to Europe in the Franco-Prussian War is how it stood on the cusp of change for foreign newsgathering, with two operational logics apparently in place for the minutely detailed telegraphic dispatches and the analytical letters. Even as they were spending fortunes on being first with the news via cable, some correspondents seem to have struggled with the speed requirement for longer, analytical writing. One correspondent in Paris for the *Times* apologized to his readers: "With my fellow-*chroniclers of the hour*, I must content myself with giving a superficial glance and a hasty record of what is passing under my own eyes."[107] A colleague there for the *Tribune* even apologized for writing twice in two days: "I witnessed a scene so extraordinary that, although I wrote you only yesterday, I must write again to describe it to you."[108] That kind of measured approach to world news would be definitively outmoded by the time the next generation of correspondents wrote about the events that led to the United States' own war with a European power.

The 1890s Cuban Revolution: Taking It on as a Reluctant World Power

In an interview with a correspondent from the *New York Times*, Cuban rebels' leader Máximo Gómez is quoted as saying, "I am pleased to welcome an American newspaper man . . . but I don't know what I might do to an American Congressman who might come to my camp."[109] Just more than two years after the interview, the U.S. Congress authorized President McKinley to fight against colonial Spain on the side of Cuban insurgents, and media historians have long argued about the power of the yellow press of the 1890s to push a hesitant country into war and, consequently, an inescapable world presence. Historians of foreign policy, however, argue that McKinley was much more adept at manipulating public opinion through an unprecedented relationship with the press than any of his predecessors, using the growing White House press corps

104 "The French on the Rhine," *New York Herald*, August 9, 1870; "Invaded France," *New York Times*, August 29, 1870.
105 "War Letters," *New York Times*, August 25, 1870; "War Correspondence," *New York Times*, August 18, 1870.
106 "War News by Mail," *New York Times*, August 9, 1870.
107 "War Letters," *New York Times*, August 24, 1870; emphasis added.
108 "Scenes in Paris," *New York Tribune*, August 22, 1870; see also Mathews, 29.
109 "Gomez Near Caimito," *New York Times*, January 26, 1896.

as his persuasion instruments by increasing their reliance on the president's office for news.[110]

Either way, the U.S. press of the late nineteenth century was at the forefront of the political shift that entrenched the United States as a major world power. There is abundant literature on the circulation battle between two New York publishers – William Randolph Hearst of the *Journal* and Joseph Pulitzer of the *World* – who, with their sensationalized reporting of Spanish wrongdoing as well as belligerent calls to arms, turned American public opinion in full support of Cuban insurgents.[111] Politicians and the public recognized that the new journalism of the late nineteenth century gripped the masses as no medium had done before. One of the most enduring consequences of the war was the establishment of the media as a necessary factor in diplomacy and international politics. This section examines U.S. correspondents' work in Cuba well before the worst of the jingoist propaganda and the war, which was covered by more than 200 correspondents with no restraint in expense, flamboyance or enterprise, and which has been amply studied elsewhere.[112]

As early as in 1895, when Cubans reignited an insurgency against Spain and their supporters lobbied Washington, American and European journalists traveled to the island, some to stay in Havana and others to ride among the rebels. Among the latter were Sylvester Scovel for the *New York Herald* and, in a strange twist on politics as journalism, Winston Churchill, writing for the London *Daily Graphic* and republished in the *New York World* and other U.S. newspapers.[113] In late 1895, the Cuban insurgents, led by Gómez and his lieutenant Antonio Maceo, battled over the western half of the island, destroying as much as they could of the sugarcane crops, the island's source of wealth, and growing their ranks with now-unemployed farmers.[114] In typical guerrilla warfare, the skirmishes with Spanish troops led by Captain-General Arsenio Martínez de Campos were relatively bloodless. Morale, however, plummeted as the rebels advanced on Havana in early 1896, pushing Campos to resign and be replaced by the new military governor, Valeriano Weyler. That change quickened the pace toward the larger war – many of Weyler's harsh tactics, including the concentration camps, would be seen as casus belli by the American public.

110 Herring, 2010, 26.

111 For a summary, see Giovanna Dell'Orto, *The Hidden Power of the American Dream: Why Europe's Shaken Confidence in the United States Threatens the Future of U.S. Influence* (Westport, CT: Praeger Security International, 2008), 18–19. For a specific treatment of Hearst's role in foreign policy, see Philip Seib, *Headline Diplomacy: How News Coverage Affects Foreign Policy* (Westport, CT: Praeger, 1997), 1–13.

112 See, among many others, Dabney, 347–352; Hohenberg, 49–53; Knightley, 57 ff.; Mott, 519–545; Joyce Milton, *The Yellow Kids: Foreign Correspondents in the Heyday of Yellow Journalism* (New York: Harper & Row, 1989).

113 "Churchill in a Fight," *Chicago Tribune*, December 6, 1895. Churchill's journo-military exploits were also noted by the *New York Times* correspondent; "A Defeat of Spaniards," *New York Times*, December 15, 1895.

114 Milton, 66–87.

Campos had hobnobbed with reporters, so much so that an illustration of his "farewell reception to his friends and newspaper correspondents at Havana" appeared in the *New York Herald*.[115] By contrast, Weyler's strict censorship of American reporters did not help the press carry more accurate images of the conflict. In turn, those images soured American diplomacy with Spain to the point of confrontation.[116]

Already in October 1895, editors commented on the strong interest among American readers – "interest in the struggle in progress in that island has not abated in this country."[117] They also noted how pro-Cuban American public opinion was: "Whatever some of their misrepresentatives may say, the American people sympathize with struggles for liberty against tyranny every time," and, "This Republic will be the first of all nations to extend a fraternal hand to the new republic in the Pearl of the Antilles."[118] In the same *New York Tribune* editorial containing that last quote is a revealing comment on the role of public opinion in foreign policy: "It would be an irreparable misfortune if this [U.S.] Government should either grant or deny recognition to the Cubans through impulse or on grounds of insufficient or inaccurate information" – much of which the press was sparing no effort to obtain and occasionally fabricate. The *New York Times* itself was hardly neutral, describing the Spanish ruling of Cuba as "the stupid and greedy and cruel misrule of her dependencies which is the custom of Spain."[119]

In addition to Associated Press articles and reprints from other newspapers, all five papers studied had their own correspondents in Cuba by early 1896, either in Havana or with the insurgents, except for the *Chicago Tribune*, which until 1898 only used AP and reprinted articles by the *New York World*.[120] Both editors and correspondents railed against Spanish censorship and hailed journalistic scoops. The *Chicago Tribune* told of how Scovel had "outwitted" Spain.[121] The Havana correspondent of the *New Orleans Picayune* scoffed, "A sure sign of the weakness of a cause is the attempt to muzzle the press" and, reporting on the detention of a colleague, warned American journalists

115 *New York Herald*, January 29, 1896. Campos had also held a press conference with U.S. reporters to announce his departure; "Campos to Newspaper Men," *New York Tribune*, January 19, 1896.

116 John L. Offner, *An Unwanted War: The Diplomacy of the United States and Spain over Cuba, 1895–1898* (Chapel Hill: University of North Carolina Press, 1992).

117 "The Cuban Revolution," *New Orleans Picayune*, October 8, 1895.

118 "Pity Oppressed Cuba," *Chicago Tribune*, October 2, 1895; "Recognition of Cuba," *New York Tribune*, October 14, 1895. On the *Tribune*'s editorial move toward American intervention, see also Bingham Duncan, *Whitelaw Reid: Journalist, Politician, Diplomat* (Athens: University of Georgia Press, 1975), 177–195.

119 "The Condition of Cuba," *New York Times*, October 16, 1895.

120 Lloyd Wendt, *Chicago Tribune: The Rise of a Great American Newspaper* (Chicago: Rand McNally, 1979), 346. For example, the December 20, 1895, edition of the *New Orleans Picayune* has stories datelined Havana by the AP and the *New York Herald*.

121 "Scovel Escapes from Spaniards," *Chicago Tribune*, January 21, 1896.

not to expect in Cuba "all manner of civilities [that] were used both in the federal and confederate camps towards the newspaper correspondent."[122] A colleague with the *New York Herald* commented that it "seemed strange... to submit my despatches to the press censor."[123] In an ironic twist, the Havana correspondent of the *New York Times* wrote that local papers were so "wholly unreliable" in their stories about Maceo's battles that "even the Government censor of the cable office refuses to allow correspondents to telegraph them to the American press."[124]

A few stereotypes emerge from the correspondence, from attacks on the Spaniards (with their "obtuse mind" and "no idea of what constitutes civil and personal liberty") to descriptions of Cubans as the "beautiful savages" ("the athletic Cuban who, from boyhood, had wielded the machete at his home, in the canefields, or riding through the brush. It is as much an adjunct to the Cuban boy as the penknife is to the youth of our own country.").[125] The correspondence, however, is for the most part very straightforward and focused on the battles rather than their social and political outcomes, with virtually no discourses specific to Cuba. Sensationalism appears almost exclusively in headlines that hardly match the matter-of-fact tone of the articles. A *New York Herald* article, headlined "Amazons in Rebel Ranks: Beautiful Women Fight Side by Side with Men in the Cuban Revolution," simply states that according to a local newspaper, "thirty-eight women dressed as men" accompanied one insurgent group.[126] One of the most striking aspects of this batch of correspondence is the prominent display given to lengthy interviews with either Spanish or Cuban leaders. The *New York Herald*'s editorial on its correspondent's talk with Campos, for example, is nearly as long as the interview itself.[127]

The *New York Times* in particular appears to have presented itself as a conduit for diplomatic exchanges. In addition to the three-column interview with Gómez noted previously, the paper also carried interviews with Campos and Salvador Cisneros de Betancourt (president of insurgent-occupied Cuba) and a letter by insurgent leader José María Rodríguez Rodríguez. In all of them, one theme dominates – the United States is the natural ally of the insurgents, who greatly admire it. Rodríguez's letter, unedited, unequivocally ends: "But I feel certain the United States will recognize us very soon, because free Cuba would mean an increase in the commercial and friendly relations between the two countries."[128] After describing Cisneros as "a great admirer of the American Nation," the correspondent concluded, "President Cisneros desires to express

[122] "Happenings in the Cuban Country," *New Orleans Picayune*, January 23, 1896.

[123] "Spanish Victory over Maceo," *New York Herald*, January 22, 1896.

[124] "Antonio Maceo's Tactics," *New York Times*, January 29, 1896.

[125] "Happenings in the Cuban Country," *New Orleans Picayune*, January 23, 1896; "Horrors of the Cuban War," *New York Times*, January 1, 1896.

[126] "Amazons in Rebel Ranks," *New York Herald*, January 29, 1896.

[127] "Interview with General Campos," *New York Herald*, December 30, 1895.

[128] "Cuban Rebels Confident," *New York Times*, December 8, 1895.

his kindest regards and deepest esteem for President Cleveland and the American Congress."[129] Little wonder that Campos turned to the *Times*' correspondent to explain he was trying to "give no excuse to the American Congress for the recognition of the insurgents": "I confide, however, . . . in the friendly disposition and pledged neutrality of President Cleveland, and I may say that, although Congress, prompted by public opinion, may force a recognition of such rights, such a result would have no serious consequences for Spain."[130] The evidence that both Spanish and Cuban leaders would recruit American foreign correspondents to speak directly to Washington, and to acknowledge the role of public opinion on foreign policymaking, clearly marks a shift in the role of the U.S. press as mediator in international affairs just as the United States was about to irrevocably step into them.

The Boxers at Beijing's Foreign Compound: American Intervention in Asia

"No one who has not lived or traveled in China can estimate the power of the Boxers," *Chicago Tribune* Paris correspondent Grace Corneau wrote in the summer of 1900, when the world's attention was riveted by the Boxers' attempt on the foreign diplomatic compound in Beijing.[131] Corneau, who had earlier spent time in China and the French colonies in Southeast Asia, was an unlikely critic of Westerners' misperceptions of Asian populations – she is most famous for being an ardent proponent of women going along with men in the French possessions. Like virtually all other correspondents studied here, however, she adamantly believed in the power of eyewitness news reporting from foreign lands.

No American journalist, however, was in Beijing to cover the siege of the European embassies in China's imperial capital at the hands of the Boxers. One of the main news items for the nearly two months it lasted was the lack of reliable information. Lasting from June 20 to August 14, with more than 500 Europeans, Americans and other foreigners huddled in the British Legation awaiting rescue, it was one of the most prominent episodes in the rebellion of the Society of Righteous and Harmonious Fists (as the Boxers called themselves). The secret society aimed to forcibly eliminate foreign traders and missionaries from across China, likely with the hidden blessing of the dowager empress and with support from the Chinese army. Reports that all foreign diplomats and their families had been massacred caused consternation across the world, even though they eventually proved false. Concerned that Europeans would use the rebellion as an excuse to carve up the Chinese empire into protectorates, and already enmeshed in Asia through the Philippines, the McKinley administration sent a few thousand American troops in a multinational rescue mission that sparked deadly confrontations with the Boxers. The U.S.

129 "Capital of Cuba Libre," *New York Times*, January 30, 1896.
130 "Martinez Campos on the War," *New York Times*, December 8, 1895.
131 "China's Defiance of the World," *Chicago Tribune*, July 8, 1900.

administration then followed it up with an Open Door note, stating that the U.S. interests were the maintenance of trade and Chinese territorial integrity.[132] For Washington, despite the military involvement in China and the ongoing consequences of conquests from the Spanish-American War, the policy marked the difference between America's disinterested interventionism and imperialism.

In editorials, the newspapers studied supported American forces' joining in the rescue mission, but most warned against any partitioning of China at American hands.[133] The *New York Herald* argued that the conflict was "a case of order against anarchy, Western progress against Eastern stagnation, European civilization against Asiatic mediaevalism," and that "China, after all, is not a nation, but an ancient mosaic." The newspaper urged the European Powers to "secure China from the dead past and give it civilization."[134] Even though its own correspondent in Shanghai urged the United States "to take a commanding position in the interest of the civilized world and China," the paper's editor starkly condemned any intervention: "If there is one people on earth that has no right and ought to be ashamed to meddle in China's internal affairs it is the American."[135] The rationale appeared twofold: "unchecked" "imperial McKinleyism" would tie the United States "hand and foot" to Europe, with more "disastrous" consequences as in Cuba, Puerto Rico and the Philippines; in addition, Americans were mistreating Chinese citizens in the United States (with violence against immigrants and restrictive laws), and yet "China has not sent an expeditionary army to enforce the rights of her subjects to that justice which is due to all human beings, civilized or uncivilized."

The *Chicago Tribune* also opposed intervention, arguing that the United States preferred "the integrity of the Chinese Empire, not only on the grounds of a traditional policy but for commercial reasons."[136] The same paper also argued that the "chief role of the United States in Asia has been as the sponsor for China, Japan, and Corea [*sic*] as nations," detailing in a long article how "this country has always led in Asiatic affairs," beginning with Perry's expedition.[137] Similarly, the *New York Tribune*, while encouraging "outside Powers to intervene in China and impose a stable and orderly government," also argued that all the United States wanted was to keep its "commercial and industrial rights," and that it would not join in partitioning but rather would consider it "no small triumph for American diplomacy" to prevent others from doing it.[138]

132 Combs, 159–160.

133 "The Trouble in China," *New Orleans Picayune*, June 19, 1900.

134 "The Chinese Crisis a Blessing in Disguise," *New York Herald*, June 20, 1900.

135 "Leader of Boxers Is Ruling China," *New York Herald*, June 29, 1900; "What Business Have McKinley and the Republican Party in China?" *New York Herald*, July 6, 1900.

136 "How Much of China is Left?" *Chicago Tribune*, June 24, 1900.

137 "The United States and China," *Chicago Tribune*, June 24, 1900.

138 "The Duty of the Powers in China," *New York Tribune*, June 20, 1900; "Hard Fighting in China," *New York Tribune*, June 24, 1900: "American Policy and the Powers," July 12, 1900.

While several Western reporters accompanied the relief expedition and documented the violence and the looting, the only Western correspondent in Beijing during the siege seems to have been George Morrison of the London *Times*, whose reports were widely reprinted in August 1900 and treated "as having the value of diplomatic messages."[139] Deprived of eyewitnesses, the U.S. press tried all means to get news of the happenings in China, using AP reports, letters by missionaries and soldiers, cables from London correspondents, and its own or British correspondents in Shanghai.[140] In a strikingly modern effort to domesticate and localize the news from far-off lands, nearly all newspapers published stories about the fear of retaliation felt in Chinese communities in the United States. The *New York Times* had a story about the "nervousness" of Chinese Chicagoans as well as an Italian boy's attack against a Chinese man in lower Manhattan.[141] The *Chicago Tribune* praised "the action of the Mayor and Superintendent of Police in instructing the officers of the department to protect the Chinese residents of [Chicago] from molestation" and reported on a dentist in Fond du Lac, Wisconsin, who had shot a Chinese laundryman there over "an argument over the Boxer trouble."[142]

Editors kept news of the Boxer Rebellion on the front pages, even as they constantly lamented the confusing and contradictory reports, the lack of direct news from Beijing, and the difficulties of making sense of transliterated Chinese names. The editors of the *Chicago Tribune*, for example, published a "key to names used in Boxer rebellion," while the *New York Tribune* promised its readers it would handle Chinese names "as intelligently, consistently and accurately as is possible in the storm and stress of publishing in New York at 2 o'clock in the morning the news that it gathers in London as late as 6 o'clock the same

[139] Robert Bickers and R.G. Tiedemann, eds. *The Boxers, China, and the World* (Lanham, MD: Rowman & Littlefield, 2007), 101–104. For Morrison's account, see "China's Infamy Shown," *New York Tribune*, August 2, 1900. For comments on the diplomatic value, "Terrible Story of Chinese Duplicity," *New York Herald*, August 2, 1900. Wilbur J. Chamberlin of the *New York Sun* took off for China in August, but only arrived in Beijing in October to find the city in ruins; Wilbur J. Chamberlin, *Ordered to China* (New York: Frederick A. Stokes, 1903), 96.

[140] For example, front-page articles with "copyright, 1900, by Associated Press" appeared from Yantai (Che-Foo) in the *New York Times* (August 4, 1900) and from Tongzhou (Tung-Chow) in the *New Orleans Picayune* (August 18, 1900). A letter from "a Chicago boy who was with Admiral Seymour's unsuccessful expedition" was published in the *New York Times*, "Seymour's Relief Expedition," August 14, 1900. The *New York Herald* reprinted articles from its European edition and praised its correspondents in China, Japan and Russia; "Missionaries Tell of Unrest in South," July 1, 1900, and "The Herald's Chinese Service," July 24, 1900. The *Chicago Tribune* had numerous articles by its correspondents in European capitals, including London (e.g., "American Troops Land at Taku; More Riots Reported in Pekin," June 20, 1900) and Vienna (e.g., "Growth of Pekin Crisis," July 5, 1900).

[141] "Chicago Chinamen Nervous" and "New York Chinaman Attacked," *New York Times*, July 16, 1900.

[142] "Protecting the Chinese," *Chicago Tribune*, July 18, 1900; "Tries to Shoot a Chinaman," *Chicago Tribune*, July 19, 1900.

morning."[143] All editors complained that "nothing but rumors" or dispatches of "contradictory and unintelligible nature" were arriving from Beijing.[144] The U.S. administration also pressed the Chinese government to allow direct communication with its ambassador in Beijing, leading some correspondents to smugly comment on "the ability of the American government to secure news ahead of the rest of the world."[145] The lack of reliable information led all newspapers to publish first the false reports that "foreigners in Pekin all dead" and then details about just how confusing reports had been, for example in a long *Chicago Tribune* article trying to establish a timeline of "the mystery of the century behind the walls of Peking."[146] The *New York Tribune*'s London correspondent accused "the enterprise of halfpenny journalism in London in describing in harrowing detail the massacres which did not occur. That enterprise has been 'yellower' than anything in China, let alone in America."[147]

It seems plausible that the lack of firsthand information also led to sensational headlines, such as the following from the *New York Times* introducing an article from London's *Daily Express*: "More Awful Details of Peking Massacre: Women Hacked to Pieces and Children Carried on Spears."[148] The descriptions in telegraphic dispatches were also sensational. The *New York Herald* wrote of the Boxers' "fanatical thirst for blood" and the Chinese authorities' "duplicity and unreliability."[149] Editorials clearly reinforced the image of the Chinese as utterly uncivilized in the contrast at Beijing between the "lust-maddened, ravenous Chinese mob" of "incomprehensible rustics" and "the elite, the noble, the cultured of the six most powerful and enlightened states of the modern world, . . . each in its way representative of the science and progress of the nineteenth century."[150]

The difference between such constructions of the Chinese and those found in the correspondence of the few reporters who had been in China is striking. Corneau's article, for example, blamed European colonization for stirring anger in China.[151] On the basis of her "personal experience of living among the Chinese in their own land," she defended Chinese civilization as "older than that of the Western world," "founded upon the respect of children for their parents, and upon the fundamental principle that education is a universal

[143] "Key to Names Used in Boxer Rebellion," *Chicago Tribune*, August 12, 1900; "Of Chinese Names," *New York Tribune*, July 20, 1900.

[144] "China in a State of Anarchy," *New Orleans Picayune*, June 22, 1900; "Is the Trouble Spreading?" *New York Times*, August 17, 1900.

[145] "China Must Let Conger's Message Come," *Chicago Tribune*, July 12, 1900; "Suffer under Fire of Allies," *Chicago Tribune*, August 14, 1900.

[146] "Foreigners in Pekin All Dead; Last of the Legations Burned," *Chicago Tribune*, July 5, 1900; "Mystery of the Century behind the Walls of Pekin," *Chicago Tribune*, July 21, 1900.

[147] "Blow to Sensational Papers," *New York Tribune*, July 31, 1900.

[148] "More Awful Details of Peking Massacre," *New York Times*, July 20, 1900.

[149] "South China May Rise, Edict Calls for War," *New York Herald*, July 17, 1900.

[150] "Mystery of the Century behind the Walls of Pekin," *Chicago Tribune*, July 21, 1900.

[151] "China's Defiance of the World," *Chicago Tribune*, July 8, 1900.

necessity," which led to high literacy rates among men and women as well as to a legal code that was "a marvel to European lawyers who have studied it." Corneau went on to say that the "cultivated" Chinese also was contemptuous of Western civilization and found "the corset more barbarous than the small shoes of China."

As noted in the Cuban rebellion, the newspapers assumed a quasi-diplomatic role. The *New York Tribune* splashed on its entire front page news of a cable directly from Li Hongzhang, a high Qing official, stating that the foreign legations were safe. The paper duly noted that it was "the first direct communication from any high official in the Chinese Empire to an American newspaper since the present trouble began."[152] In an editorial the following day, the paper crowed that the cable "had been appropriately sent to The Tribune, which the great Viceroy, in common with men of light and leading throughout the world, has long recognized as the most authoritative medium through which to communicate with the thoughtful and intelligent masses of the American people."[153]

Those "thoughtful and intelligent masses," however, needed a little extra prodding from journalists. So the *New York Tribune* editors appeared to think, judging from the revealing editorial note that introduced a summary of the Boxer Rebellion in that paper: "[The events] are here briefly reviewed for the benefit of those readers of The Tribune who *did not pay that attention* to them which they would have done *had they appreciated* the grave historical importance which now attaches to them."[154] By the turn of the twentieth century, even when they had no correspondents where news broke, the five newspapers studied assumed a responsibility to bring to American readers full accounts of the world – so that they could "pay attention" as they should.

Conclusions

This chapter analyzes the first professionally organized foreign correspondence for the first truly mass-oriented American newspapers in five consequential nineteenth-century international events – the 1848 revolution in France, the opening of Japan to trade in 1853, the Franco-Prussian War of 1870–1871, the Cuban revolt in 1895–1896, and the Boxers' siege of the foreign legations in 1900. From the earliest event, getting the most accurate, fastest news was a matter of great pride and competition among the newspapers, which implies that the editors believed Americans were interested, or at least should be made to be so. The correspondents prized their enterprise in getting first-hand, eyewitness knowledge of foreign countries and their peoples, sometimes even when it led them to conclusions at odds with their newspaper's editorial

[152] "Li Hung Chang to the Tribune," *New York Tribune*, July 28, 1900.

[153] "The Message from Li," *New York Tribune*, July 29, 1900.

[154] "Story of China's Crime," *New York Tribune*, July 20, 1900; emphasis added.

line. To appropriate Taylor's description of the expedition in Japan, U.S. press correspondents were tackling the world "with the cool assurance natural to Americans."[155]

Their correspondence, however, reflected more analysis of the United States than of the foreign realities encountered, leaving readers with the distinct impression that the most salient characteristic of the rest of the world was its inability to measure up to exceptional America. The most prominent discursive formation was of what it meant to be American, rather than any specific identity of covered countries and regions. In summary:

- In the 1848 revolutions, the focus was on the United States as the exemplar democracy that Europe might finally be imitating. There was no specific call for U.S. policy action, but one editor dubbed the movement "the newspaper revolution," hinting at the impact of news media.
- In the 1853 trade expedition, the focus again was on the United States as the exemplar trade model, bringing enlightenment to "picturesque" Japan.
- In the Franco-Prussian War, once more the focus was on the United States – this time explicitly the enterprise of American journalists. No discussion was found of what the rise of Germany would mean for world politics.
- In Cuba and China, beyond "exotic" constructions of the two countries, the discussion does shift to U.S. role toward them, with an explicit recognition that public opinion would matter to Washington and that newspapers were the conduit to the American people.

It is not entirely surprising that a newly formed country should be focused on self-definition. Nevertheless, those dominant constructions in foreign news are of American superiority, and that inevitably had consequences for the boundaries of interpretation of foreign realities available to the American public and policymakers. It is this book's basic premise that the press maintained broad frameworks of understanding that gave meanings to foreign realities and provided the frames within which foreign policymakers positioned the new country vis-à-vis the rest of the world. Both major diplomatic trends – neutrality, culminating in the Open Door policy, and expansion, culminating in the 1898 war – find clear parallels in these nineteenth-century correspondence discourses of disdain for all foreign countries (Europe included) and U.S. unique global superiority. The United States, as the model republic, was the friend of freedom and republican governments everywhere – from Paris to Havana – but not at the cost of sustained entanglement, especially because it was not entirely clear that non-Americans would know what to do with liberty. Washington, an exceptional power, had no dog in the Great Powers' imperial fights – from the Rhine to the Forbidden City – beyond protecting its trading and commercial interests, in which it was emerging as a global leader.

[155] Taylor, 372.

Such blissful self-centered focus, however, was forever altered by the Spanish-American War. Even though isolationism and the consistent denial of an imperial aim would remain constants in American foreign policy, the next fifty years would catapult the United States to the role of sole Western superpower. Journalists would be eyewitnesses to this change, as the next chapter shows. Already, they considered themselves an essential link between foreign realities and the American people. One of the most enduring consequences of reporting nineteenth-century foreign events was the establishment of the media as a necessary factor in diplomacy and international politics. At times, U.S. journalists assumed quasi-diplomatic status, albeit, crucially, in a disinterested manner – foreign leaders from China to Cuba were speaking directly to the readers through correspondents. The latter's job remained to give accurate and fresh news of the world, and to make sure that people understood that it mattered.

Their narratives oscillated from literary travel writing to nearly incomprehensible jumbles of cabled dates and places, rarely providing informed constructions of the world that were more than reflections of the United States. Especially when narrating armed conflicts, these writers tended to focus on military rather than sociopolitical outcomes, leaving readers with little understanding of specific foreign countries. They had particular difficulties with cultures far from their own, such as in Japan and China, although some correspondents' willingness to let their preconceptions be challenged by their observations suggests a hint of that opening toward understanding foreign cultures that is an essential and unique contribution provided by foreign correspondents. Moreover, the foreign correspondents seem to have assumed that they had a unique and critical role in the public sphere as mediators between foreign and national discourses, a role only destined to increase in social importance as the United States came to assume global leadership in the first half of the twentieth century.

3

America Takes Global Center Stage

The Ascent of a Political and Communication Power

> It may be said broadly that no American newspaper has prospered long or exerted permanent influence which has not worked, according to its honest convictions, for the public welfare.... [Newspapers'] progress is intertwined with the country's progress. They will keep the faith. In a nation such as ours there is no fear of an injurious commercialization of the press or of its successful use to color news, corrupt opinion and undermine American ideals and character.[1]

As this *New York Herald Tribune* editorial noted in 1925, the first half of the twentieth century saw both the United States and its press catapulted into unprecedented power. Such a meteoric rise, however, buttressed as it was by what some were beginning to see as "an injurious commercialization," was accompanied by uneasiness about its enduring consequences for both the public welfare and American ideals. By the time the United States affirmed its Great Power status with the 1898 war with Spain over Cuba, the American press was right there in the frontlines – instrument, recorder and symbol of the nascent superpower. Just as policymakers debated how to handle new global responsibilities without entirely relinquishing the isolating protection two oceans had afforded the country, journalists struggled to define and defend the new recognition of the mass media's pervasive influence. By 1945, both America's superpower status and the power of the mass media would be pivots of twentieth-century life.

American journalism from the turn of the twentieth century to the end of the Second World War established itself among the professions and in higher education, embracing the golden rule of objectivity – the strict separation of news, analysis and commentary – that distinguished it from other international

[1] "The American Newspaper," *New York Herald Tribune*, January 19, 1925, 12.

models of the press. Multiple revolutions and conflicts, including two world wars, presented new challenges for an increasingly celebrated corps of foreign correspondents, ranging from new technological logistics – and the beginning of the decline of print – to unprecedented governmental interventions. This chapter analyzes America's, and its foreign correspondents', rise to superpower to continue to answer the fundamental questions that guide this book: What discourses of the world have emerged in the American press? Do they belong to the same general frameworks of understanding of the world as major foreign policy trends contemporary to them? What can the images of the world created in the media tell us about the role of the press in international affairs?

The focus is on how newspapers in New York, Chicago and Baltimore, as well as the Associated Press, covered five events with lasting consequences: the Mexican Revolution of 1910; the Russian Revolution of 1917; Benito Mussolini's takeover of the Italian government in 1925; the Japanese assault on Shanghai in 1932; and the siege of Madrid in the Spanish Civil War in 1937. As noted previously, the world wars are excluded because the focus here is on narratives about the world, not the coverage of American military efforts, even though U.S. armed forces eventually intervened in both the Mexican and the Russian revolutions. This era has been considered a "golden age" for foreign correspondents and for relatively uncontroversial U.S. intervention against totalitarian regimes, at least compared to the multiple debacles of the Cold War. It is also a period marked by an unusually close collaboration between Washington and the press, something that would disappear in the second half of the century. Between 1901 and 1945, American policymakers and journalists seemed both intent on testing the reach of their power vis-à-vis one another and the rest of the world – the following two sections set the stage for the discussion of media discourses of the world by tracing major developments in journalism history and foreign relations.

The Power of the Press: Taking on the World, in the Public's Interest

Reacting to the excesses of the "yellow press" of the late nineteenth century, American journalists sought to establish guidelines for the profession – and indeed to cement its definition as a profession – that continued to characterize journalism for more than a hundred years. Even as the press became big business, it portrayed itself as the guardian of the public interest, an objective observer and investigator that would expose corruption and undeceive its readers from the manipulations of the commercial and political elites.[2] The first half of the twentieth century saw devastating crises – from the Great Depression to world wars – push Americans into deeply divided perspectives on the future direction of the country. Internationally, isolationism battled

[2] Leonard Ray Teel, *The Public Press, 1900–1945: The History of American Journalism* (Westport, CT: Praeger, 2006), 4.

Wilsonian limited interventionism until Pearl Harbor, while progressive reformers and pro-business laissez-faire exponents fought over domestic issues.

The mass media painted themselves as the mediators between this fraught world and the ordinary citizen, serving the public in capacities ranging from "muckraking" to disinterested facilitator even as their own industry was increasingly monopolistic.[3] In the words of a 1911 manual, one of many written then about journalism practice and education, "In its highest sense journalism is not trade nor business, but profession, the profession of the interpreter."[4] Although never a profession regulated like law or medicine, journalism in the early twentieth century started to have its official training grounds in newly established journalism schools, such as the University of Missouri's that was founded in 1908, and especially in the tools with which it approached telling the news, foremost among them the objective or at least impartial report.

Unlike the literary penchant of their European colleagues, American journalists relied on "inverted pyramid" storytelling that got out the most important facts first, in short, easy to understand, if often decontextualized, bites that would become routine across media platforms once they naturally fitted radio practices. In one of the recurring paradoxes of the U.S. model, it was the newspapers' increasing ability to operate on solid, independent budgets – because of their growing business strength and mass circulations – that allowed reporters to focus on being journalists exclusively, separated from politics.[5]

The history of journalism's mantra – objectivity – is rife with contradictory interpretations that emphasize either the press's steady ascent toward democratic ideals or its steady descent toward commercial corruption.[6] In the interwar era, both newly founded professional organizations like the American Society of Newspaper Editors and broadcasting organizations like CBS insisted in their standards and policies that news stories should be free from opinion or bias.[7] In fact, the defining of a code of ethics for journalism has been called the most important change affected by this era.[8] One recent study, however, suggested that by removing the blatant party line and introducing instead journalistic practice as the decisive logic with which to select and present stories

3 Michael Emery, Edwin Emery and Nancy Roberts, *The Press and America: An Interpretive History of the Mass Media* 9th ed. (Boston: Allyn and Bacon, 2000), 213; Frank Luther Mott, *American Journalism: A History of Newspapers in the United States through 260 Years: 1690 to 1950* (New York: Macmillan, 1950), 546 ff.; Teel, 50.

4 Walter Williams and Frank L. Martin, *The Practice of Journalism: A Treatise on Newspaper Making* (Columbia, MO: E.W. Stephens Publishing, 1911), 10.

5 Mitchell Stephens, *A History of News* 3rd ed. (New York: Oxford University Press, 2007), 248; Paul Starr, *The Creation of the Media: Political Origins of Modern Communications* (New York: Basic Books, 2004), 264.

6 For a historiography of journalistic objectivity, see Richard L. Kaplan, *Politics and the American Press: The Rise of Objectivity, 1865–1920* (Cambridge: Cambridge University Press, 2002).

7 Stephens, 251; Paul W. White, *News on the Air* (New York: Harcourt, Brace and Co., 1947), 199.

8 James Melvin Lee, *History of American Journalism* (Boston: Houghton Mifflin, 1923), 388.

as the news of the day, the turn to objectivity only obscured an even stronger reliance on cultural common sense and elite-driven understandings.[9]

Perhaps in reaction to objectivity's strictures, interpretative reporting took off in the 1930s and 1940s, particularly among foreign correspondents trying to explain increasingly far-reaching developments across the globe, something nearly impossible if one stuck to the facts without context. A more analytical, if still factual, style of journalism might also have been engendered by the presence of many novelists flocking to Europe in the interwar period who dabbled in journalism (like Ernest Hemingway) and as a response to the rising power of radio in news. After the unsuccessful press-radio wars of the early 1930s, radio had become the go-to medium for Americans by the start of the Second World War, and its strength and immediacy brought changes to reporting across media.[10] It was in the uneasy merging of these contradictory tendencies – reaching for multicultural masses, striving for impartiality, and interpreting sweeping sociopolitical changes – that the mass media established their power as modern institutions, detached from politics and yet central to political life in the United States. With little competition from the still disorganized governmental Foreign Service and the infant scholarship in international relations, foreign correspondents in particular became primary sources of foreign affairs information for the American public.[11]

Two of the clearest indications of the growing power of the press were the care the U.S. government took in making sure it toed the line and its incipient use of the media as one of the tools of global expansion, particularly during the two world wars.[12] In both wars, the government established committees that would handle both censorship and propaganda; the widespread cooperation and self-censoring in the Second World War largely stemmed from lessons learned from the first one, which had witnessed the resurgence of the kind of broad suppression – particularly with the Sedition Act of 1918 – unseen since the end of the eighteenth century. The act was used after the war to snuff any suspicion of Communist sympathy in the aftermath of the Russian Revolution, creating in the early 1920s a Red Scare similar to the McCarthy years. Just as consequential as the ingrained distrust of anything coming from Russia, however, was the reaction by the U.S. Supreme Court, which started broadening expression safeguards under the First Amendment that would eventually protect the watchdog function of the press into the rest of the

[9] Kaplan, 191–194.

[10] Michael S. Sweeney, *The Military and the Press: An Uneasy Truce* (Evanston: IL Northwestern University Press, 2006), 95.

[11] Morrell Heald, *Transatlantic Vistas: American Journalists in Europe, 1900–1940* (Kent, OH: Kent State University Press, 1988), xi.

[12] On the U.S. government's effort to use broadcasting as a strategic resource, see Starr, 192; for a study of censorship of photographs during World War II, see George H. Roeder, Jr., *The Censored War: American Visual Experience During World War Two* (New Haven, CT: Yale University Press, 1993).

century.[13] While the courts defended the public service provided by the press, another threat started right after the First World War that would also set the pace for modern journalism – consolidation of ownership and the rise of "press lords," which early critics blamed for an anti-progressive editorial line and a pandering to titillating tales that were the prototypes of today's "infotainment."[14]

Underlying both press developments and press criticisms, victories for the First Amendment and flashes of suppression, was the growing realization that the press had a vast effect on public opinion – and that public opinion really mattered to the conduct of government. Government officials realized this new power and extended wartime news management to domestic matters, institutionalizing the practice of public relations.[15] Journalists also debated their new responsibilities. In a 1920 letter to his editors at the *Chicago Daily News*, European correspondent Paul Scott Mowrer wrote, "The United States is governed by public opinion. If public opinion is to conduct our foreign affairs wisely, it must be rightly informed, by expert observers. This responsibility should be accepted by leading newspapers."[16] The first half of the twentieth century saw the highest readership in U.S. journalism history, with a daily in circulation for each family.[17]

The first large-scale academic studies of communication and its effects on people and politics started in this era, trying to answer questions that have only grown more relevant since: Should the news media be the guardians of the public sphere as a democracy needs? Can they fulfill their role despite the pulls of easy mass persuasion in the interest of growing capitals? The philosophical debate between Walter Lippmann, who believed that professional journalists needed the help of "expert" researchers to present trustworthy information, and John Dewey, who trusted in the unfettered marketplace of ideas for rational opinion formation, originates in these tumultuous interwar years, and its relevance continues to this day. Perhaps no question has seemed more pressing, as noted elsewhere in this book, than the influence of the press, via public opinion, on matters of war and peace. And war, from social revolutions to large-scale invasions and full-out world conflict, was never in short supply for American correspondents to cover from 1901 to 1945.

Golden Age of Foreign Correspondence

The foreign correspondent of the first half of the twentieth century was "charged with duties in the highest realm of newspaper work," Edward Price

13 Starr, 268.

14 Emery, Emery and Roberts, 289, 299; Starr, 254; Mott, 635.

15 Teel, 104.

16 Cited in Jaci Cole and John Maxwell Hamilton, eds. *Journalism of the Highest Realm: The Memoir of Edward Price Bell, Pioneering Foreign Correspondent for the* Chicago Daily News (Baton Rouge: Louisiana State University Press, 2007), 328.

17 Thomas C. Leonard, *News for All: America's Coming-of-Age with the Press* (New York: Oxford University Press, 1995), 177.

Bell, the London-based chief of the *Chicago Daily News*'s foreign service from 1900 to 1922, wrote to his publisher, Victor Lawson, in 1924.[18] Some historians have argued that visionary publishers like Lawson and Adolph Ochs of the *New York Times* started their exemplary foreign newsgathering operations well before the world wars captured Americans' attention, and therefore their commitment shows that they believed that providing news of the world was a necessary public service more than it was a circulation-boosting maneuver.[19] By the start of the First World War, the major newspapers on the East Coast and in Chicago, as well as the wire services, had bureaus in Europe.[20]

Such a presence would only grow over the next few decades, with the Second World War seeing the mobilization of more than 500 full-time American correspondents in what many considered the best-covered war to date.[21] Unlike their predecessors, these war correspondents faced a much better organized government censorship and propaganda machine that controlled newsgathering as never before, especially since the press also embraced self-censorship almost unanimously.[22] The media's impact, nevertheless, grew exponentially. World War II was the first radio war, and the immediacy and intimacy of front-line radio reporting, together with combat photography and the G.I.-centric reporting exemplified by Ernie Pyle, made foreign news in the 1930s and 1940s unprecedentedly real to Americans – even though the vast majority of the coverage was meant to bolster the public's spirit in support of the war effort, not to introduce doubts as later wars would.

Even aside from the two world wars, foreign news became an increasingly solid part of Americans' daily reading in the first half of the twentieth century. That was particularly true for the readers of the four newspapers selected for this chapter's study, where the sporadic, if assiduous, foreign news coverage of the early 1910s became a formidably thorough, multipage reportage by the late 1930s. The *New York Times* and the *New York Herald Tribune*, which a 1930 study described as "in a class by themselves" in terms of column space devoted to foreign news, also ran syndicated news services.[23] The *Baltimore Sun* was among the top five newspapers recorded in that study, and the *Chicago Daily News* in this era is considered a pioneer of foreign service, although its history is lamentably ill-recorded.[24]

The first decades of the twentieth century were particularly momentous for the *New York Times*. Under the guidance of publisher Adolph Ochs, who

18 Cited in Cole and Hamilton, xxxix.

19 John Maxwell Hamilton, *Journalism's Roving Eye: A History of American Foreign Reporting* (Baton Rouge: Louisiana State University Press, 2009), 164.

20 Mott, 615; Teel, 55.

21 Emery, Emery and Roberts, 345; Mott, 705, 741.

22 Sweeney, 33, 63.

23 Julian Laurence Woodward, *Foreign News in American Morning Newspapers: A Study in Public Opinion* (New York: Columbia University Press, 1930), 71; Hamilton, 194.

24 Hamilton, 157; Emery, Emery and Roberts, 312; Cole and Hamilton, xv–xvi.

came up with the slogan "all the news that's fit to print," the paper returned to lead the American press by avoiding the sensationalism of the yellow press and betting instead on solid news coverage aimed for the country's elites.[25] Its blooming foreign service mirrored its editorial position, which staunchly supported the League of Nations and condemned isolationism.[26] The *New York Herald* had also built a remarkable news enterprise, but it disappeared into one of the earliest mergers in the industry, with the *New York Tribune* in 1924, and the combined paper's foreign service built on that of the *Tribune*.[27] The combined paper's ascendance coincided with the demise of the *New York World*, putting it into competition only with the *Times*, although by the late 1930s it had withdrawn from that battle.[28]

The *Daily News*'s prodigious coverage started under Lawson, was syndicated to up to 100 American newspapers, and would be widely respected as a more expansive, adventurous addition to the *Times*'s record until it folded in the late 1970s.[29] Foreign Service Chief Bell instructed correspondents to focus on analytical news of political relevance, even when they generated in places far from Chicagoans' minds.[30] "Be *historians*, not *partisans*. Be *reporters*, not *advocates*" was Bell's instruction, according to his memoir, so that the *Daily News* might carry "journalism which was a clean mirror not of what we *wished* to see but of what we *saw*."[31] Finally, the *Baltimore Sun* began to develop its network of correspondents in the 1920s, starting with hiring foreign journalists and signing sharing agreements with English papers.[32] Over the next few decades, it founded one of the largest numbers of foreign bureaus of any U.S. newspaper that did not also have a syndicate.

Despite the strengths of all these newspapers, as historian John Maxwell Hamilton put it, "no one expected the *New York Times* [or any other newspaper] to have a correspondent everywhere a coup might break out, but they did expect the AP to have someone there."[33] The Associated Press established itself as the unsung giant of foreign correspondence, bringing a constant stream of world coverage not only to the newspapers discussed earlier, but also to the smallest dailies in the American countryside. The cooperative was started in the

25 Emery, Emery and Roberts, 233–234; George H. Douglas, *The Golden Age of the Newspaper* (Westport, CT: Greenwood Press, 1999), 123.

26 Elmer Davis, *History of the* New York Times, *1851–1921* (New York: The New York Times, 1921), 371.

27 Mott, 639.

28 Richard Kluger, *The Paper: The Life and Death of the* New York Herald Tribune (New York: Alfred Knopf, 1986), 256, 296.

29 Hamilton, 157; Donald R. Shanor, "CDN: What We'll Miss about the Chicago Daily News," *Columbia Journalism Review*, May/June 1978, 35–37.

30 Cole and Hamilton, xxiv.

31 Cole and Hamilton, 148.

32 Harold A. Williams, *The Baltimore Sun, 1837–1987* (Baltimore: Johns Hopkins University Press, 1987), 330.

33 Hamilton, 278.

1840s, but its modern version, with all members sharing news from their area plus a staff of reporters and editors delivering international and national news, took shape in 1900 after years of infighting between various regional APs.[34] By 1923, the nonprofit cooperative had twenty-seven international bureaus, and, in the 1930s, it was transmitting more than 20,000 words of foreign news per day.[35]

It appears that then as now, breaking news was the unfettered domain of the AP, while newspaper correspondents labored to provide further analysis and more personal observations. Bell remembered Lawson instructing him, "The bedrock principle of our Special Service will be, 'Don't duplicate the Associated Press'" – even though AP stories constituted approximately two-thirds of the *Daily News* foreign news stories under Bell's reign.[36] Similarly, *Herald Tribune* Paris Bureau Chief John Elliott was instructed by New York managers to "hold down coverage to high spots leaving routine to AP and UP."[37]

With the AP dominating breaking news and seasoned newspaper correspondents providing background and context, the American press entered the 1940s at the apex of its ability to provide readers with thorough, professional, eyewitness news from across the world. In 1945, the U.S. government entered the international news flow, too, by establishing a "foreign information service" in several dozen countries as an arm of propaganda for American values.[38] It was a sign of the portentous shift witnessed in the first half of the twentieth century, which saw the isolationists' last stand before a decidedly muscular – and communication-supported – approach to foreign involvement that would dominate the rest of the century.

Taking the Lead: American Policy Goes Global

By the turn of the twentieth century, American policy had clearly become global – some would say imperial, although of a much different shade from the territory grabbing of European Great Powers. Global perception of American power even preceded its reality in the wake of the Spanish-American War; a British journalist, for example, published a best-seller book titled "The Americanization of the World" in 1901.[39] At first, its most significant arena of

[34] Emery, Emery and Roberts, 245; Reporters of the Associated Press, *Breaking News: How the Associated Press Has Covered War, Peace, and Everything Else* (New York: Princeton Architectural Press, 2007), 408.

[35] Reporters of the Associated Press, 265.

[36] Cole and Hamilton, 112, xxv.

[37] Cable cited in Kluger, 296.

[38] Teel, 230.

[39] George C. Herring, *From Colony to Superpower: U.S. Foreign Relations since 1776* (Oxford: Oxford University Press, 2008), 342. On Europe's reaction to the emergence of U.S. power, see Giovanna Dell'Orto, *The Hidden Power of the American Dream: Why Europe's Shaken Confidence in the United States Threatens the Future of U.S. Influence* (Westport, CT: Praeger Security International, 2008).

influence was trade, relentlessly pursued from China – as noted in Chapter 2 – to Panama, where the United States built the canal in time for the opening of the First World War.[40]

The business-driven policy of the United States in the Americas, particularly in Mexico and Cuba where economic stakes matched strategic interests, led to bitter cultural clashes. The majority of Americans believed Latin Americans to be if not racially at least culturally inferior, even though they might, under U.S. intervention, establish capitalist and therefore democratic regimes. The problem with such "dollar diplomacy" espoused by President William Howard Taft was that U.S. investments ended up buttressing elite regimes while widening the gulf with the poor majorities, thus fomenting both dictatorial tendencies and anti-American-tinged popular unrest. President Woodrow Wilson's "missionary diplomacy," as critics dubbed his form of idealistic interventionism, led the United States into confrontation with Mexico, where a revolution began in 1910 and lasted, according to some counts, for decades, as described in the next section. Such forceful interventions bred a lingering anti-American sentiment and instability in the region that continued despite the inauguration of the Good Neighbor policy of cooperation rather than intervention in the 1920s.

Some historians argue that the crisis between the United States and Mexico – with moments like the U.S. occupation of Veracruz and U.S. troops fighting in northern Mexico against its army and one of the revolutionary leaders – did not escalate into open war only because the United States by the late 1910s was being drawn into the First World War. That war marked the end of a rule that had guided U.S. foreign policy since its inception – the United States became actively, permanently, and costly involved in Europe's affairs on European soil. As it was desperately trying to remain out of the conflict during the First World War years, the United States also found itself faced with a new kind of upheaval that would dominate its agenda for nearly a century – the revolution in Russia in 1917. It was the double threat of world war and communist revolution that eventually sold the Wilson administration, and the American people, on the necessity to join in the fight to "make the world safe for democracy." Furthermore, Wilson's decision to challenge the Russian Revolution, ideologically and militarily in a little-known intervention in two northern Russian ports, set the tone for the American challenge to Soviet-led communism that would be the defining characteristic of the post-1945 world. A recent study called Wilson's policy toward Russia the "first cold war" because it framed the conflict ideologically and inaugurated a sort of proto-containment economic doctrine.[41]

[40] Unless otherwise indicated, sources used for this general review of U.S. policy from 1900 to 1945 include Herring; Jerald A. Combs, *The History of American Foreign Policy* vol. I and II, 3rd ed. (Armonk, NY: M.E. Sharpe, 2008); Walter LaFeber, "The US Rise to World Power, 1776–1945," in *US Foreign Policy*, ed. Michael Cox and Doug Stokes (Oxford: Oxford University Press, 2008), 45–62.

[41] Donald E. Davis and Eugene P. Trani, *The First Cold War: The Legacy of Woodrow Wilson in U.S.-Soviet Relations* (Columbia: University of Missouri Press, 2002).

Shortly after the Bolsheviks took power, Washington and Western European Powers started crafting their policies in response to that perceived threat. Some decisions were immediate – the Russian withdrawal from the war necessitated American boots on the ground to bolster the Western front. After the war, Wilson strove for generous policies toward Germany and its allies in fear that desperate populations would turn to revolution, while other peace negotiators fought his League of Nations proposal arguing that any delay in the treaty would cede too much grounds to the Bolsheviks. Historians disagree as to whether Wilson was masquerading a crusade against communism under a drive for peace in Europe or genuinely wanted the latter and was a recalcitrant convert to intervention against Russia. Either way, the 1917 revolution had set up a parameter with which Washington would examine global affairs for the rest of the century, supported by an American public opinion that, despite the disaster of the Depression years, stayed faithful to the promises, and institutions, of the American dream and never turned en masse toward class unrest.[42]

The dramatic domestic economic problems of the Great Depression further destabilized the international system in the 1920s and 1930s, nipping international cooperation in the bud. Washington, which had relied on its economic might and cooperation with the two regional leaders in Europe and Asia, Germany and Japan, hardly reacted to the emergence of aggressive, expansionist regimes in those two countries. Whether this amounted to a new surge of isolationism, a reliance on economic means paralleling the rise of multinational companies, an involvement without commitment, or a unilateral, "lone hand" approach to international security is a matter of debate.[43] As the horrors of the Japanese invasion of China, the civil war in Spain, and Nazi Germany's takeover of Europe eventually transpired, the United States would regret its idle policies that culminated in the 1938 Munich crisis appeasement, which it did not directly participate in but became another ideological benchmark with consequences still felt in the twenty-first century. To cite just one shameful oversight, a 1938 *Fortune* survey found that 95 percent of Americans were not willing to raise immigration quotas in favor of refugees from Nazi Germany, including Jews.[44] Even as strange bedfellows Great Britain and the Soviet Union took the lead in stopping Hitler from overriding Europe with little U.S. help, American neutrality was increasingly challenged by the segment of the public who followed Roosevelt,[45] and it was shattered by Pearl Harbor.

[42] This paradox is detailed in David M. Kennedy, *Freedom from Fear: The American People in Depression and War, 1929–1945* (Oxford: Oxford University Press, 1999), 322.

[43] See Bear F. Braumoeller, "The Myth of American Isolationism," *Foreign Policy Analysis* 6 (2010): 349–371; and David A. Lake, *Entangling Relations: American Foreign Policy in Its Century* (Princeton, NJ: Princeton University Press, 1999).

[44] Kennedy, 415.

[45] Adam J. Berinsky, *In Time of War: Understanding Public Opinion from World War II to Iraq* (Chicago: University of Chicago Press, 2009), 52.

Historians argue that the Japanese attack was driven by an attempt to force the United States to recognize Japan's domination in China, which under the so-called Stimson Doctrine, U.S. administrations had refused because it contradicted long-established open door policies there. (Some historians have argued that the doctrine was more about principle than material interests, of which the United States had little in China; on the other hand, the United States had done very little to deter Japan's aggression in China, which spread from Manchuria to Shanghai and infuriated world opinion.) World war, then, engulfed the United States on all fronts, but because the mainland remained unscathed, the United States found itself the de facto greatest global power at the conflict's end, and the question became what the country should do with it. A consensus emerged in Washington that U.S. power should be used to facilitate a free-trading, democratic reconstructed world, led by the United States and buttressed by international organizations like the newly founded, U.S.-financed World Bank and International Monetary Fund, as well as the United Nations. To some historians, this marks a decisive shift in policy based on "entanglement" in durable security alliances across the world, and it entailed an unprecedented role for the military in deciding foreign policy. As one historian put it, it was a "novel presumption that the United States should and could dictate solutions to global problems."[46]

However, Stalin – the only leader who emerged from the Great War to lead a major power into the Second World War and remained in office after its end[47] – threw a spanner in the wheels by refusing to cooperate in such postwar order. The widely divergent Soviet and American worldviews quickly moved from the economic to the political realm along the fault line of occupied Germany. As detailed in the next chapter, winning two world wars and trying to redo the globe in its image had put the United States straight into another "cold" conflict that would last half a century, with the world fractured in two spheres of influence. In fact, some historians have argued that Americans overreacted to the post-1945 Soviet Union's takeover of its sphere because Roosevelt had continued to promote his policies under the guise of democratic peace while in reality he had already begun to play the cold war game of balance-of-power politics. Such an appraisal suggests that realist interests and ideals were continuing to clash in the formulation of foreign policy – and the frameworks for both interests and ideals were being forged, in part, in the voluminous world coverage in the American press, whose discourses are discussed in the next section.

America Covers the World: Media Discourses in the World Wars Era

In the first half of the twentieth century, as the United States took on global responsibilities by intervening in conflicts small and large across the world while

[46] Herring, 572.

[47] Kennedy, 852.

trying to exert dominant influence on peace outcomes, the press was becoming a similarly formidable institution. Vast corps of foreign correspondents were dispatched to try and make sense of the gathering storms and the U.S. role in them, obeying new ethics of public service while increasingly aware of the news media's influence on the public's mind. This book's principal argument is that the press has functioned as the public arena where meanings for things literally foreign become understood within general frameworks that in turn inform political actions. What, then, were the images of the world and, by reflex, of the United States that were created and negotiated in American foreign correspondence as the United States fought its way to superpower status? In the coverage of five formative events from 1911 to 1937, what discursive formations emerge about a generalized "other," the non-American; the construction of American that that implies; and the specific identity of covered countries and regions? The findings reflect analysis of approximately 500 news articles and editorials selected from coverage by the Associated Press, *New York Herald* and *New York Tribune* (which merged and became the *New York Herald Tribune* in 1924), *New York Times*, *Chicago Daily News* and *Baltimore Sun*.[48]

The Mexican Revolution of 1910: Too Close for Comfort

> One Mexican revolution, such as the one just ended, is enough for a while, not only for Mexico but for the United States, which suffered heavily by damage to American interests, loss of lives, crippling of commerce and the cost of the army mobilization.[49]

As the Washington correspondent of the *Baltimore Sun* wrote in the article just quoted, Americans had a direct interest in the upheaval that shook Mexico beginning in 1910 and lasting, by some counts, thirty more years. Unfortunately, U.S. journalists still tended to see events there mainly through the lens of what repercussions they would have on the United States, and they provided very little analysis of the social causes and consequences of the various phases of the Mexican Revolution. Unlike the other events analyzed in this chapter, the focus here rarely shifted from a detailed account of elections and battles, thus giving readers little context for understanding the larger issues involved and how they would affect future relations.

[48] The dates selected for study are: November 1–30, 1911, for the revolution in Mexico; November 1–30, 1917, for the revolution in Russia; January 1–31, 1925, for Mussolini's takeover in Italy; January 28 to February 3, 1932, for the Japanese attack on Shanghai; and January 1–17, 1937, for the Madrid bombing. For the first two events, both the New York *Herald* and the *Tribune* were searched; the papers merged in 1924, so for the last three events, the *Herald Tribune* was analyzed. The only available online database used was for the *New York Times* (its own and ProQuest); the search terms were as follows: Mexico; Russia; Mussolini; Shanghai; and Madrid. In all other cases, microfilm was used; every newspaper issue for the dates selected was then examined. The Associated Press corporate archives have no articles from this era; therefore, AP articles were searched in the other newspapers studied for this chapter.

[49] "Heads Off New Revolt," *Baltimore Sun*, November 20, 1911, 12.

The Mexican Revolution is considered the earliest and most puzzling of the social revolutions of the twentieth century, arguably because, unlike the Russian and Chinese movements, it was not dominated by a tight ideological program.[50] The grievances that sparked revolution stemmed from a dictatorial government's effort to achieve economic expansion through foreign investors – mostly Americans, who had poured hundreds of millions of dollars in the country's resources – and land privatization, without allowing for popular political and production empowerment. Crop failures and a general economic contraction generated widespread famine and unemployment, and violence erupted when General Porfirio Díaz tried to hang on to power by arresting his opponent in the presidential election, Francisco Madero, in the spring of 1910. Madero escaped and, with promises of labor and agrarian reforms, managed to rally peasants throughout the country to engage in guerrilla warfare, led by rebel leaders like Emiliano Zapata and Pancho Villa. In fall 1911, Díaz caved in and Madero took office, but Madero's effort to isolate his revolutionary supporters and his disappointing land reforms immediately backfired. Less than a month after Madero took office, in November 1911, Zapata introduced his Plan of Ayala, a much more radical reform program that won him the sympathy of the rural working classes and that would set the agenda for peasant rebellion for a decade.[51]

Starting to fight as Zapatistas, these revolutionaries carried on the struggle into civil war that would last through the 1910s despite violent attempts from the central government to put it down. In 1914, the United States intervened and took the port city of Veracruz. Although that action did little but further enflame Zapata's and Villa's supporters, it signaled a major shift in American policy – whereas American presidents had tended to give revolutionary governments at least the benefit of the doubt, Wilson "introduced a moral and political test" of a government's fitness to exist.[52] Washington then decided to side with the Constitutionalist leaders that represented the milder wing of the revolutionaries. In their aid, and to punish raids by Villa in New Mexico, the United States sent troops into Mexico – a move that further alienated the Mexican people, made Villa into a hero, and ended with a sheepish withdrawal. By 1917, the Constitutionalists had defeated Villa and Zapata, even though their movements did not entirely stop. They crafted a constitution, still in effect today, that protected workers' rights, national ownership of Mexican resources much to the chagrin of Americans, and some land reforms. It became the basis

[50] Michael C. Meyer and William H. Beezley, eds. *The Oxford History of Mexico* (Oxford: Oxford University Press, 2000), 433–465; Thomas E. Skidmore, Peter H. Smith and James N. Green, *Modern Latin America* 7th ed. (New York: Oxford University Press, 2010), 52–58.

[51] Friedrich Katz, *The Secret War in Mexico: Europe, The United States and the Mexican Revolution* (Chicago: University of Chicago Press, 1981), 43.

[52] Herring, 391.

for reconstructing the country, starting in 1920, into one of the most politically stable powers in Latin America.

Americans all the way up to Wilson were caught by surprise by the revolution, which they failed to understand in its broad social dimensions even though Zapata himself had written to Wilson to explain why his movement was promoting full political participation.[53] Instead, they tended to see it as affirmation of the long-standing prejudice that Mexicans were hopelessly violent and incapable of democratic governance.[54] Given that U.S.-Mexican relations had also been generally hostile in the nineteenth century, the revolution only solidified mutual mistrust that endured to the Second World War, as successive American administrations threw their support behind various Mexican leaders only to see them implement reforms that U.S. business interests found detrimental.[55] American journalists did not help Washington or the U.S. public understand the beginning of the Mexican Revolution.

Despite the proximity, the first phases of the revolution – including the promulgation of the Plan de Ayala in November 1911 – were not covered in any depth by any of the newspapers studied here. Most relied on reports from U.S. border towns or brief Mexico City dispatches by the Associated Press that tended to focus on narrow events.[56] A brief notice in the *New York Tribune*, for example, tersely noted that Madero was elected president with a 153–19 vote – hardly enough to help American readers appreciate the turmoil behind the vote.[57] The *New York Herald* relegated a brief mention about Zapata, whose "expected surrender... is delayed," to the bottom of a long cable from Mexico City relaying the hardly momentous story of a duel between two foreign diplomats there.[58]

The few correspondents in Mexico complained about the news that reached the United States, which one blamed on "the sensational and irresponsible Mexican newspapers which print as facts all the rumors without investigating their truth."[59] Other newspapers criticized Madero for declaring that he would "receive newspaper men only on special occasions" – although both the *New York Times* and the *New York Tribune* apparently managed to interview him – and they criticized the administration in general for adopting

[53] Meyer and Beezley, 464; Lloyd C. Gardner, *Safe for Democracy: The Anglo-American Response to Revolution, 1913–1923* (New York: Oxford University Press, 1984), 51.

[54] John A. Britton, *Revolution and Ideology: Images of the Mexican Revolution in the United States* (Lexington: University Press of Kentucky, 1995), 25; Sergio Aguayo, *Myths and [Mis]Perceptions: Changing U.S. Elite Visions of Mexico* (La Jolla: Center for U.S.-Mexican Studies, University of California, San Diego, 1998), 33.

[55] Jorge I. Domínguez and Rafael Fernández de Castro, *The United States and Mexico: Between Partnership and Conflict* 2nd ed. (New York: Routledge, 2009), 10; Katz, 564.

[56] For example, "Federals Kill 62 in Mexico," *Chicago Daily News*, November 25, 1911, 2.

[57] "Victory for Madero," *New York Tribune*, November 3, 1911, 2.

[58] "Turk Agrees to Duel in Mexico," *New York Herald*, November 12, 1911, 19.

[59] "Madero Gratified at U.S. Attitude," *New York Tribune*, November 20, 1911, 10.

"a policy of secrecy, which has been one of the worst defects of former Mexican Governments."[60] When longer articles made it out, they were mostly straightforward, detailed, blow-by-blow jumbles of names and actions that provided no analysis but gave the impression of a country out of control. For example, a long article in the *Herald* was a litany of paragraphs like the following: "Governor Ambrosio Figueroa, of Morelos, to-night received a telegram from the acting Governor, Señor Velasquez, saying there was a battle yesterday at Santa Ana lasting seven hours between 400 rurales and 800 Zapatists under command of Jesus Morales."[61] But no mention was found of the Plan de Ayala or the demands of the revolutionaries and the consequences for Mexicans.

The dominant discourses constructed the revolutionaries as "brigands" and Mexico as incapable of carrying on democratic reform. Dispatches and editorials in the *New York Times*, for example, referred to "lawlessness," "brigandage," and "marauding bands" led by the likes of a Zapata, whom it was impossible to induce "to take a reasonable view of the situation."[62] One editorial, echoing U.S. assessments of many countries in the grip of revolution, as noted in Chapter 2, stated, "The Mexican capacity for self-government has yet to be proved."[63] Similarly, a writer for the *New York Herald* in Mexico City dismissed the "rebels" as "semi-civilized Indians of the mountains" who were "sacking the business houses of Mexicans," and editors of the same paper wrote that Mexicans had not yet learned "the lesson of settling differences without recourse to revolutionary measures."[64] But referring to American involvement, the same editorial urged Washington to stay out unless "the fighting on which the Mexicans seem to be bent" came too close to the border.

Even the *New York Tribune*, which was more sympathetic than other newspapers, still described events with condescension and vastly underestimated the social unrest that boiled under the political developments and that would generate U.S. involvement. An editorial asserted that Mexico was an "inspiring example" of what "a Spanish-American state, even of most unsatisfactory antecedents, can accomplish."[65] The paper's correspondent called Mexico a "sister nation" and the United States its "best friend... in maintaining the

60 "1,000 Rebels Slain, Is Mexican Report," *New York Herald*, November 8, 1911, 10; "President Madero's Troubles," *New York Times*, November 18, 1911. (Occasionally, the electronic archive of the *New York Times* does not have page numbers.) For the interviews with Madero, see "Reyes's Mysterious Trip," *New York Times*, November 16, 1911, 2; and "Mexico's New Regime under Madero Begins," *New York Tribune*, November 6, 1911, 3. See also "General Madero Takes Oath To-Day," *New York Herald*, November 6, 1911, 6.

61 "Mexican State in Open Revolt about to Secede," *New York Herald*, November 25, 1911.

62 "Madero's First Duty," *New York Times*, November 10, 1911; "Special Cable to the New York Times," November 15, 1911, 1; "Zapata to be Suppressed," November 14, 1911, 1.

63 "The Mexican Situation," *New York Times*, November 29, 1911.

64 "240 Mexicans Dead in Oaxaca, Troops Rushed for Battle," *New York Herald*, November 9, 1911, 1; "Is Mexico to Be a Second Cuba?" *New York Herald*, November 9, 1911, 10.

65 "Mexico's New Era," *New York Tribune*, November 7, 1911, 6.

integrity and dignity of the nation."[66] He also seemed taken aback by the lack of pomp and circumstance in Madero's inauguration, which showed almost the same kind of "republican simplicity" as the United States, but argued that the revolution was now over and Madero would undertake the next day the "work" of settling "the Zapatist troubles."[67] A dispatch in the *Baltimore Sun* similarly noted that the inauguration had brought "no serious disorder" – unexpectedly for those rowdy Mexicans, implicitly – and that Madero's installment was the "culmination of a revolution."[68]

Other than a general dislike for disorderly Mexicans who disrupted Americans' legitimate business there and cast doubts on whether any democratic government would hold, readers of the newspapers studied here came away with very little understanding of a major social and political movement that drastically changed their southern neighbor for the rest of the twentieth century. America's role was not a part of the journalistic discourse. That did not favor public debate over government policies that would prove contradictory and that skirted the disastrous, as both the news media and policymakers appeared reluctant to conceptualize global influence. When the next major revolution broke out across the world in Russia in 1917, U.S. foreign correspondents showed a lot more interest and analytical skill, even if the Bolshevik movement was even harder to comprehend – so much so that one editorial lumped Mexicans and Russians together in their "aimless and unnecessary riot."[69]

The Russian Revolution of 1917: Rise of a Menace

> Civil strife is going on throughout Russia. The soviet is attempting to stop the bloodshed and makes suggestion after suggestion, but the bourgeoisie, failing to realize that the masses are out of control, are creating obstacles. I am convinced that the disturbances are the birthpains of a new free Russia, rather than its death throes. If Russia is to evolve a great free democracy she needs American help more than ever before and I take the liberty of suggesting that America show sympathy and not bitterness toward the struggling people.[70]

In one of the earliest academic studies of news bias, Lippmann blasted the *New York Times* coverage of the Russian Revolution as a case of "seeing not what was, but what men wished to see."[71] The *Chicago Daily News* correspondent from St. Petersburg quoted at the beginning of this section also seems to have been guilty of wishful thinking. Whatever the analytical faults of U.S. journalists covering the events in November 1917, however, they did provide an

66 "Mexico's New Regime under Madero Begins," *New York Tribune*, November 6, 1911, 3.

67 "Madero Sworn in as President of Mexico," *New York Tribune*, November 7, 1911, 5.

68 "Madero Is Inaugurated," *Baltimore Sun*, November 7, 1911, 2.

69 "How Kerensky Fell," *New York Times*, November 20, 1917.

70 Louis Edgar Browne, "Five Days' Battle Rages in Moscow; Casualties, 5,000," *Chicago Daily News*, November 17, 1911, 1.

71 The 1920 study is quoted in Starr, 396, and Teel, 91.

unprecedented number of eyewitness accounts and explanations from Russia that sought to explore the wider implications of the Soviet Revolution, not only for the allied efforts in World War I but for Russians themselves.

Much like journalists did at the time, historians have framed the Russian Revolution in the context of the gigantic European upheaval of the First World War, which Russia entered under a tsar and left under Lenin.[72] From the beginning of the war, American journalists covering the Russian front had written sympathetic reports that generated great public interest in the country.[73] By early spring 1917, U.S. diplomats and journalists were expecting popular anger at war-engendered food shortages to lead to upheaval, but they seemed caught unprepared by the magnitude of the revolution that toppled the emperor and replaced him with a provisional government, which the United States promptly recognized in hopes that democracy would now sweep the former empire.[74] As the war continued poorly for Russia, however, and the economic collapse worsened, popular unrest took a more radical form under the leadership of Vladimir Lenin and Leon Trotsky, who became suspected in U.S. eyes of being German agents trying to get Russia out of the conflict.

That suspicion compounded the overwhelmingly negative reaction that Americans had to the "October Revolution," when the Bolshevik Party took over the government and declared its intention of withdrawing from the war and turning over the land to peasant communes. The declared Soviet attempt to promote worldwide socialist revolution particularly irked Washington and the American public, who had long shown antipathy to socialism and communism as challenges to the American way of life.[75] After much indecision – a Washington correspondent of the *New York Times* pithily wrote, "the State Department is unable to understand what is occurring in Russia"[76] – Wilson eventually decided to join the Allies in a halfhearted mission to loosen the Bolshevik grip as Russia plunged into civil war. Unable to find a viable on-the-ground alternative despite overt and covert interventions, U.S. troops left the country in 1920 and the Soviet government continued its wartime "total mobilization" into permanent class struggle with the goal of a purely socialist society. What some have called the "first cold war" was well on its way, with mutual distrust cemented on both sides.[77]

[72] See Peter Holquist, *Making War, Forging Revolution: Russia's Continuum of Crisis, 1914–1921* (Cambridge, MA: Harvard University Press, 2002).

[73] Norman E. Saul, *War and Revolution: The United States and Russia, 1914–1921* (Lawrence: University Press of Kansas, 2001), 50–52.

[74] William Allison, *American Diplomats in Russia: Case Studies in Orphan Diplomacy, 1916–1919* (Westport, CT: Praeger, 1997), 9.

[75] David S. Foglesong, *America's Secret War against Bolshevism* (Chapel Hill: University of North Carolina Press, 1995), 45.

[76] "Francis's Messages Held," *New York Times*, November 17, 1917, 3.

[77] Davis and Trani, 206; Holquist, 286; Allison, 149; Foglesong, 298.

Just like U.S. diplomats and policymakers, the journalists studied here often failed to see the global resonance of the revolution – in fact, many kept arguing that the Bolshevik movement would quickly "have played out their brief role" and that "the most pathetic thing of all will probably be the situation of these peasants when they awake from their unrealizable dream."[78] Contrary to some scholarship, however, this research suggests that the readers of these newspapers never lacked news, even though war and censorship certainly posed significant logistical challenges.[79] Two AP staffers in St. Petersburg, for example, were injured in the turmoil, the cable office was closed for a few days, and Bolshevik censors wielded their blue pencils over any negative news.[80] At the height of the Bolshevik takeover, Louis Edgar Browne of the *Chicago Daily News* wrote, "This, I am told, is the first telegram leaving Petrograd in twenty-four hours."[81] Occasionally, it fell on control bureaus in London to patch together different reports, complaining that they gave "a partial and by no means clear view of the situation in Russia" and that censorship must have been rampant in St. Petersburg.[82] From the beginning, the Soviet regime had a tight control on information, curtailing the number of foreign correspondents and the news available to them.[83]

Despite those challenges, just like their nineteenth-century counterparts, editors crowed at their correspondents' successes. The *Chicago Daily News* ran this editorial on Louis Edgar Browne's coverage of the coup:

This long special cable dispatch, vividly presenting remarkable glimpses of the men, the methods and the ideas that now hold sway in the Russian capital, reached this

78 "Kerensky at Head of Soldiers from the Front Gives Battle to Bolsheviki from Petrograd," *New York Herald*, November 13, 1917, 1; "Russia," *Baltimore Sun*, November 11, 1917, 8. For a very critical account of journalists, see Phillip Knightley, *The First Casualty: The War Correspondent as Hero and Myth-Maker from the Crimea to Iraq* (Baltimore: Johns Hopkins University Press, 2004), 148–184; and Paul Moorcraft and Philip M. Taylor, *Shooting the Messenger: The Political Impact of War Reporting* (Washington: Potomac Books, 2008), 49–50. For an account of U.S. diplomacy in Russia, see Allison; Gardner, 151; Davis and Trani, 58.

79 On censorship, see Michael Emery, *On the Front Lines: Following America's Foreign Correspondents across the Twentieth Century* (Washington: American University Press, 1995), 30. Knightley argues that "the public was not kept informed," 148. For a much more sympathetic account of the correspondents' work, founded on primary sources, see Edward W. Pearlstein, ed. *Revolution in Russia! As Reported by the New York Tribune and the New York Herald, 1894–1921* (New York: Viking Press, 1967).

80 Pearlstein, xviii–xix.

81 Louis Edgar Browne, "Kerensky Defeated in Decisive Battle; Petrograd Burning," *Chicago Daily News*, November 15, 1917, 1. The *Baltimore Sun* also lamented the lack of news from Petrograd; "Latest Developments of the War," November 17, 1917, 1.

82 "Premier Has Disappeared," *New York Times*, November 18, 1917, 1; "Situation in Russia Still in Doubt; No Direct News from Petrograd," *New York Times*, November 15, 1917, 1; also "Kerensky at Head of Loyal Troops Seizes Tsarkoe-Selo," *New York Herald*, November 12, 1917, 1.

83 John Hohenberg, *Foreign Correspondence: The Great Reporters and Their Times* 2nd ed. (Syracuse: Syracuse University Press, 1995), 109.

> country ahead of all other dispatches dealing with the same subject through the special energy and enterprise of Mr. Browne. His feat is entitled to rank high in the history of journalistic enterprise. Readers of Mr. Browne's famous dispatches in the past accept him as a most satisfactory eyewitness of great events. His picture of the congress of soviets – the delegates wearing fur overcoats and fur caps in a superheated room blue with tobacco smoke, workmen and common soldiers laboriously deciding upon a policy for the vastest nation on earth amid the clatter of hobnailed boots on the wooden floor – deserves to live as a classic bit of reporting.[84]

The *New York Times*, *New York Tribune* and *Chicago Daily News* had their own correspondents in St. Petersburg (then called Petrograd). All newspapers studied also carried bulletins and long articles by AP correspondents there, all of whom took great pride in detailing their exploits to get firsthand news of what would turn out to be one of the defining moments of the twentieth century.

Correspondents gave verbatim reports of Lenin's speeches and interviewed the most important characters, including the head of the provisional government Alexander Kerensky and revolutionary leader Trotsky, to report "frank" discussions of the Russian situation.[85] Several of those interviews were lengthy question-and-answer articles, apparently little edited, that seemed to allow readers to hear reports straight from the source as well as to witness the confrontational style journalists were beginning to embrace. The AP interview with Kerensky, for example, printed by both the *New York Tribune* and the *New York Herald*, contained this rare insider view: "The correspondent called attention to widely contradictory reports on Russian conditions and asked the Premier for a frank statement of facts."[86] When correspondents' reports contained mystifying references, possibly the work of censors, editors inserted their own explanation, as in this example from the *Chicago Daily News*: "Petrograd is possibly on the eve of racial disorders. [The last sentence in the above dispatch may be an intimation that anti-Jewish riots are feared in Petrograd.]"[87]

In a preview of the highly personal, vivid style employed by 1930s battlefront reporters, correspondents showed readers what it meant to be in St. Petersburg during the revolution. An AP correspondent wrote of the street fighting visible

84 "Great Story from Petrograd," *Chicago Daily News*, November 12, 1917, 8. See also "London Gets News from Russia," *Chicago Daily News*, November 17, 1917, 8.

85 "Bolsheviki Get Moscow; Offer 3 Months Truce for Peace Conference," *New York Tribune*, November 10, 1917, 1; "Russia Doing Best to Win, Says Kerensky," *New York Tribune*, November 7, 1917, 8; Louis Edgar Browne, "'Force Peace with Guns,' Says Trotsky," *Chicago Daily News*, November 5, 1917, 1.

86 "Russia Won Out by Long Strain, but Is Not Out of War, Says Mr. Kerensky," *New York Herald*, November 3, 1917, 11; "Russia Not Quitting, but Needs Help, Says Kerensky," *New York Tribune*, November 3, 1917, 3. For an AP interview with Trotsky in the same style, see "No Separate Peace, Trotsky Declares," *New York Times*, November 24, 1917.

87 Louis Edgar Browne, "Race Riots Feared in Russian Capital," *Chicago Daily News*, November 23, 1917, 2.

"from the windows of the Associated Press headquarters."[88] A fellow AP staffer wrote: "The correspondent made a tour of the battlefield in a Petrograd droshky whose driver calmly directed his fat horse over the military road, dodging huge lorries and Red Cross motors homeward bound with wounded.... The droshky passed numerous sentries unquestioned, the soldiers apparently considering the ludicrous conveyance of the correspondent above suspicion."[89] The *New York Tribune*, which had its own correspondent, nevertheless praised AP dispatches for giving "a remarkable picture of the fighting in the streets of the capital."[90] Harold Williams of the *New York Times* claimed to have "traversed Russia from south to north."[91] Louis Edgar Browne ventured a dangerous trip away from the capital: "I have just returned to Petrograd from Moscow, where I went especially to obtain personal evidence of the ravages of civil war. I spent only fifteen hours in Russia's second capital, yet that short time was sufficient for a glimpse of the appalling results of the war between the classes."[92]

"War between the classes" was one of the constructions of the Russian Revolution in the American press, which tended to frame Bolshevism as something that would appeal "to uneducated Russians" – the AP correspondent confessed himself "surprised to find aristocratic officers commanding the Bolsheviki."[93] Other descriptions compared it to the revolution in the spring and noted that it was "totally unlike the first. Then every one was happy and smiling, full of joy and filled with glorious hopes for the future."[94] The revolution in November, an article in the same paper claimed, was "almost a repetition of the scenes in Paris during the French Revolution."[95] Indeed, several journalists argued that bloodshed was eliminating sympathy for the revolutionary cause – one reporter for the *New York Times* wrote that the "senseless destruction" in the Winter Palace "was certainly calculated to qualify revolutionary sympathy."[96] Similarly, Browne reported "tales of untold horror" and destruction at the Kremlin, "which even the Tartars regarded as sacred."[97] Several

88 "Cadets Attack Bolsheviki in Petrograd; Crowds in Nevsky Prospekt See Fighting," *New York Herald*, November 13, 1917, 1.

89 "Battle of Petrograd Is Told," *Chicago Daily News*, November 17, 1917, 2.

90 "French Cabinet Upset by Socialists; Lenine [*sic*] Still Holds Petrograd," *New York Tribune*, November 14, 1917, 1.

91 Harold Williams, "People Want a Strong Man," *New York Times*, November 18 1917, 2.

92 Louis Edgar Browne, "Maximalist Chief Becomes Dictator," *Chicago Daily News*, November 19, 1917, 1.

93 Louis Edgar Browne, "'Force Peace with Guns,' Says Trotsky," *Chicago Daily News*, November 5, 1917, 2; "Kerensky Defeated after Three Days' Hard Fighting," *New York Tribune*, November 18, 1917, 2.

94 "Loyalists Urge Russia to Refute Bolsheviki Rule," *New York Tribune*, November 12, 1917, 2.

95 "Forces of Kerensky Approaching Capital from Two Sides," *New York Tribune*, November 14, 1917, 1.

96 "City Council Foils Reds," *New York Times*, November 13, 1917, 2.

97 Louis Edgar Browne, "Maximalist Chief Becomes Dictator," *Chicago Daily News*, November 19, 1917, 1.

reports focused on widespread anarchy that would "send a shudder throughout Russia."[98]

Some correspondents rightly saw the revolution as the presage to civil war and Lenin as a dictator who "makes the laws and directs more or less the destinies of 180,000,000 people with the ease of a juggler tossing Indian clubs."[99] But even Browne, the author of that description, mistakenly assumed that "soldiers and the more intelligent workingmen" would soon realize "the scheme of government by the masses is not working out well," and his editors insisted that "the bolsheviki's wild adventure is bound to fail."[100] The journalists who constructed the revolutionaries as "extreme radicals," "reckless extremists" and "fanatics and renegades" led by "radical agitator" Lenin were even more likely to dismiss the Bolshevik takeover as fleeting.[101] In one of the earliest articles from Petrograd, Browne made the equation a matter of translation: "The bolsheviki (extremist) leaders..."[102]

Perhaps least conducive to a broad understanding of the revolution was the tendency by both correspondents and editors to focus on its repercussions on World War I instead of on Russia itself. The *New York Herald* editors, for example, had peace with Germany in mind when they warned readers that, "Russia is far away. Lack of knowledge of conditions there has inclined many Americans to dismiss the Bolsheviki as having no direct interest to the United States, when as a matter of fact their actions have very direct bearing upon this country."[103] A cartoon on the front page of the *Baltimore Sun* portrayed Russia as prostrate Samson in front of socialism as Delilah, with German soldiers looking on.[104] Harold Williams, reporting from Petrograd for the *New York Times*, condemned the Bolshevik movement as having no "constructive power" but "enormous power for destruction" in the name of

98 Harold Williams, "Rebels Destroy Shrines of Moscow," *New York Times*, November 19, 1917, 2; "Anarchy in Petrograd," *Baltimore Sun*, November 22, 1917, 2; "The Russian Overturn," *New York Times*, November 9, 1917.

99 "Maximalists Depose Kerensky; 'Force without Mercy,' Cry," *Chicago Daily News*, November 8, 1917, 1; "Maximalist Chief Becomes Dictator"; Louis Edgar Browne, "Worst Upheaval Yet Due in Russia Soon," *Chicago Daily News*, November 26, 1917, 2.

100 "Portents in Russia," *Chicago Daily News*, November 28, 1917, 8.

101 "Russian Government Upset by Revolutionists, Premier Flees; 'Reds' to Ask Immediate Peace," *New York Herald*, November 9, 1917, 1; "Lenine's [*sic*] Ideas on Peace," *Chicago Daily News*, November 12, 1917, 8; "Russia and the Rebel Pacifists," *Chicago Daily News*, November 10, 1917, 8; "Votes Rebuke Bolsheviki," *New York Times*, November 2, 1917, 1; "Russian Tide Has Turned," *Baltimore Sun*, November 14, 1917, 1; "Extremists' Rise to Power in Russia," *New York Times*, November 9, 1917.

102 Louis Edgar Browne, "Use Arms to Oust Kerensky, Is Plea," *Chicago Daily News*, November 3, 1917, 2.

103 "What We Owe to the Bolsheviki," *New York Herald*, November 4, 1917, 16. For a very similar editorial assessment, see "Time to Put Away Illusions," *New York Tribune*, November 10, 1917, 12.

104 *Baltimore Sun*, November 28, 1917, 1.

dishonorable peace.[105] The editors of the *New York Herald* referred to "the unspeakable Lenine [*sic*], known to be a Prussian agent" and argued that such "traitors" would be deposed by the Russian people: "Backward as they are, slow to think and slow to move, nevertheless the masses of the Russian people are patriotic."[106]

Such a characterization of the Russian people seems to underlie both the journalists' predictions that the revolution would not last but also the engrained uneasiness with which they regarded socialist revolution. Williams argued that Russia continued to function despite the revolution "by force of habit, by virtue of some common irrefutable, irrational belief."[107] This is what the *New York Times* editor reduced the class conflict to: "[The Bolsheviks] represent the most ignorant classes in an uneducated country, and what these most ignorant classes want is a millennium in which everybody will receive immense bonuses without doing any work and in which everybody who has anything will have to hand it over to anybody who has nothing and wants something."[108]

Nevertheless, a few correspondents tried to understand the movement, the "soviet point of view," as Browne put it, even as they wrote about the dangers to the Allied cause. Without denying a dose of "German intrigue," Browne told readers that "the largest contributing factor in the soviet's movement is a sincere and idealistic belief in internationalism."[109] In the detailed dispatch that won his editors' praise as noted previously, Browne described speakers at the Soviet congress sympathetically: "They probably are idealists and perhaps dreamers, but down in their hearts they believe that they are helping to pave the way to the universal brotherhood of man."[110] As Lenin's hold on power consolidated, Browne seemed less sure it would not last than he had been in the early days, when he had written, "That the bolsheviki regime will be transitory is certain, but it is thought probable that much bloodshed will occur before the rebels are superseded by a saner and more practical administration."[111] Even the staunchly anti-Soviet Williams confessed himself at a loss to understand Russian developments: "This combination of the sixteenth and twentieth centuries grows disconcerting. One has to develop new mental kinks to secure a grip on the situation."[112]

105 Harold Williams, "Explains Russian Parley," *New York Times*, November 26, 1917, 1.

106 "If Russia Is to Remain Russia," *New York Herald*, November 24, 1917, 8.

107 Harold Williams, "Russia, Minus a Government, Still Goes On; Petrograd Council Proposes National Election," *New York Times*, November 21, 1917, 1.

108 "The New Marats," *New York Times*, November 11, 1917.

109 Louis Edgar Browne, "Cleavage of Allies and Soviet Widens," *Chicago Daily News*, November 30, 1917, 2.

110 Louis Edgar Browne, "Lenine [*sic*] Russ Premier; How Cabinet is Made, Told by Eyewitness – L.E.B. Vividly Describes Soviet Congress in Action and Battle for Winter Palace," *Chicago Daily News*, November 10, 1917, 2.

111 Louis Edgar Browne, "Armored Cars Used by Keresnky Troops in Petrograd Battle," *Chicago Daily News*, November 12, 1917, 2.

112 Harold Williams, "Chaos in Russia Is Getting Worse," *New York Times*, November 23, 1917, 2.

Despite such correspondents' genuine efforts at understanding, and extraordinary exploits to get, the news, the dominant discourse that emerged from the coverage of the Russian Revolution was that the Bolshevik movement was extreme and unrepresentative of Russia, and, at the same time, that Russians seemed destined for a "terrible fate" by their tragic history and impotence to use revolution to bring liberty to their country.[113] "The attempt is to substitute the despotism of the Socialist proletariat for the overthrown despotism of the Czardom," wrote the editors of the *New York Times*.[114] They appeared prescient when they added that the Bolsheviks had created an abyss between Russia and the West: "The Bolsheviki, by their madness, and the Russian people, in weakly permitting them to seize upon authority, have given Russia a bad name among nations which it will live down only through many decades of stability and civil order."[115] Such discourse, however, could also be self-fulfilling – the focus on total ideological incompatibility and stubborn disbelief in socialist revolt laid the ground for the hostility and incomprehension of the Cold War. The only role left discursively open for the United States was that of enemy of all the Bolsheviks stood for – and indeed, the Soviet Revolution and the entry into World War I marked a pivotal shift in U.S. foreign policy. No longer the disinterested friend of popular revolutions everywhere, Washington would now rely on anti-communism as the lens to judge developments in a world from which it was increasingly impossible to remain aloof.

Mussolini's Takeover: Are Timely Trains Worth a Dictatorship?

> While a believer in republican government could scarcely approve all of Mussolini's methods, which are rather more tyrannical than democratic, yet no student of human nature can fail to find something attractive in this man.... Whether history will write his name as one who saved Italy from the woes of being a second Soviet Russia, or whether he will be recorded as a consummate bit of selfishness, no one can tell today.[116]

History's verdict on Benito Mussolini, the leader of Italian Fascism who allied the country with Hitler's Germany, has been significantly more negative than the *New York Times* correspondent just quoted predicted. That his takeover of power in 1925 should be described in the American press as the alternative to the Soviet menace, however, is indicative of how the Russian Revolution had forced a worldview on the United States that, with the exception of the Second World War, would drive opinion and policy for the majority of the twentieth century.

Italian politics, ruled by fractious alliances and swinging between the right and the left, had been in turmoil for decades. The southern regions had been

[113] Harold Williams, "People Want a Strong Man," *New York Times*, November 18, 1917, 2.

[114] "Despotism, Not Liberty," *New York Times*, November 27, 1917.

[115] "Outside the Pale," *New York Times*, November 25, 1917.

[116] Edwin L. James, "Mussolini's Power Remains Unshaken, While Foes Falter," *New York Times*, January 26, 1925, 1.

decimated by emigration since the 1880s, and the majority of the country relied on agriculture to survive, leading to violent clashes as industrialization took hold at the turn of the century. Hundreds of thousands of World War I deaths – mostly from the lower classes – further deepened social unrest, and Mussolini used it to enter politics with a populist program. The Fascist Party first showed its strength in October 1922, when the march on Rome by militias cowed the king into asking Mussolini to form a government.[117]

The appearance of legality was maintained until summer 1924, when the assassination of an opposition leader charging electoral fraud threw the government into disarray. In a historic speech to the Chamber of Deputies on January 3, 1925, Mussolini assumed personal responsibility for the Fascist movement – "I, and I alone, assume the political, moral and historical responsibility for all that has happened" – and, after daring the opposition to remove him, promised to take charge of restoring Italy to order.[118] Historians have considered that speech to mark the beginning of Mussolini's totalitarian dictatorship.[119] Throughout the rest of the 1920s, Mussolini worked on reinforcing his domestic hold by dissolving the Chamber of Deputies, outlawing all non-Fascist political parties (even though the monarchy was preserved), suppressing the opposition press, and forcing political opponents into exile or prison.

At the same time, however, Mussolini was much more guarded in his foreign policy and courted Washington, not only to obtain more favorable treatment for Italian emigrants, an issue found in some of the coverage studied,[120] but also to use American backing when dealing with other European powers. Initially, Western powers, including the United States, where ethnic groups were an increasingly powerful voice in foreign policy,[121] chose to ignore Fascism, hoping it might still be an ally against Hitler's rising tide. The Spanish Civil War, as noted later in this chapter, would change that, but Americans, and the U.S. press, greeted Mussolini with some enthusiasm for what they saw as having saved Italy from Bolshevism.[122]

Furthermore, U.S. correspondents' attention was riveted on Il Duce – who granted several interviews to American journalists – to the detriment of the larger phenomenon of Fascism.[123] It was the first time in the correspondence

[117] Harry Hearder, *Italy: A Short History* (Cambridge: Cambridge University Press, 1990), 227.

[118] Adrian Lyttelton, *The Seizure of Power: Fascism in Italy, 1919–1929* 2nd ed. (Princeton, NJ: Princeton University Press, 1987), 265.

[119] Stanislao Pugliese, ed. *Fascism, Anti-Fascism and the Resistance in Italy: 1919 to the Present* (Lanham, MD: Rowman & Littlefield Publishers, 2004), 69.

[120] "Italy Welcomes Kellogg," *New York Times*, January 12, 1925, 2; "Italy Hopes for Change in Immigration Stand," *Baltimore Sun*, January 12, 1925, 2.

[121] Herring, 351.

[122] John Booth Carter, "American Reactions to Italian Fascism, 1919–1933" (PhD diss., Columbia University, 1954), 29; Gian Giacomo Migone, *Gli Stati Uniti e il Fascismo: Alle origini dell'egemonia americana in Italia* (Milan: Feltrinelli, 1980), 54.

[123] Carter, 456.

analyzed in this book that broad historical movements were reduced to one figure, a journalistic shorthand that does not generally help the formation of nuanced discourses. The *Chicago Daily News* star correspondent, Edward Price Bell, for example, interviewed Mussolini in 1924. In his memoir, Bell described him as a "transcendent human dynamo and constructive influence on modern Italy," who found time for journalists because he had been a "brilliant and influential editor" and he "believed in the Press, though none more than he knew its shortcomings and its not infrequent sins."[124] One exhaustive study of Americans' reaction to Mussolini argued that it was influenced by U.S. images of Italy in general – a romantic picture of Italy as the cradle of art and culture intertwined with disparaging for the poor and oppressed Italians washing ashore by the millions.[125] Relying on those images, many Americans, and the majority of the press, tended to see Fascism as the only way to ensure that Italians would become a bit more civilized, a bit, even, Americanized – that perhaps a dictator would finally make trains run on time, a point made in an AP front-page story published in the *New York Herald Tribune*.[126]

All newspapers studied, and the AP, had their own correspondents covering Mussolini's January 1925 grab for power. That readers' interest in Italy was intense can be assumed from the fact that even with such major political crisis driving the news, some newspapers found space for reports on the arts, such as a memorial to opera composer Giacomo Puccini.[127] Even the *Baltimore Sun* sent its London correspondent to interview Mussolini in Rome, to "induce" him "to explain, for American readers, the reasons for the governmental acts which have so divided public feeling toward Mussolini, both at home and abroad."[128] The coverage was almost as intense as that of the Russian Revolution – journalists followed not only the speech but its opposition and further measures inaugurated by Mussolini, through interviews, observation and, occasionally, using Italian newspapers as sources.[129] An AP correspondent commented sarcastically on the practice that in the twenty-first century would be called "parachuting" correspondents: "Despite the lull in the political situation, a flock of foreign newspaper correspondents, including many from the United States and England who poured into Rome from other European capitals to watch the fireworks this week, refused to be convinced that the 'shooting' is over, and they are still trying with might and main to interview

[124] Quoted in Cole and Hamilton, 278–280.

[125] John P. Diggins, *Mussolini and Fascism: The View from America* (Princeton, NJ: Princeton University Press, 1972), 6–73.

[126] "Blackshirt Militia Maneuvers to Awe Italy as Machine Guns Guard Rome," *New York Herald Tribune*, January 5, 1925, 1.

[127] "King at Memorial to Giacomo Puccini," *New York Times*, January 20, 1925, 21.

[128] John W. Owens, "Upheaval in Italy Frothy Affair, Says Premier Mussolini," *Baltimore Sun*, February 1, 1925, 1.

[129] For example, the AP quoted the newspaper *Sereno* in an article reprinted in the *New York Times*, January 20, 1925, 4.

Mussolini."[130] As many of his predecessors and successors would do, the correspondent seemed to imply that only journalists in place were suited to grasp complex events.

Apparently the same correspondent also poked fun at the reporting by some of his colleagues who had predicted that Mussolini would quickly fall – a pattern of American coverage of unsavory foreign leaders that, as noted in the two previous sections, hardly helped readers appreciate the historic events:

> The peaceable adjournment of the Chamber, coming without the breaking of the expected storm, caused discomfiture mostly to the dozens of foreign correspondents who had rushed to Italy a few days ago to be on hand to describe the wreckage of the Mussolini regime.... The session of the Chamber, however, came and went without the spectacle of Mussolini's falling, so the special writers have begun to trickle out of the country one by one, although they all apparently had enjoyed the few days of basking in Italy's balmy Winter sunshine.[131]

The correspondent's own assessment as one of the "impartial observers" was that "Mussolini will remain at his post for many moons to come." As discussed earlier, such a development was hardly interpreted as bad news because it was constructed as a victory for law and order. Editorials in the *New York Herald Tribune* argued that Mussolini was "the only Italian statesman of the post-war period who has done anything worthwhile for Italy," and therefore the "Italian nation owes him a very great debt." It was Mussolini who "gave Italy public order and new virility.... Italy's prestige abroad has been immensely increased. These are the results of Fascism."[132] An article in the *New York Times* compared the Fascist takeover to that of the Soviets, because they both emerged from violent revolution, and praised Mussolini for "an attitude of generosity" "without indulging in any acts of political vengeance."[133] John Owens, the *Baltimore Sun* correspondent who interviewed Mussolini, wrote that the Fascist leader "sees his Government as having introduced order and stability and sees the Italian people as gratefully intent upon making their living and indifferent to more or less doctrinaire and partisan contentions over governmental methods." Owens's own description: "The chosen leader of Italy or its ruthless dictator, as you please."[134]

130 "Mussolini Asserts No Elections Will Be Held This Year," *Baltimore Sun*, January 11, 1925, 11.

131 "Mussolini Victor on Electoral Bill," *New York Times*, January 18, 1925, 2. The same AP story was reprinted as "Mussolini Wins as Session Ends" in the *Baltimore Sun* (January 18, 1925, 1), but with a few changed phrases, suggesting editors took liberties with AP content. For an example of stories predicting Mussolini's fall, see "Liberals Give Way to Fascisti in Rome Cabinet," *Baltimore Sun*, January 6, 1925, 1.

132 "The Italian Election," *New York Herald Tribune*, January 9, 1925, 14; "Taking Chances with Mussolini," *New York Herald Tribune*, January 6, 1925, 8.

133 "Marching Fascisti Acclaim Iron Hand as Mussolini Acts," *New York Times*, January 5, 1925, 1.

134 John W. Owens, "Upheaval in Italy Frothy Affair, Says Premier Mussolini," *Baltimore Sun*, February 1, 1925, 1.

The main discourse about Italy found in the correspondence was that of a country plagued by the "tumultuous caldron" of its internal politics, run by leaders, including Mussolini, who were "picturesque" and fascinating, and inhabited by a fickle people "susceptible to fiery phrases" – and it was hard to take it all seriously when even in the midst of crisis both Fascists and their opponents were out "enjoying a rest at the countryside."[135] The Fascists were reported to react with "ironical laughter" to opponents' challenges, and the confrontations were described as "a dramatic scene" full of shaking, pummeling, mad cheers and vehement oratory on the part of Mussolini, "his face red with anger, his eyes blazing with fury."[136] The shorthand for Mussolini's opposition was frequently "Reds" who "invoked the spirit of Lenin" – hardly a construction that would inspire the sympathy of American readers, and indicative of how quickly the shadow of communism had spread in the public's imagination.[137]

Coverage of Mussolini, however, was not as uncritical as some scholars have charged. Hiram Kelly Moderwell of the *Chicago Daily News* condemned the "police searches in the houses of many opposition leaders and societies" that he saw as "only a prelude to more radical action that will place fascismo in complete control of Italy."[138] The press suppression was covered in all newspapers, although in some cases the description seemed to justify the measures ("the seizures of newspapers printing *false or alarming* news").[139] The *New York Times* correspondent called it "the policy of the iron fist," the *Baltimore Sun* the "iron hand," and the AP noted Fascists "displayed the old warlike spirit unabated" and Mussolini showed "the characteristic role of aggressor."[140]

135 "Mussolini Asserts No Elections Will Be Held This Year," *Baltimore Sun*, January 11, 1925, 11; "A Slipping Dictator," *Baltimore Sun*, January 8, 1925, 8. Mussolini was also defined a "picturesque braggart" in the editorial "Mussolini the Magnificent," *Baltimore Sun*, January 5, 1925, 6.

136 "Italian Communists Return to Chamber after Long Absence," *Baltimore Sun*, January 15, 1925, 11; "Chamber Backs Mussolini on Electoral Bill," *Baltimore Sun*, January 17, 1925, 1; "Mussolini Defies Foes," *Chicago Daily News*, January 3, 1925, 1; "Blow by Mussolini to Crush His Foes," *New York Times*, January 4, 1925, 1.

137 "Reds Raise Tumult in Italian Chamber; End 2-Year Boycott," *New York Times*, January 15, 1925, 1; "Mussolini Jeers as Reds 'Doom' Him in Chamber," *New York Herald Tribune*, January 15, 1925, 2.

138 Hiram Kelly Moderwell, "Strike Proposed to Italian Newspapers," *Chicago Daily News*, January 2, 1925, 2; Moderwell, "All Mussolini Foes Sternly Repressed," *Chicago Daily News*, January 7, 1925, 3.

139 "Mussolini Rebuilds a Fascist Cabinet," *New York Times*, January 6, 1925, 1; emphasis added. For articles on suppression, see, among many, "Opposition Press Harried," *New York Herald Tribune*, January 8, 1925, 3; "Mussolini Keeps Down Opposition with Iron Hand," *Baltimore Sun*, January 7, 1925, 11.

140 "Rioting Flares Up throughout Italy," *New York Times*, January 3, 1925, 15; "Sudden Quiet in Italy Is Regarded as Ominous," *Baltimore Sun*, January 14, 1925, 1; "Fascists Wreck Newspaper Plant Fire Buildings," *New York Herald Tribune*, January 1, 1925, 3; "Mussolini Strikes at Free Masonry," *Baltimore Sun*, January 13, 1925, 7.

In a suggestion that censorship might have extended to foreign reporters, an editor's note in the *Baltimore Sun* warned that "although foreign correspondents were theoretically at liberty to cable what they like there is a very practical Government censorship."[141] Edwin James inserted the following disclaimer at the end of one of his articles: "Mussolini's foes say there is a discreet censorship which halts all newspaper dispatches not entirely favorable to him. I am filing this from Rome to see."[142] Editors at the *New York Times* also clearly stated that the Mussolini government was a "dictatorship" and it risked plunging the country into civil war, even though James retorted that, whereas "in most countries" a leader who needs to "squelch the opposition" and is "tainted with the stain of scandal" would not survive long, "the Italian situation is exceptional."[143]

In the end, the overall impression was conveyed that it was hard to take happenings in Italy seriously. The AP noted that "the bitter political struggle between the Fascist Government and its foes has been unable to prevail as a week-end attraction against the Springlike weather which the capital is now enjoying."[144] James, writing that France was better off economically than Italy, quipped: "Express such an opinion to the average Italian and you run the danger of having a couple of yards of spaghetti wound round your neck."[145] Moderwell wrote a lengthy article about Pasquino, an ancient statue still in place in downtown Rome on which locals post witticisms about current events. Moderwell joked, "And what did Pasquino say recently? Did he sentence the government to death, or graciously grant it a reprieve? Mere newspaper men cannot know."[146]

That narrative levity is a very dangerous framework for foreign policy, given that Italy would not only be a major combatant in the Second World War but also one of the most contested terrains in the Cold War confrontation between communism and liberalism. The inability to take the situation seriously, based apparently on images of Italians as so picturesque that a firm leader might be advantageous, fits with the 1920s strong American reluctance to get involved in global politics. Similarly, the "Red" moniker attached to all matters of unrest provided a very rigid frame that left little movement for insightful analysis. In fact, discourses about Mussolini's Italy merge two pervasive threads of American understanding of the world: the nagging suspicion that Americans were the only people capable of handling democracy coupled with the urgent perception

[141] "Mussolini's War on Masons Held Bid for Church Support," *Baltimore Sun*, January 19, 1925, 1.

[142] Edwin L. James, "Mussolini's Power Remains Unshaken, While Foes Falter," *New York Times*, January 26, 1925, 4.

[143] "Fascist Confusion," *New York Times*, January 7, 1925, 24; Edwin L. James, "Mussolini's Power Remains Unshaken, While Foes Falter," *New York Times*, January 26, 1925, 1.

[144] "Election Next Year Is Mussolini's Plan," *New York Times*, January 11, 1925, 7.

[145] Edwin L. James, "Italy Is Fearful of Debt Reminder," *New York Times*, January 24, 1925, 4.

[146] Hiram Kelly Moderwell, "Famous Rome Oracle Breaks Long Silence," *Chicago Daily News*, January 19, 1925, 2.

of necessary anti-communist involvement. In the much more menacing world of the 1930s, complacent neglect and ideological fervor would both be submerged by a different set of threats that mandated massive U.S. intervention.

Japan Attacks Shanghai: Feeling China's Pain

> China, the world's greatest geographic national entity, occupying an eighth of the world's land surface and inhabited by a fourth of the world's population, tonight presents the most tragic aspect known to mankind since the cessation of the European war thirteen years ago.... Even admitting that China today does not really constitute a nation, the events of the last four days, surprisingly to many observers, indicate that the Chinese are one people and may prove to be a people of tougher fibre than has been imagined.[147]

Correspondents like the *New York Times*' Hallett Abend, just quoted, who covered the Japanese attack in Shanghai in early 1932, graphically described the gathering storm that would in a few years burst into the Second World War. They did so with little pretense for objectivity and an unprecedented focus on the suffering of civilians that would soon spread from China to the rest of the world. For the first time in coverage studied in this research, journalists abandoned the horse-race approach to military action and provided instead vivid personal accounts of tragedy and analytical explanations of global repercussions. The dramatic constructions of a torn world erupting in unfathomable violence in the correspondence from China and Spain, as discussed in the next section, gave Americans reason to try to stay as removed as possible – and to intervene with overwhelming force to take the reins of a hopelessly devastated world when it became the only possible safe course.

While Japan had pursued an aggressive policy of regional expansion throughout the early twentieth century, its assault on Manchuria in the fall of 1931 was in evident violation of post-WWI treaties.[148] President Herbert Hoover, while condemning Japanese actions, tried to keep the United States uninvolved and to reprimand Japan through nonrecognition. Japan pressed on and, on January 28, on the pretext of protecting Japanese interests against Chinese mobs, attacked Shanghai, the trading capital of China, with a large contingent of armed forces and overwhelming air power. U.S. warships steamed to Shanghai to protect Americans and other non-Chinese living in the city's international settlement even as Hoover continued to affirm that Washington would not meddle in Asia but would insist on China's territorial integrity, and that he fervently hoped that the Chinese would do enough to defend themselves. China, however, was in the midst of conflict between the Nationalist

[147] Hallett Abend, "China's Woes Reach Climax at Shanghai," *New York Times*, February 1, 1932, 3.

[148] Dorothy Borg and Shumpei Okamoto, eds. *Pearl Harbor as History: Japanese-American Relations, 1931–1941* (New York: Columbia University Press, 1973), 25.

government and communist forces, both fueled by anti-imperialism, and the resistance it put up in Shanghai, with "unusual valor and tenacity" (according to the *New York Times* correspondent), surprised many observers.[149]

With world opinion enraged but unwilling to support Western action, Japan let Shanghai go in May, but strengthened its hold on Manchuria by establishing a puppet state there, Manchukuo. Hoover and his successor Roosevelt continued the policy of nonrecognition and moral pressure while avoiding economic or military sanctions against Japan, and Japan continued its expansion in East Asia, further destabilizing U.S.-Japanese relations and fostering a tentative, uneasy alliance between the United States and China.[150] By the time the Japanese renewed their assault on China in 1937, the U.S. Navy had started a buildup in the Pacific and the Spanish Civil War was raging in Europe – the world stood on the brink of global conflict again.

Editorials on the Shanghai Crisis tended to support the U.S. "moral sense... without any threat of force" approach and to consider it the right way to "deflate this preposterous flare-up of Japan's inflated national ego," thus minimizing the discussion of China and even arguing that the attacks must have been a sad military blunder.[151] *New York Herald Tribune* editors defined the United States' "most urgent task" as ensuring that Americans would be unharmed in Shanghai and argued, rather astonishingly, that Japan, with this "savagery and slaughter," was descending "to a level about like that on which China stands."[152] The *Chicago Daily News* editors argued that an international intervention would only please "the Chinese, who have hoped to entangle the powers in their paralyzed nation's affairs," and Russia, "which relies upon strife between capitalistic powers to further its revolutionary aspirations."[153] At the *Baltimore Sun*, editors, while sympathetic to the plight of China, "that tortured land," felt that moral pressure, "in conjunction with the enormous capacity of the Chinese millions for deadly passive resistance," would right Japan's course.[154] With disturbing callousness, they argued that responding with war "would not even rebuild the flimsy Chinese shacks burned in the conflagration that followed the bombing."[155]

149 Hallett Abend, "Foreign Zone Is Shelled," *New York Times*, January 30, 1932, 1; Christopher Thorne, *The Limits of Foreign Policy: The West, the League and the Far Eastern Crisis of 1931–1933* (New York: G.P. Putnam's Sons, 1972), 202. The change in foreign opinion after the Chinese "staunch resistance" was also noted in Hallett Abend, "Japanese Checked in Taking Shanghai," *New York Times*, January 29, 1932, 2.

150 William L. Neumann, *America Encounters Japan: From Perry to MacArthur* (Baltimore: Johns Hopkins Press, 1963), 190.

151 "Moving for Peace," *New York Times*, February 3, 1932, 18; "The Powers Combine for Peace," *Chicago Daily News*, February 3, 1932, 8; "The Pity of It," *New York Times*, January 30, 1932, 16.

152 "In Defense of Shanghai," *New York Herald Tribune*, February 1, 1932, 12; "The Appeal to Force at Shanghai," *New York Herald Tribune*, January 31, 1932, 6 (section II).

153 "New Perils in the Far East," *Chicago Daily News*, January 28, 1932, 12.

154 "Cool Heads Needed," *Baltimore Sun*, January 29, 1932, 8.

155 "Crowning Infamy," *Baltimore Sun*, January 31, 1932, 8.

But the correspondents' heartfelt tales of Chinese suffering – and a few pointed references to the Japanese tearing down an American flag[156] – seemed to shame such American detachment, as in this story by Reginald Sweetland of the *Chicago Daily News*: "Surrounded by marines from California, Texas and Virginia, I watched the Japanese bomb the defenseless city.... Hundreds of Chinese jammed their faces against the huge steel gates leading into the American quarter, hoping to enter the lines of exit from the Chinese city, but they were not allowed to do so."[157] As one dispatch in the *New York Times* put it, civilian and military authorities in the Shanghai diplomatic corps watched the "harried and harassed stream of ignorant and innocent [Chinese] folk" aghast at "the deliberate campaign of Japanese terrorism."[158]

Unlike the Boxer Uprising some thirty years earlier, the Japanese attack on Shanghai, referred to as the "mounting tale of horror" in "this greatest of Chinese cities," was witnessed and reported by a robust corps of U.S. correspondents stationed there, many of whom had come out of one of the first university journalism programs, at the University of Missouri.[159] Their gripping, outraged descriptions of the Japanese assault, combined with a rather condescending admiration for the Chinese, gave readers an unprecedented emotional perspective on the conflict, and a staunchly anti-Japanese one. Perhaps in response to then-beginning radio reporting, the correspondents wrote so that readers could not only see but also hear the battle – "At 4 A.M. there was a sharp increase in the tap-tap-tap of machine gun bursts," the AP reported.[160]

This description of the army assault on the city by Victor Keen of the *New York Herald Tribune* is representative of the seething outrage across the press:

> Many innocent Chinese coolies were shot down when, through ignorance or terror, they failed to heed Japanese orders to halt. Not a few Chinese women were shot or bayoneted – seemingly needless sacrifices involved in the Japanese program against snipers.... Yet the necessity for ruthless measures to hunt down snipers hardly excuses or explains hospital cases of Chinese women shot in the back, stabbed or bayoneted when attempting to escape from homes not in the active firing zone. Many of these cases can be explained only as the result of irresponsible hysteria or merciless racial hatred.[161]

156 "Japanese Tear Down an American Flag," *New York Times*, February 2, 1932, 16; the story also appeared in the *Chicago Daily News*, February 1, 1932, 1.

157 Reginald Sweetland, "Daily News Man Witnesses Slaughter in Chinese City; Tells of Death from Air," *Chicago Daily News*, January 29, 1932, 1.

158 "Chinese Lose Homes," *New York Times*, February 1, 1932, 2.

159 "Chinese Threaten a General Strike," *New York Times*, February 2, 1932, 16; Victor Keen, "Shanghai Awaits Attack; Foreign Area Barricaded; 13 More Warships Arrive," *New York Herald Tribune*, January 28, 1932, 1. On the Missouri connection, see Stephen R. MacKinnon and Oris Friesen, *China Reporting: An Oral History of American Journalism in the 1930s and 1940s* (Berkeley: University of California Press, 1987), 23–36.

160 "Japanese Admit Withdrawal," *New York Times*, January 30, 1932, 2.

161 Victor Keen, "4 Powers Draft Peace Formula; Japanese Reject 2 of 5 Points; Shanghai Artillery Duel Reopens," *New York Herald Tribune*, February 3, 1932, 2.

The same issue also carried a story by Elizabeth Keen – presumably the correspondent's wife, who is mentioned in another article as reporting with Keen[162] – that took a distinctly personal tone and hauntingly described civilian suffering through interviews with "three of these innocent victims" in the women's ward of the Chinese Red Cross hospital. The women, Keen wrote, "were aware of the 'war,' but none had any comprehension of why it had started or why it still continued."[163] She was not alone in inserting herself in the story. Victor Keen wrote that he spoke Japanese and described his efforts to get eyewitness information from the frontlines; in the same issue the day after the attack, his paper also printed a story by a United Press reporter, headlining it, "Correspondent Braves Shower of Machine Gun Bullets to See Shanghai Battle."[164] Abend also told of his close calls, including stepping onto a sidewalk just as "five or six shots from the second-story window of the building opposite were fired."[165] The *Chicago Daily News* headlined its correspondent's first story, "Daily News Man Witnesses Slaughter in Chinese City; Tells of Death from Air."[166]

Total war on civilian populations – and journalists – was to become a grim constant of twentieth-century conflicts, but in Shanghai correspondents still considered the "lethal aerial bombardment of a densely populated and unfortified metropolitan area" an "unexampled spectacle."[167] Given the horrors witnessed, it is not surprising that the dominant discourse in this coverage was pitiful, innocent "luckless" Chinese – in Keen's words[168] – ravaged by unfathomably aggressive Japanese. Incensed correspondents highlighted that they had personally seen "scores of cases of wounded non-combatant Chinese."[169] Even though journalists clearly sided with China, however, they still constructed it as a poor, backward, folkloristic country barely capable of understanding the conflict – and, by implication, to fully defend itself.

162 Victor Keen, "Japanese Invade Shanghai, Drop Bombs; Chinese Defend Barricade, Many Slain; U.S. Warns Tokio [*sic*] to Respect Its Rights," *New York Herald Tribune*, January 29, 1932, 1.

163 Elizabeth Keen, "Chinese Carries Wounded Wife and Their Baby 3 Days to Safety," *New York Herald Tribune*, February 3, 1932, 2.

164 H.R. Ekins, "Dogged Chinese Fought All Way, Says Witness," *New York Herald Tribune*, January 29, 1932, 2.

165 Hallett Abend, "Japanese Checked in Taking Shanghai," *New York Times*, January 29, 1932, 2.

166 Reginald Sweetland, "Daily News Man Witnesses Slaughter in Chinese City; Tells of Death from Air," *Chicago Daily News*, January 29, 1932, 1.

167 Hallett Abend, "Japanese Checked in Taking Shanghai," *New York Times*, January 29, 1932, 1.

168 Victor Keen, "Shanghai Faces New Menace in Jobless Chinese," *New York Herald Tribune*, February 2, 1932, 2.

169 Victor Keen, "U.S. Sends 1,600 Troops and 9 More Ships to Shanghai; British Add to Forces There; Settlement on War Basis; Harbin's Fall Near," *New York Herald Tribune*, February 1, 1932, 2.

Abend thus described a city scene:

> Countless incidents were witnessed which in times of peace would have had a comic element but today were imbued with deep tragedy. A white-haired grandmother, her feet bound, was hobbling along with a raw cabbage under one arm and a blue bowl of rice soup in the other hand, spilling at every step. Near by a toddling boy infant was panting after his family, clutching in one hand a fresh-water crab. These pitiful salvages probably were the only worldly possessions of these penniless folk. Further along three coolies were attempting to carry to safety a small office safe slung on ropes from bamboo shoulder poles.[170]

In a later article about the Japanese occupation, Abend described "Chinese women with their bound feet and with babies in their arms... attempting to run to safety as their faces streamed in tears."[171] AP reports were similarly both heartbreaking and deeply patronizing of the Chinese, "a blood-smeared, terror-stricken, cringing crowd":

> The hours brought terror to the civilian population as the flames, started by Japanese bombs, licked at the ancient, ramshackle structures and filled the tortuous streets and alleys with smoke and firebrands.... The terrified people were faced with a dilemma of terror. They had the choice of staying in their huts and being burned to death or fleeing into the open to be shot or torn to pieces by bursting bombs.... The flames licked their way through the narrow, warren-like streets of the mud-hut and cobblestone city as a prairie fire might attack the *nests of a colony of field mice*.... There were boxes and bundles and household goods, chickens and dogs and cats piled high in the conveyances. One-way traffic regulations in the narrow streets were powerless to stem the avalanche of misery. Family groups of three or four clung together, clutching their small bundles of possessions. Scores of them were wound up in rough, dirty bandages which covered wounds inflicted by rifle and machine-gun bullets and by bursting bombs.[172]

The AP's Morris J. Harris scathingly wrote of the "heartrending" plight of Shanghai's refugees as they met Japanese soldiers who "swept the streets with machine-gun fire. Their work was finished by Japanese in civilian clothes swinging clubs and baseball bats. These invaders declared they were searching for snipers, but how they separated snipers from the civilian population was not apparent."[173]

[170] Hallett Abend, "City Also under Shell Fire," *New York Times*, February 3, 1932, 12.

[171] Hallett Abend, "Wild Turmoil in City," *New York Times*, January 31, 1932, 1.

[172] "People of Shanghai Throng Roofs to Watch Fighting in Chapei, Swept by Bombs and Fire," *New York Times*, January 30, 1932, 2; Morris J. Harris, "Chinese Force Japanese to Partial Withdrawal in Fighting at Shanghai," *Baltimore Sun*, January 30, 1932, 1; untitled article, *New York Times*, January 31, 1932, 24. Emphasis added. The latter article was also printed, with a few changes, as "Chapei Chinese Flee in Terror to Settlement," *New York Herald Tribune*, January 31, 1932, 7. For similarly heartfelt AP descriptions, see also "Shells Fall in Settlement, Six Killed in Clash," *New York Herald Tribune*, January 31, 1932, 2.

[173] Morris J. Harris, "Japanese in Neutral Area," *Baltimore Sun*, January 31, 1932, 2.

In addition to their vivid eyewitness accounts, some correspondents also provided analysis of the larger repercussions. One article in the *New York Herald Tribune* described Shanghai's "great industrial and commercial importance" and dug into the roots of Chinese resentment against foreign employers who tended to become invaders.[174] Abend made reference to China's demographic power, or what he labeled "incalculable reservoirs of humanity," and, most presciently, he called the potential effect of the Japanese assault on the large parts of China controlled by communist forces "a problem staggering to the imagination."[175] Correspondents also sounded the alarm for a rather complacent American public on the threat of aggressive Japan. The lead quotation in a *New York Times* story about an interview with China's foreign minister, conducted in Shanghai's French Concession during the Japanese aerial bombardment, exemplifies that: "Japan's next war will be for the mastery of the Pacific, which means war against America."[176]

With in-depth reporting, thoughtful analysis and, predominantly, the pathos of their observations, U.S. correspondents in Shanghai brought home the horrors of modern warfare to American readers. Even though they rarely referenced the United States, their discourses of a helpless backward population suffering atrociously at the hand of aggressive savages implied a world spinning out of control as well as clear sides to take when it would be inevitable for America to intervene. The correspondents covering the Spanish Civil War continued along the same lines, with the increased urgency of the late 1930s and without the condescension that had marred some discourses about the Chinese.

The Spanish Civil War: The Correspondents' Fight

> This dispatch was interrupted for half an hour by a shell that crashed just above the room in the Telephone building in which we newspaper men are working. The shell sent a shower of stone and glass to the street. The shelling had begun half an hour previously, but General Franco's gunners were landing their shells on adjoining buildings. Several times since then our building has been hit and at the precise second this sentence was written another shell crashed. Still another shell has just hit the building, and the writer is leaving this exposed room for the relative safety of the center of the building.... It has been a day of excitement for the newspaper men and, since what happens to us is typical of what thousands of residents of the city go through every day, it is worth relating.[177]

Correspondents like the *New York Times*' Herbert L. Matthews did not simply vividly describe fighting in the Spanish Civil War – they were in that fight,

174 "Shanghai Fame As East's Paris Hides Industry," *New York Herald Tribune*, January 29, 1932, 3.

175 Hallett Abend, "Shanghai Expects Battle," *New York Times*, February 2, 1932, 16; Hallett Abend, "City Also under Shell Fire," *New York Times*, February 3, 1932, 12.

176 "Chen Says Japan Seeks War with US," *New York Times*, January 30, 1932, 3. See also Hohenberg, 160.

177 Herbert L. Matthews, "Madrid Is Rocked in Severe Shelling," *New York Times*, January 7, 1937, 12.

recording every near miss as they labored away at their stories, and reporters' detachment disappeared with every Franco shell hitting the besieged Spanish capital. The personal, visual, trim style most famously exemplified by Hemingway, who also wrote about this war, often alongside Matthews,[178] was common in the correspondence of all journalists studied. Again perhaps trying to compete with radio reporters, they took a ground view of conflict, the horrors it visited on civilians, and the shattering incongruity of modern warfare blending into daily life.

At the beginning of the conflict, the American public seemed not to care about it or the larger implications detailed by both journalists and diplomats like the U.S. ambassador in Madrid, who called the war "a foreign war of the Fascist Powers against the Government of Spain." In fact, as bombs rained on the Spanish capital in January 1937, a Gallup poll reported that two-thirds of U.S. respondents had no opinion on the events in Spain.[179] In February 1937, 95 percent of Americans felt that the United States should stay out of any future conflict, according to another poll.[180] The deluge of correspondence from Spain, however, with its adamant identification between observers and combatants, helped change the public's mind, and many Americans started support campaigns for the Republican cause, even volunteering to fight for it.[181]

Since the turn of the twentieth century, Spain had been increasingly plagued by violent social unrest, fomented by the unlivable conditions of landless peasantry and met with armed intervention by the conservatives. With the country under national emergency, political factions on the right – dominated by Fascists and Catholics – and left – dominated by anarchists and communists – hardened their positions into a common will to revolutionize the infant Spanish Republic. Sporadic clashes became outright war in the summer of 1936 when the military-supported Insurgents (also called Nationalists) started coordinated uprisings across Spain and their leader, General Francisco Franco, obtained aid from Germany and Italy, while the Soviet Union armed the Republican (also called Loyalist) side. Both sides committed violent purges and ferocious hate-driven acts of terrorism that shocked the world.

Some of the fiercest battles took place in the capital, Madrid, where the Republicans put up the most desperate resistance during a siege begun in the fall of 1936. Insurgent air strikes on the city of more than a million people, combined with street fighting, laid ruin to the city until March 1937, when the Nationalists withdrew. War, however, continued across the country – including, most notoriously, at Guernica. The ultimate victory went to

178 Herbert L. Matthews, *The Education of a Correspondent* (New York: Harcourt, Brace and Company, 1946), 7, 95.

179 Quote and poll are cited in Kennedy, 398; for problems with the early polls in the interwar era, see Berinsky, 34–35.

180 Quoted in Herring, 504.

181 Dominic Tierney, *FDR and the Spanish Civil War: Neutrality and Commitment in the Struggle That Divided America* (Durham, NC: Duke University Press, 2007), 58–64.

Franco in 1939, establishing a Fascist regime that dominated Spain for nearly forty years, longer than those of Germany or Italy that had been its ideological godparents.[182] Some historians have blamed the nonintervention policy of France and Great Britain for the Republican defeat, and American appeasement has also been condemned.[183] Others, however, have noted that London and Washington had mistrusted the Spanish government before the war, fearing it would not be able to hold back leftist tendencies – again using the Russian Revolution as analogy – and those antipathies, combined with fears of provoking a wider war, cemented the policy of nonintervention.[184] By the time Roosevelt started seeing a Franco victory as not in America's best interest, in conjunction with the Munich crisis and the spread of Fascism, the Spanish Republic was already on its deathbed.[185]

Foreign correspondents covered the civil war with great passion, such that some scholars have called them propagandists, and at great personal risk, witnessing daily terror both in besieged Madrid – where Matthews stayed at the Hotel Florida with the likes of Hemingway, John Dos Passos, and Martha Gellhorn – and Nationalist-controlled areas.[186] Newspapers printed daily updates on the Spanish war during the siege of Madrid, each from their own correspondent there, and often used the AP for perspectives from Franco's lines (which newspapers chose to dateline Fascist or Insurgent or Rebel Forces), defeating censorship on both sides. One article by James M. Minifie of the *New York Herald Tribune* contained this parenthetical statement: "(One line was censored here.)"[187] There were occasional light, humorous stories: A plane drop of a "big sack containing sausages" had landed in enemy lines, "critically injuring a militiaman but giving his comrades an excellent supper"; some Loyalist leaders, sitting down for an AP interview in the dining room of a lavish estate, "carefully wip[ed] their feet before stepping on Persian rugs."[188]

Outrage and tragedy, however, dominated the breathless accounts of the violence and terror that writers experienced firsthand, as shells exploded outside their windows, briefly interrupted dinner, or "shook the reporter's bed

[182] For the domestic consequences of Franco's victory, see Stanley G. Payne, *Fascism in Spain, 1923–1977* (Madison: University of Wisconsin Press, 1999).

[183] Helen Graham, *The Spanish Republic at War: 1936–1939* (Cambridge: Cambridge University Press, 2002).

[184] Douglas Little, *Malevolent Neutrality: The United States, Great Britain, and the Origins of the Spanish Civil War* (Ithaca, NY: Cornell University Press, 1985).

[185] Tierney, 160.

[186] Hohenberg, 181; Heald, 183. For a critical take, see Moorcraft and Taylor, 52–55, and Knightley, 207–235. On journalists' coverage of the Nationalist areas, see Herbert Rutledge Southworth, *Guernica! Guernica! A Study of Journalism, Diplomacy, Propaganda, and History* (Berkeley: University of California Press, 1977).

[187] James M. Minifie, "Loyalists Still Holding Line," *New York Herald Tribune*, January 11, 1937, 1.

[188] "Leftists Enjoy Sausages Dropped by Rebel Fliers," *New York Times*, January 15, 1937, 13; "Set for Attack, Says Foreign Chief of Leftists," *New York Herald Tribune*, January 4, 1937, 6.

and rattled the windows."[189] "There is something particularly terrifying about night air raids, for one feels especially helpless in the dark and his imagination works overtime," Matthews confessed in a story.[190] Experience seemed to be translated into knowledge, as reporters repeatedly wrote that their stories were validated by "aural evidence" provided by the explosions and "sound of firing" they could hear.[191] In some cases, correspondents traveled to the frontlines – sometimes so close they could go by subway – to verify or disprove claims made by propagandists on either side of the conflict.[192] Such direct experience of war was what correspondents believed they had to undertake in order to fulfill their professional call. Matthews later confessed that Madrid had taught him, "once and for all, the necessity for being on the spot, to know what was really happening."[193] Minifie, explaining why U.S. correspondents were among the Americans refusing to heed the State Department's call to evacuate Madrid, wrote, "They are here, as in the case of eight newspaper men, because they have their jobs to do."[194]

Matthews did defend his task as objective observation, writing from Madrid that "[the war's] moral and ethical aspects are for each reader or observer to make up his own mind about. A newspaper man describing affairs here has nothing to do with morals or ethics. He is here to tell what he sees and not what he thinks or feels. And what has happened here is open for every one to see."[195] But the undeniable sympathy for the besieged people of Madrid shaped a discourse dominated by the contrast between daily life and modern warfare, imbuing everyday acts with heroic, desperate resistance that left little to be impartial about.[196]

The sound of cannons had become to Madrilenians and correspondents alike as common as the sound of traffic in a busy city, Matthews wrote.[197] War was so close that for "15 centimos (slightly less than 5 cents) one can go by

189 Richard Mowrer, "Air Raids Mark Rebel Offensive against Madrid," *Chicago Daily News*, January 9, 1937, 2; James M. Minifie, "Rebels Bomb British Embassy in Madrid," *New York Herald Tribune*, January 9, 1937, 1.

190 Herbert L. Matthews, "Defenders Fight with Fury," *New York Times*, January 10, 1937, 1.

191 James M. Minifie, "Loyalists Repel Landing Force Headed for Attack on Malaga," *New York Herald Tribune*, January 17, 1937, 1.

192 "Madrid Shelled by Fascists on Children's Day," *New York Herald Tribune*, January 7, 1937, 10; "Madrid's Civilian Fight Begins," *New York Herald Tribune*, January 12, 1937, 8; George Axelsson, "Insurgents Repel 18 Madrid Tanks," *New York Times*, January 14, 1937, 8.

193 Matthews, 1946, 94.

194 James M. Minifie, "No Americans Answer Call to Leave Madrid," *New York Herald Tribune*, January 14, 1937, 6.

195 Herbert L. Matthews, "Move to the Left Speeds Up in Spain," *New York Times*, January 3, 1937, E5.

196 For references to "desperate opposition" and "historic resistance," see, among many, Richard Mowrer, "Madrid Battle Rages Unabated on Fourth Day," *Chicago Daily News*, January 7, 1937, 1; James M. Minifie, "Rebels Hurling Every Resource against Madrid," *New York Herald Tribune*, January 8, 1937, 7.

197 Herbert L. Matthews, "Madrid Is Warned Crisis Is Near as Insurgents Broaden Attacks," *New York Times*, January 19, 1937, 3.

streetcar from the center of town to within a few hundred yards of the line," Richard Mowrer of the *Chicago Daily News* explained.[198] On a tour of town, Mowrer found two men

> blocking up the cellar windows of their house with blocks and stones, a miserable attempt to make the basement a place of comparative safety. These people in the devastated zone do not want to go away, and if they did where would they go? they ask. It would take a lot to turn them away from their homes and in such cases they still live in houses whose upper stories have been hit by shells.[199]

The AP described how "crowds of women shoppers, with their children, dashed for shelter in doorways and subways as the planes came into view to escape the spray of shrapnel," but one bomb hit a subway entrance, where the "blood of the wounded seeped through the wreckage" – a detail so graphic the *Baltimore Sun* deleted it from its reprint of the story. "The total of the deaths of those buried beneath twisted wreckage and crumbled buildings may never be known," the writer concluded.[200]

The holiday season gave writers some of the most poignant portraits of such incongruity:

> For Madrid the year opened with the sound of shells dropping around the Puerta del Sol, the central square, at midnight. Instead of the traditional gathering of thousands of residents of Madrid to wait for the clocks to strike twelve there were only a few militiamen and journalists, who had expected General Franco to send his New Year's greetings that way.[201]

The bombardment on January 6, the feast of Epiphany celebrated by children across Spain, particularly incensed correspondents who declared it could "hardly be explained on military grounds."[202] Readers were faced with haunting images of children with their holiday toys taking refuge in cellars and subways, doll and toy soldier peddlers abandoning their "colorful wayside stalls" as shells started landing.[203] It was hard not to sense Matthews' rage as he concluded his Epiphany story this way: "For Spain's children today was equivalent to Christmas Day, for they received their toys from Three Kings

198 Richard Mowrer, "Fog Halts Firing in Madrid; Defenders Start Digging In," *Chicago Daily News*, January 15, 1937, 1.

199 Richard Mowrer, "Madrid Battle Resumed After Night of Quiet," *Chicago Daily News*, January 8, 1937, 2.

200 "Madrid Suffers Heaviest Bombardment of War," *Baltimore Sun*, January 10, 1937, 14; "200–300 Wounded," *New York Herald Tribune*, January 5, 1937, 8; "Big Powers Alarmed by 'Undeclared War'; 100 Die in Madrid Raid," *Baltimore Sun*, January 5, 1937, 1.

201 Herbert L. Matthews, "Madrid Is Shelled as New Year Opens," *New York Times*, January 2, 1937, 2. A similar story on New Year's Eve is by James M. Minifie, "Madrid Greets 'Year of Victory' under Shelling," *New York Herald Tribune*, January 1, 1937, 2.

202 "Madrid Shelled by Fascists on Children's Day," *New York Herald Tribune*, January 7, 1937, 1, 10.

203 "Fascist Guns Give Madrid Day of Terror," *Baltimore Sun*, January 7, 1937, 6.

after having left their shoes on mantels and window sills. I was reading the following poster when the bombers came over: 'War should not spoil childish joy. Joys are as necessary to children as bread. Playing children forget the horrors of war.'"[204]

The *New York Times* correspondent did also provide political analysis, detailing for example a "swing toward radicalism" among the Republicans and arguing, in a long piece for the *Times* magazine on Loyalist leaders, that "no greater mistake could be made today than to consider this struggle merely as a localized conflict."[205] On the six-month anniversary of the start of the war, Matthews speculated that ultimate victory would depend on "international developments."[206] Other correspondents likewise focused on the larger implications of the conflict. Mowrer described Madrid as "the battle ground of Europe's two conflicting political ideologies, fascism and antifascism," and relayed that Madrilenians believed that Franco could not win without outside help – perhaps a jibe at American nonintervention.[207] Minifie also agreed that Spain was the first "application of the Nazi method," which would only spread if left unchecked.[208] H.N. Brailsford, writing for the *Baltimore Sun* from London, called the war an "indirect duel between the Democratic and the Fascist Powers," and feared that smaller European states would follow Franco in availing themselves of Hitler's protection.[209]

Whereas astute political analysis was not lacking, the largest contribution correspondents in war-torn Madrid made to the American public was arguably their visceral accounts of what total ideological war meant to civilians and, incidentally, to journalists, who were all desperately seeking to go about their daily tasks. Here is Matthews covering yet another air raid on a Madrid street and trying to interview survivors:

> There were many other signs of damage in that stricken district, above all the weeping faces of terrified and grief-stricken women standing on corners or hurrying forlornly through the streets. It was impossible to get a coherent story from those frantic women or from men too furious and bitter to know what they were saying. Details were plentiful to the eye, however.... This was perhaps the most terrible single act as yet committed against the population – for the machine-gunner turned his deadly spray of

[204] Herbert L. Matthews, "Madrid Is Rocked in Severe Shelling," *New York Times*, January 7, 1937, 12.

[205] Herbert L. Matthews, "Move to the Left Speeds Up in Spain," *New York Times*, January 3, 1937, E5; "Free Lances of Madrid," *New York Times*, January 3, 1937, SM4.

[206] Herbert L. Matthews, "Half Year of War Ends in a Stand-Off in Spain," *New York Times*, January 17, 1937, 63.

[207] Richard Mowrer, "Drive against Madrid Stops after a Week of Fighting," *Chicago Daily News*, January 11, 1937, 2.

[208] James M. Minifie, "Germans Lead Rebels in New Madrid Thrust," *New York Herald Tribune*, January 6, 1937, 10.

[209] H.N. Brailsford, "Says 11,000 Foreign Recruits Aid Madrid," *Baltimore Sun*, January 16, 1937, 9.

bullets straight into a long line of women who had stood patiently for hours, as Madrid women have to these days, waiting their turn to enter a butcher shop. Several of them were wounded and some perhaps are now dead. Yet such are the recuperative powers of this indomitable people and such, too, the imperative need to buy food that when your correspondent arrived the line had already reformed at the butcher shop.[210]

Readers of such stories, made even more powerful by the lack of condescension that had marred similar accounts from Shanghai, were given a heartfelt picture of what a new European conflict would be like – and whose side correspondents were on, their professional neutrality shattered by total war. By their identification with suffering civilians, foreign correspondents made Spain's civil war America's ideological testing ground, providing the necessary discursive prelude to Washington's irrevocable assumption of global leadership. It was a monstrous world, and it all but begged for U.S. full-fledged intervention to the aid of heroic peoples in the grip of evil.

Conclusions

If there is one constant among the tumultuous, foundational years between 1901 and 1945, it is that both the United States and the American press – ensconced in democratic ideals of public interest, variedly defined – came to recognize and even cherish their unprecedented power on the global stage. It was a power uniquely defined in terms of ideology and pragmatism – the ideals of democracy and business would end up inextricably, if uncomfortably, linked both in media and in government affairs. This chapter analyzes how the AP and four leading American newspapers covered five consequential international events – the 1910s revolution in Mexico, the 1917 revolution in Russia, the Fascist takeover in Italy in 1925, the Japanese attack on Shanghai in 1932, and the siege of Madrid in 1937. From Mexico to Spain, correspondence changed greatly in response to the professionalization of journalism, the growth of foreign services, and the technological changes ushered in by instantaneous wireless communication and the birth of radio broadcasting. Objectivity, the golden standard of American journalism, was no sooner established than it came under fire, and for correspondents in Shanghai and Madrid it seemed to mean personal observation, not moral neutrality.

The sheer amount of foreign correspondence increased by leaps and bounds in this period, sustained by the growth of the Associated Press and the establishment of foreign bureaus by various media outlets, and became capable of providing continuous, solid reporting that – as the correspondents themselves liked to highlight – was far more useful than that by occasional writers. Starting with the Russian Revolution, correspondents clearly espoused their role as

210 Herbert L. Matthews, "100 Killed, 200 Hurt in Madrid Air Raid," *New York Times*, January 5, 1937, 5.

mediators of foreign realities, giving readers numerous clues to their involvement in foreign affairs that culminated in the vivid personal storytelling of the Spanish Civil War.

This period is also remarkable for the amount and variety of American intervention in foreign crises, despite professions of neutrality and detachment. It seemed to have become a truism in Washington that America could and should take a hand in dangerous situations across the world, first, traditionally and unremarkably, to protect its interests – as in Mexico – and gradually, after World War I, to steer world events toward the presumed triumph of democracy and capitalism. So do the discourses of the world in the American press construct the kind of world where Washington should intervene? The constructions found in this chapter are highly suggestive.

In the early stages of the Mexican Revolution, Mexico was a threat to American interests, proof of how incapable of self-government "Spanish America" was. Beyond that suspicion, which had been well established in the nineteenth century, U.S. journalists had little apparent interest in social revolution. There was no construction of a U.S. role, let alone a media role, in the turmoil other than to acknowledge that here, once again, went inferior people creating trouble for U.S. businessmen.

The 1917 Russian Revolution changed all that, moving discussion to the sphere of ideology. Correspondents – and, one infers, Americans at large – seemed incapable of understanding that discontent toward monarchical tyranny would produce a Vladimir Lenin and not a George Washington. Communism was so incomprehensible that the only expectation was that a Soviet regime would not last, just like socialism would not survive the Red Scare in the United States. The construction of Soviet Russia as an extreme manifestation of radicalism, of devastating class unrest of the kind that never happened in the United States despite war and the Great Depression, clearly reinforced the sense of uniqueness that Americans had long held. More portentously for foreign policy, it created a paradigm with which to assess the rest of the world, from Italy to China.

The predominance of the "Soviet threat" discourse from such an early date suggests the power of narratives and ideas to influence and delimit policy options, particularly in Europe. Mussolini's dictatorship in Italy, for example, was portrayed as a good way to stem the "Reds," particularly keeping in mind that fickle, picturesque Italians needed an iron hand to get the country moving. Italy, with its peculiar dual image in U.S. minds discussed earlier, was an exception to the affinity that Americans still clearly felt for Europe (now excluding the Soviet realm) as compared to the rest of the world. In all three of these cases, the press discourse revealed little explicit direction for U.S. policy or recognition of the power of journalism, with the exception of the usual satisfaction in correspondents' censorship-defeating efforts.

The impassioned outrage that burned through correspondence from war-ravaged Shanghai and Madrid represents a discursive coming-of-age. Explicit policy commentary was by now delegated to the editorial pages, but the dramatic news stories represented clarion calls for the United States to intervene to prevent such atrocious civilian suffering. The differences in the constructions in China and Spain are revealing of the condescension with which U.S. correspondents continued to approach Asian cultures. Nevertheless, both cases, and most evidently the construction of the Spanish Civil War as the correspondents' – and, by default, democratic America's – own fight, are suggestive of how far the conceptualization of U.S. global power had spread.

If being American had meant staying aloof and unconcerned from an inferior world's troubles, it now signified unrelenting moral and ideological involvement. Roosevelt's change in his position vis-à-vis Republican Spain can be seen as a microcosm of the change that Washington undertook in its approach to foreign affairs in the first half of the twentieth century – shedding the last vestiges of uneasiness with entangling alliances and assuming the position of leader of the free world. The moral outrage correspondents reflected at dictatorial regimes in war-ravaged countries with heroic but ultimately helpless populations made such a change palatable, even necessary. Furthermore, if other peoples had been constructed as making a mess of democratic revolution – Mexicans still were in 1911 – then the little-understood Russian uprising opened a worse possibility, that they might choose the Soviet instead of the American way to modernity. Thus, in the correspondence constructions as in foreign policy, ideology and realist interests fused in trying to keep the world "safe for democracy." Coverage of the Spanish Civil War suggests that Fascism might have temporarily muted the "first cold war," but mistrust for the Soviets was just lying dormant, to reemerge with a vengeance in the post-1945 era discussed in the next chapter.

Finally, how did the press function in this momentous epoch? Already journalists had come to believe themselves essential to the public's understanding of the world, and they undertook to explain foreign affairs with unprecedented passion. Beginning with Russia, they focused on the country at hand, not just, or even primarily, on the United States. They became part of the story even as they tried to get all sides of it. Despite scholarly arguments to the contrary, they covered the world in a depth that was unmatched before and that would not be easily replicated in the following decades, when governments everywhere would become much more adept at managing the news. Even as they defended their role as observers, correspondents clearly positioned themselves as the eyes and ears of America. Their political analysis could be spot-on, as when forecasting Japan's imperial aims in China, or badly off-mark, as when expecting the Russian Revolution to implode, but they increasingly tried to move beyond the recording of events and to provide readers a feel for the present and informed speculation on the future. The United States had become a superpower, and the press was ready and eager to scout the world with parallel influence.

4

The Media Are American in the American Century

The Apex of American Political and Communication Power

> PESHAWAR, Pakistan–Afghan resistance leader Gulbeddin Hekmatyar makes U.S. officials wonder whether the $2 billion of covert aid they funneled to the insurgents over the past eight years may end up merely substituting one sort of trouble for another.... Even his appearance is disturbing: His dark eyes are piercing darts, his turban is charcoal black, and he fingers white prayer beads in a manner so deliberate as to be disquieting.... [Even if he creates a fundamentalist regime,] Afghanistan's history of weak central governments and its moderate, Sunni tradition ensure that the country will never be a second Iran. Any U.S. effort to stop Islam in Afghanistan would be futile, anyway.[1]

The *Wall Street Journal* diplomatic correspondent's article just quoted, on the Soviet withdrawal from Afghanistan in 1988, seems both tragically incorrect and eerily prescient in 2012, more than ten years into a U.S.-led war in that country against the fundamentalist regime of the Taliban and its supporters. It symbolizes the best and the worst of American foreign correspondence in the Cold War era. By constructing the world as the floor mat in a Twister game between the United States and the Soviet Union, American correspondents often failed to portray essential local realities – in this case, misjudging the rise of Islamic fundamentalism in Afghanistan. Heavily weighing on the plus side, however, is journalists' engagement with the world, providing extensive reporting from virtually everywhere, and their increasing willingness to take on Washington and serve as a watchdog. The United States came out of the Second World War as a superpower, and in less than fifty years it struggled through the Cold War to find itself the global hyperpower. When the Soviet Union dissolved in late 1991, Washington stood on top of the world, and its

[1] Frederick Kempe, "Afghanistan: Not a Second Iran," *Wall Street Journal*, May 16, 1988, 1.

media with it, although even then not everybody was convinced that a new era of Pax Americana was dawning.

This chapter carries through the Cold War era the essential concerns of this book – how the U.S. press constructed the world, whether those discourses belong to the same paradigms that shaped foreign policy, and what role the U.S. media assumed in international affairs from the 1950s to the early 1990s. The focus is on how the Associated Press and four newspapers in New York, Washington and Los Angeles covered five events with lasting consequences: Castro's revolution in 1959; the Six Days' War between Israel and a coalition of Arab countries in 1967; the reopening of full diplomatic relations with China in 1979; the Soviet withdrawal from Afghanistan in 1988; and the collapse of the USSR in 1991.

Those events were chosen not only to represent different areas of U.S. interest but also to avoid "hot wars" that the United States fought, principally Vietnam, which dominates studies of the media and foreign policy in these years. As the next two sections detail, the Vietnam era, together with the turbulent domestic social disputes of the 1960s and 1970s, established in practice and in law a watchdog role for the press and transformed its relationship to the government. But just as the press was becoming more aggressive, new technologies – television and eventually cable – were eroding its grip on the American public, and the acceleration of industry consolidation was putting stronger pressures on its ability to provide independent hard news content. Much like the country itself, the U.S. press found its overwhelming global presence standing on a pedestal that would turn out to be much more fragile than most would have anticipated at the end of the Cold War.

The Bulldog: U.S. Journalism Tackles the Cold War

The triumph of the immediate postwar period, when New York newspapers, among others, saw record circulations in the millions, was short-lived.[2] The Cold War began ominously for the American press with the McCarthy wave of manipulation and suppression rivaling that of the Red Scare of the 1920s and with military censorship in the Korean War. Even the 1950s, under their veneer of prosperity and accord celebrated in images of suburban families with their cars and TVs, were more complex than the increasingly powerful PR and advertising messages made apparent. The press took it on itself to delve into such contradictions and explain them to the American public, even if it meant abandoning strict objectivity, to try and carve a role for itself that made it different from booming television.

In the 1960s, assassinations, protests, violence and civil rights campaigns all raised disturbing questions about the status quo, and the press gave them

[2] Michael Emery, Edwin Emery and Nancy Roberts, *The Press and America: An Interpretive History of the Mass Media* 9th ed. (Boston: Allyn and Bacon, 2000), 352; David R. Davies, *The Postwar Decline of American Newspapers, 1945–1965* (Westport, CT: Praeger, 2006), 2.

unprecedented coverage. Newsrooms witnessed their own desegregation along race and gender lines in these years, broadening not only the content but also the production and the audience for journalism.[3] Investigative journalism, which had been relatively dormant since the 1910s, sprung up with renewed, perhaps unprecedented force.[4] Two watershed events represent the critical power that the American press reached by the late 1960s and 1970s – Vietnam and Watergate. In Saigon, a relatively uncensored press corps staunchly fought with the military and with its home desks to get news out of a war that was not going as Washington wanted, exposing a credibility gap that shocked many Americans. The open conflict between the government and the press came to a head in the 1971 Pentagon Papers case, when the administration tried to restrain publication of leaked Vietnam documents in the *New York Times*. The U.S. Supreme Court ultimately ruled against the administration, and Justice Hugo Black, in a ringing endorsement of the aggressive press of the time, wrote that "paramount among the responsibilities of a free press is the duty to prevent any part of the Government from deceiving the people.... In revealing the workings of government that led to the Vietnam war, the newspapers nobly did precisely that which the Founders hoped and trusted they would do."[5]

Other legal developments were also extending new, stronger protections to a confrontational press hot on the trail of deceptions and cover-ups. The 1964 Supreme Court decision in *New York Times v. Sullivan* significantly weakened public officials' libel claims against journalists, encouraging the latter to take on even entrenched figures like segregationists in the South. The 1966 Freedom of Information Act gave the press access to troves of government documents. The Nixon presidency saw the combustion of two explosive tendencies – an investigative press ever more mistrustful of government and an executive that abhorred it and wanted total control. Richard Nixon, the first president who hired staff to craft his public image, became the first president to resign after the Watergate scandal had been brought to light by the persistent digging of two *Washington Post* reporters.[6] Journalists everywhere, aspiring to be the next Woodward and Bernstein, started going after public officials' wrongdoing with all resources available, from anonymous whistleblowers to sophisticated database mining made possible by the new invention of personal computing.

It is the greatest paradox of this era that just as the press basked in the recognition of its role as paladin of the public interest, its aggressiveness created a backlash among the public that would ultimately cripple much investigative journalism. Blaming the messenger, many Americans faulted the press for its

[3] James Brian McPherson, *Journalism at the End of the American Century*, 1965–Present (Westport, CT: Praeger, 2006), 6–16.

[4] Jon Marshall, *Watergate's Legacy and the Press: The Investigative Impulse* (Evanston, IL: Northwestern University Press, 2011), 42.

[5] Quoted in Margaret A. Blanchard, *Revolutionary Sparks: Freedom of Expression in Modern America* (New York: Oxford University Press, 1992), 410.

[6] Marshall, 54.

focus on bad news, on violence, on the ugly side of domestic and foreign problems, and preferred television as their news source.[7] In reaction, outlets of journalism review and criticism were established (like the *Columbia Journalism Review*, founded in 1961) and professional standards reinforced, like the Society of Professional Journalists' 1973 Code of Ethics that mandates being truthful, independent and accountable. The influence of journalism schools and the booming academic field of communication and media studies also exerted itself more on the newsroom. Government and the corporate world, however, were increasingly sophisticated in their attempts to tell their stories through public relations campaigns. President John F. Kennedy allowed live broadcasting of presidential press conferences, and President Ronald Reagan started the first White House News Service, serving smaller newspapers and radio stations, both efforts to bypass the press that would exponentially accelerate in the Internet age.[8]

Browbeaten by the elites and the public, and frequently rendered obsolete in breaking news by television, the press made two choices. Some newspapers turned to more features and interpretive analysis and even, in the case of a few journalists for whom the mainstream press was not going far enough, to a literary journalism or "new journalism" movement that challenged writers to get inside the head of protagonists and not stay bound to the conventions of he-says-she-says reporting. The other choice, to the satisfaction of most media managers, was to answer the credibility crisis by staying away from controversial news, focusing on entertainment and "soft" stories, and doing so in a blitz of nonstop coverage. CNN started the first twenty-four-hour news cable service in 1980, and *USA Today* – much maligned as the McDonald's of the press but quietly imitated – took the same approach to print in 1982, using color, easy-to-read graphics and simpler, shorter stories. The Reagan years pushed along the attempt to make Americans "feel better about themselves – and worse about the press," in the words of a media historian.[9]

The pressures of increasing concentration of ownership in the hands of stockholder-beholden media corporations made turning a profit the unspoken mantra of many news organizations, with a drastic increase in homogenization and trivialization of content. In some cases, marketing reasons led even major newspapers like the *Los Angeles Times* to abandon subscribers from the wrong (to advertisers) demographics, challenging whether any paper would really bring news to all.[10] In another sad paradox for the press, the fact that vast corporations owned media pushed Americans to begin to see journalism as part of the establishment they had learned to trust at their peril. Notorious

[7] Emery, Emery and Roberts, 417, 479; Marshall, 110.
[8] Davies, 102; Marshall, 141.
[9] McPherson, 81.
[10] Thomas C. Leonard, *News for All: America's Coming-of-Age with the Press* (New York: Oxford University Press, 1995), 174.

journalism scandals like the fabrication of the Pulitzer Prize–winning *Washington Post* story about a child addicted to heroin fomented the lack of trust. The press's share of the public's attention plummeted in the Cold War era, with one series of polls showing that whereas 85 percent of respondents had read a newspaper the day before in 1946, only 55 percent had in 1985.[11]

A mid-1980s analysis of public knowledge of world affairs found that people were a little better informed about the world if they used print and not television, the predominant news medium, and concluded that media should do a better job at engaging the audience, rather than selling it stories.[12] A study of Americans' knowledge about politics from 1940 to 1994 showed that whereas about half the public had some understanding of key actors and foreign affairs, U.S. citizens lagged behind many other nationals in political awareness.[13] The authors also found for those years a paradox that would most clearly define the Internet age's dilemma of quantity versus quality. The news media provided more information than ever before, albeit largely contextless, but analyzing it required sophisticated sorting skills that not all have equally, so in the end citizens were not more or less informed about the world in 1994 than they had been in 1940.[14]

By the early 1990s, the glory days of the press seemed to be waning under the onslaught of public indifference or worse and the pressures of corporate logic and an image-driven communication environment. To use two popular cinematic versions of true media events, journalism seemed to have gone from *All the President's Men* – the apotheosis of powerful investigative impact – to *The Insider*, the caving in of the public's right to know in the interest of the corporate stockholders' bottom lines. Those changes inevitably would affect one of the best services the press had provided in this era – foreign correspondence.

On All Fronts of the Cold War

In a way, all foreign correspondents in this era were war correspondents – covering all fronts of the global struggle between Soviet-led communism and American-style democracy and capitalism.[15] As scholars of media and war have pointed out, news values play an important role in determining what conflicts get covered, on the basis of feelings of affinity for a culture, distance, scale and

[11] Mitchell Stephens, *A History of News* 3rd ed. (New York: Oxford University Press, 2007), 285.

[12] John Robinson and Mark Levy, *The Main Source: Learning from Television News* (Beverly Hills, CA: Sage, 1986), 232–236.

[13] Michael X. Delli Carpini and Scott Keeter, *What Americans Know about Politics and Why It Matters* (New Haven, CT: Yale University Press, 1996), 85–89.

[14] Delli Carpini and Keeter, 133.

[15] John Maxwell Hamilton, *Journalism's Roving Eye: A History of American Foreign Reporting* (Baton Rouge: Louisiana State University Press, 2009), 352.

the tendency to domesticate news.[16] Therefore, there are vast disparities in the ways countries embroiled in Cold War tensions were covered. A sociological analysis of how U.S. journalists in the 1960s and 1970s chose what to report found that news values were overt in foreign stories, which focused on the threat of communism and therefore the relevance of any particular country to Americans.[17] Such values included ethnocentrism, a sense of missionary democracy and capitalism, and an emphasis on social order and individualism, tempered by competition with other media outlets and values that newsrooms believed would resonate with the public, including novelty and action.

The Cold War shaped understanding of all foreign events from the 1950s through 1991 for both journalists and policymakers, and correspondents had the difficult task of seeing through the simplification inherent in that frame to get at local realities. The souring of press-government relations during the Vietnam War also led journalists to analyze more critically the global role of the United States and its essential core, often independently of home editors' preferences. The difficulty and expense of international communication in the pre-digital era meant that correspondents had a lot more say in what to cover and how, often going weeks without direct contact from top managers in New York and Washington. Incensed with the foreign desk's questioning of his stories from Vietnam, for example, star *New York Times* correspondent David Halberstam cabled that if the queries did not stop, "I will resign repeat resign and I mean it repeat mean it."[18] The debate over whether the media "lost" Vietnam still flares up in some Washington circles, but so do the accusations that foreign correspondents and the media in general did not really sway public opinion and policy in consequential ways.[19]

One tangible consequence of Vietnam was estrangement between the military and the press, which was perceived as not having become part of the team as it had in World War II, so that in wars in the 1980s, including U.S. interventions in Grenada and Panama, journalists had extremely restricted access to the frontlines and the combatants.[20] In the Persian Gulf War of 1991, the military restricted journalists to pools under escort by officers who would choose where to take correspondents (except for the handful who had been in Baghdad before

16 Susan L. Carruthers, *The Media at War: Communication and Conflict in the Twentieth Century* (New York: St. Martin's Press, 2000).

17 Herbert J. Gans, *Deciding What's News:* A Study of CBS Evening News, NBC Nightly News, Newsweek *and* Time (New York: Random House, 1979), 31–37.

18 Quoted in Hamilton, 391.

19 Daniel C. Hallin, *The "Uncensored" War: The Media and Vietnam* (New York: Oxford University Press, 1986); Philip Knightley, *The First Casualty: The War Correspondent as Hero and Myth-Maker from the Crimea to Iraq* (Baltimore: Johns Hopkins University Press, 2004), 465.

20 Knightley, 484–485; Michael S. Sweeney, *The Military and the Press: An Uneasy Truce* (Evanston, IL: Northwestern University Press, 2006), 151–179; Paul L. Moorcraft and Philip M. Taylor, *Shooting the Messenger: The Political Impact of War Reporting* (Washington: Potomac Books, 2008), 94–97.

the war), showing the kind of tight news management that, critics argue, led the public to see war as a "deadly video game."[21] One result, according to a study of *New York Times* and other U.S. media coverage of U.S. military interventions from Grenada in 1983 to Haiti in 1994, was that the press mirrored the debates in Washington without adding any independent contribution that might have enlarged the discussion.[22]

Outside of wars that the United States fought, studies have found that the Cold War frame hurt journalists' ability to see other realities on the ground. A study of the press coverage of Iran from the 1950s through the 1970s, for example, found that U.S. correspondents failed to understand Iranian politics and therefore missed the story because it did not fit the democracy versus communism parameter.[23] Many such examples will be detailed in the rest of this chapter. Despite these failings, Mort Rosenblum, an AP foreign correspondent in the 1960s and 1970s, perhaps summed it up best in his 1979 book: "This [foreign correspondence] system is geared as much to amuse and divert as it is to inform, and it responds inadequately when suddenly called upon to explain something so complex and menacing as a dollar collapse – or a war in Asia. Yet it is the American citizen's only alternative to ignorance about the world."[24] His prescription was to make news more relevant to U.S. audiences by explaining it better, focusing more on what life in foreign countries was like, and analyzing larger trends instead of providing a steady diet of "coups and earthquakes," the title of his book.

The media outlets chosen for this chapter were trying to do just that in the Cold War era, and in the eyes of some of their own editors, as discussed in Chapter 6, they experienced the finest hour of foreign correspondence in this period. The *New York Times* and the Associated Press consolidated their dominance on the entire system. *Times* coverage of foreign events became the standard to read, to match, and to study in these years. One study of its articles on foreign policy crises from the 1960s through the 1980s found that its foreign correspondents were remarkably more critical, analytical and alert to repercussions than its Washington staff.[25] The AP's presence was often out of the spotlight but arguably even more pervasive, providing the record of what

[21] See W. Lance Bennett and David L. Paletz, eds. *Taken by Storm: The Media, Public Opinion, and U.S. Foreign Policy in the Gulf War* (Chicago: University of Chicago Press, 1994); Bradley S. Greenberg and Walter Gantz, eds. *Desert Storm and the Mass Media* (Cresskill, NJ: Hampton Press, 1993).

[22] Jonathan Mermin, *Debating War and Peace: Media Coverage of U.S. Intervention in the Post-Vietnam Era* (Princeton, NJ: Princeton University Press, 1999).

[23] William A. Dorman and Mansour Farhang, *The U.S. Press and Iran: Foreign Policy and the Journalism of Deference* (Berkeley: University of California Press, 1987).

[24] Mort Rosenblum, *Coups and Earthquakes: Reporting the World for America* (New York: Harper & Row, 1979), 1.

[25] Nicholas O. Berry, *Foreign Policy and the Press: An Analysis of the* New York Times' *Coverage of U.S. Foreign Policy* (New York: Greenwood Press, 1990), 155–157.

was happening even while trying to contextualize it and explain its meaning for the thousands of member newspapers and broadcasting stations. A mix of American correspondents and local hires, AP staffers were in Budapest in 1956 when Soviet tanks fired on demonstrators, in newly independent Congo in 1960, in Santiago during the 1973 coup against Allende, and at the Berlin Wall when people started tearing it down in 1989.[26] They closed the last foreign news agency bureau in China in 1949 and reopened the first thirty years later. In 1985, an AP chief of bureau, Terry Anderson in Beirut, was kidnapped and held for nearly seven years by militants affiliated with Hezbollah.

Throughout this period, newspapers across America printed AP stories of the world, even when they had their own correspondents. Among the latter, three upstarts in the 1950s would become dominant by the end of the Cold War: the *Los Angeles Times*, the *Washington Post* and the *Wall Street Journal*. Until the opening of a bureau in London in 1954, the *Post*, founded in 1877, had not had its own foreign correspondents, and the young upstart, buoyed by financial success, slowly developed its network of bureaus in the 1960s under publisher Katharine Graham.[27] By the late 1960s, the newspaper had become a formidable competitor – it won the Pulitzer Prize for reporting on the Six Days' War, which is discussed later in this chapter, and, with the demise of the *New York Herald Tribune*, for a while it provided the only major East Coast competition to the *New York Times*, even though the latter continued to field many more correspondents.[28] Another latecomer to foreign news was the *Wall Street Journal*, founded in 1889 in New York as a strictly business newspaper that only started seriously chasing other news in the 1940s, when it began printing short AP news summaries from around the world on a front-page column titled "World-Wide News."[29] Expansion began through the London bureau in the late 1950s, the same years in which the staunchly conservative editorial line shocked many readers by supporting civil rights; in the 1960s, it established itself as a national newspaper, reaching more than one million subscribers, and covered the major international news of the era with its own correspondents, starting regional publications across the world in the 1970s.[30]

Finally, on the West Coast, the *Los Angeles Times*, founded in 1881, really started imitating the East Coast giants only in the 1960s, under publisher Otis Chandler, vastly expanding its international reporting and adding nine

[26] Reporters of the Associated Press, *Breaking News: How the Associated Press Has Covered War, Peace, and Everything Else* (New York: Princeton Architectural Press, 2007), 257–305.

[27] Chalmers M. Roberts, *The Washington Post: The First 100 Years* (Boston: Houghton Mifflin, 1977), 334, 359.

[28] Roberts, 378, 394.

[29] Lloyd Wendt, The Wall Street Journal: *The Story of Dow Jones and the Nation's Business Newspaper* (Chicago: Rand McNally, 1982), 277, 289.

[30] Wendt, 332, 341.

foreign bureaus, from Bonn to Tokyo, in the space of a couple of years.[31] The expansion continued in the 1970s, when it was one of the most widely read and followed newspapers in the country. By 1991, it fielded fourteen reporters to cover the collapse of the Soviet Union, winning widespread praise.[32]

Even for these newspapers, however, the pressures on journalism that had been building since the 1980s – especially the race for corporate profits – started hurting foreign correspondence, setting the stage for a serious retrenchment after the end of the Cold War. To look at foreign correspondence in this era, then, is to see it at its peak strength, and to get a glimpse of its future troubles. Much the same can be said for the United States as a global power, as the next section explains.

From a Bipolar to a Unipolar World: Winning the Cold War

The United States emerged from the Second World War with an unprecedented power in global affairs that had no real challengers except the Soviet Union. The Cold War is both the simplest and one of the most controversial eras for U.S. foreign policy. On the one hand, a single, clear threat to national security was perceived – the Soviet Union, with its entourage – and all crises were defined in terms of this overarching trouble between the only two superpowers in a bipolar world. On the other hand, profound disagreements developed over how to face it, which have continued to haunt the country for decades.

The conflict had a purely geopolitical basis, starting in divided postwar Europe and hitting strategically pivotal areas in the Middle East, East Asia and even Latin America.[33] It was also greatly influenced, however, by politics and ideology, giving the United States a singular challenge when it tried to remake the postwar world in its image, not least as a challenge to the capitalist economy Washington sought to export. The strong anti-communism that most Americans had shared since 1917 clouded some strategic considerations and enlarged the Soviet menace. From the 1940s through the 1960s, U.S. presidents stoked the public's anti-communist flame with repeated reminders that the Soviets were the aggressors and Americans needed to, and would, overcome because they stood for universal values.[34] The need to sell Americans and foreign allies

[31] Dennis McDougal, *Privileged Son: Otis Chandler and the Rise and Fall of the* L.A. Times Dynasty (Cambridge, MA: Perseus Publishing, 2001), 249.

[32] McDougal, 404.

[33] Unless otherwise indicated, sources used for this general review of U.S. policy from 1946 to 1991 include Jerald A. Combs, *The History of American Foreign Policy*, vol. II, 3rd ed. (Armonk, NY: M.E. Sharpe, 2008); George C. Herring, *From Colony to Superpower: U.S. Foreign Relations since 1776* (Oxford: Oxford University Press, 2008); Richard Saull, "American Foreign Policy during the Cold War," in *US Foreign Policy*, ed. Michael Cox and Doug Stokes (Oxford: Oxford University Press, 2008), 63–87; Klaus Larres, ed. *The US Secretaries of State and Transatlantic Relations* (London: Routledge, 2010).

[34] Kenneth Osgood and Andrew K. Frank, eds. *Selling War in a Media Age: The Presidency and Public Opinion in the American Century* (Gainesville: University Press of Florida, 2010), 94.

on the constant Soviet threat created a program of news management and propaganda that centered on mass communication and included founding newspapers reflecting American values in fault-line countries like Germany. In yet another historical irony, American dominance in the news and entertainment global infrastructure often became a focal point of resentment, particularly in developing countries.[35]

Beginning with the Truman administration, strategic and ideological considerations merged in one general benchmark of all Cold War policies – containment of communist expansion globally. Containment meant, broadly, two commitments: military defense of U.S. allies, most clearly in the 1949 establishment of NATO, a radical step in security cooperation that broke with a tradition of unilateralism;[36] and domestic development of those same allies, with unprecedented large-scale economic aid programs like Europe's Marshall Plan. Where policy got much more contentious, however, was in the attempt to take the same commitments beyond Europe and aggressively militarize them. Every post-colonial conflict that flared up in revolutionary movements smacked of Soviet influence to Washington, regardless of the local socioeconomic and political aspects. Fear of Soviet attacks ran high among the U.S. public; according to one poll, 74 percent of respondents in 1948 believed the United States would be at war again within ten years.[37] Two events pushed Washington to take an increasingly active military interventionist role in Asia, one that ultimately led to profoundly hurtful failures like Vietnam. China, which many U.S. leaders had assumed would be a steadfast ally, went communist in 1949, and immediately afterward North Korea invaded South Korea. In deciding to send U.S. troops to repel the northern communists, Truman changed containment into a military doctrine, one permanently in the shadow of nuclear showdown.

Hence the so-called domino theory – the need to stop communist regime change across the world before it spread to neighboring countries, even though the original location might be of little economic or strategic interest to the United States, because any gain by the communists anywhere was a defeat for the free world. It became U.S. policy to draw the line, quite literally, at where the Soviet influence was allowed to extend. To do so, the United States frequently supported disreputable right-wing and colonial regimes against nationalist challengers, even as it believed it would take charge of the postcolonial world to

[35] Philip M. Taylor, *Global Communication, International Affairs and the Media since 1945* (London: Routledge, 1997). For one example of a U.S.-government-launched newspaper in Germany, see Jessica C.E. Gienow-Hecht, *Transmission Impossible: American Journalism as Cultural Diplomacy in Postwar Germany, 1945–1955* (Baton Rouge: Louisiana State University Press, 1999).

[36] David A. Lake, *Entangling Relations: American Foreign Policy in Its Century* (Princeton, NJ: Princeton University Press, 1999), 128.

[37] Osgood and Frank, 140. Poll quoted in Gabriel A. Almond, *The American People and Foreign Policy* (Westport, CT: Greenwood Press, 1960), 91.

push toward modernization along American, not Soviet, lines.[38] Most administrations in the 1950s and 1960s, the "heyday of decolonization," believed that "Third World" peoples were irresponsible and vulnerable to communist propaganda.[39]

The CIA did not stop even at assassination attempts, including targeting the leader of the closest communist regime to the United States and a genuine strategic threat, Fidel Castro, who had ousted the U.S.-backed dictator Fulgencio Batista in Cuba in 1959, although it is not clear that such efforts had executive mandates. The closest call in nuclear war came three years later in Cuba, after Soviet leader Nikita Khrushchev sent nuclear missiles there capable of reaching the United States. The most influential and contested U.S. intervention came in Vietnam, ending in a withdrawal of U.S. troops back to a United States that had grown extremely hostile to the war. As one historian put it, the war replaced appeasement in the Munich crisis "as the most potent symbol of what America should avoid in foreign policy,"[40] and its echoes still reverberated nearly thirty years later when the United States invaded Iraq.

The Cold War also dragged the United States into the quagmire of the Middle East, where, since its founding in 1948, the Jewish state of Israel was in permanent conflict with the Palestinian Arabs it had displaced into refugee camps as well as its neighboring countries. The traditional colonial powers in the area withdrew after the Second World War, leaving the United States to represent the West in a part of the world that at the time sat on two-thirds of proven oil reserves. Moved both by a powerful Jewish lobby that had existed since the early 1900s and a sense of moral obligation, Washington rushed to recognize the new state of Israel, establishing what would become a "special relationship" that infuriated the Arab world.[41] Eventually, Khrushchev further stoked the fire by reversing Stalin's policy and putting Soviet support behind the Arab states. When Israel won a quick and devastating victory against Egypt and its allies in 1967, with the full moral, although not military, support of President Lyndon Johnson and most Americans, much of the Arab world saw confirmation that the United States was an enemy to it. The question of the 1967 borders and intermittent U.S. efforts to negotiate a lasting peace between Israel and Palestinians have not abated since, providing an enduring strain between the United States and Western Europe, which, even more dependent on Middle Eastern oil, pointedly disassociated itself from Washington.

Significant breakthroughs in the Cold War came during the Nixon presidency, when his administration, under the leadership of Henry Kissinger

[38] On modernization, see Michael E. Latham, *The Right Kind of Revolution: Modernization, Development, and U.S. Foreign Policy from the Cold War to the Present* (Ithaca, NY: Cornell University Press, 2011).

[39] Herring, 652, 671.

[40] Combs, 219.

[41] Herring, 353, 629.

and using as an opening China's strained relationship with the Soviet Union, reopened relations with Beijing in an effort to demoralize North Vietnam and push the Soviets to negotiate with the Americans. Nixon traveled to China in 1972, and President Jimmy Carter officially opened the U.S. embassy in Beijing in 1979, leading the way to a wave of "Westernization" in the country.[42] Indeed, the Soviet Union did move closer to cooperation with the United States, and the Cold War slowly ground to a halt in the 1980s just as the American public grew vastly disillusioned with global involvement and Congress clamored for a larger role in foreign policy. Even though the conservative administrations of Presidents Ronald Reagan and George H.W. Bush still ordered small-scale U.S. interventions in the developing world, Washington was losing the desire for nation building and development of earlier years.

In 1980, Reagan still believed that the "Soviet Union underlies all that is going on. If they weren't engaged in this game of dominoes, there wouldn't be any hot spots in the world."[43] Eventually, however, Reagan's policy shifted toward negotiation, especially after Soviet President Mikhail Gorbachev came to power in 1985. Gorbachev started pushing for reform of the collapsing Soviet economy, and he refused to intervene when opposition parties in Eastern Europe took power away from the communists. The television-ready defining moment of the end of the Cold War was the breaking through of its most despised symbol, the Berlin Wall, on November 9, 1989, which marked an epochal shift also in U.S.-European relations, as will be discussed in the next chapter. Much to the world's surprise, the USSR imploded two years later, opening the way for an entirely different configuration in Washington of the world and its role in it. Such a quick, drastic and utterly nonviolent change in the balance of power had little precedent in history, making it hard to conceptualize for policymakers.[44]

Despite much fanfare, some American diplomats and, as discussed later in this chapter, journalists, feared, paradoxically, that this imbalance might actually be a bigger threat to the United States than the Soviets had been. A unipolar world was fraught with dangers, but Americans' interest in it was dramatically decreasing – whereas a peak of more than 50 percent of poll respondents had cited "international affairs and foreign aid" as "the most important problem" facing the country in the early 1950s, that number had plummeted to single digits in the 1970s and barely reached 10 percent in 1991, only to drop further in the 1990s, according to Gallup polls.[45] Furthermore,

[42] Herring, 901.

[43] Quoted in Combs, 282.

[44] Herring, 861.

[45] Data from Gallup's "Most Important Problem" surveys, retrieved online from the University of Texas at Austin's Policy Agendas Project, http://www.policyagendas.org/page/datasets-codebooks#gallups_most_important_problem. Many thanks to the University of Minnesota's Rodrigo Zamith for data elaboration.

increasingly fewer correspondents would be there to cover the world than had roamed the various Cold War fronts.

America Covers the World: Media Discourses in the Cold War

The United States clearly dominated the second half of the twentieth century – militarily, politically, economically and, increasingly, in its communication power. Just as Washington got entangled in conflicts across the world under the overarching ideology of the fight against Soviet communism, so did journalists chase the story in remote corners of the globe. They challenged progressively tighter efforts by governments to manage the news, basked in newly affirmed power in the Vietnam era, and started reeling under pressures to lay off the hard news in the Reagan years. Sometimes journalism shone as a dogged watchdog that opened the public's eyes to deception and dangers; many other times, the media missed the stories that did not fit the Soviet threat frame. The five episodes discussed in this chapter show such accomplishments and missed opportunities – times when the press functioned and malfunctioned as the public arena where meanings for things literally foreign became understood within general frameworks that in turn informed policymaking. This chapter focuses on the coverage of five defining events from 1959 to 1991 to uncover what discursive formations emerged about a generalized "other," the non-American, about America itself, and the specific identity of covered countries and regions. The findings reflect analysis of more than 640 articles and editorials selected from coverage by the Associated Press, *New York Times*, *Washington Post*, *Wall Street Journal* and *Los Angeles Times*.[46]

Castro's Cuba: Still the Pearl of the Antilles

> The [anti-American] rancor that will remain below the surface for years will never be personal, nor will it handicap future relations. Cuba is a country extraordinarily favored by nature. Her sugar and metals will always guarantee a high income in foreign currency. Her fertility will always prevent hunger, even among the

[46] The dates selected for study are: January 1–15, 1959, for the revolution in Cuba; June 5–12, 1967, for the Six Days' War; March 1 through April 30, 1979, for the reopening of relations with China; May 10–31, 1988, for the Soviet withdrawal from Afghanistan; and December 8–26, 1991, for the dissolution of the Soviet Union. Online databases (ProQuest and Lexis Nexis) were used for all dates for the *New York Times* and *Los Angeles Times*; starting in 1979 for the *Washington Post* and in 1988 for the *Wall Street Journal*. The search terms were as follows: Cuba; Israel; China/Shanghai/Peking in the dateline field; Afghanistan and Soviet Union. In the other cases, microfilm was used; every newspaper issue for the chosen dates was then examined. For the Associated Press copy, AP microfilm archives in New York were studied for the Cuban Revolution and 1967 war; no microfilm record was found on China in 1979, so stories were culled from the newspapers used. Starting with the 1988 case study, AP stories were found using the same search words (listed earlier in this note) in the internal digital archives.

poorest of Cubans. Her hot or balmy climate makes the problem of clothes easy. What the Cuban Republic has thus far lacked is honest, efficient government.[47]

New York Times star correspondent Herbert L. Matthews had courageously reported gripping stories from the Spanish Civil War, as discussed in Chapter 3, and with similar disregard for personal danger, he had found and interviewed Castro in 1957 when he seemed little more than an adventurous rebel doomed to failure.[48] That Matthews could write in 1959 the analysis just quoted suggests that American journalists were still enmeshed in discourses dating back at least a century, especially in the developing world. Matthews's postrevolutionary Cuba would have been perfectly recognizable to his 1890s colleagues who had dubbed it the Pearl of the Antilles, an island so bountiful that it essentially feeds itself while the population basks semi-nakedly in the tropical sun and smiles on its northern neighbor. The newspaper even ran a description of the island for its readers titled, tellingly, "Scene of Revolt Is a Lush Green Island."[49] Matthews did admit in the article just quoted that Washington's support for the previous dictator, Batista, might have left a taste of "anti-Yankeeism" among Cubans, but that would soon dissipate if Castro's new era of "liberty, democracy and decent government" took hold. Nothing in this analysis prepared readers to imagine that the world would stand on the brink of nuclear war over Cuba in three years, nor, for that matter, that Cuba might be more than a palm-fringed pawn for either superpower.

In the 1950s, Cuba had a relatively healthy although sugar-dependent economy, but its high standards of living were starkly different between the capital, Havana, and the impoverished rural areas.[50] Discontent brewed among the working class and the peasants, and it led to support for radical social and economic transformations proposed by populist leaders like Fidel Castro. Castro, who had staged a failed attack on military barracks in Santiago de Cuba in 1953 and had gone into exile after being released from prison in an amnesty two years later, landed with a small group of rebels in Cuba in December 1956. On and off for the next two years, his followers (a motley coalition also supported by Cuba's Communist Party) and Batista troops battled in the countryside, and Castro grew vastly popular.

The United States had been involved in Cuban politics and dominated its economy since the nineteenth century, generating enduring and little-understood resentment among Cubans. Washington had tried to persuade

47 Herbert L. Matthews, "Cuba: First Step to a New Era," *New York Times*, January 4, 1959.

48 John Hohenberg, *Foreign Correspondence: The Great Reporters and Their Times* 2nd ed. (Syracuse, NY: Syracuse University Press, 1995), 262; Thomas G. Paterson, *Contesting Castro: The United States and the Triumph of the Cuban Revolution* (New York: Oxford University Press, 1994), 74–78.

49 "Scene of Revolt Is a Lush Green Island, Largest and Most Populous of Antilles," *New York Times*, January 2, 1959, 7.

50 Samuel Farber, *The Origins of the Cuban Revolution Reconsidered* (Chapel Hill: University of North Carolina Press, 2006), 20–21.

Batista to hold fair elections in a last-ditch effort to stop Castro's revolution, which it feared it would not be able to control. President Dwight Eisenhower responded to Batista's refusal by stopping his supply of U.S. arms, and the besieged dictator fled to the Dominican Republic. Castro triumphantly took over in January 1959, remaining the most powerful man in the country even though a former judge formally headed the first government. Eisenhower hoped that Castro would not go fully communist and would stop assailing American influence on the island. When Castro became staunchly anti-capitalist, collectivized Cuba in 1960 along the Soviet model, and reached out to Moscow with a trade deal, Washington began an overtly hostile relationship that peaked in the fiasco of the Bay of Pigs and the eyeball-to-eyeball confrontation with the Soviet Union over nuclear missiles; the hostility ended up outliving the Cold War itself. Thousands of Cubans also fled the island for the United States, creating one of the most powerful lobbies in U.S. foreign policy.[51]

The confusion that initially prevailed among the U.S. foreign policy establishment over Castro's Cuba was shared by the journalists who covered the regime change in January 1959. The AP, the *New York Times* and the *Wall Street Journal* had or flew in reporters to Cuba, while the *Los Angeles Times* and the *Washington Post* still relied on domestic reports and wire stories, although a reporter of the latter claimed to have interviewed Castro a few months before the takeover.[52] Most journalists seemed enamored with a folkloristic image of Castro's "recklessly brave" "beaded rebels" – a detail they repeated endlessly, and "Dr. Castro," as the *New York Times* occasionally called him, even appeared in a live telecast by CBS from Havana.[53] Giving credit to the new government, an AP cable dispatch noted that it was leaving Cuba "free of censorship," and a reporter with Castro's "victory caravan" making its way to Havana wrote that Castro had pointed at the correspondents as a sign that his regime would not allow censorship.[54] Some reporters, however, raised questions about the new government's intentions and tactics.

[51] Thomas M. Leonard, *Castro and the Cuban Revolution* (Westport, CT: Greenwood Press, 1999), 17.

[52] Karl E. Meyer, "Castro's Triumph over Batista Leaves Cuba's Future Blurred," *Washington Post*, January 2, 1959, 1. A *Wall Street Journal* story datelined Havana mentions that the writer "with several other newsmen flew to Cuba from Miami by chartered plane"; Ed Cony, "Castro Calls Off General Strike in Cuba as Fighting Subsides; Urrutia Is Installed as Provisional President," *Wall Street Journal*, January 5, 1959, 3.

[53] "Castro Declares Trials Will Go On," *New York Times*, January 14, 1959, 1; "Castro, on TV, Predicts Arms Will Be Given Up," *New York Times*, January 10, 1959, 2; "Battle for Santa Clara Decisive in Cuba," *New York Times*, January 4, 1959, 4. For a particularly striking reference to "three giant, bearded rebels" who dressed as the Three Kings to distribute Epiphany toys to children, see "All Quiet in East, Raul Castro Says," *New York Times*, January 8, 1959, 3.

[54] "News of Cuba Uncensored," *New York Times*, January 2, 1959, 7; Ben Funk, "Cuban Separate," Associated Press, January 5, 1959. There are no AP headlines in the record for 1959; the titles given here for reference are the internal "signatures" reflecting time of filing and type of story.

AP staffers seemed singularly unimpressed by Castro, perhaps because three of them had been arrested and threatened by the new regime.

An AP reporter just arriving from Miami walked into the office as the following was unfolding:

> Trigger-happy young Cuban rebels today stormed and shot their way into the Havana Post building and, at gunpoint, threatened to kill three Associated Press newsmen.... They kicked open the door of the AP bureau and leveled their weapons at George Kaufman, Havana chief of bureau; correspondent Larry Allen; and Harold Valentine, photographer from the Miami bureau.... Kaufman and Allen had spent some time flat on the office floor, trying to write news and keep up with teletype dispatches while bullets peppered the floor.[55]

Allen himself, eventually returned to the office by the rebels, wrote the AP's main story, reporting that AP newsmen had been the victims of the first (and the tone clearly implied not the last) "incident involving Americans."[56] Another AP staffer, a photo editor from New York, wrote that his welcome to Havana had been the muzzle of a machine gun poking through the chartered airliner.[57]

As their predecessors had, editors in 1959 gloated about their correspondents' exploits, their access to Castro, their language skills, and their supposed expertise on Latin America. A story by a *Chicago Tribune* reporter, printed in the *Los Angeles Times*, was prefaced by an editor's note highlighting that he was the first to interview Castro after the "rebel victory" and that he had "a wide acquaintance with leading figures in many Latin-American countries."[58] As in the Spanish Civil War, reporters also pointed out when their direct observations contradicted official sources. A brief note in the AP news roundup published in the *Wall Street Journal* noted that Castro's government "refused to confirm" news of mass executions of Batista supporters, but "Associated Press correspondent Stanford Bradshaw said he saw a big mound of fresh earth at the reported scene."[59]

Editorially, coverage seemed greatly optimistic that Castro would usher in democracy for the island and continue good relations with the United States, showing no understanding that U.S. policies might have generated ill will or that Cold War politics would make it a testing ground. *New York Times* editors, after bidding "good riddance" to Batista, dubbed Castro "the extraordinary young man" and called for American aid to a people unsurpassed in the hemisphere for "friendly feeling toward the American people" and "respect for the

55 Bob Clark, "Night Lead Newsmen," Associated Press, January 2, 1959.

56 The story ran in the *Los Angeles Times*, "Heavy Fighting in Havana Streets," January 3, 1959, 1.

57 Robert Tieken, Associated Press, January 3, 1959.

58 Jules Dubois, "Castro Tells Aim in First Interview," *Los Angeles Times*, January 5, 1959, 2.

59 "What's News," *Wall Street Journal*, January 13, 1959, 1; Stanford Bradshaw, "Second Night Lead Cuban," Associated Press, January 12, 1959.

United States as a nation."[60] Similarly, the *Washington Post* editors blamed Batista, turned Castro into David, because "armed originally with little more than the biblical slingshot, [he] had felled a seasoned and ruthless dictator," and argued that this "should be weighed against the charges that Castro's movement is a nursery for Cuban communism."[61] Editors at the *Los Angeles Times* and the *Wall Street Journal* were a bit more cautious, arguing that it was not clear what regime Castro would install, and that Batista too had been considered the savior from tyranny originally.[62] Perhaps the most striking editorial construction of the Cubans' "colorful history," one this research found all the way back to the revolutions of 1848, was the following – could it be, "this cannot be positive yet – that the Cuban people have reached that stage of political and social maturity where they demand and will fight for decency in government as well as for freedom"?[63]

In correspondence from Cuba, some of the same discourses appear, showing very little understanding of the legacy of U.S. intervention there and almost no conceptualization that the "red menace" could strike so close to the homeland. The closest Matthews came to exploring the latter was an interview with Castro aide Ernesto Che Guevara, in which the latter, his voice "remarkably low and his smile unexpectedly gentle," denied any communist leaning, something the journalist himself would later also do under attack by conservative American critics. Matthews added that Havana's La Cabaña fortress, where the interview took place, "is more picturesque than a Hollywood director could make it, for it is swarming with 'the bearded ones' – the fighting troops of the Guevara column."[64] In an analysis, the *New York Times* journalist concluded that the big difference between the Mexican and the Cuban revolutions was that the latter was not "as radical in terms of the political left and right. If anything it is conservative."[65] In a longer magazine piece, Matthews – the *Times*' expert on Latin America – insisted that there was no possibility of communists even sharing government in Cuba.[66] The *Chicago Tribune* correspondent also

60 "A Cuban Dictator Falls," *New York Times*, January 2, 1959, 24; "Aftermath in Cuba," *New York Times*, January 3, 1959, 16.

61 "Castro at Floodtide," *Washington Post*, January 3, 1959, 6. Also "Aftermath in Cuba," *Washington Post*, January 10, 1959, 12, and "Climax in Cuba," *Washington Post*, January 2, 1959, 20.

62 "The Rise and Fall of Sgt. Batista," *Los Angeles Times*, January 2, 1959, B4; "The Lesson from Cuba," *Wall Street Journal*, January 5, 1959, 12.

63 "End of an Epic," *New York Times*, January 11, 1959, E10; "Cuba in Transition," *New York Times*, January 6, 1959, 32.

64 Herbert L. Matthews, "Top Castro Aide Denies Red Tie Leaders Say They 'Await Fidel'," *New York Times*, January 4, 1959, 7.

65 Herbert L. Matthews, "Cuba Course Unclear under Castro Regime," *New York Times*, January 11, 1959, E6.

66 Herbert L. Matthews, "A New Chapter Opens in Latin America," *New York Times*, January 11, 1959, SM13.

praised Castro's "unmistakable sincerity" and "sharp" mind when he said his movement had no association with communists.[67]

Other stories focused on the repercussions for U.S. trade, business and even tourism (especially to Cuba's casinos); in an early case of the frequently absurd domestication of news, one story focused on American tourists in Havana who, "disappointed by a revolution's disruption of their holiday," vowed never to come back to the island.[68] Such descriptions implicitly reinforced a construction of Cuba, "an island located literally at this country's doorstep,"[69] as a bountiful pseudo-colonial terrain for American investment. Some reported predictions that "normalcy" would be promptly restored – again ignoring the strong undercurrents of nationalist uprisings in Cuba and elsewhere.[70] Other correspondents, like the *Wall Street Journal*'s, were less optimistic, finding that unrest seemed menacing to private property (reporting an AP detail that crowds destroyed parking meters to celebrate the revolution), and Castro and Guevara, although "sincere" in their annoyance at continually being asked whether they were communist, had not been "encouraging" to U.S. business.[71]

The coverage that focused the most on social and political unrest, rather than the picturesque and the colonial, was the AP's – although the wire service still mentioned "Castro's storybook warriors, with their long waving hair and beards" and even devoted one story to the leader's facial hair.[72] The AP foreign news analyst, who had been out of the office when rebels attacked it, described how Castro's followers had "embarked on a wild orgy of celebration, looting, burning and killing in Havana."[73] In his profile, Allen described Castro as "a professional rebel who has been in revolt most of his life," who had carried on his revolution by "burning plantations, shattering communications lines, kidnaping [*sic*], striking where and how he could."[74] The reporter who found the alleged site of mass executions wrote that Castro "warned sternly against any U.S. intervention in Cuban affairs" and threatened, in case of an invasion, to kill "gringos" – which, the AP helpfully explained, "is a term used by some Latin Americans, often in a derogatory sense, for U.S.-citizens."[75] Still, even

67 Jules Dubois, "Castro Tells Aim in First Interview," *Los Angeles Times*, January 5, 1959, 2.

68 Bob Clark, "Americans," Associated Press, January 4, 1959.

69 Karl E. Meyer, "Castro's Triumph over Batista Leaves Cuba's Future Blurred," *Washington Post*, January 2, 1959, 1.

70 R. Hart Phillips, "Castro's Victory Lifts Cuba's Hope," *New York Times*, January 14, 1959, 49; Hart Phillips, "Cuba May Have A Tourist Season," *New York Times*, January 11, 1959, X23.

71 "What's News" and "Batista Flees Cuba, Temporary President Named; Castro's Forces Move to Take Over," *Wall Street Journal*, January 2, 1959, 1 and 3; Ed Cony and Henry Gemmill, "Cuba's Future," *Wall Street Journal*, January 8, 1959, 1, 3.

72 William L. Ryan, "Cuban Interpretive," Associated Press, January 3, 1959; George Kaufman, "Castro Beard," Associated Press, January 11, 1959.

73 William L. Ryan, "Fourth Night Lead Cuban," Associated Press, January 2, 1959.

74 Larry Allen, "Personality in the News," Associated Press, January 1, 1959.

75 Stanford Bradshaw, "Third Night Lead Cuban," Associated Press, January 15, 1959.

the AP repeatedly noted, "There is no point now in Washington worrying about whether communist elements are involved in the revolution. The rebel leaders have indicated they intend to keep the reds at arms' length."[76] Ten years later, in 1969, Castro would order the AP correspondent out – the last resident American newsman to leave the communist island.[77]

With the partial exception of the AP, then, coverage of Castro's Cuba still reflected some of the nineteenth-century imperial gaze even as it tried, unsuccessfully, to gauge its relevance to the twentieth-century Cold War. The United States was constructed as the friendly and beloved neighbor, in a vast misunderstanding of its actual role on the island and of its perception there. The continued references to communism, and the failure to grasp its implications, show how prevalent it had become as an organizing frame for global affairs – and how difficult it still was for Americans to conceptualize its allure, especially at the United States' doorstep. Less than ten years later, the Cold War frame entirely dominated U.S. press discourses about conflict in another area of great trade, emotional and strategic significance: the Middle East.

The 1967 War: Stunning Victory, Impossible Peace

> TEL AVIV, Israel AP – In six short days, a little nation of 2.5 million has humbled 100 million Arabs, jolted their topmost leader into an emotional offer to step down, and amazed the watching world with military efficiency. For Israel and the Middle East it really was the week that was – the most momentous since the Jewish state was hammered into existence over the bitter anvil of Arab resistance 19 years ago.... The Soviet Union, five years after looking down the gun barrel of the Cuban missile crisis, once again backed away from a showdown. Russia and the United States, for the sake of world safety, both used their influence in trying to stop the fighting.[78]

In extensive coverage, the U.S. press constructed the six-day 1967 war between Israel and Egypt with its allies much along the lines of the AP dispatch just quoted. It clearly cheered on the "little guy" Israel against a broadly defined (and stereotyped) "Arab" mass. It inevitably saw the crisis in terms of the Soviet versus American conflict, so much so that the war seemed to have four combatants – in a front-page summary of Middle East developments in the *New York Times*, the capitals listed were Tel Aviv, Cairo, Washington and Moscow.[79] There was no question that the United States had to be involved somehow, although many journalists argued that there would be a most strenuous peace out of a little war – indeed, the question of the 1967 Israeli borders was still at the core of international mediation nearly fifty years later. Two

[76] William L. Ryan, "PMs Budget Cuban," Associated Press, January 5, 1959.

[77] Reporters of the Associated Press, 295.

[78] Hal McClure, "Blitz War Recap," Associated Press, June 10, 1967.

[79] "Fighting Is Raging in Gaza and Sinai; Action in Air Heavy," *New York Times*, June 6, 1967, 1.

other trends emerging here would also prove enduring – overt news management by governments and, not unrelated, a homogenization of stories across media.

Since the creation of the state of Israel in 1948, tensions in the Middle East between Arabs and Israelis had been brewing, exacerbated by disputes over Arab Palestinians displaced by the Jewish state and over access to the commercially vital Suez Canal.[80] They unexpectedly exploded in an open war between Egypt, Syria and Jordan against Israel in June 1967, which immediately became a Cold War front with the Soviet Union warning the United States not to intervene and Arab countries threatening an oil embargo against anyone helping Israel. After days of tense mobilization, Egyptian threats and Palestinian attacks, the Israelis launched an air strike that singlehandedly destroyed the Egyptian Air Force in a matter of hours on June 5. Secure from the air, Israeli troops went on to take the Sinai desert from Egypt, the West Bank and the old city of Jerusalem from Jordan, and the Golan Heights from Syria – nearly quadrupling their territory – in less than a week.

What to do with those occupied territories has remained the sticking point since postwar negotiations through the United Nations, with Israel arguing it should hold on to as much as its security warrants and Arab states making renunciation the starting point for recognition of Israel's existence. The United States, starting with the Johnson administration, while generally supportive of Israel, has tried to mediate a "land-for-peace" compromise that would ensure self-determination for Palestinians, many tens of thousands more of whom had been made refugees by the war. Washington, making an Arab-Israeli settlement the centerpiece of its policy in the Middle East, usually met with little success and aroused strong backlash from Arab countries. Americans, especially the extremely active Jewish lobby, remained strongly and emotionally involved in both sides of the ongoing conflict. The unrest stemming from a six-day war dragged on for more than forty years.

The media studied in this chapter gave exhaustive coverage to the war, which suddenly made the Middle East a staple of foreign news – the AP established a full bureau in Israel in 1967.[81] The newspapers apparently could not get enough from the various fronts of the war; on the first day, the *New York Times* ran two nearly identical stories, one by AP and one by its own correspondent, on the front page.[82] Throughout their stories, and in the majority of the Western press, reporters came very close to "cheerleading" for Israel, as one study put

[80] See Combs, 253–266; Michael B. Oren, *Six Days of War: June 1967 and the Making of the Modern Middle East* (New York: Oxford University Press, 2002); Richard B. Parker, *The Six-Day War: A Retrospective* (Gainesville: University Press of Florida, 1996); Steven L. Spiegel, *The Other Arab-Israeli Conflict: Making America's Middle East Policy, from Truman to Reagan* (Chicago: University of Chicago Press, 1985).

[81] Reporters of The Associated Press, 287.

[82] Terence Smith, "Fighting Is Heavy," and "Army and Planes in Action," *New York Times*, June 5 1967, 1.

it, because of the horrors of the Holocaust and a sense of biblical affinity.[83] As for Arabs, studies found that stereotypes of "orientalism" – such as fatalism, backwardness, and resistance to modernity – dominated U.S. media coverage of the war and of all matters related to Islam in this era.[84]

Editorially, the overarching discourse, framed in Cold War terms ("the world today has a new war on its hands," according to the *Los Angeles Times*), was the fundamental, insurmountable difference between Arabs and Israelis, which made permanent peace "improbable" or at a minimum "a long, tough job," in the words of the *Washington Post*.[85] A cartoon next to that editorial showed the United States, USSR and the UN looking at a sandy expanse inscribed with "hatred, permanent 'state of war,' threats of extermination" and, standing under a crane with a large cornerstone called "Middle East Peace 1967," asking, "this time, how about a solid foundation?" *Wall Street Journal* editors, referencing oil and Soviet threats, also argued that relations between Israel and its Arab neighbors were likely to get worse and the United States should "exert such influence as it can" for negotiating a long-term "modus vivendi" in the region.[86]

The *New York Times* repeatedly referenced that the war's "fuse... goes back to the dawn of history" – constructing the conflict as immutable – and, in a clear swipe at the Vietnam-embroiled White House, argued that, "military victory will be no solution in the Middle East any more than the military victory the United States is seeking in Vietnam would be in Southeast Asia."[87] *Times* editors insisted that the Soviet Union and the United States needed to work together on a "stable settlement," although Washington's professed neutrality was "grotesque both in terms of American commitments and American interests in the area."[88] The editors were hardly neutral themselves. They blamed the Arabs' loss on the lack of "soldiers of equal heart and spirit" to the Israelis, and they chastised the backwardness of the "volatile [Arab] peoples of the area," whose economy is "'camel-and-dates'" and where "the people are dependent upon village radios and word of mouth for 'facts' which are too

[83] Michael Emery, *On the Front Lines: Following America's Foreign Correspondents across the Twentieth Century* (Washington: American University Press, 1995), 213. For a critical take on Israeli rhetoric about the war, see Norman G. Finkelstein, *Image and Reality of the Israel-Palestine Conflict* (London: Verso, 2001), 123–149.

[84] Edward W. Said, *Covering Islam: How the Media and the Experts Determine How We See the Rest of the World* (New York: Pantheon Books, 1981).

[85] "Conflict in the Middle East," *Los Angeles Times*, June 6, 1967, A4; "The Lesson of History," *Washington Post*, June 6, 1967, A16; "The Job Ahead," *Washington Post*, June 9, 1967, A22. See also "Mid-East Peace," *Washington Post*, June 8, 1967, A20.

[86] "The Aftermath," *Wall Street Journal*, June 12, 1967, 16.

[87] "The Long Accounting ..." *New York Times*, June 6, 1967, 46; "Let There Be Peace," *New York Times*, June 11, 1967, 206.

[88] "A Peace with Reconciliation," *New York Times*, June 7, 1967, 46; "The Search for Peace," *New York Times*, June 6, 1967, 46.

often fiction."[89] *Times* columnist James Reston, writing from Tel Aviv, went even further, asserting that Arabs would require "a biological mutation" to be capable of peace and describing Israeli soldiers, on the contrary, "smoking and singing like Hemingway's heroes at the start of the Spanish Civil War."[90]

Unlike the gripping reportage from the Spanish Civil War, however, as detailed in the previous chapter, the swiftness of the defeat and the apparent scarcity of civilian damage turned some 1967 reports into a rather aseptic game. A few reporters, in the Madrid tradition, wrote that they could feel the blast of shells outside their hotel, that "the deep cough of heavy guns" rattled the windows as they typed, and "the explosion pushed the windshield of our car out of the frame," but the majority of the correspondence foreswore such human side of war.[91] One article from Tel Aviv called the list of destroyed Egyptian planes "the box score," another defined battles as "dogfights," yet another from a correspondent embedded "with Israeli forces on the northern front" described soldiers cheering their officers "as they might their soccer heroes after a bruising victory."[92] A story describing the Israeli blitz quipped that "the Arabs were caught with their planes down"; another reported that Israeli soldiers in a key port "watched the nonmilitary movements of a few girls in bikinis enjoying most the kicks and none of the risks of war."[93] A kibbutz visited by journalists was found to have "an air of gaiety" despite evidence from shelling.[94] The thousands of refugees, "these unhappy people," were curtly described as an "expensive" problem for Israel, noting that the territorial annexation would create a demographic time bomb for Israel – implicitly writing the refugees themselves out of the story.[95]

The construction of the uncivilized Arabs threatening Israel and the latter's "stunning," "striking" military prowess and civilian fortitude was dominant in the correspondence from Israel. Even geography was constructed as inimical

89 "The Four-Day War," *New York Times*, June 9, 1967, 44; "The Military Prospects," *New York Times*, June 6, 1967, 46; "... and the Birth of a Myth," *New York Times*, June 8, 1967, 46.

90 James Reston, "Tel Aviv: The Israeli Strategy," *New York Times*, June 9, 1967, 44; James Reston, "A War's First Hours," *New York Times*, June 6, 1967, 16.

91 Flora Lewis, "Jerusalem Shaken by Gunfire as All Israel Rallies to Call," *Washington Post*, June 6, 1967, 14; Joe Alex Morris Jr., "Heavy Fighting Erupts in Divided City of Jerusalem," *Los Angeles Times*, June 6, 1967, 15; Hans Benedict, "Mideast-Gaza," Associated Press, June 6, 1967.

92 Bernard D. Nossiter, "Israel: Army Reported Near Suez and on Jordan River Bank," *Washington Post*, June 8, 1967, 14; Hans Benedict, "Israeli Air Force," Associated Press, June 8, 1967; Dan Kurzman, "Battle Duty Became Parade," *Washington Post*, June 11, 1967, A19.

93 Hanson W. Baldwin, "48 Hours of Battle," *New York Times*, June 7, 1967, 20; Robert C. Toth, "Tense Eilat Forgets Its Boom Town Past," *Los Angeles Times*, June 5, 1967, 10.

94 James Feron, "Youth in Kibbutz Describes Attacks," *New York Times*, June 11, 1967, 17.

95 Seth S. King, "Along with Terrain, Israel Gets Burden of 900,000 Refugees," *New York Times*, June 8, 1967, 16; George Melloan, "In the War's Wake," *Wall Street Journal*, June 13, 1967, 15; "Arab Birth Rate High," *New York Times*, June 11, 1967, 20; Thomas Reedy, "Mideast-Israeli," Associated Press, June 10, 1967.

to the country – one *Washington Post* correspondent in Tel Aviv wrote of "the great bulge of Jordan that pushes into Israel," while the *Los Angeles Times* correspondent described Jordanians as "infesting" the valleys around Bethlehem and the *Wall Street Journal* writer found Israel had a lot more to lose because "the Arab lands" "are far less developed."[96] The same *Washington Post* article just quoted internalized Israel's perspective – that it was fighting "to remove the Arab threat from its borders" – without comment, question or balance. Under a façade of objective reporting, some of the correspondence also seemed aimed at convincing the White House of Israel's righteousness: "There is hope here that Washington and other capitals will remember that the Arabs were trying to liquidate Israel, not merely bring about border changes."[97]

The construction of Israelis' stoicism creates a strong contrast to the image of Arab threat. Just before the start of hostilities, for example, Terence Smith of the *New York Times* portrayed the "deliberate calm" with which Israelis in Jerusalem, "accustomed to living on the edge of a hostile border," were stacking sandbags on window sills, "as if they had always spent their afternoons that way."[98] The same reporter would later relay how Israeli soldiers had swept up glass fragments from the Dome of the Rock mosque damaged in the shelling – and so would the *Los Angeles Times* correspondent, in one of many instances of identical reporting.[99] One writer found evidence of "the national spirit" in "people in the street, the chambermaids, the taxi drivers – even the censors" – unwittingly revealing a journalist's routine sources.[100] Stories like one about a "smiling waiter in the Tel Aviv Hilton" who apologized for interruptions in the breakfast service because he had been away fighting in the Sinai – "as though it were the most natural thing in the world to bring around breakfast a day after he was part of an army that crushed about 150,000 Egyptians, supported by perhaps 1,000 tanks" – simultaneously reinforced the construction of Israel's slam dunk and massive, if ultimately futile, Arab threat.[101]

The constant references to episodes in New and Old Testament writings, to the Holy Land, and to Jerusalem as the holy or "biblical" city are also striking, revealing a discourse that implicitly reinforced Israeli claims to the area as moral and immemorial, and constructed conflict as destiny. AP writers

96 Bernard D. Nossiter, "Israel: Army Reported Near Suez and on Jordan River Bank," *Washington Post*, June 8, 1967, 14; Joe Alex Morris Jr., "Bethlehem Road Littered by War," *Los Angeles Times*, June 9, 1967, 21; George Melloan, "Israel vs. the Arabs," *Wall Street Journal*, June 6, 1967, 16.

97 Sydney Gruson, "Cabinet Confers," *New York Times*, June 12, 1967, 18.

98 Terence Smith, "Israelis in Jerusalem, Often Divided, Unite Calmly to Prepare to Defend City," *New York Times*, June 5, 1967, 3.

99 Terence Smith, "Israelis Weep and Pray Beside the Wailing Wall," *New York Times*, June 8, 1967, 1; Robert C. Toth, "Jews Worship at Wailing Wall after Capturing Old Jerusalem," *Los Angeles Times*, June 8, 1967, 22.

100 James Reston, "Determined Nation," *New York Times*, June 8, 1967, 17.

101 Sydney Gruson, "Cabinet Confers," *New York Times*, June 12, 1967, 18.

described "the haze of battle" "over the tranquil Sea of Galilee, where St. Peter once fished" and mixed legend and reporting in the capture of Jericho: "They fought another Battle of Jericho and the walls came tumbling down with hardly a shot being fired.... Joshua's men marched around the walls and then shouted them down: psychological warfare before the term was invented. This time Israeli air force planes swooped over town, dropped a few bombs to frighten the inhabitants and flew away."[102] Stories from Israeli-occupied Bethlehem called it "the legendary birthplace of David, the giant killer, as well as Christ, the bringer of peace" where, now, "tough, young, unshaven and sun-tanned Israeli soldiers" were observed by "impassive Arab adults and excited children."[103] The *New York Times* reporter in Bethlehem described almost verbatim "groups of Arabs [who] watched impassively" – and so did the *Los Angeles Times* writer, who apparently had driven together with the other two.[104] Incidentally, non-Israelis, judging from the correspondence, did nothing but "wait" in this war – as their women "were gossiping or huddling in front of their huts grinding beans with a stone," in a perfectly primitive image.[105]

Most correspondents also highlighted the emotional moment when, after taking Jerusalem's "holy" city, "Israeli troops wept and prayed... at the foot of the Wailing Wall," "repeating a tradition that goes back 2,000 years but has been denied Israeli Jews since 1948."[106] Several writers argued that, having "paid for this in casualties," Israelis would not give up Jerusalem.[107] The dateline from the city is itself a microcosm of the war – from "Jerusalem, Israel" and "Jerusalem, Jordan" to "Jerusalem, Israeli Sector" and "Jerusalem, Israeli-occupied Jordan" to, simply, Jerusalem.

For the first time in this research, journalists from the various organizations seemed to have covered the war together – probably encouraged by tight Israeli control of the media. As the *New York Times* and AP noted, censorship was in place in both Israel and Egypt, but the novelty was in journalists' writing

102 Hugh A. Mulligan, "Galilee Eyewitness," Associated Press, June 10, 1967; Lawrence Malkin, "Battle of Jericho," Associated Press, June 10, 1967. The religious element is also prominent in a book the AP published about the war, the Associated Press, *Lightning out of Israel: The Six-Day War in the Middle East*, 1967.

103 Bernard D. Nossiter, "Israelis Occupy Bethlehem," *Washington Post*, June 9, 1967, 13.

104 Terence Smith, "Even in War, Bethlehem Has Air of Tourist Town," *New York Times*, June 10, 1967; Joe Alex Morris Jr., "Bethlehem Road Littered by War," *Los Angeles Times*, June 9, 1967, 21.

105 Flora Lewis, "Jerusalem Shaken by Gunfire as All Israel Rallies to Call," *Washington Post*, June 6, 1967, 14.

106 Terence Smith, "Israelis Weep and Pray Beside the Wailing Wall," *New York Times*, June 8, 1967, 1; Robert C. Toth, "Jews Worship at Wailing Wall after Capturing Old Jerusalem," *Los Angeles Times*, June 8, 1967, 22; Eric Gottgetreu, "Israel-Jordan," Associated Press, June 7, 1967.

107 Sydney Gruson, "For the Israelis There Are Some Border Problems," *New York Times*, June 9, 1967, 18; Gruson, "Cabinet Confers," *New York Times*, June 12, 1967, 1.

about press releases and news management, too.[108] Robert C. Toth of the *Los Angeles Times* said correspondents were flooded with Israeli press releases, including one comparing Egyptian President Nasser to Hitler, and he called the Israeli release of the alleged transcript of a conversation between Nasser and the Jordanian king "admittedly a case of news management."[109] Alfred Friendly of the *Washington Post*, who complained about "the insistence of escort officers to get reporters quickly out of an area where continued military action had not been expected," joined four U.S. reporters and a few European ones on a low-flying Israeli plane to see the destruction in the Sinai, and commented that Israel had "put on view for reporters the panorama of Egyptian defeat."[110] Some copy, as previously noted, is nearly verbatim – both the *New York Times* and the *Washington Post* correspondents, for example, wrote that Israeli soldiers in Jerusalem "acted like tourists" rather than occupation forces.[111]

The discourses that emerge from the strikingly similar news reports, then, portray conflict between righteous Israel and a mass of undifferentiated "Arabs" as rooted in history and religion. The dangerous and potentially unsolvable conflict – largely because of Arab lack of "civilization" and the pesky issue of all those refugees – was described as a threat to superpower balance. The war permanently put the Middle East on the map for the U.S. press just as it became a hot spot for Washington's policy. The Cold War threat was averted, but the construction of the Arab-Israeli conflict as immemorial and even moral did little to foster innovative U.S. policy thinking. Just as in Cuba, foreign correspondence from Israel reflected more historical notions than evolving realities, and it is highly suggestive that U.S. policy toward both situations has similarly stalemated since. In a little more than a decade, another complex, influential spot on the globe would open up for American journalists to try to decipher – China – and their analysis would prove remarkably more probing.

Normalizing Relations with China: Communism, Capitalism and Peking Duck

> KUNMING, China – On Sunday morning, the narrow back lanes of Kunming swiftly filled with thousands of parchment-skinned peasants, in from the

108 "Censorship Blurs Details of Fighting," *New York Times*, June 6, 1967, 3; "Censorship NL," Associated Press, June 5, 1967.

109 Robert C. Toth, "Jordanians Again Fire into Israeli Jerusalem," *Los Angeles Times*, June 5, 1967, 11; Robert C. Toth, "Israel Issues Tape of Cairo-Amman 'Plot,'" *Los Angeles Times*, June 9, 1967, 20.

110 Alfred Friendly, "Israeli Troops Quickly Cut Off Gaza Strip from Egypt," *Washington Post*, June 6, 1967, 14; Alfred Friendly, "Fight over Sinai: Witness to Egypt's Disaster," *Washington Post*, June 11, 1967, 1.

111 Michael Lerner, "Tension Eases in Jerusalem, Tel Aviv," *Washington Post*, June 11, 1967, A19; Terence Smith, "Jerusalem Arabs Divided on Future," *New York Times*, June 12, 1967, 18.

> countryside. Squatting on the cobblestones, they assembled their cucumbers, onions and potatoes in tidy pyramids in front of them, put their plumpest fowl on display and opened for business. Open-air markets are so commonplace throughout the Third World that they rarely rate a second glance, but Kunming's thriving free market is something special.... free enterprise has only begun to make a comeback after a decade of suppression.... Thus the back streets of many Chinese towns are regularly transformed into bazaars that offer practically everything that can be found in an American supermarket – and sometimes more.[112]

When the United States and China formally reestablished relations in the spring of 1979, U.S. journalists who had been peeking into the vast country from Hong Kong rushed in. Like Linda Mathews, the *Los Angeles Times* correspondent just quoted, they ventured into China seeking vestiges of both communism and the legendary China that had long fascinated Westerners. The most remarkable finding to emerge from study of their correspondence is the overwhelming focus on Chinese business – well before the country would explode onto the global scene as a formidable economic power in the twenty-first century. To most correspondents, China still had a long way to go before emerging from the "Third World," but some places already looked as capitalistically appealing as an American supermarket – and perhaps a safer ground for Americanization than all those other ideologically committed Cold War fronts.

The United States had long considered a united, independent China a force for stability in East Asia, so in the 1940s it maintained relations with both the Chinese Communists and Chiang Kai-shek's government, hoping for a compromise, until 1946, when civil war broke out.[113] In October 1949, Mao Zedong declared victory for the communists and established the People's Republic of China, announcing it would lean toward the Soviet Union. Less than a year later, the war in Korea further complicated relations, as did the entrenchment of Nationalists in Taiwan (Formosa), both hardening Washington's opposition to Beijing, which in the confrontation got "instant great-power status."[114] In the 1950s, China became another front of communist containment for the United States, and all vestiges of American influence were pushed out of the mainland while military support grew in Taiwan. The 1960s, with the escalation of the Vietnam War, saw continued hostilities between the two countries; even though Mao began to detach China from the Soviet orbit, he started the "cultural revolution," which among many disastrous results also isolated China from the rest of the world. Finally, in the late 1960s, as Sino-Soviet relations soured and détente stalled, the Nixon administration cautiously reached

[112] Linda Mathews, "Rural China's Bazaars: Hint of Capitalism," *Los Angeles Times*, April 21, 1979, OC1.

[113] Warren I. Cohen, *America's Response to China: A History of Sino-American Relations* 5th ed. (New York: Columbia University Press, 2010).

[114] Herring, 645.

out to Beijing, Beijing put the brakes on class warfare to revive the economy, strategic interests trumped ideological divergence, and formal talks resumed early in 1970.[115] The following year, travel restrictions were lifted and China invited a group of Americans to visit – the ping-pong team.

Kissinger and Nixon also traveled to Beijing – visits considered by some historians one of the greatest diplomatic gambles of the Cold War and, in Nixon's case, precisely choreographed for maximum impact on U.S. television. Although Taiwan remained a sticking point into the twenty-first century, normalization was well under way, pushed along by a renewed interest on the part of U.S. business leaders who, in the midst of a faltering home economy, coveted the Chinese market.[116] The American public was transfixed by Nixon's trip in 1972, even though polls suggest that most Americans then had an unfavorable opinion of China.[117] The percentage of Americans who have perceived China as an enemy or unfriendly country has fluctuated since then, with a high of 69 percent in 2001 and a low of 6 percent in 1988. After a few false starts, with the blessing of Carter and Deng Xiaoping, the U.S. embassy reopened in Beijing on March 1, 1979, when Treasury Secretary Michael Blumenthal traveled there to resolve long-standing disputes over confiscated assets and to open trade negotiations. The relationship has continued to grow closer with growth in trade, educational exchanges and media presence despite strong disagreements over human rights and security.

The Associated Press, which in 1972 established an exchange of news with China's Xinhua news agency, and United Press International rushed in March 1979 to open the first two U.S. news bureaus in Beijing (then still known as Peking) since 1949, starting a trend that would make China a crucial foreign post for media worldwide.[118] Before then, American journalists had been able to observe China only from a distance, which often meant through Washington's perspective.[119] After 1979, correspondents flocked to China, even though they were often not allowed to travel freely or talk to all sources, and, according to one study, they remained bound to dominant policy interpretations.[120] In mid-April 1979, for example, Mathews reported that she and another American – most likely Jay Mathews, who wrote a nearly identical story for the *Washington Post* – had been talking for two hours with a group of youths in Kunming Zoo when the latter "became agitated and bolted as soon as they saw

[115] William C. Kirby, Robert S. Ross and Gong Li, eds. *Normalization of U.S.-China Relations: An International History* (Cambridge: Harvard University Press, 2003).

[116] Margaret MacMillan, *Nixon and Mao: The Week That Changed the World* (New York: Random House, 2007); Herring, 775.

[117] Jean A. Garrison, *Making China Policy: From Nixon to G. W. Bush* (Boulder, CO: Lynne Rienner, 2005), 210–213.

[118] "A.P. and U.P.I. Name Peking Correspondents," *New York Times*, March 23, 1979, A4.

[119] Tsan-Kuo Chang, *The Press and China Policy: The Illusion of Sino-American Relations, 1950–1984* (Norwood, NJ: Ablex Publishing, 1993), 58, 74–77.

[120] Chang, 241.

a Chinese man nearby with a camera," whom they feared to be a plainclothes policeman.[121] An analysis of U.S. coverage of China in the 1990s found the frame moved from containment to engagement to globalization, all oscillating between ideals of democratization and practical interests.[122] The correspondence analyzed for this section also presents a confusing portrait of China, torn between a quasi-colonial gaze constructing the country as an untapped market, a few enduring cultural stereotypes, and a genuine attempt to understand a country the West knew very little about.

The persistence of stereotypes and cultural cues is the most visible indicator of how daunting the task of understanding China appeared to journalists – it was easier to talk about Peking duck or "firecrackers and Coca-Cola" festivities than about a gigantic power "representing one-fourth of the world's people" in the process of remaking itself along its idiosyncratic model.[123] Following around Blumenthal as he toured his old Shanghai home gave journalists an opportunity to remind readers that the city had once been the realm of "opium sellers, pimps and beggars," a den of "rampant disease" and "rampant vice," where dead bodies were "routinely cast into the street," and where hot water had been a luxury, and perhaps still was.[124] Describing a banquet in honor of the visiting Boston Symphony Orchestra in Beijing, one writer devoted a paragraph to, yes, the lack of Peking duck on the menu.[125] Detailing the struggles of Americans trying "to blend inconspicuously into the life of this isolated Chinese city [Kunming]" – at best a quixotic task the journalist uncritically reported – Mathews seemed to bristle with her protagonists at the newly found Chinese will to "firmly make all the rules for foreigners inside their borders."[126] On a cruise on the Yangtze River, she provided this postcard snapshot of immutable China:

> As the sun slowly burns off the haze at water level, the shadowy forms on shore take shape. It becomes clear that the chanting comes from a gang of skinny men struggling upstream step by step, hauling a heavily laden barge with long

121 Linda Mathews, "China 'Democracy Wall' Is Bare," *Los Angeles Times*, April 14, 1979, A14; Jay Mathews, "Wallposters Vanish across China as Open Debate Is Muted," *Washington Post*, April 14, 1979, A12.

122 Chin-Chuan Lee, "Established Pluralism: US Elite Media Discourse about China Policy," *Journalism Studies* 3–3 (2002): 343–357.

123 William J. Eaton, "U.S. Opens Embassy in Peking Ceremony," *Los Angeles Times*, March 1, 1979, B9. The firecrackers and Coke image was also picked up by Richard J. Levine, "China Agrees to Pay Americans 41 Cents on the Dollar for Property Seized in 1949," *Wall Street Journal*, March 2, 1979, 8.

124 William J. Eaton, "Blumenthal Tours Old Haunts in Shanghai," *Los Angeles Times*, March 4, 1979, B10; Edward Cowan, "His Old Home in China Seen by Blumenthal," *New York Times*, March 4, 1979, 13; Hobart Rowen, "Nostalgia in Shanghai Blumenthal Tours Boyhood Ghetto Home," *Washington Post*, March 4, 1979, A1.

125 Harold C. Schonberg, "Boston Symphony Moves on to Peking," *New York Times*, March 17, 1979, A10.

126 Linda Mathews, "Americans Struggle to Blend In," *Los Angeles Times*, April 20, 1979, F4.

> ropes slung over their shoulders. For centuries, men have pulled boats up the Yangtze to reach the treasures of inland China, straining their muscles against the current of one of the world's mightiest streams. As a three-day trip down the river from Chonqing (Chungking) to Wuhan suggests, neither the 20th century nor the advent of Communist rule has had much impact on life along the river.... Yet, despite the ancient pace of life and the dreamlike panoramas along the river, the Yangtze is on its way to becoming one of China's economic lifelines.[127]

"Old Chinese traits" were also dragged in when correspondents perceptively tried to confront looming problems, like housing in the growing metropolises. "Family togetherness" was a virtue made out of necessity in workers' housing projects, where families of six lived in a room.[128] A story about changing divorce mores seemed "a tale out of an old Chinese novel," although the court case spoke of "life under the Communists: the strength of peer pressure, the persistence of such traditional values as filial piety and the ready resort to Communist phraseology in everyday life."[129] In fairness, a few simplistic visual cues dominated stories about U.S.-Chinese relations too, with most correspondents captivated by a "brand new" American flag fluttering under "a sparkling winter sun" as the embassy opened, an event at which a few journalists, "well traveled men who consider themselves rather sophisticated," admitted feeling "choked up."[130]

When it came to explaining modern China, journalists seemed most captivated by the spread of trade, business and entrepreneurship – a very reductive discourse that ignored seismic changes in China's cultural and political landscape. In Shanghai, "a shopper's city," correspondents found evidence of "the new interest in consumer goods."[131] "American businessmen in Peking have quickly become reconciled to the fact that the Chinese will proceed at their own pace and there isn't any way to hasten the process" – a construction of fast Westerners slowed in the march to progress by tardy Easterners that dates all the way to Perry's expedition to Japan in 1853 – but they still regarded China "as a lush new market," another typically imperialist

[127] Linda Mathews, "The Yangtze: China's Past Joins Future," *Los Angeles Times*, April 27, 1979, B1.

[128] William J. Eaton, "China Housing Project: Room to Share," *Los Angeles Times*, March 18, 1979, E3. On the housing problem, see also Hobart Rowen, "Housing for the Masses," *Washington Post*, March 24, 1979, E1.

[129] Fox Butterfield, "Chinese Law Eases Divorce – Or Does It?" *New York Times*, April 22, 1979, 13.

[130] Edward Cowan, "China Will Pay 41 Cents on Dollar for American Assets Seized in '49," *New York Times*, March 2, 1979, A5; Edward Cowan, "Vietnam Fighting Overshadows Progress in Peking Trade Talks," *New York Times*, March 1, 1979, A8; Hobart Rowen, "U.S. Formally Opens Embassy in China," *Washington Post*, March 1, 1979, A23.

[131] William J. Eaton, "Blumenthal Tours Old Haunts in Shanghai," *Los Angeles Times*, March 4, 1979, B10.

construction.[132] A *New York Times* reporter toured a bicycle factory and found it reflected the history of China, that is, "product development, improved productivity, bootstrap automation and a new sense of freedom and purpose."[133] Visiting a farming commune, the same reporter noted some residents were raising pigs "for private gain" and called it "a radical brand of doctrinal flexibility and individualism," but a colleague highlighted the difficulties of promoting efficiency without incentives.[134]

In the best tradition of foreign correspondence that problematizes realities instead of reducing them, however, most correspondents also explored the social and political contradictions that they saw, including "a campaign to clamp down on dissent" that one called "government backtracking."[135] A *New York Times* reporter noted that protestors were continuing to put up wall posters demanding human rights in Shanghai, reflecting that "the new, more open atmosphere" had not been entirely squelched by "conservative backlash from the Communist bureaucracy."[136] Two colleagues in Guangzhou (Canton) for the *Los Angeles Times* and *Washington Post*, on the contrary, found "dampened interest in political debate" and "a perceptible amount of paranoia" replacing efforts toward "Western-style political freedom" – implicitly still a foreign concept in the East.[137]

As so often before, journalists found themselves to be unwitting mediators between political groups and, by reflex, the American audience. The *New York Times* correspondent in Shanghai for a visit by the Boston Symphony Orchestra related that a group of young Chinese men wanting to get permission to return to Shanghai from their distant farm jobs "tried to publicize their cause by using an event attended not only by local notables but also by American reporters."[138] He also touched on the exceedingly controversial subject of the cultural revolution in describing one Chinese pianist who had been a victim of its "unhappy history" and was now in need of "some polish and a thorough

[132] Richard J. Levine, "China Agrees to Pay Americans 41 Cents on the Dollar for Property Seized in 1949," *Wall Street Journal*, March 2, 1979, 8; Edward Cowan, "China Needs Western Wares But Can It Pay for Them?" *New York Times*, March 11, 1979, E3.

[133] Edward Cowan, "Innovation at the Forever Bicycle Factory," *New York Times*, March 18, 1979, F1.

[134] Fox Butterfield, "China Is Trying New Incentives for Its Farmers," *New York Times*, April 26, 1979, A11.

[135] "What's News," 1, and Barry Kramer, "China Opens an Attack to Subdue Clamor for Individual Freedom and Democracy," *Wall Street Journal*, April 16, 1979, 17.

[136] Fox Butterfield, "Critical Wall Posters on View in Shanghai Despite Officials' Ban," *New York Times*, April 16, 1979, A1.

[137] Linda Mathews, "China 'Democracy Wall' Is Bare," *Los Angeles Times*, April 14, 1979, A14; Jay Mathews, "Wallposters Vanish across China as Open Debate Is Muted," *Washington Post*, April 14, 1979, A12.

[138] Harold C. Schonberg, "Shanghai Youths Use Boston Symphony Visit for Protest," *New York Times*, March 16, 1979, A11.

exposure to Western musical thought."[139] An article sought to explain the very public nature of a birth control campaign to Americans who "would be embarrassed to have their neighbors know what method of birth control, if any, they are using."[140] Others shed light on China's drive to liberalize and modernize and on its successes and failures. Correspondents described eager young Chinese trying to learn English for a shot at the global job market, the resurgence of prostitution for Western currency, and the government's efforts to control intellectuals and the flourishing counterculture.[141]

The normalization of U.S.-Chinese relations, then, brought an eager corps of correspondents to the rising power. Often, their discourse of China was weighed down by a heritage of stereotypical images, a sense of innate Western superiority and anti-communism, and a tendency to see the country only as a giant business venture. But correspondents on the ground also tried to make sense of the contradictions that they saw between a strict communist regime and openings toward freedom, and to tell their readers what daily life was like in a country that had been blacked out for thirty years. They hit on several of the themes that would prove important – economic liberalization without corresponding civil liberties, a complex love-hate relationship with American ideas, and a production juggernaut. Even though ducks and dreamscapes dominated, these pioneer correspondents' constructions of China proved remarkably perceptive. Despite the overbearing Cold War frame, so did some of their colleagues' discourses of Afghanistan, where American foreign policy was unwittingly laying the seeds for a major challenge in the post–Cold War era.

Soviet Withdrawal from Afghanistan: A Pyrrhic Cold War Win

> WASHINGTON (AP) – The United States welcomed the withdrawal Monday of Soviet troops from Afghanistan and renewed its pledge to support Moslem rebels as they fight to take control of the Kabul government.... The statement did not make clear whether the United States supported the rebels in a civil war with the pro-Soviet government or also in attacks on Red Army forces as they depart from the war-torn country.... President Najib has denounced the rebels, who are called "freedom fighters" by the Reagan administration, as "terrorists" and "barbarians" and "fanatics who laughingly preach a holy war."[142]

[139] Harold C. Schonberg, "Long-Jailed Pianist Soloist with Boston," *New York Times*, March 19, 1979, C45.

[140] Fox Butterfield, "As Population Nears a Billion, China Stresses Curbs," *New York Times*, April 24, 1979, A2.

[141] Fox Butterfield, "China Reassessing Its Liberalization Drive," *New York Times*, April 23, 1979, A3; Jay Mathews, "Easy as ABC? English-Language Craze Takes China by Storm," *Washington Post*, April 18, 1979, A1.

[142] Barry Schweid, "US Welcomes Soviet Pullout from Afghanistan; Vows to Back Rebels," Associated Press, May 16, 1988.

Few Cold War frames are as heavily laden with irony from a twenty-first century perspective as the jubilation with which Washington greeted the Soviet withdrawal from Afghanistan in 1988, pushed along by Islamist groups funded by the United States, as noted in the AP report just quoted. The war in Afghanistan had indeed weakened the once-mighty Soviet Army, and as Washington predicted, the Afghan government would be taken over by Islamic fundamentalists by 1992. But those same "freedom fighters" hailed by Reagan turned out to be indeed harboring terrorists, including Osama bin Laden, the man who changed the post–Cold War world with the 9/11 attacks on the United States. Only a few of the correspondents sounded caution, but all detailed the difficulties of traditional armed forces in Afghanistan as well as the political uncertainty that lay ahead for the country.

Soviet troops had invaded Afghanistan in late 1979 in an attempt to overthrow the government, which, although Marxist, was divided internally, disliked by the population that rejected its secular laws, and intent on reaching out to Soviet enemies, potentially destabilizing an important Soviet border. Whether Moscow's move was protective or imperialistic remains a matter for historians to dispute,[143] but the Carter administration, already riled by the Iran hostage crisis that year and unable to understand rising Islamic fundamentalism in the region,[144] saw it as a major Soviet invasion in an area already conflicted and a gateway to ports and oil. The war in Afghanistan put détente on hold, created a U.S.-Pakistan arms channel that would ultimately arm the mujahideen (including bin Laden), to whom covert aid was also authorized in a significant policy change from containment to regime change in the Soviet sphere, and committed the United States even more deeply to the region.[145] Even though they had managed to install a puppet leader quickly, the Soviets remained mired through the 1980s in guerrilla warfare in the country, which some Soviet leaders called "our Vietnam."[146] Brutal acts abounded on both sides, and Soviet public opinion soared against the war.

The diminished threat to the United States, however, did not encourage the Reagan administration to pull back. On the contrary, the U.S. military presence in the Persian Gulf area continued to grow, and the first Reagan administration reinforced a hard line against the Soviet Union while training and arming fundamentalists with sophisticated weaponry, including deadly antiaircraft missiles, at the tune of hundreds of millions of dollars each year.

[143] Combs, 270; Henry S. Bradsher, *Afghan Communism and Soviet Intervention* (Oxford: Oxford University Press, 1999).

[144] Herring, 849–853.

[145] Gilles Dorronsoro, *Revolution Unending: Afghanistan: 1979 to the Present* (New York: Columbia University Press, 2005); Roy Gutman, *How We Missed the Story: Osama bin Laden, the Taliban, and the Hijacking of Afghanistan* (Washington: United States Institutes of Peace, 2008).

[146] Hafizullah Emadi, *Dynamics of Political Development in Afghanistan: The British, Russian, and American Invasions* (New York: Palgrave Macmillan, 2010), 121.

In May 1988, largely because of U.S. support to the insurgents as well as Gorbachev's desire for better relations, the Soviet Union began withdrawing troops, completing the process in February 1989. It was a dramatic change for Soviet foreign policy toward accommodation despite, or some argue because of, little willingness to compromise on Washington's part.[147] The Soviet Union's collapse in 1991 prompted the collapse of its client Kabul, which was seized by Islamic fundamentalists in the spring of 1992, and violent struggles for internal supremacy continued to mar Afghanistan. The Taliban prevailed in the mid-1990s, but the world had ceased paying attention.

The Soviet invasion catapulted the fractured, underdeveloped country into the global media spotlight, which stopped probing in its corners as soon as the Soviets were gone in what one researcher called "one of the great lapses in the history of the profession."[148] It was a particularly ironic case of missed opportunities to report from a place that would become a top global preoccupation for the first decade of the 2000s, but one increasingly likely to happen as foreign correspondents were pulled away in the age of crisis in journalism, which is discussed in the next chapter. One study of U.S. press coverage of the Soviet war in Afghanistan found that coverage took cues from the evolution in U.S.-Soviet relations, with less negative portrayals of Moscow's acts as the withdrawal drew near.[149] The coverage analyzed in this section focused pointedly on the Soviet Union – the "spheres of influence" partition, as the *New York Times* correspondent put it – and it did exhibit a bit of gloating over the Soviets' first "taste of military failure" and how the withdrawal was timed for a Reagan-Gorbachev meeting.[150] It also constructed, however, a complex picture of Afghanistan that left very much open to question whether seeing the Red Army's back would be the end of the story.

The correspondents' interest was clearly in the Soviets, not the Afghanis, and articles succinctly captured the Cold War repercussions of the military actions. A long analysis in the *Los Angeles Times* focused on the shift in Soviet policy that the withdrawal represented, the first time since 1917 that the Union was

[147] Andrew Bennett, *Condemned to Repetition? The Rise, Fall, and Reprise of Soviet-Russian Military Interventionism, 1973–1996* (Cambridge, MA: MIT Press, 1999); Sarah E. Mendelson, *Changing Course: Ideas, Politics, and the Soviet Withdrawal from Afghanistan* (Princeton, NJ: Princeton University Press, 1998).

[148] Gutman, 261–262.

[149] Jothik Krishnaiah, Nancy Signorielli and Douglas M. McLeod, "The Evil Empire Revisited: *New York Times* Coverage of the Soviet Intervention in and Withdrawal from Afghanistan," *Journalism Quarterly* 70–3 (Autumn 1993): 647–655.

[150] Steven R. Weisman, "Soviet Strengthens Economic Links to Northern Afghanistan," *New York Times*, May 20, 1988, A9; Rone Tempest, "U.S. Hopes for Fast Rebel Takeover; Soviet Pullout to Test Afghan Hold on Cities," *Los Angeles Times*, May 13, 1988, 1. On the timing, see Steven R. Weisman, "25% of Russians in Afghan Force Will Leave in May," *New York Times*, May 15, 1988, 1; Richard M. Weintraub, "Soviet Gives Details on Pullout; Afghans to Inherit Facilities, Equipment Worth $1 Billion," *Washington Post*, May 15, 1988, A1.

"retreating from the front line" of "worldwide socialist revolution."[151] The same writer also reflected the changed mood among the Red Army, making them sound and look very similar to U.S. soldiers in Vietnam in their being "troubled by doubts about why they were sent here, about the mission they were given and about the way they carried it out."[152] Another Soviet soldier told reporters "that Afghanistan was 'a beautiful but terrifying place' that he was happy to leave."[153] The dominant construction of Soviet soldiers focused on human and universal traits, as in the episode of a Russian wife rushing police lines to plant a "swooning kiss" on her returning soldier husband: "The kiss of Oxana Gerasimenko made it official: Eight years and 143 days after Soviet troops invaded Afghanistan, the first of the boys were home and the rest were on their way."[154]

One of the most striking features of reporting from Afghanistan in 1988 is how clearly articles identified U.S. covert aid to the insurgents – variously called the "U.S.-backed moujahedeen," "U.S.-backed moujahedeen rebels," "U.S.-backed guerrillas," "American-backed guerrillas," and "U.S.-backed Moslem rebels." (The AP explained in a story that "Mujahedeen, or holy warrior, is a term the rebels use to describe themselves.")[155] The *New York Times* quoted a "Western diplomat" saying of the arms available to the guerrillas, "They're really stuffed to the gills," and explained that they were "largely supplied by the Central Intelligence Agency."[156] The *Washington Post* hypothesized that "Soviet inability to develop an effective countermeasure to the Stinger missiles" – courtesy of the United States – might have caused the withdrawal.[157]

U.S. support for the rebels was stated repeatedly and with such a matter-of-fact tone that it clearly points to an overarching discourse of U.S. legitimate interest in stopping the Soviets anywhere, at any costs, even this late in the Cold War. One reporter, "strolling the streets" in rebel-leaning Mazar-i-Sharif, wrote that "several residents, some speaking broken English, thanked him for

[151] Michael Parks, "Analysis: Retreat in Global Revolution; Afghan Quagmire Brings Basic Soviet Policy Shift," *Los Angeles Times*, May 14, 1988, 1.

[152] Michael Parks, "'Sick of This War,' 'What Was It All For?' a Soldier Asks," *Los Angeles Times*, May 16, 1988, 1.

[153] Steven R. Weisman, "Soviet Formally Pulls First Troops out of the Long Afghanistan War," *New York Times*, May 16, 1988, A1.

[154] Rone Tempest, "Cheers and Tears Greet Returning Soviet Soldiers," *Los Angeles Times*, May 19, 1988, 1.

[155] Bryan Wilder, "Guerrilla Commander Outlines Plans for Future Afghan Fighting," Associated Press, May 15, 1988.

[156] John Kifner, "Several Garrisons Are Said to Fall to Afghan Rebels," *New York Times*, May 23, 1988, A12; John Kifner, "With Afghanistan Guerrillas: Rocket Raid in Heady Times," *New York Times*, May 27, 1988, A1.

[157] Richard M. Weintraub, "Afghan Combat Offered Soviet Army Some Painful Lessons," *Washington Post*, May 15, 1988, A28.

the U.S. government's aid to the rebels.... 'America is beautiful,' one man said."[158] A *New York Times* correspondent even managed to ride with a group of insurgents and reported about their fervent prayer rituals, their "traditional flat wool Afghan cap that looks something like a rolled-up paper bag," and their commander, "a sturdy 35-year-old from a merchant family in Jalalabad who managed an air of dignity even while simultaneously smoking and shouting into his walkie-talkie."[159]

Who exactly the rebels were puzzled correspondents, like the one cited at the beginning of this chapter. The construction of Afghanistan itself seems shrouded in mystery both geographical and social, "this arid, inhospitable terrain in Central Asia, land of the Pushtun warrior and the Hindu Kush Mountains," in the words of a *Los Angeles Times* writer in Kabul.[160] In that context, a few stories give hints that Washington's victory might prove more elusive than immediately recognized. The same reporter just quoted described "several hundred schoolchildren" in Kabul chanting "Death to the CIA" outside the U.S. embassy. Others found that most of the country's "more educated, westernized elite have chosen to cast their lot with neither side in the bitter Afghan conflict."[161] The young, who had grown up in a country at war, were torn between "conflicting ideologies," Marxism and Islam, which would be difficult to reconcile.[162]

Kabul residents were described as feeling "intensely personal" and yet fatalistic as they witnessed the departure of the Soviets, "the latest of many outsiders who, over the centuries, have overstayed their welcome among an intensely proud people." They were tired of war, the article continued, "even though it runs against the image often portrayed in the West of the fierce Afghan warrior bent on revenge, or the guerrilla fighting a holy war for Islam or the dedicated communist battling for the survival of his regime."[163]

The prevailing mood was one of "cynicism, frayed nerves, anguished speculation and helplessness" – hardly the victory portrait painted by U.S. diplomats.[164] The AP reporter stuck in Peshawar, Pakistan, by the

[158] Rone Tempest, "Northern Area Seen as Fallback Position for Afghan Regime," *Los Angeles Times*, May 20, 1988, 24.

[159] John Kifner, "With Afghanistan Guerrillas: Rocket Raid in Heady Times," *New York Times*, May 27, 1988, A1.

[160] Rone Tempest, "U.S. Hopes for Fast Rebel Takeover; Soviet Pullout to Test Afghan Hold on Cities," *Los Angeles Times*, May 13, 1988, 1.

[161] Richard M. Weintraub, "New Afghan Premier Seen as Reconciliation Force," *Washington Post*, May 29, 1988, A37.

[162] Scheherezade Faramarzi, "The Two Educations of Afghanistan's Youth," Associated Press, May 17, 1988.

[163] Richard M. Weintraub, "Kabul's People Fear the Future," *Washington Post*, May 23, 1988, A14.

[164] Steven R. Weisman, "In Kabul, Rising Fear and Cynicism," *New York Times*, May 23, 1988, A12.

government's ban against the AP discussed later in this section, found that people believed "peace was still far away," and he wondered what it would take for peace to "ever [return] to the mountains and deserts of Afghanistan."[165] When an AP correspondent was finally allowed back in Kabul at the end of May, her lead, while straightforward, set up such a contrast that it implicitly spelled more trouble for the country: "President Najib opened a multi-party national Parliament with a call to rebels to abandon their eight-year war and join the government. Also Sunday, a guerrilla leader claimed anti-government forces control 90 percent of the Afghan countryside."[166] Some of the discourse seemed to encompass all superpower actions in the country, not just the Soviets'. Afghans had resisted communism because they "would not reject their feudal and tribal traditions in favor of coerced modernization," which left open the question of how they would react to U.S. influence.[167] And perhaps the war provided a series of lessons "to a superpower that became involved in the civil conflict of a small neighbor" – a construction that hardly applied only to the Soviets in the Cold War era – most important of which was winning "the necessary backing from the local population to deny that same support to [its] foes."[168]

As many times before in many countries, U.S. journalists became part of the story, played by political actors on all sides who were increasingly conscious of the power the media had in public opinion and international affairs. For *Los Angeles Times* editors, glasnost and Soviet defeat meant "a Soviet officer on Sunday, feeling free to tell Times correspondent Michael Parks in Kabul that it had all been a mistake."[169] For the Associated Press, a question posed by a correspondent during a news conference with the Afghan government meant all its reporters were barred from traveling to the country to cover the withdrawal.[170] As noted in the 1967 war, journalists reported on Soviet media management: The return of the first soldiers in the border town of Termez was "a show for the media," with about a hundred foreign reporters "bused up to the border from Kabul" and allowed into the Soviet Union without visas. Even U.S. intelligence satellites had noted the preparation of the parade grounds,

165 Bryan Wilder, "Soviet Withdrawal Is a Great Day but Peace Is Far Away," Associated Press, May 15, 1988; Bryan Wilder, "Peace in Afghanistan Will Require Massive Reconstruction," Associated Press, May 16, 1988.

166 Earleen Fisher, "Najib Convenes Parliament, Calls for Guerrilla Cease-Fire," Associated Press, May 30, 1988.

167 Steven R. Weisman, "In Afghanistan, Communists Stand Alone and Divided," *New York Times*, May 22, 1988, 147.

168 Richard M. Weintraub, "Afghan Combat Offered Soviet Army Some Painful Lessons," *Washington Post*, May 15, 1988, A28.

169 "Afghanistan as History," *Los Angeles Times*, May 17, 1988, 6.

170 "Associated Press Barred from Covering Afghan Withdrawal," Associated Press, May 11, 1988.

and American officials "had advised reporters that the Soviets were planning something out of the ordinary."[171]

That Cold War intelligence should pick up PR information for reporters is a fitting comment on the role of the media, and on the evaporating atmosphere of terror that had ruled the world for nearly fifty years of superpower struggle. Correspondence from Afghanistan is particularly striking for how rarely it was about that country compared to the Soviet Union, but a few stories did probe into the Islamist rebels and might have led readers to question the blindly anti-communist line Washington had taken. The last Cold War act – the dissolution of the Soviet Union – also happened under the U.S. media glare, and it raised even more serious doubts about the world order.

Soviet Union Collapses in 1991: Pax Americana, or a Scarier World?

> After sitting down in front of the camera, but before it began to roll, Gorbachev realized he'd forgotten to tuck a pen in the pocket of his black suit. So [CNN president Tom] Johnson fished from his own pocket a shiny black Mont Blanc ballpoint and handed it to the 60-year-old Soviet leader, who used it to sign the decree giving up his post as commander-in-chief and transferring authority over the country's nuclear arsenal to Yeltsin.... As the TV crews were headed to the exit, they ran into a pair of guards rushing down another corridor, away from another pack of photographers. Camera flashes showed something large, and bright red, in the guards' arms. It was the Soviet Union's hammer-and-sickle flag, just lowered from atop the Kremlin.[172]

There could be no better vignette of the power of U.S. media at the end of the Cold War than the story just quoted. Under the gaze of an AP correspondent – the only print journalist to witness Gorbachev's resignation inside the Kremlin, according to the AP editor's note – the last Soviet president used a pen provided by CNN to sign his resignation from commanding the Red Army and Moscow's powerful nuclear arsenal. At that moment, with the Soviet Union dead and formally buried, the United States stood on top of the world as the sole superpower, and its news media were right there with it. And yet, there is something almost wistful, dare one say painful, in the reporter's telling of the two guards that, having lowered the once mighty red flag one last time, try to scurry away from the "pack" of journalists.

The most striking aspect of the discourse in U.S. coverage of the last days of the Soviet Union in December 1991 is its complete lack of cheering in front of a nearly fifty-year-old enemy that had collapsed, taking a powerful ideology with

[171] Rone Tempest, "Cheers and Tears Greet Returning Soviet Soldiers," *Los Angeles Times*, May 19, 1988, 1. The *New York Times* also discussed the invitation to see the withdrawal; Steven R. Weisman, "A First Soviet Unit Quits Afghanistan," *New York Times*, May 19, 1988, A1.

[172] Alan Cooperman, "Gorbachev's Final Moments in Office: Calm, Dignified, Ready to Go," Associated Press, December 25, 1991. The pen episode is also relayed in David Remnick, "At the End: 'For Me, They Have Poisoned the Air,'" *Washington Post*, December 26, 1991, A1.

it.[173] Rather, correspondence constructed new lurking dangers as even scarier than the defunct evil empire, as Reagan had called it as recently as 1983 – "yes, evil empire," the *Washington Post* editors insisted, "imposed by force, destroyed by the popular will."[174] The construction derived in part from a discourse of Russian apathy, which was the latest incarnation of the "can they do democracy?" frame. It was sometimes stated explicitly, as in an article that referred to the "somewhat inhospitable Russian soil" where democracy struggled to take root, and another that complained the commonwealth agreements all lacked "a ringing historic quote in the vein of the American Declaration of Independence."[175] The construction was also shaped by the perceptive realization that fragmentation, exacerbated nationalisms and ethno-religious strife made the future ahead murky.

In 1985, Gorbachev became the leader of a Soviet Union he quickly realized was nearing economic collapse with its overwhelming emphasis on defense spending. He immediately embarked on a series of negotiations with the Reagan administration on arms control, and, after a few false starts, the two leaders signed a major reduction agreement on nuclear forces. Shortly after, Gorbachev also substantially reduced Soviet arms and troops in Eastern Europe, effectively allowing for the end of the arms race in the divided continent. In 1989, the litmus test of Gorbachev's reform spirit came in Poland. As freedom movements spread there and in other countries in the Soviet orbit, Gorbachev stunned the world – as many reporters would put it – by refusing to interfere and even ordering the Polish Communist Party to respect the results of free elections that overwhelmingly voted into power a noncommunist government. The Soviet grip on Europe was shattered, with the Berlin Wall coming down a few months later, communist governments being voted out of office in one country after the other, and East and West Germany reuniting.

The three Baltic republics of Estonia, Latvia, and Lithuania agitated for independence from the Soviet Union in 1990, beginning to chip away at the USSR and raising fears of civil strife in other republics that had nuclear warheads. Gorbachev struggled to retain power over a Soviet population to whom he had allowed freedom of dissent and religion in the name of "glasnost" and "perestroika," or openness and reconstruction, but whose quality of life was in free fall with the economy. The Bush administration started fearing that such a rapid collapse of the Soviet Union might threaten global stability and endanger arms reduction, so Washington refrained from any gloating at the archrival's troubles.[176] In 1991, President Bush even traveled to Ukraine, another

[173] Contrary to the argument in Moorcraft and Taylor, 101.

[174] "A Post-Soviet 'Commonwealth,'" *Washington Post*, December 10, 1991, A20; Herring, 866.

[175] Michael Dobbs, "Reformed out of a Job; Gorbachev Is Left Ruling Kingdom of Air," *Washington Post*, December 15, 1991, A1; Serge Schmemann, "Hard Realism Wins the Day," *New York Times*, December 22, 1991, 13.

[176] Herring, 906, 913.

republic chomping at the bit, to suggest it should move slowly on independence. Shortly after, however, hardliners in Gorbachev's government, fearing he was losing control over the republics, staged a coup. As Russians rose against the plotters, Gorbachev returned to power and kicked the Communist Party out of government. By December, however, the three biggest, richest republics – Russia, Ukraine and Belarus – broke away from the Soviet Union and formed a much looser Commonwealth of Independent States. Most of the other republics joined them and, after making one last try to salvage the central government, Gorbachev resigned on December 25, 1991, writing "the end" to the Cold War era.

For the historic reformer, it was a bitter end.[177] For the United States, it was a relatively short-lived triumph – durable peace among great powers seemed ensured, in a way that it had never been, but Pax Americana was a fleeting illusion.[178] The guiding principle of U.S. foreign policy – containment – was gone, and new challenges arose, from nationalism to terrorism to the rise of new economic powers. Correspondence and editorials from the last days of the USSR were tinged with the sober realization of many of those dangers and the need for continued U.S. global presence. The *Washington Post* editors, for example, urged "people who live in fortunate places like the United States" to provide aid in response to upcoming economic hardships for former Soviet citizens, and they cautioned U.S. diplomats that their work was only getting harder.[179] Similarly, *Wall Street Journal* editors called for "practitioners of Western capitalism and banking" to step up and help ensure "that the political institutions of this huge land mass should not again assume a structure wholly inconsistent with those of the Free World" but rather would move closer to "the politically civilized world."[180] At the *Los Angeles Times*, editors worried about nuclear control and "major urban riots," and they bleakly concluded that the "fracturing of the Soviet Union could imperil international security" – surely not a victorious statement on the end of the Cold War.[181] *New York Times* editors sounded the alarm on "narrow nationalism unleashed by democratization."[182]

U.S. journalists flocked to Moscow and the agitating Soviet republics and covered the collapse of the Soviet Union breathlessly – one *Washington Post*

177 Mendelson, 126; Don Oberdofer, *From the Cold War to a New Era: The United States and the Soviet Union, 1983–1991* (Baltimore: Johns Hopkins University Press, 1998).

178 John Lewis Gaddis, *The United States and the End of the Cold War: Implications, Reconsiderations, Provocations* (New York: Oxford University Press, 1992), 15.

179 "The Rubble of the Ruble," *Washington Post*, December 8, 1991, C6; "... Mr. Yeltsin Takes Over," *Washington Post*, December 26, 1991, A22.

180 "Goodbye USSR, Hello CIS," *Wall Street Journal*, December 13, 1991, A14; "Absolutely, Positively Over," *Wall Street Journal*, December 10, 1991, A14.

181 "A Bit of Haste at the Creation: Will New Commonwealth Prove a Short-Lived Dream?" *Los Angeles Times*, December 10, 1991, 6.

182 "Out of the Soviet Wreckage," *New York Times*, December 10, 1991, A30.

correspondent said this was the stunning end of an era of "breathtaking change for both the Soviet Union and the world."[183] They interviewed everybody from leaders to workers in Moscow's train stations, and focused on everything from nuclear warheads to increasingly rare chunks of meat in state-run stores. In a sign of journalistic convergence to come, the correspondence was the most self-referential encountered yet in this research, routinely citing Soviet news agencies like Tass and Interfax, Soviet newspapers like *Izvestia*, Soviet and international television broadcasts, and the international press. That led to most articles using the same short quotes from the main actors, such as Gorbachev's warning that the collapse of the Soviet Union would make the ongoing civil war in Yugoslavia look like "a joke," and focusing on the same images, including the hammer-and-sickle flag making its last stand at the Kremlin, that "timeless fortress of czars and general secretaries."[184]

Among the most revealing constructions are the definitions of the Soviet Union and the "boilerplate" paragraphs in which the U.S. press summarized its historical importance – an interesting hint that readers might need a refresher on what the Cold War had been about. "Boilerplates" are nonattributed, brief descriptive summaries that, while aiming to be uncontroversial and repetitive, provide the major framing of the issue at hand.[185] Already at the beginning of December 1991, correspondence gave the Soviet Union up and called it "imploding," "crumbling," "fallen," "worn out," "a mortally wounded empire," "the former Communist superpower," "the ruins of the Soviet empire," "one-time military superpower," "decaying superpower," "closer and closer to becoming a relic," "shattered union," "wreckage of 74 years of Communist rule," but also "a geopolitical colossus straddling one-sixth of the Earth's surface." The Gorbachev years were described as extraordinary, a period in which the Soviet Union "metamorphosed from proud, totalitarian superpower into a fledgling democracy that no longer hid the truth about its hopeless economy and shameful past."[186]

183 Michael Dobbs, "Gorbachev to Quit If States Take Over; Shifting of Power Speeds Up in Moscow," *Washington Post*, December 13, 1991, A1.

184 Michael Dobbs, "Slavic Republics Declare Soviet Union Liquidated," *Washington Post*, December 9, 1991, A1; Francis X. Clines, "Soviet Union's Last Rites: New Year's Eve the Goal," *New York Times*, December 18, 1991, A1. On the flag, see Michael Parks and Carey Goldberg, "Soviet Union Set to End Dec. 31," *Los Angeles Times*, December 18, 1991, 1; Elisabeth Rubinfien, "Gorbachev Agrees to Cede Soviet Structures to Russia – Moving of Certain Entities Expected by Year End; Some Disputes Remain," *Wall Street Journal*, December 18, 1991, A3; Thomas Ginsberg, "Gorbachev Promises Decision Soon on Stepping Down," Associated Press, December 22, 1991.

185 Colleen Cotter, *News Talk: Investigating the Language of Journalism* (Cambridge: Cambridge University Press, 2010), 176–181.

186 Peter Gumbel, "Fading Beacon: As Soviet Events Seem to Bypass Gorbachev, Talk Is of His Legacy – He Set Change in Motion, Say Muscovites, Then Failed to Stay at Its Forefront – Maybe a Role for Him Still," *Wall Street Journal*, December 13, 1991, A1.

Here is how the *Los Angeles Times* summarized the Soviet Union: The "continent-sized state created by V. I. Lenin 69 years ago, which came to be the vanguard of Communist revolutions across the globe, the greatest power in Europe and the chief Cold War threat to the United States."[187] For the *New York Times*, it was simply "a state that had fascinated and frightened the world for 70 years."[188] The AP inserted this boilerplate in its story about the Alma-Ata agreement that ended the Soviet Union: "Born in the Bolshevik revolution of 1917 and forged in the fire of Stalinist terror, the Soviet Union was a political and military colossus of this century. Its people suffered under repressive Communist rule, but its influence was felt in every corner of the world, with half of Europe under its sway for four decades."[189] (The AP also distributed a pronunciation guide to the "less familiar republics of the former Soviet Union" – much like newspapers had for Chinese names when covering the Boxer Rebellion in 1900.)[190] These obituaries of the Soviet Union discursively established its key feature in the Western press: a formidable historical power that had seemed unassailable.

As to what brought it down, in a chronology of "key events" in the breakup of the Soviet Union, created by the AP, the first date was March 11, 1985 – Gorbachev's election to general secretary of the Communist Party.[191] Indeed, strikingly, the correspondence clearly constructed the cause of the collapse as its internal combustion and the new air let in by Gorbachev – "reform communism turned out to be a contradiction in terms, like fried snowballs," one reporter wrote – but it gave no credit to U.S. policies or leaders, previewing later historians' assessments.[192] Sounding struck by the rather tragic end of Gorbachev's days in power, most correspondents wrote he held his place in history as the man who, simply, "ended the Cold War" – a construction that challenged Washington's view of its own accomplishments.[193] The desire for

[187] Elizabeth Shogren, "Slavic States Call Soviet Union Dead, Form a Commonwealth," *Los Angeles Times*, December 9, 1991, 1.

[188] Celestine Bohlen, "This Way Out: Yeltsin Leads a Bold Move to Replace the Soviet Union," *New York Times*, December 15, 1991, E1.

[189] Alan Cooperman, "11 Republics Sign Agreements on Commonwealth, Ending Soviet Union," Associated Press, December 21, 1991.

[190] "Soviet-Politics-Pronouncers," Associated Press, December 21, 1991.

[191] "Chronology of Breakup of Soviet Union," Associated Press, December 9, 1991.

[192] Michael Dobbs, "Reformed out of a Job; Gorbachev Is Left Ruling Kingdom of Air," *Washington Post*, December 15, 1991, A1; Herring, 862. See also Margaret Shapiro and Fred Hiatt, "Snubs Helped Seal Old Union's Fate; Soviet President Kept in Dark as Leaders Created Commonwealth," *Washington Post*, December 14, 1991, A1; Elisabeth Rubinfien, "Gorbachev Resigns as Soviet President with Dignity, Defiance, and Warnings – U.S. Recognizes Republics, Immediately Establishes Relations with Russia," *Wall Street Journal*, December 26, 1991, A3; Michael Parks, "Commonwealth a New Creature – with Echoes," *Los Angeles Times*, December 14, 1991, 1.

[193] Elizabeth Shogren, "Slavic States Call Soviet Union Dead, Form a Commonwealth," *Los Angeles Times*, December 9, 1991, 1.

independence was linked to rebellion against both seven decades of communist central rule and "centuries of Moscow's czarist rule," a construction of the Russian space as always oppressed that reinforced questions about the viability of freer regimes.[194] Correspondents argued that a "smooth transition" from "centralized dictatorship to a loose confederation of democracies, remains far from certain."[195] "A disjointed people, freed from their decades of dictated misery, faced a frightening new course of shedding collectivism for the promises of individual enterprise. It is a course that remains a mystery for most of the commonwealth's 280 million people," a *New York Times* correspondent summarized.[196]

The pessimism derived from the construction of ordinary Soviet citizens as so backward and dispirited that the fast-track political and economic reforms left them bewildered, unable to understand change or even care. There was an "astonishing nonchalance" in people "so exhausted by their own daily trials and their confusion and despair over the future," whose "daily grind required to put food on the table is too all-consuming to allow time for the contemplation of politics."[197] One correspondent in Yaroslavl found it resembled "the fictitious city of Glupov (Stupidtown)" depicted by a nineteenth-century Russian author, its citizens reacting to change with their "traditional defenses," "skepticism and suspicion."[198]

The assessment of a colleague was at best a backhanded compliment: Despite "traditional Russian gloom about the future," for most people "the taste of freedom seems to have been at least as important as the availability of sausage."[199] The AP's Moscow chief of bureau, however, found that the commonwealth might "remove the Kremlin's traditionally heavy hand from the lives of 285 million people, but it will do little immediately to fill their stomachs or ease their anxiety."[200] A correspondent at Moscow's Food Store No. 4 found that people did not talk about the disintegrating Soviet Union but about how long

194 Fred Hiatt, "Minsk Is No Moscow, and That's the Point for New Grouping," *Washington Post*, December 9, 1991, A16.

195 Fred Hiatt, "Russia, Ukraine See Commonwealth Differently," *Washington Post*, December 13, 1991, A1.

196 Francis X. Clines, "Communist Flag Is Removed; Yeltsin Gets Nuclear Controls," *New York Times*, December 26, 1991, A1.

197 David Remnick, "At the End: 'For Me, They Have Poisoned the Air,'" *Washington Post*, December 26, 1991, A1; Wendy Sloane, "Weary Muscovites Apathetic about Dissolution of Union," Associated Press, December 17, 1991. See also James F. Clarity, "On Moscow's Streets, Worry and Regret," *New York Times*, December 26, 1991, A13.

198 Michael Dobbs, "Crawling toward Revolution," *Washington Post*, December 22, 1991, A1.

199 Peter Gumbel, "Taking Stock: Russians Remember the Gorbachev Years with Mixed Feelings – Ruble Is Worthless, Sausage Is Scarce and Expensive, but Freedom Is Priceless – the Winners and the Losers," *Wall Street Journal*, December 20, 1991, A1.

200 Bryan Brumley, "Slavic Commonwealth Appears to Be Death Blow to Soviet Union," Associated Press, December 9, 1991.

they would have to wait in line to get "fatty hunks of beef."[201] The food shortages were so severe that the United States delivered aid to hospitals, an ironic twist captured by a correspondent: "The American military, after decades of cold war training to fight a hot war against the Soviet Union, arrived here to help this country feed its hungry."[202] Giving the Russian fish might work, but correspondents wondered (again not a little ethnocentrically) whether the Soviets could be taught how to fish. Would American-style capitalism take root, when the most entrepreneurial Muscovites seemed to be the traffic cops who had upped the price of bribes?[203] Would a citizenry accustomed to "incompetence, sloppiness and corruption," who had learned that to "do the minimum and challenge nothing" was "the most effective way to get along," be able to handle freedom?[204]

The whole country was constructed as in shambles, "Tens of millions of [Soviets] were worrying about finding decent and adequate food for the coming week, and about the likelihood that in the grip of a frigid December, the power or heat might fail."[205] "The one thing in the state Lenin founded that is not breaking down, Sergei S. Debov believes, is Lenin," a *New York Times* correspondent wrote referring to the caretaker of Lenin's preserved body in its Moscow mausoleum.[206] One reporter recalled that food shortages in 1917 had been one of the causes of the Bolshevik Revolution but concluded that today's citizens were "only edgy" – people who experienced "civil war, famine, war, mass murder and repression still seem to prefer the humiliation of endless lines, empty shops and political inaction to the terrible unknown," a colleague surmised.[207] An AP correspondent was much more ominous: "A divided military and downtrodden citizenry could explode during the long Russian winter.... For now, the streets are calm. Under a perpetual gray sky, Russians silently slog through a brown mush of snow and mud, ignoring what seem to

201 Steven Gutterman, "Public Wants Food, Not Politics," *Los Angeles Times*, December 10, 1991, 10.

202 James F. Clarity, "U.S. Military Delivers Food to Moscow's Hungry," *New York Times*, December 23, 1991, A11.

203 Charles P. Wallace, "Doing Business: On Going Discount in Soviet Union," *Los Angeles Times*, December 17, 1991, 3; Serge Schmemann, "The Future Is Now, With Russia Unready," *New York Times*, December 22, 1991, E1; Francis X. Clines, "The Free Market Inflates Moscow Traffic Bribery," *New York Times*, December 19, 1991, A14.

204 Thomas Kent, "Soviet State Mixed Achievement and Façade as Its Dream Failed," Associated Press, December 22, 1991.

205 John-Thor Dahlburg, "Gorbachev: President Left without a Country; Upheaval: He Has Brought about His Own Downfall, a Former Aide Says," *Los Angeles Times*, December 9, 1991, 1.

206 Serge Schmemann, "Preserving Lenin, the High-Tech Icon," *New York Times*, December 17, 1991, A14.

207 James F. Clarity, "Moscow's Main News: Prices Will Go Up Jan 2," *New York Times*, December 25, 1991, 6; Serge Schmemann, "The World according to Gorbachev Disappears," *New York Times*, December 8, 1991, E3.

be a thousand daily incitements to riot: shoving in line to buy shoes, paying a day's wages for a few tomatoes, watching limousines race down special lanes reserved for the Kremlin elite. How much longer will they take it?"[208]

Journalists also questioned the redrawing of borders, because many Soviet citizens lived outside their ethnic republics, and raised the specter of "the potentially explosive mix of ethnic tension and territorial disputes."[209] All media mentioned the deadly street violence that erupted in Georgia in late December, and while they objectively stated it was not clear if it was related to the commonwealth, its presence in stories about the Soviet Union made it a part of the ominous discourse. Most journalists seemed skeptical of Russia's "more equal" status in the commonwealth, and they feared it would "supplant the Union as an enterprise that continues to trouble the West."[210] In this context, the repeated references to the nuclear arsenal – with many missiles "still pointed at the United States" – and the confusion over which leader would hold the "button" for nuclear attacks reflected the dominant U.S. policy concern and again emphasized the sense of impending doom.[211] So did the prominence given to Gorbachev's concerns that the end of the Soviet Union would mean anarchy.[212] The search of "a new political organization" was almost secondary

208 Alan Cooperman, "Russian Winter Forecast: Cold, Stormy and Explosive," Associated Press, December 11, 1991.

209 Michael Dobbs, "Gorbachev's Position Erodes Further; 5 Asian Republics Choose to Join Commonwealth," *Washington Post*, December 14, 1991, A1. On ethnic strife, see also Michael Dobbs, "Gorbachev Rejects Commonwealth; Soviet President Faces New Fight for Survival," *Washington Post*, December 10, 1991, A1; Laurie Hays, "Cracks Appear in Yeltsin's New Union," *Wall Street Journal*, December 13, 1991, A1; Michael Parks, "New Entities Now Must Find Their Identities," *Los Angeles Times*, December 22, 1991, 1; Bryan Brumley, "Gorbachev and Yeltsin Set Date for Kremlin Funeral: For the Soviet Union," Associated Press, December 17, 1991.

210 David Remnick, "In New Commonwealth of 'Equals,' Russia Remains the Dominant Force; Historical Status, Space-Age Arms Ensure Regional Primacy," *Washington Post*, December 22, 1991, A39; Michael Parks, "Questions, Answers on Crumbling Old Union," *Los Angeles Times*, December 21, 1991, 17; Celestine Bohlen, "The Union Is Buried: What's Being Born?" *New York Times*, December 9, 1991, A1.

211 Fred Hiatt, "Leaders Vie for Drifting Soviet Army," *Washington Post*, December 11, 1991, A1. Most articles made reference to nuclear issues. For a sample, see Margaret Shapiro, "Gorbachev Rejects Commonwealth; Declaration by Slavic Republics Is Called 'Illegitimate, Dangerous,'" *Washington Post*, December 10, 1991, A1; Fred Hiatt, "Nuclear Control Responsibility Remains Unclear," *Washington Post*, December 10, 1991, A34; Laurie Hays and Elisabeth Rubinfien, "Gorbachev Struggles to Preserve Union," *Wall Street Journal*, December 10, 1991, A11; Elizabeth Shogren, "Won't Launch 1st Strike, 4 States Pledge," *Los Angeles Times*, December 22, 1991, 1; William J. Broad, "Nuclear Designers from East and West Plan Bomb Disposal," *New York Times*, December 17, 1991, C1; Francis X. Clines, "Yeltsin Reported to Gain Advantage on Commonwealth," *New York Times*, December 12, 1991, A1; Bryan Brumley, "Russian and Soviet Officials Give Assurances That Nuclear Weapons Secure," Associated Press, December 9, 1991.

212 Many articles reflected concerns about anarchy. For a sample, see Peter Gumbel, "Fading Beacon: As Soviet Events Seem to Bypass Gorbachev, Talk Is of His Legacy – He Set Change in

to the search for "an entirely new identity" in this "latest dramatic twist in the extraordinary saga" of Russian history.[213] The perspective that the country would turn into Yugoslavia, "with thousands of nuclear weapons tossed in for good measure" – an "apocalyptic future" – led one correspondent to wistfully note that the "old Cold War standoff... never seemed more stable or attractive than it does now."[214]

The discourse of the Soviet Union portrayed a shattered country on the verge of chaos, inhabited by apathetic citizens so trained by terror and totalitarianism that they cared little about ideology and a lot about not being able to feed themselves. With a trace of the ethnocentrism noted in virtually all correspondence in this book, U.S. reporters wondered whether the former Soviets could do democracy – but also gave them credit for ending the Cold War. The confrontational frames remained in this coverage almost by reflex – most evident in the concern about nuclear warheads – but the dangers of a postwar world were also evident. With the major toolbox of the Cold War suddenly gone, Washington policymakers would similarly struggle to engage the world they now dominated. The following exchange, related by a *New York Times* reporter in Moscow, contrasts supposed Soviet cynical apathy and American hopeful eagerness – but also, perhaps unselfconsciously, the ultimate difficulty for journalists to see reality on the ground as locals live it: "One man, calling an American reporter to have dinner, was not put off when his friend said he would have to work. 'We can't have dinner,' the American said. 'Your country is falling apart.' 'How about tomorrow?' rejoined the Russian, unperturbed."[215]

Conclusions

The differences between the U.S. press coverage of Castro's Cuban Revolution in 1959 and the collapse of the Soviet Union in 1991 indicate how far American foreign correspondence had come professionally in the Cold War era. In the 1950s, most reporters seemed still fascinated with the exotic aspects of the

Motion, Say Muscovites, Then Failed to Stay at Its Forefront – Maybe a Role for Him Still," *Wall Street Journal*, December 13, 1991, A1; Carey Goldberg, "Gorbachev Fires Restive Army's Chief of Staff; Soviet Union: With Discontent Growing in Military, a Conservative is Replaced by a General Who Resisted Coup," *Los Angeles Times*, December 8, 1991, 1; Carey Goldberg, "Amid Chaos, Ministries Don't Know Where to Turn," *Los Angeles Times*, December 12, 1991, 19; Deborah Seward, "August Coup Plotters in Jail, but Are New Plotters Lurking?" Associated Press, December 9, 1991.

213 Serge Schmemann, "But Alas, There's No Union of Minds," *New York Times*, December 11, 1991, A19.

214 John-Thor Dahlburg, "National Agenda When the Lights Go Out at the Kremlin; There Are Several Scenarios, None Good, for the Former Union," *Los Angeles Times*, December 10, 1991, 1.

215 Celestine Bohlen, "Gorbachev Struggles to Put a Saving Face on His Once and Former Union," *New York Times*, December 10, 1991, A18.

Caribbean island, like all those long-bearded warriors; insouciant about the political ramifications for Cubans; and concerned with how the United States would best benefit from the latest change in its backyard. In 1991, correspondents scoured the Soviet Union to understand what this stunning change would mean, trying as hard as they could to see it through the eyes of ordinary citizens. They put their fingers on the major problems that were likely to emerge, and indeed did. Perhaps most importantly, the correspondence was about the Soviet Union, not just or even predominantly a reflection of the United States, whose role in the end of the Cold War was conspicuous in its absence. The one constant construction was that of foreign people as perhaps incapable of true democracy – an implicit discourse of the superiority of American ideals that is a uniting thread in both the journalism and policy history related in this book.

After all, America had proclaimed itself the leader of the world after the Second World War, and in many ways by the early 1990s it had succeeded in overcoming the main strategic challenges of the Cold War. In doing so, however, it had created a deep ideological fracture both at home, where the public had grown disenchanted with political and media institutions, and abroad, where resentment against American "imperialism" was peaking. The frame of the Cold War confrontation between two superpowers, which in this chapter emerged clearly in the 1967 Middle East war, had been so dominant that its sudden collapse created the great anxiety reflected in 1991 correspondence. In the Cold War, the discourse about America was that it was adamantly a global leader with an unquestionable role to play in affairs big and small across the world – until 1991, when new and old doubts combined in a sense of "the end of the world as we know it." Not only did constructions of the Soviet people cast suspicion on whether they could handle freedom, but the correspondence was suddenly mute on the role of the United States, and of the media, in the post–Cold War era. As to the rest of the world, the discourse defined it either as a helpless prey or a dangerous ally of the archenemy, the Soviet Union. That renders specific discourses of different countries that emerged from some correspondence all the more important to understand for the post–Cold War era.

Take the Israeli-Arab dilemma. The 1967 conflict left geopolitical and humanitarian questions still unsettled nearly fifty years later, but it also established a definition for the two main actors that endures, at least as found in correspondence. Discursively, Israel had the moral upper hand and the spunky charm of David against Goliath; the Arabs were an uncivilized and stumbling undifferentiated mass, which per se is an extremely problematic simplification. Their mutual hatred, based on religion, was immutable and immemorial. All three of those constructions clearly also shaped U.S. policymaking, which subsumed most considerations, except oil and including the perpetual refugees, to a penchant for Jerusalem and its problems. In fact, some 1967 correspondence appeared keen to remind Washington that Israel was heroically defending itself from unreasonable, fatal persecution, a clear call for one-sided U.S. policy.

Or take China, as it opened its doors to the world again in the 1970s. Not unlike their colleague accompanying Commodore Perry to the Far East in 1853, U.S. correspondents told of a legendary China that constituted a great investment opportunity for Americans. U.S.-China policy, too, has privileged economic relations. It is striking that, already in 1979, the confrontation with China seemed to revolve around the business, not ideological, battle between communism and capitalism, although journalists recognized that those Chinese who protested human rights abuses did so trying to attract the sympathy of U.S. reporters. In fact, China's contradictions – economic laissez-faire coupled with strict control of political and ideological expression – were as clear in 1979 correspondence as they are today, and they complicated Washington's simplified image of the rising power in the East.

Finally, Afghanistan – U.S. policy there in the 1980s was as simple as it got in the Cold War, based on arming local rebels to overthrow the communist regime and contain Moscow's advance. The correspondence made overt news of that covert aid, and much like policymakers, most journalists seemed oblivious to the reality of Afghanistan itself, its people, its customs, and its fundamentalist leaning; several, however, strove to show that the reality on the ground was more complex. Constructing the mujahideen-ruled future as uncertain and potentially dangerous, some stories questioned both whom the United States had chosen to support as well as, in a few rare cases, whether Americans should be involved at all. Sadly, the press left Afghanistan together with the Soviet Army – the withdrawal was very much media-ready, as the journalists duly noted in an implicit assertion of the power of the media – only to rediscover it urgently a decade later when the traits it had brushed over became the dominant preoccupations of the early twenty-first century.

The discourses in the Cold War press, then, clearly belong to the same framework of understanding of the world shared by U.S. policymakers, namely, containment at all costs, everywhere. Until 1991, none seriously questioned the United States' prominence in global affairs, its right and even responsibility to intervene anywhere with almost any means, and its standing for universal rights, most importantly democracy and free markets, to contain the Soviet menace. In the cases of both Cuba and China, there is a trace of the economic discourse that positions foreign countries as business opportunities for Americans. Most significantly, the discourse of foreign people as incapable of being trusted with democratic self-government, found in discussions about postrevolutionary Cuba as well as 1991 post-Soviet republics, not to mention the Middle East, clearly buttresses the unique role of the exceptional American superpower.

In this golden era for foreign news, however, correspondents also proved that they could provide insights into foreign affairs that were not available through other mass channels and that thus had the chance of broadening readers' perspectives. With the startling exceptions of Castro's Cuba and the 1967 war, correspondence occasionally probed at specific questions for the countries covered that, although outside the main frames of the Cold War, allowed local realities to become part of the discourse. Correspondence from China constructed a country in the middle of great internal turmoil, taking different tracks in politics and economics. Coverage from Afghanistan suggested that the country remained a mystery to outsiders, where fierce allegiances made superpower interventions futile ventures. Stories from the Soviet Union clearly showed the dangers rising from poverty, nationalism, ethnic strife and the rise of extremism that, kept under the lid by the Soviet machine, would boil to the surface after its demise. While Cold War correspondents helped shape the paradigm of containment on the part of the righteous superpower, then, they also proved this book's argument that journalists on the ground could provide missing pieces of the puzzle that better reflected the world – even though apparently with little effect on policy.

Ultimately, those pieces hinted at the fragility of the basis on which American superpower stood at the end of the Cold War. The media history explored in this chapter also points to fissures in the pedestal holding up the kind of watchdog journalism that shone its light in all remote corners of the world. The homogenization and outside management of stories clearly began with the 1967 war case, suggesting an increasingly sophisticated effort on the part of U.S. and foreign governments to shape the story and chip away at independent journalistic observations. Tightly controlled not by censors but by public information officers, reporters started covering the same angles and citing the same sources across media outlets. The focus on a few, made-for-TV details – the Coke and firecrackers at the Beijing embassy opening, the endlessly repeated hammer-and-sickle flag coming down the pole at the Kremlin – suggest a burgeoning trivialization of news. Those traits, combined with the very flood of correspondence from the dying Soviet Union, point to one of the dilemmas that journalism would incur in the 1990s and 2000s – quality versus quantity. In the Cold War, a great quantity of foreign correspondents produced high-quality copy that, while resonating with the same concerns that informed policy, did its best to complicate overly simplistic discourses of the world. In the post–Cold War era, bottom-line conscious media companies would withdraw from the world by downsizing foreign assignments, privilege the homogenized trivial over the controversial, and damage the ability of quality reporting to stand its own ground against the torrent of online information.

5

A Web of Disentanglements

American Policy and Media Struggle to Engage the Post–Cold War World

> The flood of information about the attacks – on TV, cellphones, the Internet – seized the attention of a terrified city, but it also was exploited by the assailants to direct their fire and cover their origins.... When [live coverage of rescue operations] was cut, residents panicked.... "I was immediately on the phone speaking to a lot of senior politicians in Delhi. The public needed it put back on. But we also had to be restrained," [Times Now Chief Editor Arnab] Goswami said, adding that his station refused to show photographs of bodies being brought out at captured sites, which could have boosted the morale of the attackers. He will participate in a summit of television stations Thursday to study their role in the crisis. The Mumbai attacks also lit up the blogosphere, and Web sites such as YouTube and Twitter kept the data going without interruptions and blackouts. For residents of Mumbai, TV coverage was riveting. Madhuri Raghuveer said her family could not get enough of it.... Days later, with Indian news stations repeatedly replaying scenes from the attacks, her husband, who goes by the initials H.R., cut off the cable. He said it just got to be too much.[1]

Seismic changes in both global policy orientations and journalism greeted the end of the Cold War, both underwritten by the shrinking importance of institutions – be they nation-states or newspapers – and the rise of diffuse power organizations ranging from religious fundamentalism to social media. Global events – such as the 2008 terrorist attacks in India described in the *Washington Post* story just quoted – played out in the media glare. But the United States and U.S. media lost much of their prominence in the confused world that turned out to be a far cry from the "end of history" Pax Americana that some had suggested would follow the collapse of the Soviet Union. Both American

[1] Emily Wax, "Gunmen Used Technology as a Tactical Tool; Mumbai Attackers Had GPS Units, Satellite Maps," *Washington Post*, December 3, 2008, A1.

journalism and the country's role as the world's sole superpower came under increasing attack, from within and from without. In both policy and the media, after the unprecedented involvement of the Cold War era, the tendency was, to paraphrase the Mumbai resident quoted at the beginning of this chapter, to go for quick solutions and then turn off the world when it simply got to be too much.

After the damned if you do, damned if you don't vacillations of the 1990s, the dominant policy paradigm of the first decade of the twenty-first century was the "war on terror," inaugurated by the terrorist attacks against the United States on September 11, 2001. Solid consensus over it lasted mere months, however, and the struggling American journalism industry could spare only a handful of correspondents to make sense of the web of interconnected global factors that rose to play a major role in the new era. Just as Washington struggled to redefine its place in the world, journalism fought to stay relevant and viable under the onslaught of new technologies that risked making professional reporting a relic of the past.

This chapter examines how the American press constructed the world in the turbulent first two decades of the post–Cold War era, thus bringing up to the present the historical analysis of the role that U.S. foreign correspondence assumed in international affairs. It also contrasts media discourses with the emerging paradigms that have reshaped foreign policy, finding both parallels and new spaces that support this book's fundamental premise – that foreign correspondence helps define how we see the world we act in, and it does so in ways that can provide insight difficult to find in other discourses. The focus is on how the Associated Press and four newspapers in New York, Washington and Los Angeles covered five events that symbolize post–Cold War trends: The Bosnian War in 1993; the end of apartheid with the election of Nelson Mandela in South Africa in 1994; the end of one of the world's longest-ruling one-party regimes with the election of Vicente Fox in Mexico in 2000; the currency switchover to the euro, one of the most ambitious transnational projects of the European Union, in 2002; and the terror attacks in Mumbai in 2008.

The events reflect changes in U.S. interests in the world, such as globalizing economics, new engagement with Africa, and the rising influence of Asian powerhouses like India, while steering clear of the areas where the United States fought prolonged wars, such as Afghanistan and Iraq. The latter conflict brought a storm of criticism against the U.S. media for having failed to live up to their watchdog role and for renewed efforts by the government to control them.[2] The controversy put under the spotlight a journalism system in crisis, where concerns for the bottom line translated into widespread trivialization of news, and professional newsgathering and editing were challenged by

[2] Among many critical accounts, see W. Lance Bennett, Regina G. Lawrence and Steven Livingston, *When the Press Fails: Political Power and the News Media from Iraq to Katrina* (Chicago: University of Chicago Press, 2007).

unprecedented competition from online, consumer-generated communication. A 2007 drawing by Pulitzer Prize–winning cartoonist Mike Luckovich captured the widening gulf between the U.S. media's ideal public service role and the reality: An assistant rushes to an anchorman to announce, "Another copter down in Iraq," but the anchorman sternly replies, "Sorry, no time. [Pop star] Britney [Spears] shaved her head." The next two sections detail the struggles of the journalistic and policy establishments in the post–Cold War era.

Clicks for All: U.S. Journalism Stumbles into the Twenty-First Century

The technological revolution that transformed journalism starting in the mid-1990s was unprecedented in both speed and depth. Never before in the history of humankind had an individual been able to receive and send so much information so instantaneously across such wide distances, at almost no cost either financially or socially under the cloak of anonymity, as in the age of the Internet. Newspapers, radio and television stations – the standard news producers and distributors – risked going the way of papyrus as digital media chipped away at their advertising-based business model, their slow distribution network, and, most significantly, their social and political relevance. After spending more than a century building a profession and fighting for its democratic role in the courts of law and public opinion, journalists entered the twenty-first century offering a public service that media owners wanted only as a profitable sell while droves of consumers went elsewhere to find it for free. For perhaps the first time in history, the biggest quandary about communicating information was not how to get more of it faster, but how to find a sensible thread to make sense of the deluge of separate pieces competing for our limited attention.[3]

In the early 1990s, news media were fighting off enduring challenges: consolidation, often at the hands of large multinational corporations with holdings in many industries; credibility issues with a disenchanted public; and polarization of content to target narrow audiences instead of a national public.[4] But in the mid-1990s, an innovation that had started at the confluence of military, scientific and academic research turned the media world upside down – the World Wide Web and its browser programs, allowing unlimited amounts of files to be shared and searched remotely and easily over the Internet for the fast-growing percentage of Americans who owned a personal computer. In less than twenty years, a geeky pastime became a necessity of daily life for millions of people across the world. The defining characteristics of the digital world were instantaneousness, interactivity and a diffused lack of structure

[3] Mitchell Stephens, *A History of News* 3rd ed. (New York: Oxford University Press, 2007), 292.

[4] Michael Emery, Edwin Emery and Nancy Roberts, *The Press and America: An Interpretive History of the Mass Media* 9th ed. (Boston: Allyn and Bacon, 2000), 479–507; David R. Davies, *The Postwar Decline of American Newspapers, 1945–1965* (Westport, CT: Praeger, 2006), 2.

that empowered individuals to the point of near elimination of all kinds of middlemen, including the now-called "traditional" media.

Newspapers suddenly had competition where none had existed before. Online auction sites such as eBay rendered classified advertising obsolete, devastating the most solid basis of revenue. Big corporations and the government, which had provided the rest of advertising income, increasingly could reach their intended audiences directly online instead of relying on the press. Chat rooms, discussion pages and eventually social media such as Facebook gave a whole new meaning to the public sphere, undermining the philosophical raison d'être of the press. Most ominously for journalism, by the late 1990s, non-journalists got in the business of news by posting often-unverified information on blogs, which further eroded the professionals' share of the public's interest.

Media companies struggled with these changes from the beginning, starting to provide online content very slowly and cautiously. Even the first newspaper Web sites were careful not to scoop their print editions.[5] By 1998, when a blogger posted information *Newsweek* was working on about President Bill Clinton's affair with an intern, the role of the Internet in the media system became impossible to ignore.[6] Newspapers tried to establish their presence online despite competition from both self-publishing and, increasingly in the 2000s, from newsmakers directly reaching out to the public. The White House trend to overrule the media and present its message directly to the people, noted in Chapter 4, reached an unprecedented scale in the administration of President Barack Obama, worrying many journalists about the ability of news media to serve as a fact-check on political statements.[7] Both the George W. Bush and the Obama administrations restricted access to the press, and government agencies at all levels found ways to ignore those Freedom of Information Act requests that had been a bedrock of investigative journalism.[8]

Journalists struggled to define their professional role, and courts debated whether protections and privileges traditionally intended for the press extended to bloggers and their kin. News media became exponentially more reactive to news consumers emboldened by the ease with which they could participate in the public exchange of information usually dominated by elites. From the flourishing of comments sections published below articles to the reliance on public contributions such as iReport on CNN, the public had an increasing say in news production. It did so also indirectly, as "most-clicked" and "most-emailed" stories became easier to track, and therefore the pressure grew on

[5] Elliot King, *Free for All: The Internet's Transformation of Journalism* (Evanston, IL: Northwestern University Press, 2010), 156, 207; James Brian McPherson, *Journalism at the End of the American Century, 1965-Present* (Westport, CT: Praeger, 2006), 138.

[6] King, 208–209; McPherson, 142.

[7] Clint Hendler, "Message Control: Is Obama's White House Tighter Than Bush's?" *Columbia Journalism Review*, July/August 2010, 19–20.

[8] Jon Marshall, *Watergate's Legacy and the Press: The Investigative Impulse* (Evanston, IL: Northwestern University Press, 2011), 169–175.

journalists to follow the public taste in what to report. The assumption that readers would be satisfied with whatever news editors and reporters provided them crashed in this era, leading some to praise new media as more democratic and many others to bemoan the end of a profession skilled at selecting a manageable summary of the important happenings of the day for the broadest possible audience.[9]

As news production changed, therefore, so did content. Speed often translated into homogenization of news as all outlets copied one another incessantly. The erosion of professional boundaries, of a general recognition of differences between news, analysis and opinion, widened the credibility gap. The pressures of both "soft news" and analytical pieces led to a further erosion of objectivity in favor of openly partisan news, evidenced not only in the creation of media outlets clearly targeting narrowly defined political audiences but in a more personal style across all media. There was nothing of Lippmannesque expert detachment in the single-word, brutally effective *San Francisco Examiner* headline on September 12, 2001: "BASTARDS!" Most worrisome of all for the future of the press, the news media's desperate effort to reinvent themselves to please more consumers seemed not to be paying off. In the early 2000s, less than 20 percent of young Americans followed general interest and political news in newspapers, and not many more did so on television or even the Internet.[10]

The double challenge from the business and the public service sides combined in the late 2000s with an economic recession to threaten newspapers with extinction.[11] Several flagship newspapers, such as the *Seattle Post-Intelligencer* and the *Christian Science Monitor*, stopped publishing print editions. Major newspaper conglomerates such as the Tribune Company, which owned such stars as the *Los Angeles Times* and the *Chicago Tribune*, filed for bankruptcy. The apparently unflappable *New York Times* got a $250 million loan from a Mexican businessman. Punishing layoffs and cutbacks hit newsrooms across America – and among the first to go were foreign correspondents.

Retrenching Foreign Correspondence

Foreign news, inherently more complicated, more expensive to get and less immediately relevant than local stories, was first on the block as media managers shrank budgets.[12] Already in 1998, international news coverage in most American newspapers had "almost reached the vanishing point," according to

9 Thomas C. Leonard, *News for All: America's Coming-of-Age with the Press* (New York: Oxford University Press, 1995), 138–146.

10 David T.Z. Mindich, *Tuned Out: Why Americans Under 40 Don't Follow the News* (New York: Oxford University Press, 2005), 3.

11 King, 256–257.

12 Jaci Cole and John Maxwell Hamilton, "The History of a Surviving Species: Defining Eras in the Evolution of Foreign Correspondence," in *The Future of Newspapers*, ed. Bob Franklin (London: Routledge, 2010), 176.

Peter Arnett, who had won a Pulitzer for his AP reporting from Vietnam.[13] The tendency grew to "parachute" local staff abroad when a crisis occurred – thereby killing precisely the kind of longtime experience and explanation that made understanding crises possible. For the few correspondents who remained abroad on behalf of major U.S. news organizations, the technology-enabled shrinking of the world brought much more control from the home desks and a lot more pressure to get short stories out quickly instead of pursuing investigative projects. In 1998, one count found nearly 300 full-time foreign correspondents working abroad for a dozen newspapers and newspaper chains like Cox and Hearst.[14]

Ten years later, the four newspapers selected for this chapter – the *New York Times*, *Washington Post*, *Los Angeles Times* and *Wall Street Journal* – were the only U.S. newspapers left with a network of foreign bureaus, according to the Pew Research Center's Project for Excellence in Journalism.[15] Among them, perhaps the one that underwent the biggest change in this period was the *Wall Street Journal*, which was taken over in 2007 by Rupert Murdoch's News Corporation, the controversial owner of Fox News, and which reached top circulation in the United States by the late 2000s. The Associated Press maintained a dominant position with its network of correspondents – Bob Reid, a particularly peripatetic staffer, for example, reported from besieged Sarajevo in 1993 and took fire in Baghdad in 2005 – although it increasingly relied on local hires for both reporters and editors.[16] One study also suggested that more U.S. media grew to rely on the AP in this period, compared to other, non-American news agencies.[17] Despite such dominance, being a cooperative owned almost entirely by its newspaper members, it also had to sell its international service harder to them. As discussed in the next chapter, all five organizations experienced some retrenchments in their foreign affairs operations and endured mounting criticism for their performance in the late 2000s.

The drastic cut in print journalists abroad raised burning questions about the major sociopolitical issue discussed in this book – the relationship between the media, public opinion and international affairs. The period from 1993 to 2008 – the date range of the events analyzed in this chapter – is particularly striking because it spurred the creation of diametrically opposed theories, ranging from the CNN effect to the sobering realization that maybe most Americans only get interested in foreign issues if they happen to hear about them from

13 Peter Arnett, "Goodbye, World," *American Journalism Review*, November 1998, 52.

14 Arnett, 62–63.

15 Quoted in Michael Anft, "The World, in Eight Weeks," *Johns Hopkins Magazine*, February 2009, 33.

16 Reporters of the Associated Press, *Breaking News: How the Associated Press Has Covered War, Peace, and Everything Else* (New York: Princeton Architectural Press, 2007), 257–260.

17 Tsan-Kuo Chang, Brian Southwell, Hyung-Min Lee and Yejin Hong, "A Changing World, Unchanging Perspectives: American Newspaper Editors and Enduring Values in Foreign News Reporting," *International Communication Gazette* 74–4 (June 2012): 367–384.

the likes of Oprah and Jay Leno. In the early 1990s, the pervasiveness of then-new media like CNN prompted many to study what their impact might be on foreign policymaking. New opportunities for non-state actors to drive policy seemed to open up after the Cold War, and media were deemed decisive factors in U.S. military interventions during humanitarian crises ranging from Africa to Eastern Europe. A simplistic theory of the "CNN effect" – that media coverage can pressure Washington into action – has been widely criticized. A lighter version of the theory, positing that through coverage of great human suffering the media can have some influence in an uncertain policy environment, has proven more enduring.

It seemed to fit well, after all, a world where the disappearance of the Soviet Union and the flare-up of ethnic hatred worldwide certainly discombobulated policymakers. Correspondents still roamed the world trying to learn the history and new geographic configurations of the post–Cold War, the trends of ethnic strife, the rising importance of religion in political affairs, and economic interconnectedness. But the task often proved impossible, given the financial strains media were under and the difficulty of persuading the American public that foreign affairs still mattered.[18] Then, the post-9/11 "war on terror" provided another durable strategic frame for U.S. policy; and the media, according to some critics, readily embraced the new enemy as a generic jihadist to substitute the generic communist of old, largely abandoning the in-depth analyses of realities on the ground that were perhaps more urgently needed than ever.[19] Foreign correspondents themselves were substituted by bloggers and soft news peddlers, and the direct influence of journalists on policy seemed to be waning. As one *New York Times* columnist put it in 2005, in order for journalists to preserve public trust and influence, "we need to show that we serve the public good – which means covering genocide as seriously as we cover, say, Tom Cruise."[20] At the same time, the media became even more of a tool and a battlefield in the diffused power struggles of the twenty-first century, if often in unexpected guises.

A thought-provoking recent study suggested that the majority of politically unengaged Americans in the post-9/11 world focused on foreign policy issues presented in "soft news media," ranging from *The Tonight Show* to Oprah, so that serious information became the by-product of a search for entertainment, and therefore potentially calibrated the Internet tendency of exposing users only to information they seek.[21] The author cautioned, however, that violence

[18] Henry A. Grunwald, "The Post–Cold War Press: A New World Needs a New Journalism," *Foreign Affairs* (Summer 1993): 12–16.

[19] Philip Seib, ed. *Media and Conflict in the Twenty-First Century* (New York: Palgrave Macmillan, 2005), 222.

[20] Nicholas D. Kristof, "All Ears for Tom Cruise, All Eyes on Brad Pitt," *New York Times*, July 26, 2005, A17.

[21] Matthew A. Baum, *Soft News Goes to War: Public Opinion and American Foreign Policy in the New Media Age* (Princeton, NJ: Princeton University Press, 2003).

and human drama, the elements that made foreign events the fodder of non-public affairs programs, also made people less inclined to having the United States get involved in them, least of all multilaterally, and turned them into easier preys to political actors savvy enough to use entertainment programs to sway them.[22]

In fact, several critics have argued that for all its apparently democratic leveling and opportunities, the digital age has meant that major global events are in the media glare, but one easily controlled and manipulated. The U.S.-led war in Iraq that started in 2003, for example, has been criticized as one in which the breadth of coverage did little to mitigate its lack of depth, and the practice of "embedding" journalists with specific military units raised new questions about the military's control of the media for propaganda purposes.[23] One study has suggested that the war in Iraq has also been the "extreme realization of the power of partisanship" – with public opinion, enabled by polarized media, blindly following domestic party politics in forming its opinion of the events in Iraq.[24] An analysis of public opinion surveys before and at the beginning of the conflict found that Americans harbored pervasive misperceptions about the rationales for war, which led them to support it, and that erroneous understandings were strongly related to partisan news sources.[25] Months into the Iraq war, for example, 33 percent of viewers of the staunchly pro-Republican television cable channel Fox mistakenly believed that the United States had found weapons of mass destruction in Iraq – one of the rationales the Bush administration had used to promote intervention – compared to 17 percent of respondents who got their news from newspapers and 11 percent who used public broadcasting. Further, Fox viewers' misperceptions increased the more they had paid attention to the news.[26]

In a counterpoint revealing the increasingly borderless nature of online media, another study suggested that U.S. residents most opposed to the war in Iraq went to non-American online sites to get news about the conflict, possibly to find information consistent with their views that was not available in

22 Baum, 270, 283.

23 Michael S. Sweeney, *The Military and the Press: An Uneasy Truce* (Evanston, IL: Northwestern University Press, 2006), 183–185; Philip Knightley, *The First Casualty: The War Correspondent as Hero and Myth-Maker from the Crimea to Iraq* (Baltimore: Johns Hopkins University Press, 2004), 529. For a critique specific to the *New York Times*' performance before the Iraq war, see Howard Friel and Richard Falk, *The Record of the Paper: How the* New York Times *Misreports US Foreign Policy* (London: Verso, 2004).

24 Adam J. Berinsky, *In Time of War: Understanding Public Opinion from World War II to Iraq* (Chicago: University of Chicago Press, 2009), 217.

25 Steven Kull, Clay Ramsay and Evan Lewis, "Misperceptions, the Media, and the Iraq War," *Political Science Quarterly* 118/4 (2003–2004): 569–598.

26 Kull, Ramsay and Lewis, 584, 586.

the U.S. media.[27] Even though coverage of other conflicts, particularly those involving massive human rights violations and gruesome civilian casualties, showed growing reliance on nonofficial sources that focus on the plight of ordinary people, government voices still prevailed in foreign news.[28] Journalism in the digital age fared perhaps worst of all when there was no lethal conflict to cover.[29] No alluring drama means no parachuting journalists and entire regions disappearing from the radar until something catastrophic happens there. Even major news stories like the wars in Afghanistan and Iraq faded rapidly from news cycles and, presumably, the public's attention. This correspondence environment left Americans who rely on general-interest media with a picture of the world as a strife-ridden, unpredictable mess. It is little wonder that searing doubts should accompany the question of America's own role in it, as discussed in the next section.

Redefining Power: Global Leadership in the Twenty-First Century?

Once the lid of the superpower duel was removed by the end of the Cold War, festering regional strife fed by poverty, underdevelopment, fundamentalism and ethnic hatreds exploded all over the world. For the United States, perhaps no policy debate has been more essential than that of American global leadership and power in such a world – a question stemming from a belief in American exceptionalism that has always accompanied U.S. foreign policy.[30] The sole superpower of 1991 was devastatingly struck ten years later, and even if the "war on terror" rallied consensus toward a go-it-alone, good-versus-evil perspective, the prolonged conflicts in Iraq and Afghanistan again called into

[27] Samuel J. Best, Brian Chmielewski and Brian S. Krueger. "Selective Exposure to Online Foreign News during the Conflict with Iraq," *The Harvard International Journal of Press Politics* 10/4 (2005): 52–70.

[28] John Maxwell Hamilton and Regina G. Lawrence, "Bridging Past and Future: Using History and Practice to Inform Social Scientific Study of Foreign Newsgathering," *Journalism Studies* 11/5 (2010): 683–699.

[29] Paul L. Moorcraft and Philip M. Taylor, *Shooting the Messenger: The Political Impact of War Reporting* (Washington: Potomac Books, 2008), 213.

[30] Unless otherwise indicated, sources used for this general review of U.S. policy from 1993–2008 include Jerald A. Combs, *The History of American Foreign Policy* vol. II, 3rd ed. (Armonk, NY: M.E. Sharpe, 2008); George C. Herring, *From Colony to Superpower: U.S. Foreign Relations since 1776* (Oxford: Oxford University Press, 2008); John Dumbrell, "America in the 1990s: Searching for Purpose," in *US Foreign Policy*, ed. Michael Cox and Doug Stokes (Oxford: Oxford University Press, 2008), 88–104; Klaus Larres, ed. *The US Secretaries of State and Transatlantic Relations* (London: Routledge, 2010); Thomas H. Henriksen, *American Power after the Berlin Wall* (New York: Palgrave Macmillan, 2007). On American exceptionalism in the twenty-first century, see Meghana V. Nayak and Christopher Malone, "American Orientalism and American Exceptionalism: A Critical Rethinking of US Hegemony," *International Studies Review* 11–2 (2009): 253–276.

question whether U.S. national interests were best served by the kind of extensive global intervention that had marked the twentieth century. The very question of whether America had the power to act as a global leader stoked fears of U.S. decline and provoked calls for a return to more isolationist policies. Events seemed to validate the pessimistic predictions by some American diplomats and journalists that the challenges of the post-Soviet world – extremism, terrorism, ethnic hatred, economic disruptions and environmental catastrophes – might prove even more dangerous for the United States than the nuclear standoff had been. Most importantly, the uncertain experimentation of the 1990s and the polarizing new conflicts of the 2000s – furnishing evidence of wide mistrust and even hatred of the United States in the world – raised doubts among Americans about what global leadership could and should accomplish.[31]

Such confusion stemmed from the contradictory post–Cold War reality, where horrifying barbaric violence seemed to disintegrate parts of the world even as others shed the last vestiges of colonialism and, on the cultural and economic levels, a quickening era of globalization seemed to foster development, integration and a modicum of human rights protection. In a single year, Washington was confronted, to take but two extreme examples discussed later in this chapter, with mass killings and torture in the Balkans just as it cheered the peaceful dissolution of South Africa's apartheid regime. Would the new world reflect "the end of history," with all countries progressing until they became free capitalistic democracies like the United States, or would people be in for a "clash of civilizations," where long-simmering cultural differences would translate into deadlier wars?[32]

To further confound policymaking was the appearance that none of the turmoil of the 1990s constituted a direct threat to U.S. security, so public opinion lost what little appetite it had for active world leadership. The Clinton administration, lasting from 1993 to 2001, set the new parameters of Washington's engagement, focusing on economic policies rather than military power to limit politically unpalatable boots-on-the-ground actions while not abandoning the tradition of moral purpose and humanitarianism. The justification for meddling in regional disputes, then, became not containment of communism but a proactive stance to help spread democracy on the back of free markets. In the march toward globalization, the United States would be, in the words of Secretary of State Madeleine Albright, the "indispensable nation."

Until the shock of 9/11, however, almost all interventions abroad and even peaceful international agreements such as the North American Free Trade

[31] For an interesting, bipartisan dialogue on the repercussions of this "crisis of confidence" on U.S. foreign policy, see Zbigniew Brzezinski and Brent Scowcroft, *America and the World: Conversations on the Future of American Foreign Policy* (New York: Basic Books, 2008).

[32] Michael E. Latham, *The Right Kind of Revolution: Modernization, Development, and U.S. Foreign Policy from the Cold War to the Present* (Ithaca, NY: Cornell University Press, 2011), 192.

Agreement entered into force in 1994 faced widespread skepticism from the American public. NAFTA was also unpopular among many Mexicans, who feared that it would only feed the country's grave problems of unemployment and poverty, and instability continued there, disproving the optimistic predictions of hand-in-hand free-market development and democratization. The Clinton administration, like the George H.W. Bush one before it, was reluctant to be involved in the Bosnian War, although it eventually did take the lead in brokering a peace agreement. It also organized NATO forces against Serbia, but U.S. military involvement was restricted to air strikes, which limited U.S. casualties but also the ultimate effectiveness of peace measures on the ground. The inability of the increasingly integrated European community to deal with the civil war, and American willingness to step in, cemented the public perception on both sides of the Atlantic that America and Europe were on different tracks, with unchallenged American military power countered by Europe's soft diplomatic approaches.

The same Washington vacillations proved disastrous – and consequential – in Africa, where the genocide in Rwanda went largely ignored and the civil war in Somalia became the poster child of botched humanitarian intervention. Continued involvement in the Middle East broke no new ground – no peace agreement was reached between Israelis and Palestinians, who repeatedly resorted to intifada over grievances dating to the 1967 war; Iraq was air-bombed almost every year; and sporadic counter-terrorism measures did nothing to stop the preparation of the defining event of the early twenty-first century, the 9/11 attacks. Until then, America was tentatively engaged in a broadly defined, often contradicting, and sometimes unpopular attempt to maintain global leadership.

Al-Qaeda briefly brushed aside all uncertainties as the United States found a new, powerful enemy to deal with in Islamic jihadism, the face of which was group leader Osama bin Laden, who had fought the Soviet occupation of Afghanistan and had turned against the United States after the 1991 Gulf War. The vast majority of American public opinion, and most U.S. allies, supported the U.S. war in Afghanistan in fall 2001 to topple the Taliban regime that had harbored bin Laden. The government did fall quickly, but just as it had for the Soviet Army, guerrilla warfare mired U.S. forces in the country through the 2000s.

Much more controversial domestically, and vehemently disapproved virtually everywhere else, was the U.S.-led invasion of Iraq to overthrow the regime of Saddam Hussein in 2003. In 2012, the debate was still raging as to why exactly the George W. Bush administration took the "war on terror" there, inaugurating a painfully divisive doctrine of "the lone superpower," on the basis of military supremacy and aggressive, unilateral preemption of strategic threats that marked a drastic change from Cold War doctrines.[33] The

[33] Herring, 922, 944.

Bush campaign to sell the war to the American public through fear as well as appeals to spreading democratic values, as noted earlier, backfired as the conflict remained unsolved.[34] Some have argued that, as a "grand strategy," the "war on terror" relied too heavily on military solutions and lacked "concerted diplomatic, psychological and economic tools" – including public diplomacy – that were established successfully in the early years of the Cold War to fight communist expansion.[35]

The international consequences of the "war on terror" were calamitous. Violence continued to mar the main theaters of Afghanistan and Iraq years after quick military victories seemed to have been achieved, driving holes in the theory that U.S. regime change could foster sweeping, lasting reform and therefore damaging the post–Cold War ethos of U.S. involvement in the underdeveloped world. Anti-Americanism surged worldwide and U.S.-European relations plummeted, menacing the whole NATO infrastructure and transatlantic ties that had lasted centuries, as did U.S.-Latin American bonds. As the Bush administration sought to insert a wedge between Western Europe's powerhouses, particularly France and Germany, and the smaller countries in Eastern Europe, relations between Washington and Moscow also soured. Perhaps most devastating of all, the post–Cold War U.S. strategy – bringing stability through imposed democratization – seemed to have failed, with anarchy in the war zones, resentment across the world, and a marked pessimism at home.

The Obama administration struggled with this fallout even as it turned its attention to major domestic economic problems and the rising influence in globalization of non-Western countries like China and India, whose power boomed in the 2000s. When President Obama was elected in 2008, Americans still had a greatly Anglocentric view of the world, however; according to one public opinion survey, 60 percent of respondents felt that Great Britain was "very important" to the United States, while only 37 thought so for Mexico, a meager 25 for Afghanistan and India, and less than a quarter for France.[36] Furthermore, studies suggest that news coverage, especially if negative, sometimes influenced Americans' perception of a foreign country's importance to U.S. interests.[37] Importance might also correlate to lack of friendliness.

34 Kenneth Osgood and Andrew K. Frank, eds. *Selling War in a Media Age: The Presidency and Public Opinion in the American Century* (Gainesville: University Press of Florida, 2010), 252; Latham, 204.

35 Joseph S. Nye, Jr., "Public Diplomacy and Soft Power," *The Annals of the American Academy of Political and Social Science* 616 (March 2008): 94–109; Heather S. Gregg, "Crafting a Better US Grand Strategy in the Post-September 11 World: Lessons from the Early Years of the Cold War," *Foreign Policy Analysis* 6–3 (2010), 237–255.

36 Data from the 2008 Global Views survey by The Chicago Council on Global Affairs, retrieved online from http://www.thechicagocouncil.org/userfiles/file/pos_topline reports/pos 2008/2008 public opinion 2008_us survey results.pdf.

37 Wayne Wanta, Guy Golan and Cheolhan Lee, "Agenda Setting and International News: Media Influence on Public Perceptions of Foreign Nations," *Journalism and Mass Communication Quarterly* 81–2 (Summer 2004): 364–377.

American and European reciprocal feelings were lukewarm at best, according to a 2008 transatlantic public opinion survey, and so were American feelings toward India, another country discussed in this chapter's case studies. A great disparity emerged in the same survey over the perception of U.S. leadership: More than 80 percent of American respondents felt that it was very or somewhat desirable that the United States "exert strong leadership in world affairs," while solid majorities in European countries felt it was somewhat or very undesirable.[38] Overall, the 1990s and 2000s reinforced a trend of international disengagement on the part of the American public that had started in the 1970s. Never more than 10 percent of respondents said that "international affairs and foreign aid" were "the most important problem" facing the country, according to Gallup, and percentages only in the 20s called "defense" the critical problem, even in the aftermath of 9/11 and the wars in Afghanistan and Iraq.[39]

As this book was written in 2012, it was too early to tell how the era of the "war on terror" would play out. Despite the rhetoric, some doubted that the Obama administration would constitute a return to multilateralism and "renewed partnerships."[40] In fact, a consensus seemed to emerge that 9/11 was a watershed moment for U.S. foreign policy – not so much because it dramatically altered real power relations, but because it imposed an epochal reinterpretation of core driving perceptions, foremost among them America's global uniqueness, reinforcing this book's main theoretical assumption that discourses matter as much as material realities in policymaking. In fact, the twenty-first century, with its lack of obvious balance-of-power threats, has generated renewed interest in explanations for foreign policy that focus on soft power, ideas and ideological constructions, making it a particularly useful period for the purposes of this analysis. Two studies of national identity discourses in post-9/11 foreign policy suggest that the Bush White House's construction of America as the defender of freedom against the evil forces of terrorism drove foreign interventions, their initial public resonance, and their ultimate failure, when foreign realities on the ground did not develop as expected, even though the new self-definition was likely to endure.[41]

[38] Data from the 2008 Transatlantic Trends report by a collaborative project headed by the German Marshall Fund of the United States, retrieved online from http://trends.gmfus.org/doc/2008_english_top.pdf.

[39] Data from Gallup's "Most Important Problem" surveys, retrieved online from the University of Texas at Austin's Policy Agendas Project, http://www.policyagendas.org/page/datasets-codebooks#gallups_most_important_problem. Many thanks to the University of Minnesota's Rodrigo Zamith for data elaboration.

[40] David Skidmore, "The Obama Presidency and US Foreign Policy: Where's the Multilateralism?" *International Studies Perspectives* 13–1 (February 2012): 44.

[41] Karl K. Schonberg, *Constructing 21st Century U.S. Foreign Policy: Identity, Ideology, and America's World Role in a New Era* (New York: Palgrave Macmillan, 2009), 2; Dirk Nabers, "Filling the Void of Meaning: Identity Construction in U.S. Foreign Policy After September 11, 2001," *Foreign Policy Analysis* 5–2 (2009): 191–214.

Could the United States sustain a preemptive doctrine militarily, strategically and even morally? Would the "rise of the rest" reshuffle Western alliances that had shaped international relations for the past two centuries? Would the cost-benefit calculations of a cash-strapped, aging American public disentangle the United States from the extraordinary global presence it had maintained since the Second World War, as suggested by a remarkable drop from 2001 to 2011 in the percentage of Americans who said promoting democracy abroad should be an important long-range policy goal?[42] Would the twenty-first century see a "post-American world"?[43] Most crucially, whether and how American power would continue to be a presence in the world was in question – and reliable, mass-targeted news of the world to help foster informed debate was dramatically shrinking, as shown in the next section.

America Covers the World: Post–Cold War Media Discourses

The United States struggled to define its role in the contradictory new world of the post–Cold War and post-9/11 era. Most regrettably, its press often failed to provide the pervasive, consistent coverage of the world that might have helped construct a fuller policy environment. From the mid-1990s to the late 2000s, the corps of foreign correspondents abroad on behalf of U.S. newspapers shrank, and the focus turned to human interest, catchy stories that stood little chance of furnishing a nuanced picture of foreign realities. Whereas noteworthy analytical reporting still took place, the trends toward homogenization of news (and sources) and a made-for-publicity manipulation of events accelerated across the world. The frames of economic progress first and of Islamic terrorism later were as dominant as the Soviet threat frame had been. The five cases in the next sections show the progressive disengagement of the U.S. press – a dangerous threat to the media's function as mediator between the U.S. public and increasingly complex issues abroad. This chapter focuses on the coverage of five illustrative events from 1993 to 2008 to uncover what discursive formations emerged about a generalized non-American "other," about America itself, and the specific identity of covered countries and regions. The findings reflect analysis of more than 700 articles and editorials selected from

42 For a thought-provoking essay on the role of demographics on foreign policy, see Michael Mandelbaum, "Demography and American Foreign Policy," *SAISPHERE*, 2010–2011, 8–11. The public opinion data are quoted from an online resource of the Carnegie Endowment for International Peace and the Pew Research Center, retrived online from: http://carnegieendowment.org/publications/interactive/how-do-americans-view/.

43 The debate on America's relative decline continued unabated in 2012; see, among many, the three "Controversy" essays in *International Studies Quarterly* 56–1 (March 2012): Christopher Layne's "This Time It's Real: The End of Unipolarity and the *Pax Americana*," Joseph S. Nye, Jr.'s "The Twenty-First Century Will Not Be a 'Post-American' World," and William C. Wohlforth's "How Not to Evaluate Theories."

coverage by the Associated Press, *New York Times*, *Washington Post*, *Wall Street Journal* and *Los Angeles Times*.[44]

Bosnian War: New Era, Timeless Atrocities

> CITLUK, Bosnia-Herzegovina – The bureaucrats agreed on a pact and the military commanders endorsed it, but in the end it was a small army of singing children and an angry old woman who were nearly the undoing Wednesday of the United Nations' troubled mission here. Seeking for the second straight day to reach more than 35,000 stranded Muslims on the brink of starvation in nearby Mostar, a U.N. aid convoy finally rolled forward after being halted for more than six hours on sweltering back roads by dozens of Croatian women and children determined not to see food delivered to their enemies.... The daylong odyssey provided an unsettling picture of how bitter the divisions among Bosnia's population have become and how helpless the United Nations is to intervene in the hatred. Humanitarian aid is viewed by most parties to the conflict as a guise for keeping the enemy alive to fight another day.[45]

The disintegration of Yugoslavia in the early 1990s was the starkest reminder that the much-heralded post-Soviet peace in Europe was a fragile dream and that the United States was newly recalcitrant to lead. Foreign correspondents, like the *Los Angeles Times* reporter just quoted, found atrocity after atrocity in the three-way civil war in the Balkans that would become the nickname for ethnic hatred and national disintegration in the post–Cold War era. Most of their stories spared no morbid detail – the article just quoted also noted that refugees in Citluk were reduced to "drinking water from toilets" – and reflected a barely veiled sense of outrage for what American journalists saw as the impotence of the United Nations. Together, they framed a discourse that painted the Balkans as a barbaric cauldron of cruel peoples who all had hated one another forever, and whose only possible hope was a strong U.S. intervention. From quotes to editorials, it is evident that no doubts about U.S. leadership had emerged yet – but doubts about self-government in a foreign land were amplified.

A communist dictatorship, Yugoslavia had been sitting on top of century-old ethnic feuds between the dominant Eastern Orthodox Serbs, Catholic Slovenes

[44] The dates selected for study are: August 14 to September 1, 1993, for the siege of Mostar in the Bosnian War; April 25 to May 11, 1994, for the election and inauguration of South Africa's President Nelson Mandela; July 1–11, 2000, for the Mexican election; December 31, 2001, to January 7, 2002, for the switchover to the euro; and November 26 to December 5, 2008, for the Mumbai terrorist attacks. Online databases (ProQuest and LexisNexis) were used for all dates for all newspapers. Search words were: Mostar, Mandela, Fox and Mexico, euro, and Mumbai. For the Associated Press copy, stories were found using the same search words in the internal digital archives.

[45] Kim Murphy, "Anger Almost Halts Bosnia Mercy Mission," *Los Angeles Times*, August 26, 1994, 14.

and Croats, and Muslims in the Bosnian region. When the dictatorship collapsed, Serb leader Slobodan Milošević fomented nationalism and, after Slovenia, Croatia, and Bosnia declared independence, used the former Yugoslav army under his leadership to retake control of those areas. Whether the underlying cause of the war was Serbian aggression or unleashed nationalistic strife, all sides in the civil war committed atrocities against civilians in acts of "ethnic cleansing" that horrified the world.

At first, all Europeans and Americans did was help the United Nations deliver aid to besieged areas – including, notoriously, in the historical old town of Mostar, the August 1993 episode this section focuses on, where Croats and Muslims had turned against each other, as many as 35,000 civilians risked starvation, and both sides held hostage the UN aid convoy.[46] Western powers also tried to negotiate a cease-fire and impose economic sanctions on Serbia. The massacre at Srebrenica in 1995, when Serbs pushed past a UN peacekeeping mission and killed several thousand Muslims, finally resolved the United Nations and the United States to act forcefully. Putting aside the quagmire of the century's dominant analogies, from Munich to Vietnam, and ignoring public opinion, Clinton supported massive NATO bombing, wrangled a cease-fire by dividing Bosnia into ethnic enclaves, and committed thousands of U.S. troops to the region for peacekeeping. The Bosnian War was over, but profound unrest would continue in the region, particularly in Kosovo, and this U.S. intervention became the benchmark for the new era.

Thousands of journalists reported the horrors of this conflict as it was happening, including ethnic cleansing and other suffering of the civilian population.[47] Whether relentless media coverage of the carnage pushed the White House toward intervention is unclear, especially because a minority of the public remained favorable to U.S. strikes.[48] Two studies of British and American media coverage of the war found that it usually depicted Serbs as the villains and advocated Western actions against them.[49] A study of U.S. public opinion during the crisis, however, found that Americans wanted to intervene only if others shared the burden and if success was ensured.[50] Editorially, the newspapers studied here clearly identified the United States as the only possible

[46] Steven L. Burg and Paul S. Shoup, *The War in Bosnia-Herzegovina: Ethnic Conflict and International Intervention* (Armonk, NY: M.E. Sharpe, 1999).

[47] Brad Blitz, ed. *War and Change in the Balkans: Nationalism, Conflict and Cooperation* (Cambridge: Cambridge University Press, 2006).

[48] Philip Seib, *Headline Diplomacy: How News Coverage Affects Foreign Policy* (Westport, CT: Praeger, 1997), 40–43.

[49] Philip Hammond, *Framing Post–Cold War Conflicts: The Media and International Intervention* (Manchester: Manchester University Press, 2007), 51–86; Danielle S. Sremac, *War of Words: Washington Tackles the Yugoslav Conflict* (Westport, CT: Praeger, 1999).

[50] Steven Kull and Clay Ramsay, "U.S. Public Opinion on Intervention in Bosnia," in *International Public Opinion and the Bosnia Crisis*, ed. Richard Sobel and Eric Shiraev (Lanham, MD: Lexington Books, 2003), 70.

savior of the besieged Bosnian civilians, a finding consistent with a previous analysis of the *Washington Post* and *Wall Street Journal*'s role in the crisis.[51] The *Washington Post* editors, for example, urged Washington to send a clear signal to "prowling Serbs and Croats that there are after all limits to American forbearance" – implying that what America bore or not was the decisive factor.[52] Editors at the *Los Angeles Times* similarly argued that the only chance to rescue "religious tolerance and cosmopolitan culture" in the Balkans was to raise "the specter of American power."[53] The most interesting implication for this book's purposes is that these editors seemed to continue the long tradition of constructing the United States as a necessary leader for a desperately torn world incapable of helping itself.

That construction also held true in correspondence from Bosnia, where some reporters showed a keen understanding of both the very publicity that their stories were receiving and the manipulation all sides attempted. A correspondent in Sarajevo, for example, wrote a scathing story about the medical evacuation of wounded children that some UN officials accused of being "a public relations show," and that he apparently covered too:

> More than 200 reporters, television crews and photographers descended on the sick and wounded in a media event unmatched since the Serb siege of Sarajevo began 16 months ago. Television cameras rolled, their hot lights glaring at the back of a girl with meningitis as she whimpered in pain. Photographers jostled for a shot of U.N. troops from France carrying patients on stretchers from Kosevo Hospital.[54]

The AP correspondent, writing about an evacuated child, quoted doctors saying that they feared the world's interest in Sarajevo's children would evaporate "as the memory of the heart-rending TV images ... fades."[55] Another reporter in Sarajevo wrote an entire analysis on how UN officials had mounted a campaign to convince Western reporters to substitute the word "siege" with nicer euphemisms such as "enjoying a tactically advantageous position."[56] That all sides seemed aware of the importance of Western media is evident from the fact that even belligerents took reporters on "brief and closely monitored" tours, including one of a Croat detention camp near Mostar visited by AP.[57]

[51] Yaeli Bloch-Elkon, "Studying the Media, Public Opinion, and Foreign Policy in International Crises: The United States and the Bosnian Crisis, 1992–1995," *The Harvard International Journal of PressPolitics* 12–4 (2007): 20–51.

[52] "Sarajevo: Strangled Still," *Washington Post*, August 17, 1993, A20.

[53] "Reining in the Serb Victory," *Los Angeles Times*, August 16, 1993, 6.

[54] John Pomfret, "39 Patients Flown Out of Sarajevo; Recipient Countries Quarrel with U.N. over Motivations," *Washington Post*, August 16, 1993, A1.

[55] Terry Leonard, "One Child Saved, but Thousands More Await Help," Associated Press, August 23, 1993.

[56] John F. Burns, "A Siege by Any Other Name Would Be as Painful," *New York Times*, August 17, 1993, A6.

[57] "Bosnian Croats Halt Convoy from Taking Aid to Muslims," *New York Times*, August 21, 1993, 1.

Most stories in August 1993 were written from Sarajevo, and the *Wall Street Journal* stood out among the newspapers studied for the penury of articles on Mostar. During the UN convoy crisis, however, a few correspondents traveled to Mostar, which they constructed as lying outside the "world's attention" even though its "plight" was more "critical" than Sarajevo's.[58] (An AP reporter, in a rare balance effort, wrote that once the world's attention was riveted by Mostar, it would forget areas where the Croats were suffering – offering readers an all-encompassing vision of misery on all sides.)[59] In the same tradition of war-zone writers found repeatedly in this research, correspondents proudly conveyed to readers their battlefront credentials: "Three reporters were in a car several dozen feet away when the shell hit, kicking up a monstrous brown cloud of dirt and pulverized brick."[60]

Most often, correspondents relied on searing quotes from civilians, reflecting a turn to minimizing the journalist's own voice and conveying directly the participants' voices that clearly dominated this era's stories. A front-page brief in the *Wall Street Journal* constructed the role of the United States simply by quoting a sign in the "besieged Muslim quarter of Mostar" where people were holding the UN aid convoy – and apparently Western reporters – hostage: "Why did the world forget us?"[61] "We want the Americans to save us and send us parachutes of food," a public kitchen cook in Mostar told the *Washington Post* correspondent the same day she stood 20 feet away from where a Croat sniper had shot a man in the mouth, killing him.[62]

Virtually all correspondence similarly constructed the United Nations as incapable of handling the crisis and, by default or explicitly, the United States as indispensable to end Bosnia's misery. The saga of the UN aid convoy to Mostar – blocked en route by Croatians who did not want help to reach the enemy, then by Muslims who believed it might offer some protection from Croat action – was widely constructed as evidence of such failure. It showed "U.N. soldiers, caught in the middle as the world body often has been in this

58 Kim Murphy, "Mostar, Bosnia's Forgotten City, May Get 1st Relief Convoy Since June 15," *Los Angeles Times*, August 20, 1993, 10; John Pomfret, "The Hidden Agony of Mostar's Muslims," *Washington Post*, August 22, 1993, A1.

59 Snjezana Vukic, "Past Wrongs Make Bosnian Muslims and Croats Uneasy Hospital Bedfellows," Associated Press, August 24, 1993.

60 John Pomfret, "'Maybe It's Better to Die by Shelling Than of Hunger,'" *Washington Post*, August 23, 1993, A11.

61 "What's News," *Wall Street Journal*, August 27, 1993, 1. For the longer AP story the brief came from, Snjezana Vukic, "Despite Aid, Thousands of Besieged Mostar Muslims Fear the Worst," Associated Press, August 26, 1993. An AP story datelined Mostar noted briefly, "113 U.N. personnel and several reporters trapped in the city," Snjezana Vukic, "Standoff Continues over Departure of U.N. Convoy," Associated Press, August 27, 1993.

62 John Pomfret, "'Maybe It's Better to Die by Shelling Than of Hunger,'" *Washington Post*, August 23, 1993, A11.

conflict," as the *Los Angeles Times* put it.[63] The *Washington Post* correspondent in Mostar, having described how "Croat snipers" had fired at Muslims celebrating the arrival of the food convoy, quoted a teacher and mother of two as saying: "Our only hope is the Americans. The U.N. can't get anything done."[64] Making the pro-American point visually clear, when he described how the "terrified inhabitants" blockaded the convoy, believing it might offer some protection from enemy fire, he added that the "makeshift checkpoint" was "shaded by Coca-Cola umbrellas."[65]

As to discourses about Bosnia, correspondence constructed the conflict as based on religion and history, painting it as inevitable in this barbaric corner of the world – "an ethnic crazy quilt" "fated" to erupt in battles, a "multi-ethnic patchwork" before all peoples got started on "ethnic-cleansing operations."[66] Correspondence that focused on morbid details, such as a *New York Times* story describing the "dead rat floating" in water near piles of "human waste" in a popular swimming hole, further reinforced the perception of a bleak, helpless country.[67] Not even the big publicity coup of the children's rescue from Sarajevo helped the reality on the ground, when "Serbian, Croatian and Muslim armies fighting in central Bosnia to dismember the doomed republic kept up the killing over the weekend, oblivious to the much-publicized rescue."[68]

In Mostar, the "once picturesque town" – apparently a favorite correspondents' adjective over time – one reporter found ethnic hatred and division literally inscribed in the urban landscape: "Ottoman-style houses with cool courtyards, sprawling Austro-Hungarian villas and drab communist-era apartment blocks look as though they have grown mouths that seem to grin or howl."[69] "The desolation is so complete even the glass shards have vanished" from shelled storefronts, the AP reported.[70] Even the city's beloved old bridge, built in the sixteenth century and eventually destroyed in the war, "belonged in the trauma ward" – not only because sniper fire killed someone there nearly every day, but also because it symbolized a concept of multiculturalism that had

63 Kim Murphy, "Muslims Hold Up Convoy's Return," *Los Angeles Times*, August 27, 1993, 1.

64 John Pomfret, "U.N. Trucks Deliver Food to Mostar's Muslim Ghetto," *Washington Post*, August 26, 1993, A18.

65 John Pomfret, "Desperate Muslims Hold Aid Givers Hostage," *Washington Post*, August 28, 1993, A1.

66 John-Thor Dahlburg, "Weary Croats Expect Renewal of Warfare," *Los Angeles Times*, August 15, 1993, 4; Chuck Sudetic, "Bosnia Aides Ask U.S. Guarantee As Peace Talks Are Set to Resume," *New York Times*, August 30, 1993, A6.

67 Chuck Sudetic, "At Sarajevo Swimming Hole, Life Thrives in War's Shadows," *New York Times*, August 24, 1993, A1.

68 "39 Escape Sarajevo in Medical Evacuation," *Los Angeles Times*, August 16, 1993, 1.

69 John Pomfret, "The Hidden Agony of Mostar's Muslims," *Washington Post*, August 22, 1993, A1. The "picturesque" description is in Snjezana Vukic, "Standoff Continues over Departure of U.N. Convoy," Associated Press, August 27, 1993.

70 Snjezana Vukic, "Killing and Maiming Goes On, but Five Children Leave," Associated Press, August 27, 1993.

become "anathema."[71] One episode on the bridge exemplified the atmosphere of ferocity and hopelessness: A Muslim soldier told a reporter he had just killed two Croats, belonging to the same forces that had expelled his mother to the Muslim quarter, which she never reached because she died after hitting her head on the debris on the span, her younger son at her side.[72]

Civilians were described as reduced to "near-bestial" conditions, ready to "scuffle" over the rations UN soldiers "tossed" them.[73] On a larger scale, Mostar showed how Croats and Muslims were "engaged in fierce competition for the remaining crumbs of their country," going from allies against the Serbs to mortal enemies in a "brutal logic," "the kind of twist of alliances that have made the Balkans notorious."[74] Soldiers on both sides, too, were dehumanized, described as they "enthusiastically" engaged in a "deadly game of tit for tat" – a reporter told of how a Croat soldier, interrupting a game of cards fifty yards away from the front line, had seemed to want to kill a civilian who had nearly wandered into an ambush, "the man who had allowed a Muslim sniper a chance to kill him." A few seconds later, "the card game began again."[75] An AP reporter in Mostar wrote, as a matter-of-fact explanation, that a "particularly shocking feature of this war has been the practice of purging captured territory of rival ethnic groups by killing or expelling them," and added that "paranoia and exaggeration" fomented hatred on all sides.[76] Reporting from nearby Citluk, the correspondent described one English woman who had helped evacuate wounded Muslim children from Mostar and planned to move to another town to help wounded Croat children – an oasis of Western resourcefulness in the midst of indiscriminate Bosnian horrors.[77]

The correspondence from one of the most tragic fronts of the first European post–Cold War conflict, then, continued a discourse that has transpired repeatedly from this book's history: The United States was the sole global leader capable of handling a disintegrating region, whose bloodied quagmire of

[71] John Pomfret, "As Mostar Bridge Crumbles, So Does Bosnian Dream of Ethnic Unity," *Washington Post*, August 30, 1993, A1.

[72] John Pomfret, "In Mostar's War, Little Hope of Peace," *Washington Post*, August 24, 1993, A13.

[73] Maud S. Beelman, "Fierce Fighting in Mostar Leaves 33 Dead, Shells Wound 13 in Capital," Associated Press, August 17, 1993; "Convoy Reaches S. Bosnia City – but without Food," *Los Angeles Times*, August 22, 1993, 1.

[74] John Pomfret, "Complex Bosnian Alliances Sow Tragedy as They Twist and Turn," *Washington Post*, August 21, 1993, A16.

[75] Kim Murphy, "In Mostar, No Enthusiasm for Bosnia Peace," *Los Angeles Times*, August 30, 1993, 1.

[76] Snjezana Vukic, "In Shattered Mostar, Muslims and Croats Stand Off across a Street," Associated Press, August 22, 1993; Snjezana Vukic, "U.N. Denied Access to Trapped Muslims in Mostar," Associated Press, August 20, 1993.

[77] Snjezana Vukic, "Artist-Turned-Aid Worker in Mostar Driven to Help," Associated Press, August 30, 1993.

inveterate historical hatred bode very badly for a new, peaceful world. As Washington also believed, America was still the indispensable nation, although how much it could do in such a barbaric world was beginning to be questioned. The perceptive pessimism that emerged in coverage of the collapsing Soviet Union seemed to be validated. Correspondents were also still fully engaged, and they would continue to be so in what many expected to be a bloodbath and turned out to be a remarkable good story – the end of apartheid in South Africa.

Mandela's Election: The Rare African Good News

> The world's obsession with South Africa has always been odd. There's no oil here, and no foreign military bases. It's a small country, with an economy half that of Belgium and a population of 40 million. But the horrors of apartheid, the legalized system of racial segregation, sparked such moral outrage around the globe that Africa's last white-ruled state maintained an outsize grip on international attention. And the dramatic climax, Mandela's electoral triumph, has proved nearly as cathartic overseas as it has at home.[78]

This *Los Angeles Times* correspondent's evaluation of what made an African country a story is an enlightening, if probably unwitting, insight in the unspoken rules of foreign news in the 1990s. A large corps of correspondents for the media analyzed here covered the spring 1994 election of Nelson Mandela, which formally ended apartheid, writing front-page stories from across South Africa. Why did the world care about a small country that did not rank high strategically or economically – in fact, really, about a whole continent that did not meet those criteria? Because it constituted first an unapologetically bad and then an improbably good human rights story, one that seemed to fit the more positive perspective on what the end of the Cold War could mean. It certainly provided a terrific counterpoint to Bosnia. The discourses found in correspondence about Mandela's election, however, allowed room for doubts about whether all would end well in "the world's newest democracy."[79] Some constructions were tinged with the usual mistrust of foreign democratic abilities, but the pointed analyses also provided a sometimes explicit counterpoint to easy triumphalism.

In the Cold War, the United States had never made Africa a policy priority, but the institutionalized system of racial segregation in South Africa – considered not only the richest but the most strategic country in the continent – generated the recurring, if contradictory, involvement of different administrations beginning with Kennedy's. The National Party, which ruled South

[78] Bob Drogin, "Inauguration Draws World to South Africa," *Los Angeles Times*, May 9, 1994, 1. For a strikingly similar assessment of why the world cared about South Africa, see Paul Taylor, "Polecat Turns into Poster Child; Vote Transforms S. Africa's Image," *Washington Post*, May 3, 1994, A1.

[79] Bob Drogin, "S. African Leaders Call Vote Free," *Los Angeles Times*, April 30, 1994, 1.

Africa from 1948 to 1994, had made strict segregation of the races a legislative and enforcement priority, essentially forbidding any relations between whites and blacks and relegating the latter to separate "homelands," so that some 75 percent of the population ended up living in 13 percent of the territory.[80]

In the late 1970s, the Carter administration, spearheaded by its UN ambassador and civil rights leader Andrew Young, had pushed hard for the rights of blacks, suggesting that they be allowed to vote, while still protecting trade in the country by refusing economic penalties.[81] The Reagan White House, however, disliked black nationalism, which it feared a tool of communism, and told Pretoria that the United States had no business interfering with its racial policies, until it was overruled by Congress, which imposed broad economic sanctions in 1986.[82] The Bush and Clinton administrations, while not mediating negotiations directly, encouraged the drastic changes promoting the end of apartheid, which were ushered in by the last president from white supremacy rule, F.W. de Klerk. De Klerk started dismantling segregationist policies in early 1990 and freed the leader of black South Africans, Nelson Mandela, from the prison where he had spent twenty-seven years. Mandela's release, televised live, was a global media event.[83] Mandela's party, the African National Congress (ANC), was legalized, and it renounced violent resistance.

After more negotiations, Mandela and de Klerk decided to hold the first elections open to all South Africans regardless of race in April 1994 as a way to democratically elect a new, representative government. Some powerful black leaders, especially representing the Inkatha Freedom Party that wanted full autonomy for Zulu areas, resisted the arrangement, and deadly violence marred the preelection period, accompanied by sporadic terrorist acts by white supremacists. Despite the unrest, the elections were peaceful and gave the once-banned ANC a solid majority. Mandela became South Africa's president in front of a host of dignitaries, ranging from First Lady Hillary Clinton to Cuba's Fidel Castro, the crowd itself a symbol that the country was now welcome on the international stage, back into "the community of nations," as one correspondent put it.[84] Some have argued that the media played a role in this transformation, too. Television service came to South Africa only in 1976, and it carried black entertainers – such as the wildly popular Bill Cosby – who might have helped white South Africans redefine a multicultural space.[85]

80 Alex Thomson, *U.S. Foreign Policy towards Apartheid South Africa, 1948–1994* (New York: Palgrave Macmillan, 2008), 14.

81 Herring, 833, 843.

82 Combs, 286–287; Thomson, 129; Herring, 882.

83 Robert Harvey, *The Fall of Apartheid: The Inside Story from Smuts to Mbeki* (Basingstoke: Palgrave, 2001), 203.

84 Bob Drogin, "'Let Freedom Reign': Mandela," *Los Angeles Times*, May 11, 1994, 1.

85 Ron Krabill, *Starring Mandela and Cosby: Media and the End(s) of Apartheid* (Chicago: University of Chicago Press, 2010).

This section focuses on correspondence from the election to Mandela's inauguration to offer insight into how U.S. journalists constructed an image for the African country that had most captivated America's attention – in fact, the AP had opened its first African bureau there in 1957.[86] The discourses are intrinsically contradictory – celebration for democracy coexists with fears of what black rule might do to the rare African economic success story, and the insistence on the lack of violence seemed to imply that it should have been expected in such a major racial upheaval. Similarly, the newspapers' editors hailed the peaceful election, calling it a victory of "hope, optimism and pragmatism" over "revenge," a possible "nightmare" that had turned into "a peaceful festival of democracy," and arguing that it showed South Africa had "turned the corner toward the rest of humanity."[87] The very act of voting, editors wrote, "instilled dignity and pride" in black South Africans – an interestingly passive construction.[88] Editorials, however, also warned that in the African "crucible of colonialism, racism and greed," "old hatreds" and "deep-seated fears" would not disappear, much as Mandela and de Klerk labored for peace – a reduction of the whole process to two figures that was recurrent in the coverage and tended to obscure the larger social and political implications.[89]

The very terminology used to describe the election was revealing of contrasting constructions of a society that would find itself suddenly integrated – it was variedly called "free" election or "liberation" election, "all-race," "multiracial" or "nonracial." The correspondents' portrayal of the two leaders focused so much on their "grace" and statesmanship that it seemed to imply it could hardly be expected, especially from Mandela, who "sounded more like the country's president than the liberation leader," suggesting the two were antithetical.[90] It was ironic, one reporter found, that Mandela should call for calm during elections when he "once headed a guerrilla army that used car bombs and other terrorist tactics in its battle against apartheid."[91] Only a few references were made to Mandela's communist supporters, a sign that Cold War frames were no longer relevant.[92] Rather, some correspondents reported on his "adaptive" skills on par with "an American pol working the ethnic

86 Reporters of the Associated Press, 282.

87 "Words of Hope, Not Revenge," *Los Angeles Times*, May 3, 1994, 6; "South Africa, Reborn," *New York Times*, April 30, 1994, 22; "Bombs Won't Win in South Africa," *New York Times*, April 26, 1994, A22.

88 "The Hope and the Temptation," *Wall Street Journal*, May 3, 1994, A1.

89 "Dawn of a New Era for South Africans," *Los Angeles Times*, April 25, 1994, 6. See also "A New South Africa," *Washington Post*, May 3, 1994, A22.

90 Scott Kraft, "Mandela Urges Reconciliation as He Ends Historic Campaign," *Los Angeles Times*, April 25, 1994, 6.

91 Bob Drogin, "Car Bomb Kills Nine as S. Africa Vote Nears," *Los Angeles Times*, April 25, 1994, 1.

92 Bob Drogin, "Joyous Mandela Claims Victory: 'Free at Last!'" *Los Angeles Times*, May 3, 1994, 1; Francis X. Clines, "South Africans Take a Draught of Democracy," *New York Times*, May 1, 1994, E5.

smorgasbord from blintzes to tacos," even though he had also "behaved like a tribal chief" in his first campaign to negotiate with the government.[93] One sure sign of Mandela's presidential manners, one jaded reporter found, was that he "deflected sticky questions with ease from reporters speaking every possible language in every possible accent."[94] Mandela, the "former saboteur who became the world's best-known political prisoner," cast his vote "in front of hundreds of journalists, dozens of television cameras."[95]

The end of apartheid was constructed in many stories as the achievement of the two national leaders and South African whites, revealing a discourse of their black compatriots as needing help to obtain their rights. A lead summary of apartheid's history in a *Washington Post* story about voting did not mention antiapartheid efforts but only that the country's "white leaders" had begun to dismantle the system.[96] Another story in the same newspaper portrayed whites and blacks as equal victims, and argued that whites had stood aside in hopes that the black government would take care of brewing black anarchy.[97] One reporter noted that a white woman had "brought" her black maid to the polls – and quoted the woman as saying she had to insist.[98] Another told of whites who had "filled in as bartenders at a country club bar so the black staff could take time to vote," something the reporter found indicative of the "grace" with which "many white South Africans are taking the shift to multiracial democracy," which implies white agency and also fear of violence.[99] Even in the rural areas where racial clashes had been virulent, reporters found blacks going to vote on tractors lent them by their "white bosses," who had also given them the day off.[100]

De Klerk was credited with having "unlocked the chains of black leaders, freed black political groups and, most important, persuaded the majority of whites to accept an all-race democracy in a country where they are outnumbered 5-to-1" – a construction privileging white concessions over black

93 Francis X. Clines, "How Pride in Election Eases Fear," *New York Times*, April 25, 1994, A6; Bill Keller, "Mandela, from Jail to Freedom, Patient Consensus Builder," *New York Times*, May 1, 1994, 1.

94 Tina Susman, "Mandela as President: China, Israel, George Bernard Shaw," Associated Press, April 26, 1994.

95 John Daniszewski, "Bomb Rocks Johannesburg Airport, Mandela Votes," Associated Press, April 27, 1994.

96 William Claiborne, Michelle Singletary, Lynne Duke and DeNeen Brown, "S. Africans Vote in Hospitals, at Embassies, Behind Bars," *Washington Post*, April 27, 1994, A26.

97 Paul Taylor, "S. Africa's New Race; It's against Time, and Election Was Only 1st Hurdle," *Washington Post*, May 8, 1994, A1.

98 Bob Drogin, "Pride Marks Peaceful S. African Voting," *Los Angeles Times*, April 28, 1994, 1.

99 David Crary, "Fanatic Fringe Aside, Whites in South Africa Take Change in Stride," Associated Press, April 28, 1994.

100 John Daniszewski, "Right-Wing Campaign Crushed, but Vote Threatened by Numbers," Associated Press, April 27, 1994.

rights.[101] Mandela's inauguration was described as "the last and most orderly *relinquishment* of white dominion on the continent."[102] Similarly, a correspondent noted that most "of the 5 million whites seemed ready to accept the rise of the 30 million blacks," who were celebrating their "ascension from the hard subjugation of apartheid."[103] Even though the correspondence unanimously constructed white supremacy as abhorrent, a few stories minimized it – for example, arguing it had been created by "a handful of whites" – and implied that its worse effect had been shunning the country from the civilized world.[104] The peaceful transition was so hard to believe that for "the day, at least, blacks and whites were united by the mutual strain of taking in the recently unimaginable."[105] With pervasive "intolerance and violence," many feared that the new South Africa would not really be "much different from the old," still divided by "a gulf of inequality, mistrust and, sometimes, hatred" – the "fairy tale" of the election might not last.[106]

In contrast to the "amazingly" peaceful elections, South Africa was constructed as a violence-ridden country, where according to one article, some 14,500 people died in "political violence... since the ANC was legalized in 1990" – a chronology that can suggest causation.[107] In this "long-divided land," "a nation where political murder and mayhem often seems a way of life," where "chronic violence resounds in rat-a-tats of post-colonial mania," it was nothing short of miraculous that "pride and hope" should trump "violence and fear."[108] The "degree of peace and civility" that marked the voting was "unforeseen," even though there were still "by-now-familiar scenes of panic, twisted metal, broken glass and bloodied pavement."[109] South African blacks

101 Scott Kraft, "Grace Marks Concession by De Klerk," *Los Angeles Times*, May 3, 1994, 1.

102 Bill Keller, "De Klerk Concedes," *New York Times*, May 3, 1994, A1; emphasis added.

103 Francis X. Clines, "After 300 Years, Blacks Vote in South Africa," *New York Times*, April 27, 1994, A1.

104 Bob Drogin, "It's a 'New Era,' Says Officially Elected Mandela," *Los Angeles Times*, May 10, 1994, 1.

105 Bill Keller, "De Klerk Praised," *New York Times*, May 11, 1994, A1.

106 Thomas Kamm, "On the Eve of South Africa's Elections, Turning Bullets into Ballots Isn't Easy," *Wall Street Journal*, April 25, 1994, A8; Thomas Kamm and Joe Davidson, "Black Township Joyfully Greets Vote in South Africa; Nearby Whites Somber," *Wall Street Journal*, April 28, 1994, A6; Joe Davidson and Thomas Kamm, "Calm Transition for South Africa Cheers Many but Concerns Remain," *Wall Street Journal*, May 9, 1994, A10.

107 Bill Keller, "Blacks Seizing Their Moment: Liberation Day," *New York Times*, April 28, 1994, A14; Scott Kraft, "Mandela Urges Reconciliation as He Ends Historic Campaign," *Los Angeles Times*, April 25, 1994, 6.

108 Bob Drogin, "Pride Marks Peaceful S. African Voting," *Los Angeles Times*, April 28, 1994, 1; Francis X. Clines, "How Pride in Election Eases Fear," *New York Times*, April 25, 1994, A6. For similar remarks about "violence and racial hatred," see Bob Drogin and Scott Kraft, "No Room for Anger, Mandela Declares," *Los Angeles Times*, May 2, 1994, 1.

109 Bill Keller, "Leading Candidates Tell Backers to Put Faith in Election," *New York Times*, April 25, 1994, A6; John Daniszewski, "Right-Wing Campaign Crushed, But Vote Threatened by Numbers," Associated Press, April 27, 1994.

emerged as primitive from some descriptions of the electoral victory celebration. They surprised police because "little violence or vandalism" had marred their celebrations.[110] They "ululated and swayed to the irresistible African rhythm," bursting into the "boogie steps of the 'toyi-toyi'" that had become an ANC trademark.[111] "Zulu chiefs in leopard skins and feathered headbands" were greeted in Parliament as "grand leaders of new voting blocs, much the way visiting Rotarians or Knights of Columbus lobbyists are fawned over in American statehouses."[112] Archbishop Desmond Tutu arrived in the chambers "in a state bordering on delirium"; a police officer "laughed" as a woman, "a baby tied to her back with a crocheted shawl, swiveled her hips and turned in circles, singing 'Mandela, Mandela.'"[113]

Given that discursive background, many stories debated how the "economic and social chasm between the races" would be narrowed while averting economic destruction – how the "lives of the newly enfranchised electorate" could be lifted "without bringing down Africa's richest economy."[114] The implicit assumption there is that social programs for blacks would derail South Africa's white-led economic success story, an economic spin on the old trope that foreign countries might not be able to handle democracy, but also a remarkable, if pessimistic, focus on the future of the country itself that avoided easy simplifications. The biggest challenge for the new government was handling black impatience, without having citizens "weaned on the politics of ungovernability" resort to "their traditional tactics" – presumably violence and disruptive protests.[115] Several stories argued that black demands were "as modest as a flush toilet, as elementary as human dignity," and that South Africans in "squatter shacks" had no aspiration to "be served poolside cocktails by their

110 Bob Drogin, "Mandela Begins Shaping New Government," *Los Angeles Times*, May 4, 1993, 12; Tom Cohen, "Slow Vote Count Delays National Assembly Meeting," Associated Press, May 3, 1994.

111 Bob Drogin, "Joyous Mandela Claims Victory: 'Free at Last!" *Los Angeles Times*, May 3, 1994, 1; Francis X. Clines, "A Joy Born in Pain Dances in the Street," *New York Times*, May 3, 1994, A14; Laurinda Keys, "Multiracial Government Begins as Provincial Legislatures Meet," Associated Press, May 7, 1994.

112 Francis X. Clines, "Cape Town Sunset Leaves White Rule in Deep Shade," *New York Times*, April 26, 1994, A8.

113 Francis X. Clines, "Apartheid's Outcasts Have Come to the Fore," *New York Times*, May 10, 1994, A8; Laurinda Keys, "Sowetans Dance in the Streets at Mandela Victory," Associated Press, May 2, 1994.

114 Bob Drogin, "First Blacks Take Oaths as S. African Legislators," *Los Angeles Times*, May 8, 1994, 1; Bill Keller, "Can Both Wealth and Justice Flourish in a New South Africa? Two Old Foes Think So," *New York Times*, May 9, 1994, A6.

115 Thomas Kamm, "Great Expectations: Meeting Blacks' Needs Will Be a Challenge in New South Africa," *Wall Street Journal*, April 25, 1994, A1. For a similar assessment of the challenges of a government "made up of people who have never before been allowed a whiff of official power," see Paul Taylor, "Polecat Turns into Poster Child; Vote Transforms S. Africa's Image," *Washington Post*, May 3, 1994, A1; Donna Bryson, "Vote behind Them, South Africans Look to Road Ahead," Associated Press, April 30, 1994.

former oppressors," even though voting was enough to have "straightened their shoulders."[116] But would South Africa manage to "avoid the economic populism that has been the bane of much of Africa"?[117]

A *Wall Street Journal* story lead starkly constructed a contrast between idle blacks and productive whites as it discussed land claims: It started to describe an Afrikaner found "on his back" because it was a rainy day and therefore time to fix engines and work on his farming machines, and then proceeded to a "mud hut" across the farm where a Zulu man of the same age was also on his back, because an accident had left him paralyzed so he spent his days in bed, "talking to family, smoking tobacco rolled with newsprint and listening to his radio – when it works."[118] A *Washington Post* correspondent, acting as mediator as noted repeatedly in this research, wrote that Mandela had used an interview with him and four other American reporters hoping to "assure minorities (i.e., whites) who live here and potential investors abroad that there will be nothing to fear from the economic policies of a government led by his African National Congress."[119] Mandela, the writer concluded, "needs whites' skills to lift the lot of blacks."[120] Similarly attuned to foreign perceptions, the AP bureau chief (and future international editor) wrote that Mandela had picked reporters "with special attention to those from industrialized countries that can help with South Africa's development."[121]

Unlike most other correspondence studied so far, this coverage hardly mentioned American involvement or the American role as the beacon of democracy, with only a few exceptions such as an AP story describing a drawing of Martin Luther King in a Soweto home.[122] A *New York Times* editorial suggested that "Americans can legitimately join in the cheering," but a reporter for the same newspaper seemed disappointed that the opening of the new provincial legislatures had "about as much vox-pop panache as a C-span hearing from inside the Washington Beltway" – democracy got boring quickly.[123] A *Washington Post* editorial warned against expecting the kind of progress in South Africa "that neither America nor any other nation on earth saddled with deep-seated

[116] Bill Keller, "Mandate for Human Dignity," *New York Times*, April 27, 1994, A1.

[117] Thomas Kamm, "Foreign Investors Reweigh South Africa – Some Firms Wait for Stability, Others Jump to Market," *Wall Street Journal*, May 2, 1994, A2.

[118] Joe Davidson, "Gray Area: South Africa Ponders Its Next Controversy: Who Owns the Land?" *Wall Street Journal*, May 4, 1994, A1.

[119] Paul Taylor, "Mandela Frets While He Waits; Possible Landslide Worries S. Africa's Next President," *Washington Post*, May 1, 1994, A1.

[120] Paul Taylor, "S. Africa's New Race; It's Against Time, and Election Was Only 1st Hurdle," *Washington Post*, May 8, 1994, A1.

[121] John Daniszewski, "All-but-President Mandela Meets the Press," Associated Press, April 29, 1994.

[122] Donna Bryson, "From Center of Struggle, Three Generations Contemplate Change," Associated Press, April 27, 1994.

[123] "Free at Last!" *New York Times*, May 4, 1994, A22; Francis X. Clines, "South Africa Slips Quickly into Parliamentary Routine," *New York Times*, May 8, 1994, 10.

racial problems" had fully achieved – hardly a model discourse of the United States.[124]

A *Washington Post* correspondent, writing about the African-American delegation observing the election together with "the cream of the African American media," acerbically concluded that for "some American strugglelistas, there is also a danger of a different sort: being exposed for knowing too little about the struggles here, and worrying too much about the folks back home."[125] Foreign correspondents throughout this research often bragged about knowing best by virtue of their position, but rarely with the open disdain for American politicos that showed in that article's conclusion: "Encountered by a journalist in the lobby of the Carlton, [the Reverend Al] Sharpton was asked whether he had come to observe or be observed. 'A little of both,' the activist from New York replied, smiling. 'Where are you going to watch the voting?' he was asked. 'So-weee-to,' he replied. 'You mean So-weh-to?' the journalist inquired. 'That's right,' Sharpton said." U.S. leadership certainly did not shine when personalities could not even pronounce the name of the black township where a turning-point antiapartheid protest had been held.

Most strikingly, some articles constructed South Africa as continuing to belong to a different realm, where civilization and Africa met – with "Africa" standing in, presumably, for its antithesis. The *New York Times* Chief of Bureau (and future Executive Editor) Bill Keller wrote that the vote was "like South Africa itself, a hybrid of high-tech and make-do, of anxiety and expectation, of Europe and Africa."[126] The theme echoed elsewhere in the correspondence. An AP reporter described how the election was "something different" because it entailed finding "tribal runners" to guide helicopters carrying ballots to rural areas, educating voters on how to put down their X on those ballots, and then "teaching vote-counters what a valid ballot looks like" – all under the threat of civil war, in best Third World fashion.[127] Would the elected government be able to pull off a "near miracle on a continent littered with black-ruled nations still struggling to overcome the effects of colonialism," or would South Africa be "another African basket case of civil strife, corruption and mismanagement"?[128] "White South Africa is a developed nation; black South Africa is a typical African country," a reporter wrote, going on to define that typicality as poverty, unemployment, lack of education and lack of basic infrastructure.[129]

124 "President Nelson Mandela," *Washington Post*, May 11, 1994, A20.

125 Paul Taylor, "The Election Onlookers, Ogling as History Happens," *Washington Post*, April 26, 1994, E1.

126 Bill Keller, "As All Go to the Polls: Who, How, Where, When," *New York Times*, April 5, 1994, A7.

127 Drusilla Menaker, "Multiracial Election: They've Never Done It Like This Before," Associated Press, April 29, 1994.

128 Tina Susman, "When the Lights Dim, the Work Begins," Associated Press, May 10, 1994.

129 Thomas Kamm, "Great Expectations: Meeting Blacks' Needs Will Be a Challenge in New South Africa," *Wall Street Journal*, April 25, 1994, A1.

Several themes, then, emerge from coverage of the formal end of apartheid. Some are recurrent, such as the doubts that foreign peoples might not know what to do with the democracy given them (as opposed to earned) and that any lack of violence was surprising and probably temporary. Specific to Africa was its use as a simple stand-in for the opposite of civilized – in no other case presented so far in this book was the implicit assumption so clear that all a writer needed to do was say that South Africa was an "African country," and readers would conjure up the rest. Also different is the construction of the United States, which is unusually minimal and even negative, unlike the discourse of America's global role found thus far. As to the role of journalists, they continued to show awareness of being used for publicity in an increasingly mediated world, but they also chased the story across the country, producing a veritable flood of articles and analyses that represents, in this book, a swan's song of foreign correspondence. The difference in output, and the impoverishment of discourses, in another historic election only six years later and much closer to home, is startling, as the next section illustrates.

Mexico's 2000 Election: Change to America's Neighbor

> What may startle Mexicans most is what does not change. The deepening gap between the rich and poor, the educated and the unskilled, will not easily be bridged, analysts warned. Small, armed groups are likely to continue to threaten from their hide-outs in southern Mexico. Whether or not the PRI is in power, Mexico will still be Mexico.[130]

The election of Vicente Fox in the summer of 2000 in Mexico ended the rule of the Institutional Revolutionary Party (PRI), which had governed the country since the revolution in the early twentieth century. Despite the historic occasion and the proximity, American journalists in the country produced significantly fewer stories than they had from South Africa in 1994. The focus of the majority of the correspondence was on economic repercussions for the United States – the era-of-globalization version of the colonial attention to ports and natural resources that had marked earlier foreign news, and perhaps a new recognition that news needed to be domesticated to matter. The construction of Mexican voters reflected the usual discourse of less-civilized people struggling to find a semblance of democracy. As the *Los Angeles Times* correspondent put it in the article just quoted, the occupants of Los Pinos, the Mexican presidential residence, might change, but "Mexico is Mexico." Just like Africa was Africa, this kind of journalistic shorthand drastically reduced the ability of readers to envision a real foreign country beyond a few stereotypes so widely shared that stories did not even need to spell them out.

Historians consider the 2000 election of Fox, a presidential candidate from the opposition party, as the inauguration of true electoral democracy in

[130] Jaunita Darling, "Mexico's Landmark Vote; Voters Driven by the Idea of Change," *Los Angeles Times*, July 4, 2000, 10.

Mexico, after more than seventy years of power being passed on only within the PRI.[131] That party, albeit with a different name, had come to power in the second decade of the Mexican Revolution as a way to stabilize the political succession, with each president picking his replacement, in a light version of authoritarianism that gave the country great stability and relative prosperity through the twentieth century.[132] Mexico during the PRI reign was a hybrid – there were regular elections and opposition but also systematic ruling party fraud, patronage networks and occasional use of force. Fox's National Action Party (PAN) was founded in response to the PRI's leftist, anticlerical leanings in the 1940s, but it remained out of power until the 1990s, together with more leftist parties that spurred unrest in many regions. Relations with the United States, which had been marked by what some had dubbed "bargained negligence" in the Cold War era, also entered a new era in the early 1990s with NAFTA, which prompted a flow of southward U.S. investments even as Mexican workers increasingly sought better jobs in the north.[133] Largely an economic success, the trade agreement did not solve Mexico's social ills, as became manifest when Zapatistas mounted a growing rebellion in Chiapas, a presidential candidate was assassinated, and a financial crisis spurred widespread agitation against the PRI and for democratic reforms to hold it accountable.[134]

For the 2000 election, the party held primaries, but it was still not enough. After a vigorous campaign that seemed to end in a statistical dead heat, Mexicans chose Fox, a former governor, rancher and business executive who had run on a basic platform of change. Public opinion surveys show two-thirds of Mexicans believed their country a full democracy after Fox's victory, whereas almost half of them had not thought so going into the election, and traditional vote-buying tactics by the PRI failed.[135] Some journalists, and scholars since, also saw in "the success of the telegenic Fox" the growing influence of media, which had beamed debates "even in the most remote villages."[136] The election appeared to disprove the long-held perception among Washington's

[131] Thomas E. Skidmore, Peter H. Smith and James N. Green, *Modern Latin America* 7th ed. (New York: Oxford University Press, 2010), 45; Jorge I. Domínguez and Chappell Lawson, eds. *Mexico's Pivotal Democratic Election: Candidates, Voters, and the Presidential Campaign of 2000* (Stanford, CA: Stanford University Press, 2004).

[132] Emily Edmonds-Poli and David A. Shirk, *Contemporary Mexican Politics* (Lanham, MD: Rowman & Littlefield, 2009).

[133] Jorge I. Domínguez and Rafael Fernández de Castro, *The United States and Mexico: Between Partnership and Conflict* 2nd ed. (New York: Routledge, 2009), 10.

[134] Jorge I. Domínguez and Alejandro Poiré, eds. *Toward Mexico's Democratization: Parties, Campaigns, Elections, and Public Opinion* (New York: Routledge, 1999), 2.

[135] Domínguez and Lawson, 15.

[136] James F. Smith, "Fox Rode the Gusting Winds of Change, Says Times/Reforma Survey," *Los Angeles Times*, July 3, 2000, 17. On the importance of the campaign, see Domínguez and Lawson.

elites that Mexicans were passive and apathetic when faced with authoritarian governments.[137] Among Fox's first initiatives was to take up immigration reform with newly elected President Bush, and a new era of cooperation between the two countries seemed to be dawning, but the 9/11 attacks froze those developments for the 2000s. Mexico's opposition to the Iraq war further soured relations, and illegal immigration and narco-trafficking remained flash points between Washington and Mexico City well beyond the end of Fox's term in 2006.

American editors hailed Fox's election and spurred Washington not to "miss any opportunity to help Mexico consolidate its democracy" – revealing that indeed the media had not considered Mexico a democratic state.[138] After acknowledging that Mexico was now "a full-fledged democracy," editors at the *Wall Street Journal* conceded that, after Fox and outgoing president Ernesto Zedillo, "Mexican voters also deserve credit for the emergence of their democracy" – yet another implication that a few prominent figures created democracy, with the people at most a supporting cast, as they had been in South Africa.[139] Similarly, editors at the *New York Times* found that Mexico's citizens had come "into contact with the democratic currents sweeping Latin America and the world," and this infusion of modernity might even "mitigate the feelings of political and economic powerlessness that have driven so many Mexicans to emigrate illegally to the United States" – "feelings" apparently accounting for immigration.[140] A *Washington Post* editorial, praising Mexicans for having "shown a remarkable democratic vocation and political maturity," still belonged to a discourse of foreign people's childish inability to self-govern that appears shockingly patronizing in the twenty-first century.[141]

American correspondents also described Fox's election as a triumph for democracy, albeit one that astonished Mexicans, and, strikingly, they focused on what a new regime in Mexico might mean for the United States, not necessarily for Mexicans themselves. The very descriptions of Mexico defined it in relation to the United States. Without even mentioning Mexico by name, the lead in one article stated that Fox had "ignited a political revolution *south of the U.S. border*."[142] The lead in another reported "the birth of a new kind of government for America's southern neighbor" – one wonders if the references

137 Sergio Aguayo, *Myths and [Mis]Perceptions: Changing U.S. Elite Visions of Mexico* (La Jolla: Center for U.S.-Mexican Studies, University of California, San Diego, 1998), 250.

138 "New Day for Mexico," *Los Angeles Times*, July 4, 2000, 6.

139 "Mexico's Moment," *Wall Street Journal*, July 5, 2000, A22.

140 "Mexico's Democratic Breakthrough," *New York Times*, July 4, 2000, A12.

141 "Mexico's Triumph," *Washington Post*, July 4, 2000, A18.

142 Peter Fritsch, Jose de Cordoba and Joel Millman, "Defining Challenge: Can Mexican Victor Prove That 'Change' Is More Than a Slogan?" *Wall Street Journal*, July 5, 2000, A1; emphasis added.

were needed because readers would not know where Mexico is or because its proximity was its most relevant feature.[143]

Fox himself was universally identified as "the former Coca-Cola Co. executive," who had honed his leadership skills in the American multinational company and seemed adept at driving the media agenda in his lengthy news conferences with foreign reporters.[144] A *Wall Street Journal* story defined Mexico as "a country of 100 million with whom the U.S. shares annual cross-border trade of nearly $300 billion" and yet plagued by poverty, inefficiency and tax evasion.[145] A *New York Times* story argued that Mexicans' "gut wariness of their neighbor," the United States, had played a role in the campaign.[146] Quite naturally, correspondents also picked up a theme of great interest to their American readers – immigration to the United States – in many stories, and the *Los Angeles Times* must have deemed its readers' interest so keen that it even ran a story about the election of Mexico City's mayor.[147]

A widely repeated construction was of Mexicans "stunned" and even "a bit fearful" by their unsuspected electoral power, because they had been "inured to years of easy – and sometimes fraudulent – PRI victories."[148] Just as in the South African election the coverage repeatedly focused on the lack of violence, here it reported the lack of fraud as newsworthy in a country with a "rich tradition" of it.[149] Corruption was described as so endemic that the election had

143 Molly Moore and John Ward Anderson, "Opposition Candidate Wins Mexican Ballot; PRI's 71-Year Grip on the Presidency Is Broken," *Washington Post*, July 3, 2000, A1.

144 James F. Smith, "Fox Burned His Own Brand on Campaign Trail," *Los Angeles Times*, July 4, 2000, 1; James F. Smith and Ken Ellingwood, "Fox Lays Out Plan to Overhaul Justice System," *Los Angeles Times*, July 5, 2000, 1; Molly Moore, "Fox Sets Priorities for a New Mexico; President-Elect Targets 'Nests of Corruption,'" *Washington Post*, July 5, 2000, A1; John Rice, "Mexican President-Elect Promises More Open Style," Associated Press, July 7, 2000.

145 Peter Fritsch and Jose de Cordoba, "Huge Upset Appears Possible in Mexican Vote – Longtime Ruling Party Is in the Closest Contest Ever for the Presidency," *Wall Street Journal*, July 3, 2000, A8.

146 Julia Preston, "Leading Candidates in Mexico as Close on Issues as in Polls," *New York Times*, July 1, 2000, A1.

147 Jose de Cordoba and Joel Millman, "Mexico Charts Shifts in Relations With U.S. – Mexico's Fox Plans for Broader Policy on U.S. Immigration," *Wall Street Journal*, July 7, 2000, A8; Mark Stevenson, "Mexico's President-Elect Pledges Straight Talk with U.S." Associated Press, July 4, 2000; Niko Price, "Mexico's President-Elect Feels Snubbed by Gore and Bush," Associated Press, July 6, 2000; Chris Kraul, "Left Headed for Another Capital Win; Mayoralty: Cardenas' Pick Is Ahead in the Country's Second-Most Important Elective Race," *Los Angeles Times*, July 3, 2000, 18.

148 Juanita Darling, "Opposition Supporters Throng the Capital to Celebrate," *Los Angeles Times*, July 3, 2000, 16; John Rice, "Mexico's New Leader Moves to Ease Apprehensions after Stunning Election," Associated Press, July 3, 2000; Peter Fritsch and Jose de Cordoba, "Huge Upset Appears Possible in Mexican Vote – Longtime Ruling Party Is in the Closest Contest Ever for the Presidency," *Wall Street Journal*, July 3, 2000, A8.

149 Sam Dillon, "Whoever Wins, Vote in Mexico Will Be Fateful," *New York Times*, July 2, 2000, 8. For similar references to fraud, see Mary Beth Sheridan, "Election May Test Faith

"ravaged not only a political party but a way of life," even as it made Mexico "a more modern society," so that Mexicans "may not know what to expect" of a democratic election.[150] One correspondent called the election "Mexico's surprising step toward achieving First World status," implicitly relegating it to the Third World, a waning terminology in the 2000s.[151] Another framed it in terms of the post–Cold War era, as part of the "global democratic wave" that had "toppled the Berlin Wall and ended one-party dominance in a host of nations" – again denying agency to the Mexican people.[152] They had found themselves converted overnight into "a self-confident democracy . . . capable of ousting a government," a remarkable change for a people who had "long settled for the appearance of democracy."[153]

A repeated theme was Mexico's backwardness, especially in the areas "bypassed by globalization," which was always constructed as a positive.[154] The United States was portrayed as the aspirational model: Some Mexicans would further pursue a "gringo willingness to take risks, lavish money on education and bypass the government to find solutions to their problems" – all characteristics gringos, apparently, had the trademark on.[155] Fox's government would have a "*U.S.*-style system of checks and balances" and an "*American* model of justice" – phrasing that implies corruption could only end by imitating the United States.[156] A Fox supporter who was quoted in the lead of a story about Mexico's rising middle class was interviewed while "grabbing a quick lunch at McDonald's before heading back to her job selling Chevrolets."[157]

in Mexico's Political System," *Los Angeles Times*, July 2, 2000, 1; Michael Cooper, "Border Balloting," *New York Times*, July 3, 2000, A6; Lisa J. Adams, "Mexican Voters Choose President Amid Rare Uncertainty of Outcome," Associated Press, July 2, 2000.

150 James F. Smith and Mary Beth Sheridan, "An End to the PRI Era – and Way of Life," *Los Angeles Times*, July 3, 2000, 1; John Rice, "Mexico's New Leader Moves to Ease Apprehensions After Stunning Election," Associated Press, July 3, 2000.

151 Chris Kraul, "Mexico Stocks, Peso Soar on Post-Election Hopes," *Los Angeles Times*, July 4, 2000, 1.

152 Ken Ellingwood, "PAN Pioneers Went from Shadows to Day in the Sun," *Los Angeles Times*, July 7, 2000, 1.

153 Julia Preston, "Joy in Streets of Capital as Reign of 71 Years Ends for the PRI," *New York Times*, July 3, 2000, A1; Julia Preston, "A Crowning Defeat: Mexico as the Victor," *New York Times*, July 4, 2000, A1.

154 John Ward Anderson and Molly Moore, "Two Mexicos Go to the Polls; a Divided Populace to Vote on Change," *Washington Post*, July 2, 2000, A1. For another "primitive" portrayal, see Amparo Trejo, "In Rural Mexican Area, Confronting Ruling Party Carries Costs," Associated Press, July 1, 2000.

155 John Ward Anderson and Molly Moore, "Two Mexicos Go to the Polls; a Divided Populace to Vote on Change," *Washington Post*, July 2, 2000, A1.

156 Molly Moore, "Fox Sets Priorities for a New Mexico; President-Elect Targets 'Nests of Corruption,'" *Washington Post*, July 5, 2000, A1; Ginger Thompson, "Victor in Mexico Plans to Overhaul Law Enforcement," *New York Times*, July 5, 2000, A1; emphasis added.

157 Traci Carl, "Long Ignored, Mexico's Middle Class Finds a Voice in Fox," Associated Press, July 6, 2000.

Perhaps now Mexico too could become a "sophisticated world player," even an "important player in the global economy" – a focus on economic aspects that reflects U.S. policy preoccupations with freedom and security riding on free-market expansion, but also echoes an older hemispheric colonialism.[158] And perhaps the new administration would no longer rule "a la Mexicana," in the words of a Virginia-based "Mexico expert" quoted in an AP story – again using a whole country as a shorthand for undemocratic governance.[159] The construction, furthermore, of "doubts regarding the governability" of Mexico persisted in 2000 coverage as it had in the earliest years studied in this book, as did the discourse of Mexico as overshadowed by history.[160] Growing out of that discourse, one story pessimistically concluded that even with a Fox victory, "Mexico will remain a strange hybrid – an electorate in pursuit of democracy with an authoritarian force at its very core."[161]

In coverage of America's neighbor at the turn of the twenty-first century, then, foreign correspondence still employed frames about foreign cultures that this research found consistently – the country made strides toward democratization despite the inability and apathy of many of its own citizens, largely through the clearly America-leaning efforts of a Coke man and his McDonald's-munching, Chevrolet-selling supporters. The most important feature of the country was its relationship to the United States, in this case trade and border exchanges. Other than analysis of how difficult it would be for Mexicans to shed the familiar corrupted system of the PRI, stories about the sociopolitical ramifications of the electoral change for the country were notable for their scarcity. The United States remained the model for any country that aspired to modernity, with traits such as a just government and entrepreneurship considered strictly gringo. Finally, the correspondence's economic development focus is noteworthy. It will be even more so in the next two sections, which focus on one of the largest financial operations in modern history and on one of the world's fast-rising economic giants.

The Euro Debut: Can Europe Really Unite and Lead?

> The euro coins and bank notes that will enter circulation Tuesday are a new sign that after centuries of insults, invasions and conquests, West European nations

158 Ginger Thompson, "Strong Feelings of Pride over Orderly Balloting," *New York Times*, July 4, 2000, A7; Kevin Sullivan and Mary Jordan, "Defeat Leaves Long-Ruling Party Shaken; Spurned after 7 Decades in Power, PRI May Turn to New Generation of Leaders," *Washington Post*, July 4, 2000, A14.

159 Lisa J. Adams, "Exiting Mexican President Paves Way for Opposition Parties," Associated Press, July 1, 2000.

160 Peter Fritsch and Jose de Cordoba, "Huge Upset Appears Possible in Mexican Vote – Longtime Ruling Party Is in the Closest Contest Ever for the Presidency," *Wall Street Journal*, July 3, 2000, A8; Sam Dillon, "Whoever Wins, Vote in Mexico Will Be Fateful," *New York Times*, July 2, 2000, 1.

161 Julia Preston, "Mexicans Get a Chance to Define Democracy," *New York Times*, July 2, 2000, WK3.

> have agreed to bury their various hatchets. But lingering animosities came to the fore when the Europeans set out to design their new money.... The coins of Greece, poorest of the eurozone countries, depict one of the most notorious exploits of the Olympian god Zeus – when he took the form of a white bull and raped a maiden. For those not up on their mythology, the coins include the name of the woman: Europa.[162]

The debut of the euro as the common currency of the majority of countries in the European Union in 2002 was the culmination of a post–World War II project of European integration that, while always supported by the United States, was drifting toward a profound alienation with America. As noted repeatedly in this book, American reactions to Europe have always been ambivalent – cultural and historical ties mitigated by an unflinching aversion to European entanglements. Much like the *Washington Post* article just quoted, the discourse of Europe that emerges from coverage of the euro was tinged with pessimism that bickering European countries would be able to carry off such a complex and symbolic financial switchover, especially given their notorious inefficiency. Even if they did manage to overcome the burden of their gory history, Europeans were not capable of mounting serious competition to U.S. global leadership. The discursive insistence on the latter reflects the times. At the end of 2001, transatlantic relations also stood on the cusp of a momentous change – the solidarity over 9/11 and Afghanistan would quickly dissipate under the strains of the Iraq war, and U.S.-European relations would plummet to historic lows.

The precursors to the European Union had formed in postwar Europe under the benign aegis of U.S. support, which saw unity as integral to its Soviet containment efforts and the Atlantic alliance.[163] Ironically, Europeans perceived the growing integration as a way to resist U.S. dominance even as Washington continued to support it, until it actually did emerge as a rival economic bloc in the 1970s. In the following decades, the relationship got rockier as the United States and Europe grew increasingly divided over the meaning of partnership versus leadership. Those tensions simmered as, from the trade integration of the Cold War era, the European Union grew to a borderless sphere in search of common policies in security, defense, and justice. Europe's failures in the Bosnian conflict, coupled with its increasingly confrontational stance on issues spanning from human rights to the environment, reinforced Washington's perception that where hard power was needed, the United States still had to rely on its own resources. The fallout over Washington's scoffing at Europe's symbolically extended helping hand after 9/11 precipitated a crisis that was not fully solved into the second decade of the twenty-first century. For the first time, faced with a break in Western Europe's support for its invasion of Iraq,

[162] T.R. Reid, "Bridge-Building Leaves Space for National Pride," *Washington Post*, December 31, 2001, A12.

[163] Mike Smith, "The USA and the EU," in *US Foreign Policy*, ed. Michael Cox and Doug Stokes (Oxford: Oxford University Press, 2008), 237; Herring, 620.

the White House in 2003–2004 actively sought to divide and diminish the European Union, even though some collaborative projects continued.

It was in this atmosphere that the most visible supranational integration in 2000s Europe happened: the January 2002 switch from national currencies to the euro, which had been traded in financial transactions since 1999 and then became legal tender distributed by ATMs and banks. The vast operation – an estimated 134 billion euros distributed in the first days, all national currencies withdrawn in six months – was a logistical success. In a nudge to national sensibilities and to skeptics of the European project who feared a loss of national identity, the euro coins had designs that vary by country, whereas the euro bills featured unidentifiable renditions of architectural elements. As a monetary measure, the euro aimed at stemming exchange volatility and inflation and, more subtly, at pressuring lower-performing economies to pursue structural reforms, such as labor market liberalization and deregulation, a move that appeared to have dramatically backfired ten years later.[164] On a broader sociopolitical level, taking out old national currencies such as Italian lire and German marks, and substituting them with a single currency for twelve states, was meant to deepen the political project of integration.[165] At its debut, the euro both reinforced and represented Europe's growing international economic weight just as transatlantic relations took a turn for the worse.

The U.S. press framing of the switchover focused, editorially, on the symbolic and international aspects, calling the euro both the "most potent and tangible symbol" of European integration and the "loss of one chunk of national sovereignty."[166] The editors of the *Wall Street Journal* spotlighted the competition with the United States: The aftermath of 9/11 had shown "America's economic resilience" and "its unchallenged position as the world's political and military leader," and Europe continued to "lag America in growth, employment and innovation."[167] Correspondence was extensive and varied from financial centers in Germany and Great Britain (which had conspicuously stayed out of the eurozone that extended over "a landmass separated from it by just a few miles of choppy water") to small towns from Finland to Portugal.[168] As noted in the quote that opened this section, the construction of European unity that emerged was problematic – from the expected debut logistical snafus to the bloody history of divisions and hatreds, the discourse portrayed a struggling Europe that could not compete, yet, with the United States. A *New York Times*

164 Alberto Alesina and Francesco Giavazzi, eds. *Europe and the Euro* (Chicago: University of Chicago Press, 2010), 57.

165 Madeleine O. Hosli, *The Euro: A Concise Introduction to European Monetary Integration* (Boulder, CO: Lynne Rienner, 2005).

166 "Here Comes the Euro," *New York Times*, January 1, 2002, A20; "Europe's Hello-Goodbye," *Los Angeles Times*, December 31, 2001, B10.

167 "Happy New Euro," *Wall Street Journal*, December 31, 2001, A8.

168 Alan Cowell, "Britain's Quandary: Hoping the Euro Neither Succeeds nor Fails," *New York Times*, January 2, 2002, A8.

correspondent in Frankfurt reflected those contradictions by writing that the shared currency was meant to "open the way to closer political union," especially because it seemed to make Europe "far more efficient, flexible and stable" than it had been thus far.[169] It was the euro's aim to give Europe a "greater voice in influencing the globalizing world economy," the AP paraphrased a European Union official as saying.[170]

Reporters found European Union citizens "bracing for confusion," filled with "anxieties" and "skeptical" on the eve of the change.[171] Much as their colleagues had marveled at the nonviolent election in South Africa and the nonfraudulent voting in Mexico, correspondents in Europe insisted that "the inevitable confusion" had not materialized and the process had "unfolded smoothly," generating a vast "sense of relief" and no anticipated "euro-rage."[172] Even in notoriously unorganized Italy, where "waiting until the last minute to deal with change is a matter of proud tradition," and where police had to calm crowds of retirees forced to deposit millions of lire they had been "hiding in their homes," "the problems were less severe than predicted."[173] One reporter who embarked on a cross-Europe, euro-testing trip found that the currency, while convenient, had "magnified the old discrepancies" that divided this "patchwork of nations" – hardly a construction of powerful unity.[174] Similarly, an AP business writer found that Europeans cared little about "the grand significance" and more about the bump-up in prices as retailers played with euro unfamiliarity.[175] Even as an economic measure, the euro was hardly a game changer, some argued, further painting a picture of the continent's "already

[169] Edmund L. Andrews, "The Euro Takes Visible Shape: Pocket Change," *New York Times*, January 1, 2002, A1.

[170] "Top EU Official Says Euro Will Give Bloc a Greater Voice in Affecting the World Economy," Associated Press, December 30, 2001.

[171] Edmund L. Andrews, "Banks in Europe Scramble to Fill Automated Tellers with Euros by Midnight," *New York Times*, December 31, 2001, A4; David McHugh, "Banks, Businesses, Consumers Make Final Preparation for Midnight Currency Switch to the Euro," Associated Press, December 31, 2001.

[172] Carol J. Williams, "As Euro Debuts, Cashiers See Trouble," *Los Angeles Times*, January 2, 2002, A6; Edmund L. Andrews, "Europeans Resolve to Embrace the Euro (as Soon as They Spend Their Old Bills)," *New York Times*, January 2, 2002, A8; T.R. Reid, "Euro's Smooth Debut Brings Official Relief amid Public Excitement," *Washington Post*, January 2, 2002, A10; "Day Two: Euro Demand Overwhelms Banks – Europe's Common Currency Rises against Dollar and Yen," *Wall Street Journal*, January 3, 2002, A2; David Rising, "Retailers Report Few Problems on First Business Day of Euro Changeover," Associated Press, January 2, 2002.

[173] Carol J. Williams, "It's Happy New Euro for a Continent," *Los Angeles Times*, January 1, 2002, A1; Melinda Henneberger, "Italy Has Some Difficulties Letting Go of the Lira," *New York Times*, January 4, 2002, A8.

[174] Alan Cowell, "On the Road, Euros Smooth the Way," *New York Times*, January 6, 2002, 10.

[175] Paul Geitner, "Holiday over, Euro Undergoes First Real Test as Europeans Head Back to Work," Associated Press, January 2, 2002.

weak economy," where competitiveness was hobbled by "oligarchical conglomerates, complex firing and hiring rules, high taxes and other rigidities."[176]

Several stories portrayed reluctance to abandon currencies that had "long histories" and that, in an effort to "modernize" individual countries, led to "a loss of national heritage," coins of the realm being one of the "few national symbols" for divided Europeans.[177] Europeans were quoted as worrying about the euro as "another step on a path toward producing a homogenized society" out of a continent "long divided by language, religion and nationalist pride," where even cheese was proudly, radically different across borders.[178] The overall discourse of such attachment reflected the long shadow of history over European countries – a trope of much U.S. foreign correspondence. An AP special correspondent traveled to Waterloo, the site of Napoleon's 1815 defeat, and drew a parallel between Bonaparte's effort to unify Europe and the euro's – finding that "despite intervening centuries, some old mistrust remains."[179] Other journalists found more recent examples of European disunity – calling it "the continent at the heart of two world wars."[180]

On the war path, a *New York Times* reporter traveled to Germany's Saarland region bordering France, a place "where French and German blood once spilled with gory regularity," to speculate about whether jingling euros in their pockets would create "a kind of coherence from the cacophonous history of wars that will make Europeans feel more European, opening the way to political union."[181] A *Wall Street Journal* journalist also chose a German town on the Rhine to talk about the "idealism" of European unity born of its "horrific past" and commented that "abstract concepts such as Europe" were hardly reliable "in an age of terrorism."[182] A *Washington Post* colleague in the European capital of Brussels merged the World Wars, competition with the United States,

176 "Euro-Optimism Continues for Retailers and the ECB – Shops Post Slight Increase in Sales, as Central Bank Keeps Rates Unchanged," *Wall Street Journal*, January 4, 2002, A6; Daniel Williams, "Euro's Circulation Spurs Gain against Dollar; 1.5 Percent Appreciation on First Day since Rollout Encourages Supporters," *Washington Post*, January 3, 2002, A14.

177 Angela Doland, "Europeans in 12 Countries Test Out Their Euros on First Day of Currency Changeover," Associated Press, January 1, 2002; Melinda Henneberger, "Reluctance in Greece to Let Go of the Coin of History," *New York Times*, December 31, 2001, A4; Edmund L. Andrews, "Germans Say Goodbye to the Mark, a Symbol of Strength and Unity," *New York Times*, January 1, 2002, A8.

178 Paul Geitner, "Europe Unites around Single Currency but Differences – Good and Bad – Survive," Associated Press, January 5, 2002.

179 Mort Rosenblum, "From Calais to Crete, Europe Wonders Whether Euro Will Spell Unity or Be Another Waterloo," Associated Press, January 1, 2002.

180 Colleen Barry, "More Than a Decade in Planning, Three Years on Paper, Euro Cash Becomes Legal Tender for 300 Million Europeans," Associated Press, December 31, 2001.

181 Steven Erlanger, "Today the Europeans Are Jingling Euros, Musing on the Unity They'll Buy Europe," *New York Times*, January 1, 2002, A8.

182 Neal Boudette, "It Takes More Than the Euro to Unite Europe – as Currency Hits the Street, Most Find the Bold Idea behind It an Abstraction," *Wall Street Journal*, December 31, 2001, A4.

and even colonialism to construct the euro's impact in terms of historical redemption and revenge.[183] The euro, he wrote, was "potent evidence" of European progress toward the "dream" of unity it first harbored after having "virtually destroyed itself in two world wars." But it also meant that "with their global empires gone and their economies dwarfed by those of the United States and Japan, countries such as France, Germany and Spain hope to win back some of the respect and influence they had when they were colonial powers."

A story by a reporter on a ten-country trip demonstrates the discourse found in this coverage. The writer found some evidence of "cultural union" – breakfast foods, marijuana and sports – as well as more "American" common ties – ketchup, English and a "firm commitment to democracy, free debate and individual liberties," if with a considerably more leftist spin.[184] But the final verdict stopped short of unity, and even shorter of competition: "What's not clear is whether these disparate elements of a pan-European culture can ever lead to a Europe that is as united as another wealthy transcontinental power, the United States. Europeans may talk, eat, travel, cheer and vote in increasingly common ways, but the continent is still a collection of sovereign nations." The *Wall Street Journal* – the preeminent source of U.S. business news – put it even more bluntly from Brussels: The "European Union has a long way to go before it produces a unified economy, let alone a unified Europe.... The result of Europe's chronic gridlock: The EU isn't likely to overtake the U.S. any time soon as the world's leading economic power."[185]

The discourses about the European Union that emerge from coverage of the changeover to the euro reveal some enduring constructions of the non-American "other" as well as some new emphases. The spotlight on history, on gruesome wars, and on long-standing, proudly affirmed cultural divisions helps paint a backward, provincial Europe that has not fully embraced modernity. As always, the focus on Europe's economic and political power, and its ability to compete with the United States, implies a construction of a superior America. The latter, however, is stated so frequently and so explicitly that it raises the question as to whether it might not betray doubts about it. Across virtually all of the correspondence analyzed for the twentieth century, American dominance was so taken for granted that it went largely unmentioned, and so did any likely competition. The uneasy question of American global leadership in the face of rising economic powers also influenced the last case examined in this chapter, a series of deadly terrorist attacks in India in 2008.

[183] T.R. Reid, "W. Europe Ready for the Euro; New Coins, Notes Signify 'More Than a Currency,'" *Washington Post*, December 31, 2001, A1.

[184] T.R. Reid, "Common Currency Builds on Common Culture; For Many Europeans, Euro's Arrival Strengthens Ties That Bind Continent," *Washington Post*, January 1, 2002, A1.

[185] Paul Hofheinz, "One Currency, Many Voices: Issues That Still Divide Europe – Policy Gridlock Remains, Hobbling EU's Clout as Economic Bloc," *Wall Street Journal*, January 2, 2002, A6.

Mumbai Attacks: Terrorism and Business among the "Rest"

> MUMBAI, India (AP) – Demands for action are being heard across India amid the anger over last week's rampage in Mumbai by militants accused of coming from Pakistan, but leaders of the two nuclear-armed neighbors are striving to keep tensions in check. Neither country has the appetite for a fourth war in six decades, and both sides seem to be hoping that U.S. diplomacy ... will defuse the situation, analysts said.... India fears the consequences a war would have on the huge economic gains it has made in recent years.[186]

The terrorist attacks that left nearly 200 people dead in Mumbai in late 2008 were identified repeatedly in the media as India's 9/11. It is fitting to conclude this analysis of the history of American foreign correspondence with a crisis that reflected both the pervasive presence of the media, as noted at the beginning of this chapter, and the overarching theme of the "war on terror," with a splash of Cold War nuclear standoff to boot. In addition to terrorism, Islamic fundamentalism, and atavistic hatreds that nuclear arms made all the more ominous, correspondence such as the AP article just quoted focused on two other themes – U.S. global leadership, returned to prominence, and India's economic power.

Modern India gained its independence in 1947, when neighboring Pakistan was also spun off into a member of the British Commonwealth.[187] Hostility between the two countries has been one of India's main foreign policy preoccupations since then, whereas India's policy of nonalignment in the Cold War influenced an early, uneasy U.S.-Pakistan alliance.[188] Washington walked a fine line, providing India with economic aid and Pakistan with military assistance even as the two countries continued their standoff and at times outright war, thereby often alienating them both. The hostility between the two countries took prominence on Washington's radar in the early 1990s, when Muslims in the Indian part of Kashmir rebelled in the wake of violence between Indian Hindus and Muslims, and jihadists came from Pakistan to help them. Increasingly in the post–Cold War era, the facts that both countries had nuclear programs, that Pakistan often functioned as a basis for Islamic terrorism, and that India's economic influence surged made their frequent conflicts a global concern and changed Washington's attitude toward New Delhi, while the partnership with Islamabad remained tense at best.[189]

186 Ravi Nessman, "India, Pakistan Tread Lightly after Mumbai Attack," Associated Press, December 2, 2008.

187 Nicholas Tarling, *Southeast Asia and the Great Powers* (London: Routledge, 2010), 16–41.

188 Harold A. Gould, *The South Asia Story: The First Sixty Years of U.S. Relations with India and Pakistan* (Los Angeles: SAGE, 2010).

189 Sumit Ganguly, Brian Shoup and Andrew Scobell, eds. *US-Indian Strategic Cooperation into the 21st Century: More than Words* (London: Routledge, 2006), 1.

Terrorist attacks, and anti-Muslim violence, had plagued India since the end of the Cold War, in Kashmir and in major cities, although hardly any had the spectacular impact and brazenness of those started on November 26, 2008.[190] Less than a dozen well-armed and trained militants from a fundamentalist group based in Pakistan attacked a series of targets in downtown Mumbai, including one of its most luxurious and historic hotels, and held off Indian police commandoes for three days, killing more than 170 people and injuring many more. The world's attention was riveted on the city, with not only mainstream foreign journalists and India's brand-new bevy of television news channels[191] but also social media users generating a constant feed of information.

The *Los Angeles Times* noted a darker side of the world's attention, speculating that the late-evening timing of the attacks "allows the story to hit news cycles in Europe and North America, with global publicity a key objective among terrorists hoping to undermine stability and spread fear."[192] For the first time in this research, the press also took notice of the information role of ordinary people. The *New York Times* published a story about how bystanders had recorded the unfolding attacks on Internet blogs, photo-sharing sites and short-message services, and called it "another case study in how technology is transforming people into potential reporters, adding a new dimension to the news media."[193] The authors wrote that such spontaneous feeds experienced none of the bureaucratic and logistical "headaches" faced by media, and they filled in the early gap when "mainstream media outlets [were] still struggling to understand the extent of the attacks" – which can be read as either an indictment of media or a dismissal of online information sharing before an understanding is reached. (Not everyone wished to be a part of the story, however: The AP described European survivors from the attack to one hotel who "waved away journalists eager for news.")[194]

In editorials, the newspapers explained why the attacks mattered through a very U.S.-centric lens that privileged the "war on terror" theme. *New York Times* editors urged Washington to intervene because the terror in Mumbai could push nuclear-armed neighbors into war, which would "divert even more of Pakistan's attention and troops away from fighting extremists on its western

[190] Ram Puniyani and Shabnam Hashmi, eds. *Mumbai Post 26/11: An Alternate Perspective* (Los Angeles: SAGE, 2010), xi.

[191] Shefali Anand and Vibhuti Agarwal, "Attack Coverage Tests India's Nascent News Channels," *Wall Street Journal*, December 1, 2008, A12.

[192] Mark Magnier and Subhash Sharma, "Attacks in Mumbai: Americans, Britons Apparently Targeted," *Los Angeles Times*, November 27, 2008, A1.

[193] Brian Stelter and Noam Cohen, "High-Tech Citizen Journalists Provide Glimpses That Transcend News Cycle," *New York Times*, November 30, 2008, A26.

[194] Ramola Talwar Badam, "Victims Speak of Night of Terror in Mumbai," Associated Press, November 27, 2008.

border with Afghanistan," and it would also be "hugely damaging to India's extraordinary economic progress."[195] At the *Wall Street Journal* and the *Washington Post*, editors saw evidence that the "war on terror is far from won, and it is migrating to democracies with weak antiterror defenses" – presumably unlike the United States with its stronger ones.[196]

The correspondence discourse about India was among the most reductive found in this book, restricting the country to essentially three images – its nuclear status, its tradition of terrorist attacks between Muslims and Hindus, and its rising economic power, including its film industry centered in Mumbai. The "hot Bollywood film industry" was one of the recurring images presented about Mumbai, probably in a nod to the popularity of entertainment news that had dramatically increased in mainstream newspapers in the 2000s.[197] The historic city of more than 16 million was constantly defined as "India's commercial capital," its "dream city," full of signs of "India's economic boom," including the "vast, heaving shantytowns" where many migrant workers attracted by the city's opportunities lived.[198] The correspondence hardly mentioned its profound sociopolitical contrasts and the disparities between the attack sites privileged by extraordinarily wealthy locals and Westerners, such as the Taj Mahal Palace hotel, whose "onyx columns and high alabaster ceilings" were portrayed in several stories, and other sites, such as a major train station, whose victims might have been more representative.[199] The disconnect between tourists' India and reality was captured in a story about Americans held up in the Taj during the siege, "their cameras filled with photos of Hindu temples and Buddhist caves."[200]

Correspondents for the *Wall Street Journal* argued that the hotel occupied "a singular place in Mumbai life" as "the center for business, entertaining, and upscale dining for the city's financial community and for visiting dignitaries," and wrote that attacks there damaged "the city's lofty ambitions of becoming

195 "The Horror in Mumbai," *New York Times*, December 1, 2008, A28.

196 "Murder in Mumbai," *Wall Street Journal*, November 28, 2008, A14; "Massacre in Mumbai," *Washington Post*, November 29, 2008, A14.

197 For example, one story focused on the lead attacks investigator, whose career had inspired Bollywood movies; Peter Wonacott and Geeta Anand, "Mumbai Cop Heralded in Film Leads Investigation of Terror Attacks," *Wall Street Journal*, December 5, 2008, A1.

198 Somini Sengupta, "For the Heroes of Mumbai, Terror Was a Call to Action," *New York Times*, December 2, 2008, A1; Tim Sullivan and Ravi Nessman, "India Terror Begins with Corpses on Train Platform," Associated Press, November 30, 2008; Emily Wax, "In Just Minutes, Mumbai Was under Siege; Young Gunmen Exploited Coastline Vulnerabilities to Slip into City and Methodically Spread Terror," *Washington Post*, December 1, 2008, A1.

199 Erika Kinetz, "Landmark Mumbai Hotel Targeted in Terrorist Spree," Associated Press, November 27, 2008; Puniyani and Hashmi, 16–22.

200 Emily Wax, "Ruthless Attackers, Desperate Victims; Survivors of Three-Day Mumbai Massacre Give Harrowing Accounts of Their Hours under Siege," *Washington Post*, November 30, 2008, A1.

an international finance capital."[201] Others said the "glitzy targets" symbolized "the new cosmopolitan face of the world's largest democracy" – the democratic moniker so common that it surfaced even in a quote from President Bush.[202] "Money drives Mumbai," a story lead pithily put it, and the correspondent went on to write that the "poor seem as traumatized as the representatives of a newer, more prosperous India that has embraced call centers, shopping malls and imported brands."[203] In speculating about the possible repercussions of the attacks, most stories argued they could hurt India's appeal to foreign investors as a "major international financial center," as well as its performance as "one of the engines of global economic growth," constructions that focused on the country's economy as its most salient feature.[204]

A *New York Times* story illustrates the construction of India as a country always in the grip of terror: The attacks are described as "particularly brazen" "even by the standards of terrorism in India."[205] India, one correspondent wrote, was unsuccessful in its battle against terror because political parties needed to "compete for the loyalty of Hindu and Muslim voters," a construction that again reinforces the perception of terrorism as endemic to certain faiths.[206] Similarly, another correspondent described Mumbai as "India's New York" because of its attractiveness to immigrants from across the country, but raised the specter of more violence among its religiously divided population.[207] Other journalists wrote that "communal violence between Hindus and Muslims" made Mumbai "no stranger to terrorist attacks," and that the whole country had "a history of violence by Hindus and criminal mafias as well as Muslim extremists" – a veritable hodgepodge of terror.[208] On the day the attacks started, the AP ran a sidebar on "some major attacks in India since

201 Peter Wonacott and Geeta Anand, "The Hunted: 'We Were Ready to Die,'" *Wall Street Journal*, November 28, 2008, A1; Geeta Anand and Jackie Range, "Terror in Mumbai: Attacks Hurt City's Bid to Be a World Finance Center," *Wall Street Journal*, November 28, 2008, A5.

202 Mark Magnier and Subhash Sharma, "Attacks in Mumbai: Americans, Britons Apparently Targeted," *Los Angeles Times*, November 27, 2008, A1; Mark Magnier, "Mumbai Takes a Deep Breath after the Crisis; the Bustling Economic Center Is Proud of Its Ability to Bounce Back. This Time, Though, the Scars Are Deep," *Los Angeles Times*, November 30, 2008, A1.

203 Mark Magnier, "Mumbai Takes a Deep Breath after the Crisis; the Bustling Economic Center Is Proud of Its Ability to Bounce Back. This Time, Though, the Scars Are Deep," *Los Angeles Times*, November 30, 2008, A1.

204 Robert F. Worth, "Lack of Preparedness Comes Brutally to Light," *New York Times*, December 4, 2008, A14; Heather Timmons and Keith Bradsher, "Violence Clouds India's Economic Future," *New York Times*, November 29, 2008, A11.

205 Somini Sengupta, "Terror Attacks Kill Scores in India; U.S. Hostages Reported Held at Hotels," *New York Times*, November 27, 2008, A1.

206 Somini Sengupta, "Crisis May Shift Political Landscape," *New York Times*, November 29, 2008, A11.

207 Emily Wax, "In a Resilient City, Hopes That Cooperation Prevails," *Washington Post*, November 29, 2008, A11.

208 Mark Magnier and Subhash Sharma, "Attacks in Mumbai: Americans, Britons Apparently Targeted," *Los Angeles Times*, November 27, 2008, A1; Sebastian Rotella and Mark Magnier,

2005," and the *Washington Post* later carried a similar rundown of terror attacks, defining Mumbai as "the scene of bombings that have killed hundreds of people since 1993."[209] In this discursive context, the city's description as famously resilient – "all too familiar with recovering from massive tragedy" – did little to alleviate the overall picture of gloom.[210]

In fact, the whole region was found to be "volatile" and a concern to Americans who were trying to mediate between Pakistan and India, in "stepped-up" efforts the attacks could "threaten."[211] After all, war seemed endemic to the region, because, as stories pointed out, the two countries – "nuclear-armed rivals" was an endlessly repeated description – had "fought three wars in the last 60 years."[212] Even worse, any deterioration of relations between India and Pakistan would "complicate matters for the U.S.," because it would "distract Pakistan" from helping out in the fight against al-Qaeda – an implicit affirmation of the importance of the "war on terror" frame that made all global events most interesting where they touched U.S. strategic interests.[213] The lead in a *Wall Street Journal* story linked the "world's largest democracy" to what it

"India Hunts for Survivors and Culprits; Commandos Launch Raids to Free Hostages; Death Toll at 125," *Los Angeles Times*, November 28, 2008, A1.

209 "A Look at Some Major Attacks in India," Associated Press, November 26, 2008; Rama Lakshmi, "Dozens Die in Mumbai Attacks; Hotels under Siege; Gunmen Said to Target Americans, Britons," *Washington Post*, November 27, 2008, A1; "India's Growing Terrorism," *Washington Post*, November 28, 2008, A16.

210 Mark Magnier, "Terrorized City Returns to Routines; Mumbai's Trains Are Full and People Are Out," *Los Angeles Times*, December 2, 2008, A4; Ramola Talwar Badam, "A Worried Mumbai Tries to Recover from Fatal Siege," Associated Press, November 29, 2008; Rama Lakshmi, "Mumbai Is Getting Back in Business; Gunmen-Hit Café Reopens; Denizens Resume Mundane Tasks," *Washington Post*, December 4, 2008, A16.

211 Emily Wax and Rama Lakshmi, "As Rice Presses Pakistan, Tens of Thousands Take to Streets," *Washington Post*, December 4, 2008, A16; Somini Sengupta and Keith Bradsher, "Indian Soldiers Seek Survivors of Terror Siege," *New York Times*, November 28, 2008, A1. See also Siobhan Gorman and Matthew Rosenberg, "Attacks Linked to Pakistan Group," *Wall Street Journal*, December 1, 2008, A6.

212 Matthew Rosenberg, "Attackers' Identity Remains Unclear," *Wall Street Journal*, November 28, 2008, A4; Laura King and Mark Magnier, "India and Pakistan Talking Tough; The Rivals Emphasize Their Right to Defend Themselves as Tension over Mumbai Grows and Leads Trickle In," *Los Angeles Times*, December 3, 2008, A3. On nuclear references, see among many Mark Magnier and Sebastian Rotella, "U.S. Leans on Pakistan; India Says Evidence in the Mumbai Attacks Increasingly Points to a Militant Group There," *Los Angeles Times*, December 4, 2008, A3; Muneeza Navqi, "India Blames 'Elements' in Pakistan for Attacks," Associated Press, November 28, 2008; Paul Peachey, "Mumbai Begins to Heal after Terrorist Rampage," Associated Press, November 30, 2008; Emily Wax, "Indian Commandos Battle Assailants; Attacks in Mumbai Commercial Center Kill at Least 125," *Washington Post*, November 28, 2008, A1.

213 Matthew Rosenberg, "Attackers' Identity Remains Unclear," *Wall Street Journal*, November 28, 2008, A4; Robert F. Worth, "India Says Pakistan Carried Out Attacks," *New York Times*, December 2, 2008, A6. On the "gravity" with which Washington viewed the fallout, see also Mark Magnier and Laura Kind, "India Challenges Pakistan to Act, Fast" *Los Angeles Times*, December 2, 2008, A1.

dubbed "a dramatic escalation of radical Islam's war" against it, again bringing the Mumbai reality in line with the major frame of the post-9/11 world.[214]

A boilerplate sentence in a follow-up story from a *New York Times* correspondent in Mumbai is highly revealing of the move away from understanding local realities and toward reducing foreign events to their "war on terror" frame that was pervasive in 2008 correspondence. The attacks are defined as having "stunned the world and left 173 people dead" – in that order.[215] The repeated reliance on the aspects of India's story that captivated the world – terrorism, business, and nukes – likely restricted the possibilities for readers unfamiliar with the country to understand its realities. Covered by a highly mobilized set of correspondents as well as local news outlets and new media users, the Mumbai attacks nevertheless brought little journalistic light to shine on India. The majority of the correspondence constructed a generic violence-torn country with ancient hatreds where the United States needed to intervene in order to bring a modicum of stability, although the problems were portrayed as so intractable as to raise doubts about Americans' willingness to do so.

Conclusions

This chapter has focused on the role of U.S. correspondence in international affairs in the post–Cold War, post-9/11 era, which witnessed a profound struggle over the global leadership abilities and intentions of both the United States and the American news media. Crushing some expectations that the end of the long standoff with the Soviet Union would usher in a globalization of U.S. economic and political values, the world in the 1990s and 2000s often seemed a little too much for Americans to take. Poignantly, in this deluge of policy preoccupations and information sources, the number of general interest publications with robust coverage of international affairs dwindled, posing a serious threat for the function of foreign correspondents as mediators that is one of the premises of this book.

For journalism, the times brought a new emphasis on speed and quantity to the detriment of in-depth investigation as well as a cacophony of competition with fewer resources to sort out trustworthy information. Those trends combined in a growing tendency to use shorthand descriptions – South Africa is like Africa, Mexico will be Mexico, and Europe is where world wars were fought – that are remarkably useless in helping readers form nuanced understandings of the world. The homogenization of news stories also progressively increased in each of the case studies from 1993 to 2008, with reporters often relying on the same quotes, the same perspectives, and the same boilerplate definitions

214 Yaroslav Trofimov and Peter Wonacott, "Terrorists Paralyze India's Business Capital," *Wall Street Journal*, November 28, 2008, A1.

215 Robert F. Worth, "Lack of Preparedness Comes Brutally to Light," *New York Times*, December 4, 2008, A14.

of everything from apartheid to Mumbai. One recalls the disdain that a correspondent in South Africa had for an American VIP election observer who could not pronounce Soweto correctly, and one wonders how many colleagues in the late 2000s still had the luxury of learning the local ways through extended international stays as opposed to parachuting assignments. Paradoxically, in all cases except for the euro's debut, reporting on reporting abounded, signaling a new awareness of the capricious role that the media – from television focusing on Sarajevo's wounded children to blogs detailing Mumbai terrorist moves – had in shaping events and global reactions to them.

These developments were fraught with danger when U.S. foreign policy, lacking the relatively easy paradigms of the Cold War, was also struggling for coherence. In the 1990s, as Washington experimented with new directions, the public space seemed more open for debate, whereas within the confines of the post-2001 "war on terror," a sharp drop occurred in discursive variety. Whether the "making the world safe from terrorism" frame would be enough to bring into the twenty-first century the "making the world safe for democracy" trend of U.S. policy, however, remained in doubt. It seemed unlikely that an impoverished correspondence discourse that reduced countries to single-word descriptions would nourish the kind of public debate that revitalized notions of enlightened American leadership. Indicative of such retrenchment is that, both in Washington's orientations and in foreign correspondence, the preoccupation with business relations dominated – from Johannesburg to Mumbai, it was increasingly the economy, stupid.

From Bosnia to India, one construction prevailed in news discourses – pessimism over whether countries had the political "maturity" and the ability to overcome racial, ethnic and historical hatreds necessary to govern themselves. The construction of the United States, however, varied greatly across the five cases, in ways that seem indicative of the self-doubting trends of U.S. policy. The discourses in correspondence from the Bosnian War drew a grim picture of the post–Cold War world, one on the verge of disintegration as apparent modernity crumbled in the faces of atavistic feuds. Such an unraveling world clearly demanded U.S. leadership, as would the nuclear tensions between India and Pakistan in 2008 in the even more hostile post-9/11 globe. For Mexico in 2000, the United States remained the model country to be imitated, just as it was the unsurpassable competitor for the European Union.

However, the constructions are crucially different in that the United States emerging from Bosnian correspondence is the much-vaunted disinterested leader of the free world trying to salvage a semblance of it, whereas the United States mediating between New Delhi and Islamabad is only interested in using both to pursue its own "war on terror" goals. Correspondence from Mexico in 2000, the European Union in 2002 and India in 2008 constructs the importance of these parts of the world – in fact, their very essence – predominantly in their relationship to the United States. Furthermore, the construction of U.S. interest is in terms of other countries' competition (from the European Union) or generation of problems, be they illegal immigration or the fight in Afghanistan, suggesting a very restricted, ad-hoc notion of U.S. leadership.

A paradox seems to be forming – as discourses about the world turn markedly inward to reflect more the United States than the foreign realities, in ways not found in this research since 1911, the uncertainty about how Washington should act toward them increases. As the United States evaluated its global options for the twenty-first century, certain themes found throughout this book remained constant – America's exceptional status, its moral obligation to disentangle ceaseless global quandaries, and the world's recurrent inability to form democratic, wealthy republics in its image. But as fewer correspondents with less time constructed more repetitive, reductive discourses about the world, the chances of having an informed debate about foreign affairs, and a broadly engaged global policy, seemed likely to diminish. The possible futures of foreign correspondence as mediator between the American public and an increasingly interconnected world on the verge of becoming too much to handle are the subject of the next chapter.

6

The Importance of Being There and Making People Care

The Troubled Present and Possible Futures of U.S. Foreign Correspondence

> PORT-AU-PRINCE, HAITI – Three weeks after converging upon the site of a devastating magnitude 7.0 earthquake, American anthropologists have confirmed the discovery of a small, poverty-stricken island nation known to its inhabitants as "Haiti." Located just 700 miles off the southeastern coast of Florida, the previously unaccounted-for country is believed to be home to an estimated 10 million people. Even more astounding, reports now indicate that these people have likely inhabited the impoverished, destitute region – unnoticed by the rest of the world – for more than 300 years.

In February 2010, the satirical U.S. newspaper *The Onion* published the front-page spoof just quoted under the headline, "Massive Earthquake Reveals Entire Island Civilization Called 'Haiti.'" A real earthquake, of course, had devastated the country in January, killing hundreds of thousand of people, but the satire in the article was directed at the media's involvement in foreign affairs, lambasting it for being so absent even from the United States' neighborhood that until tragedy struck and "experts" flocked in, nobody knew the island existed. With similarly trenchant humor, the *New York Times*–owned *International Herald Tribune* published a cartoon featuring a news anchor telling his television audience about Haiti, "A desperately poor neighbor is now the epicenter of media attention. Following a strong series of aftershocks, it will soon become invisible again." As a footnote, the cartoon added, "Unless Pat Robertson has some additional comments" – the U.S. televangelist had notoriously commented that the island was "cursed."[1]

Both satires spotlight the troubled present and the necessary future of American media involvement in foreign affairs as we enter the second decade of the twenty-first century. Dramatic human suffering stories like earthquakes

[1] *International Herald-Tribune*, January 16–17, 2010, 7; original emphasis.

continued to draw substantial journalistic attention in 2010 as they did since oral cultures began to share information.[2] Before and after such flurries of news, however, large swaths of the world disappear from America's radar as diminished numbers of correspondents, pressed for time and resources, rush off to the next crisis. The central argument of this book is that foreign correspondence is a fundamental locus of constructions about foreign countries and the United States itself, which has always helped shape the environment within which certain foreign policies were made and others excluded. The past four chapters analyzed the role of U.S. foreign correspondence in setting the discursive stage for how Americans have understood the world, and therefore evaluated options for acting in it, from 1848 to 2008.

This chapter examines the status of foreign correspondence in the American press today, why there is reason for profound concern about its ability to serve as an irreplaceable mediator, and how industry leaders are envisioning the future. A final section presents interviews with leaders of non-U.S. news organizations, offering a snapshot of their strategies for coping with challenges similar to those faced by their American counterparts. Through in-depth interviews with foreign editors, as well as with international editors, at the Associated Press, the *New York Times*, the *Los Angeles Times*, the *Washington Post* and the *Wall Street Journal*, one fundamental theme emerges.[3] It is going to be a hard sell to both penny-pinching managers and easily distracted readers, but foreign correspondents for broad-circulation media continue to bear the responsibility of telling the mass public why it should care about the world before events compel it to scramble to do so. As argued throughout this book, a restricted, ad hoc understanding of the world narrows and impoverishes the discursive environment, which in turn constrains the range of possible policies.

That responsibility is all the more important as mainstream media organizations overall today have fewer correspondents covering fewer parts of the world just when news stories affect more people more quickly than ever before. As

[2] Mitchell Stephens, *A History of News* 3rd ed. (New York: Oxford University Press, 2007), 26.

[3] Interviews were conducted by phone with: John Daniszewski, Associated Press, senior managing editor of international news, June 13, 2011; Mark Porubcansky, *Los Angeles Times*, deputy foreign editor, May 23, 2011; Greg Winter, *New York Times*, editor on the foreign desk, May 16, 2011; John Bussey, columnist and former foreign editor, *Wall Street Journal*, July 1, 2011; David E. Hoffman, part-time contributing editor (and assistant managing editor for foreign news, 2005–2009), *Washington Post*, June 7, 2011. In addition, four AP international news leaders were interviewed in person: Dan Perry, Europe and Africa desk editor (2004–2010), in London, January 9, 2009; Larry Heinzerling, deputy international editor (now retired), in New York, February 13, 2009; Charles Hanley, special correspondent, in New York, February 13, 2009; Charles Hutzler, Beijing chief of bureau, in Beijing, July 8, 2010. Finally, two former newspaper international editors were interviewed by phone for their historical perspective: Alvin Shuster, *Los Angeles Times*, foreign editor from 1983 to 1995 (May 31, 2011) and Peter Osnos, *Washington Post*, foreign editor in the late 1970s (June 1, 2011). All quotes from these journalists in this chapter are from these interviews. The author is most grateful to all of them for taking time out of exceptionally busy schedules for interviews that lasted an average of sixty minutes.

noted in the previous chapter, in less than a decade, the number of U.S. newspaper reporters based in foreign countries has declined by one-fourth, even though the United States remains engaged on multiple global fronts, starting with an active overseas conflict. Even though no hard counts of freelancers are available, the vast majority of U.S. media appear to be leaving coverage of international news to occasional stringers and wire agencies such as the AP, and some have balked at continuing their AP subscriptions, leaving their readers to scour the World Wide Web for foreign news. The five U.S. news organizations discussed in this chapter are the bright spots in this gloomy picture, but they are also adapting to the realities of the online world. Even though some see promise in the Web's potential for multiplying sources and engaging audiences, two major concerns make it unlikely that the Internet in itself can replace the function of news organizations.

The first issue is that a reader needs to actively seek information online, or else rely on preselected "my news" feeds, in both cases missing the broad exposure to issues, which are interesting but not of personal interest, that newspapers used to drop literally at one's doorstep. The second problem is that a Web deprived of trusted traditional international news sources like the AP and the national U.S. newspapers risks becoming, in the words of Google's chief executive, a "cesspool" of useless information – an especially frightening perspective for an increasingly interconnected world.[4] Survey data from 2010 showed that the Internet overtook newspapers, but not television, for the first time as the regular source for news – but virtually all the sources people go to online are either the "old" media or their aggregators.[5] That is why talking about newspapers as organizations producing news, not as printed products, matters to the future of journalism. And that is why the persistent crisis of print journalism means, in the words of *New York Times* media critic David Carr, that the "sky is falling. The question now is how many people will be left to cover it."[6]

Can the Market Save the Marketplace of Ideas? Possible Futures of Journalism

The most frightening aspect of the current crisis in journalism is that, from an institutional and economic crisis, it is fast becoming a crisis in the demand for the kind of news that sustains self-government. Every society at every time in history has wanted to know "wassup," to quote the famous Budweiser advertisement, and has developed different methods of handling that need for information gathering and distribution. Journalism as practiced by elite

4 Quoted in David Carr, "Mourning Old Media's Decline," *New York Times*, October 29, 2008, B1.

5 Tom Rosenstiel, "Five Myths about the Future of Journalism," *Washington Post*, April 7, 2011.

6 Carr.

newspapers in the United States in 2012 – reporting and investigating facts of public interest by professionals – is a relatively recent model, developed in America by commercial media over approximately the 160 years discussed in this book. While it has continually evolved, one normative facet has remained constant: the necessity of a free press providing an open public sphere for an informed citizenry in a democratic self-government.

Different ways grew over time to fulfill these responsibilities, from the stridently partisan political sheets of the early republic to gigantic operations aimed at educating a newly reading public in nationhood to today's perspective, shared by all the editors interviewed for this chapter, that the press needs to provide context for people to elaborate on important developments across the world. The platforms and styles with which the press – and its multimedia incarnations – furnish this essential public service might well be changing, but its continued functioning is critical to the preservation of democracy. If what will be called journalism in the twenty-first century moves away from it, then it is not just a crisis of a particular institution, but of the entire system of governance of which the press has been an integral part since its modern founding.

Some journalism historians, such as Mitchell Stephens, have suggested that the basic function of distributing the news might move in the future from the news media to online and social networks that many young users today rely on for information.[7] For people younger than thirty, the Internet in late 2010 inched past television and eclipsed newspapers as the main source for national and international news – although such survey data does not do justice to the role of newspapers as the original reporters of news distributed off print.[8] A scenario of newsless newspapers would leave them to provide the space for analysis and commentary, in a sort of digital-age public square, perhaps capitalizing on the ability of "soft news media" discussed in the previous chapter to interest the least-engaged Americans in public affairs information. Such non-journalistic sources have rapidly increased their politically relevant content and therefore might ultimately help foster a more engaged electorate and a more democratic information environment. They cannot substitute the agenda-setting, consensus-building function of professional journalism, however, whose standards, if sometimes unmet, sustain quality public discourse, according to Bruce Williams and Michael Delli Carpini, who researched political knowledge.[9]

[7] Speech to the joint AEJMC/AJHA journalism historians' conference held on March 12, 2011, at New York University.

[8] "Internet Gains on Television as Public's Main News Source," Pew Research Center Publications, retrieved from http://www.pewresearch.org. On survey data not reflecting the importance of print, see the testimony of the Pew Research Center's Project for Excellence in Journalism director, Tom Rosenstiel, "Where the News Comes From – and Why It Matters," September 25, 2009, also retrieved from http://www.pewresearch.org.

[9] Bruce A. Williams and Michael X. Delli Carpini, "*The Daily Show* and *The Colbert Report* in a Changing Information Environment: Should Fake News Be Held to Real Standards?" in

Increasingly individualized and specialized communication without the reach of institutional media could end up shrinking, rather than broadening, the public sphere.[10]

For professional journalism to continue to exist, however, its business model clearly needs revamping, as the layoffs, shutdowns and downright disappearance of newspapers in the late 2000s indicate. The Pew Research Center's Project for Excellence in Journalism found in 2011 that newspaper newsrooms had shrunk by 30 percent since 2000.[11] Some have suggested that commercial media outlets might rely on nonprofits or even government subsidies akin to the license fees that support the British Broadcasting Corporation. Startling many news media observers, the *Los Angeles Times* announced in May 2012 that it would use a $1 million grant from the Ford Foundation to hire reporters in several beats, including the U.S.-Mexican border and Brazil.[12] Government involvement, however, is a model the American media establishment adamantly opposes. Since the end of the party press era in antebellum America, virtually all U.S. mainstream media have relied much more on advertising than on circulation to finance their operations, and that is one of the reasons why they have suffered more than news organizations elsewhere in the world after the Internet started redirecting ad money.

In a 2009 *Columbia Journalism Review* article, Leonard Downie Jr. and Michael Schudson defended the importance of newsrooms over citizen journalists in providing "news judgment oriented to a public agenda and a general audience.... Something is gained when reporting, analysis, and investigation are pursued collaboratively by stable organizations that can facilitate regular reporting by experienced journalists, support them with money, logistics and legal services, and present their work to a large public."[13] They suggested that the American people help pay substantially for journalism as a public good through tax exemptions, philanthropic foundations, public broadcasting, university funds, and even the Federal Communications Commission. As Schudson put it a little more than a year later, such a proposal for government or interest-group funding seems "dead in the water," shot down by majorities

Will the Last Reporter Please Turn Out the Lights: The Collapse of Journalism and What Can Be Done to Fix It, ed. Robert W. McChesney and Victor Pickard (New York and London: The New Press, 2011), 306–313.

10 W. Lance Bennett and Robert M. Entman, eds. *Mediated Politics: Communication in the Future of Democracy* (Cambridge: Cambridge University Press, 2001), 474.

11 Tom Rosenstiel and Amy Mitchell, "Overview: The State of the News Media 2011," Pew Research Center's Project for Excellence in Journalism, retrieved from http://stateofthemedia.org/.

12 James Rainey, "L.A. Times Will Use $1-million Grant to Expand Key Beats," *Los Angeles Times*, May 18, 2012, AA3.

13 Leonard Downie Jr. and Michael Schudson, "The Reconstruction of American Journalism," *Columbia Journalism Review*, November/December 2009, 31. Many essays making similar points about possible public/government roles in paying for the media are in part II of McChesney and Pickard.

nearing 80 percent of news executives who are members of the American Society of News Editors and the Radio Television Digital News Association, according to a 2010 survey.[14] Suspicion of public money with strings attached by the government is enduring, even though the large companies that own most media institutions have also been widely criticized for calling the tune in coverage over editorial preferences.[15] A new history focused on the tension between "the business of news and the philosophy of journalism" argues that American journalism has always needed resources and independence – put bluntly, news media best serve society when they "build a big enough audience so that [they] can make enough money to tell anyone to go to hell."[16]

If one agrees that journalism is essential to self-governance, that solid reporting is the essence of journalism, and that financial resources are necessary for solid reporting, then the business crisis of American mainstream media, particularly newspapers, becomes a sociopolitical concern. Schudson's later, more modest forecast was "journalism on a diet with supplements" – with less reporting by staffers supplemented by online, user-generated information.[17] One major problem is that, as the time and money to do hard news and investigative reporting vanish, the reliance on PR handouts and propaganda increases.[18] Several major news organizations have been trying to fight back budget cuts, mostly by experimenting with ways to make money off their stories when used online, especially by aggregators. At a 2009 conference on economic models for news, Bernard Lunzer, the president of the Newspaper Guild, argued that preventing aggregators from getting "a free ride" was a top priority, meaning that newspapers should find ways to get revenue for their online content. Regaining some control over online revenue was also a crucial step noted by the Pew Research Center's Project for Excellence in Journalism in 2011.[19] The AP announced in 2009 that it would take legal action against Web sites that used articles distributed by the news cooperative without obtaining permission and sharing revenue.[20] The AP's financial situation is a paradox of the times – as its approximately 1,700 member newspapers slash staff, it relies

[14] Michael Schudson, "News Crisis in the United States: Panic – and Beyond," (paper presented at the annual meeting of the International Communication Association, Boston, May 28, 2011); "Tomorrow's News," Pew Research Center, April 12, 2010, retrieved from www.pewresearch.org.

[15] For a productive criticism of the spread of the commercial model as corrosive for the public sphere, see Edward S. Herman and Robert W. McChesney, *The Global Media: The New Missionaries of Global Capitalism* (London: Cassell, 1997).

[16] Christopher B. Daly, *Covering America: A Narrative History of a Nation's Journalism* (Amherst: University of Massachusetts Press, 2012), 394.

[17] Schudson, 2011.

[18] Robert McChesney and John Nichols, "Down the News Hole," in McChesney and Pickard, 105.

[19] Rosenstiel and Mitchell.

[20] Richard Pérez-Peña, "A.P. Seeks to Rein in Sites Using Its Content," *New York Times*, April 7, 2009, B1.

increasingly on its services, but ultimately also has less money to pay for them, and some editors have experimented with doing away with AP's national and international wires and focusing instead on local news.[21]

Furthermore, the growing trend on the part of media institutions to "monetize the web," appearing to curtail the free – and gratis – flow of news on the Internet, was met with skepticism.[22] The spring 2011 gamble of the *New York Times* was a potential game changer – the newspaper introduced a paywall, giving its Web site users only twenty, then ten, free articles per month and blocking content after that unless they subscribed to a payment plan. While the *Wall Street Journal* has done well with a paywall, presumably because of its financial information targeting elite audiences, survey data from 2010 showed that only 23 percent of respondents would pay a paltry $5 a month for online access if it were the only way to keep their local newspaper alive.[23] Would a public used to free content online accept having to pay for it? Would the shift signal a possible bifurcation in two news-reading publics, with those most interested and willing to invest in news having access to quality sources and the vast majority of people relegated to getting snippets of information from more dubious fonts?[24] In whichever way the financial crisis of professional journalism will be solved, one consequence was already clear in 2012 – the combination of business retrenchments and online distribution was reshaping content in overt and subtle ways even at the most traditional media.

In the simplest terms, fewer resources have meant a shrinking news hole. In 2008, with more than half of U.S. newspapers with circulations of more than 100,000 cutting between 10 and 19 percent of their staff, the makeup of the papers changed, according to data by the Pew Research Center's Project for Excellence in Journalism.[25] The most evident flip was between foreign and community news: Sixty-four percent of newspapers decreased their space for foreign news, and 62 percent increased their news hole for community news. Surveys suggest that such a strategy is risky: While only about a third of respondents in 2009 said they would miss "a lot" reading the local newspaper if it stopped publishing, 68 percent in another survey the same year said it would be an "important loss" if the large national newspapers disappeared.[26]

[21] Jon Fine, "The Scoop on the Associated Press," *BusinessWeek*, November 6, 2008.

[22] Amy Mitchell and Tom Rosenstiel, "Overview: The State of the News Media 2012," Pew Research Center's Project for Excellence in Journalism, retrieved from http://stateofthemedia.org/.

[23] "Major Trends: The State of the News Media 2011," Pew Research Center's Project for Excellence in Journalism, retrieved from http://stateofthemedia.org/.

[24] Alex S. Jones, *Losing the News: The Future of the News That Feeds Democracy* (Oxford: Oxford University Press, 2009), xviii.

[25] "The Changing Newsroom: Gains and Losses in Today's Papers," July 21, 2008, retrieved from http://www.journalism.org.

[26] "Stop the Presses? Many Americans Wouldn't Care a Lot If Local Papers Folded," March 12, 2009, Pew Research Center, retrieved from http://www.pewresearch.org; "Press Accuracy

More systematic changes, however, are affecting news production in ways that are likely to endure even if by some miracle all reporters were hired back.

In 2007–2008, the AP commissioned a study of 18-to-34-year-old news consumers in the United States and other countries. It found that people got their news as a byproduct of checking email, trying to escape boredom and multitasking, behaviors that led them to scan an excess of headlines in "largely shallow and erratic news consumption."[27] Fatigued by information overload over which they felt they had no control, but using some news knowledge as social currency, the young adults also preferred sports and entertainment, because such stories offer simple plots with easy resolution. Out of the study, the AP proffered recommendations that ranged from repackaging news so that navigation is easier online to "bringing closure to stories whenever possible." It also announced it would reshape its editorial workflow to adjust to faster reports of "what is happening, not what has happened," a perspective echoed by a competitor, Reuters, in its vaguely unsettling advertising line, "Before it's news, it's Reuters."[28] A scholarly study of print and online newsroom practices, combined with content analysis of articles, in Argentina's largest daily newspapers explored similar news consumption lessons for newspapers everywhere.[29]

Pablo Boczkowski found that a defining change in news consumption is driving a revolution in news production: People consider news a break from work to get at their computers, not a leisure home activity for the evening or weekends. To accommodate that interest, news producers are putting out more stories faster and continuously monitoring other sites, so that they end up all reproducing the same content both online and in print: "In an age of information plenty, what most consumers get is more of the same," Boczkowski concluded.[30] That homogenization leads to two paradoxical social outcomes: The more time they spend feeding the online beast, the less time journalists have to invest in investigative public affairs reporting, which is the kind of content that allows media to influence decision makers. But if they choose to disregard the public's preference – increasingly hard to do because every click is easily counted and timed online – then they could alienate the mass public, thus also losing what gives them influence.

In addition to such a lose-lose situation, Boczkowski argues that "citizen journalism," or news content generated by such an occasional, distracted public

Rating Hits Two-Decade Low," Pew Research Center for the People & the Press, September 13, 2009, retrieved from http://people-press.org.

[27] "A New Model for News: Studying the Deep Structure of Young-Adult News Consumption," Associated Press, June 2008, 42, retrieved from http://www.ap.org.

[28] "A New Model for News: Studying the Deep Structure of Young-Adult News Consumption," Associated Press, June 2008, 58, retrieved from http://www.ap.org.

[29] Pablo J. Boczkowski, *News at Work: Imitation in an Age of Information Abundance* (Chicago: University of Chicago Press, 2010).

[30] Boczkowski, 6.

interested in "sports, crime and entertainment," as he observed, can hardly be expected to make up for professional journalists' decreasing coverage of public affairs news.[31] The situation is only likely to worsen as more people get their news, whether from the *New York Times* or Facebook, on mobile applications, a trend that the Pew Research Center's Project for Excellence in Journalism called the new era of media in 2012.[32] Whereas on-the-go news consumption meant increased interest in the news overall, the report also noted as troubling "the extent to which technology intermediaries now control the future of news." Furthermore, one wonders what impact the even more cursory, literally small glance that mobile owners give their news will have on the content that organizations will privilege for smartphones and tablets. Is analysis of foreign politics likely to be seen as a revenue-creating app? Do correspondents covering a continent, who have to feed Twitter and Facebook, and perhaps also shoot photos and edit audio slideshows, have any time to investigate?

The growing, and problematic, importance of the audience to journalistic production "heightens preexisting tensions between editorial relevance and consumer taste," because even though journalists tend to privilege public affairs, most consumers do not, and the latter's preferences have crept into press work practices.[33] From journalistic routines, such consumer choices trickle into the language of news, as reporters and editors not only evaluate what stories their communities are more likely to read, but also write the texts in language, and shorthand, that their readers are supposed to share.[34] Word choices that might appear conspiratorially ideological to some readers are often selected by journalists because of their perception of what words will capture the audience's attention and facilitate their understanding, according to one study.[35] One of the language norms that mainstream journalists usually apply is word choices that minimize bias and involvement, thus reflecting the ethos of objectivity, fairness and balance.

After all, the reader – or the image of the reader that a journalist holds – has long been a paramount consideration in news judgments. A 1911 manual on "the practice of journalism" advised that news "in its broadest sense, is that which is of interest to the readers – the public," and what interested the public was prominence, proximity, unusualness, magnitude, human interest and timeliness.[36] Throughout the twentieth century, however, journalists assumed that they were trained to assess those values and present interesting news that the public needed to learn. Today, the expectation is that the newspaper will

31 Boczkowski, 182–183.

32 Mitchell and Rosenstiel.

33 Boczkowski, 143–146.

34 Colleen Cotter, *News Talk: Investigating the Language of Journalism* (Cambridge: Cambridge University Press, 2010).

35 Cotter, 84.

36 Walter Williams and Frank L. Martin, *The Practice of Journalism: A Treatise on Newspaper Making* (Columbia, MO: E.W. Stephens Publishing, 1911), 212–213.

"speak to us as friend, not as civics instructor," a study of American front pages concluded, evidenced by the growth of features with personal touches, human interest and the voices of "everyman."[37] Pressures from the online interaction, coupled with pressures to stay in business, are forcing many newsrooms to delegate news judgment to the readers who prefer infotainment, thus losing the public's trust and influence with policymakers. Some even argue that the "social responsibility model of journalism is outdated" and elitist, and media should embrace serving only specific interest audiences.[38]

Among the biggest losers in this dynamic is accountability journalism – the news stories that keep the record – that then is followed up from different angles with investigations, practices that can often seem dull and are always time consuming, but that form the core of hard news.[39] Some saw such record-keeping, following-up essence as in grave danger in fall 2009, when an AP memo was released that urged staffers to "*focus* on what gets *used* and *eliminate* the *leftovers*."[40] As an example, the memo used a chart on stories about Somali pirates that showed that the AP's "production of content often continues to coast along well after the public's interest flags. Yes, we produce a lot of copy when usage is at its highest, which should be our aim. But our production remains stubbornly high, even after usage plummets. That's wastage." Certainly, the AP editors are right that no media organization can survive if its stories are not used, and the memo went on to encourage staffers to break more news on "the big stuff." Letting the vagaries of usage determine what is the big stuff, however, and what becomes the record, can become a dangerous delegation of journalistic judgment that risks impoverishing the overall public discourse.

Another irony in the growingly interconnected relationship between news media and readers in the twenty-first century is that, whereas traditional media strive to highlight their credibility compared to other, easily found outlets on the Web, the public does not see it that way. A 2009 survey found that fewer than one in three Americans believe that news organizations "get the facts straight" and are "careful to avoid bias," whereas two out of three feel stories are "often inaccurate" and media are "politically biased," all dramatic changes from public evaluations from the mid-1980s.[41] Paradoxically, whereas national audience media had a financial incentive to keep their reporting as free from bias as possible, news organizations in today's polarized, echo-chamber media

37 Michele Weldon, *Everyman News: The Changing American Front Page* (Columbia: University of Missouri Press, 2008), 3, 43.

38 Rachel Davis Mersey, *Can Journalism Be Saved? Rediscovering America's Appetite for News* (Santa Barbara, CA: Praeger, 2010), 125.

39 Jones, 4–5.

40 Megan Garber, "The AP: Intimations of Politico," *Columbia Journalism Review*, October 16, 2009; emphasis original.

41 "Press Accuracy Rating Hits Two Decade Low," Pew Research Center for the People & the Press, September 13, 2009, retrieved from http://people-press.org.

world might find that opinion sells better, and costs less to produce, than dispassionate debate.[42] More than half of survey respondents also said they were not familiar enough with the *New York Times* and the *Wall Street Journal* to be able to say whether they trusted them or not, even though those newspapers are widely considered by elites, policymakers and scholars as the best general news and business news providers, respectively, in the country. That is a particularly discouraging finding for those who have argued that instead of aiming for the lowest common denominator, newspapers need to make quality journalism the key to business success, because readers will only buy a newspaper they trust, and advertisers will only pay a newspaper consumers read.[43]

One more feature of traditional journalism that is now imperiled is the privileges it receives under American law. Since the First Amendment to the Constitution, a free press has been integral to free speech, rights to be protected for democracy to flourish. In the twentieth century, a series of Supreme Court cases enshrined added responsibilities for the press, allowing and sometimes prescribing it the freedom to act as a watchdog of government at all levels, aggressive and even fallacious if short of malice. Protected by law and buffeted by economic success, newspapers could not only be influential but also able to afford their objective ethics, to resist the pressure to publish a story before it was thoroughly verified.[44] But as today's journalists have less time for verification, as content moves toward the less objective, tabloid, and advocacy models of communication, and as readers seem increasingly mistrustful of distinctions between factual and non-journalistic content, legal protections for a kind of journalism without public affairs news at its core might be reconsidered. That brings us back to a central issue – the interplay between forms of journalism and forms of government. Creating a marketplace of ideas, after all, is a public good, not just customer service for newspaper subscribers.

It is in this vicious cycle that the business problem of print journalism becomes a content problem on every platform and ultimately a problem of what news sees the daylight in the public sphere to guide policy formation. The vast majority of the breaking news that is circulated, commented on, and sometimes improved in the vast reaches of the Web still originates from a few institutions, such as the major newspapers, that invest millions of dollars in reporting. Information distribution might be costless, but its production is still a very expensive endeavor, so that two of the famous five Ws of journalism today might be who cares about information and what are they willing to pay

42 Jones, 81–100. For a similar point that also references neuroscience to explain why emotion sells better than objectivity, see Jack Fuller, *What Is Happening to News: The Information Explosion and the Crisis of Journalism* (Chicago: University of Chicago Press, 2010), 73.

43 Philip Meyer, *The Vanishing Newspaper: Saving Journalism in the Information Age* (Columbia: University of Missouri Press, 2004), 7.

44 Jones, 105.

for it.[45] For all their democratic potential, most news sites have a "parasitical relationship" to newspapers, in the words of a media scholar and columnist.[46] Solid journalism in the twenty-first century might not need print or even ads, but it does need cash. It is finding it increasingly hard to get that – newspaper revenues continued to plummet in 2012[47] – and ever harder to do so without betraying its public service mission in quality or reach.

If both the public sphere and the information distribution characteristics of journalism are to continue to buttress democracy in the digital age, the possible increase in public participation cannot succeed without quality reporting by professionals. In the final scene of the movie *All the President's Men*, two dogged young reporters are told that on their Watergate investigation nothing is riding, except for "the First Amendment to the Constitution, freedom of the press, and maybe the future of the country." Echoing that sentiment, the editors of a 2011 collection of essays on the future of journalism in the twenty-first century, tellingly titled, *Will the Last Reporter Please Turn Out the Lights*, wrote that "the existential crisis for news media is, in fact, an existential crisis for self-government... just about everything rides on how the crisis in journalism plays out."[48]

Given the power and the reach of U.S. influence globally in the 2010s, when it comes to foreign correspondence, a vital aspect of international relations – the ability to form some understanding of the world – is also riding on whether the American press will continue to engage foreign realities.

Staying Power: Possible Futures of Foreign Correspondence

Reporting foreign news for American audiences in the twenty-first century is more necessary, more expensive, more competitive and more endangered than at any other time discussed in this book. The step from financial to political and social is short. Media organizations are pondering a question that reflects the larger journalistic concerns discussed earlier: In the era of cheap air travel and wireless connection, of Facebook and WikiLeaks, do traditional media need to invest substantial portions of their dwindling budgets on foreign correspondents who produce lengthy analyses on obscure corners of the world?

Yes is the answer this book suggests, and so do all the editors interviewed for this research, and so should policymakers who are interested in a truly informed democratic process that goes beyond manipulation, secrecy and special interests. The simple reason is that general-interest news media with continuous

[45] James T. Hamilton, *All the News That's Fit to Sell: How the Market Transforms Information into News* (Princeton, NJ: Princeton University Press, 2004), 231, 238.

[46] Eric Alterman, "Out of Print: The Death and Life of the American Newspaper," in McChesney and Pickard, 14.

[47] "Key Findings: The State of the News Media 2012," Pew Research Center's Project for Excellence in Journalism, retrieved from http://stateofthemedia.org/.

[48] McChesney and Pickard, ix.

foreign coverage are uniquely positioned to give readers global perspectives that are vital in forming a productive discursive environment. As some editors argue, in today's world of migration, Skype, and borderless trade, it is difficult even to distinguish "foreign" news from other kinds of hard-hitting reports. What is vastly more complex is how to continue to produce quality foreign correspondence that is not drowned out by soft news and non-journalistic production.[49]

"Virtually anyone can board an airplane to anywhere. And when they land, they can flip open a laptop and begin to blog. Correspondents are not so *special* anymore," John Maxwell Hamilton muses in his masterful history of U.S. foreign correspondents.[50] Hamilton and others see increased democratic potential and development opportunity in the assertion that anyone can be a foreign correspondent, pointing out that citizen journalists and "parachuted" reporters can uncover fresher, less formal perspectives than established news bureaus.[51] Richard Sambrook, formerly of the BBC, wrote that, as more people and institutions, including governments, take to the Web, "anyone with an interest in the [foreign] event can hear direct from the protagonist rather than via an edited version from a newspaper or broadcasters."[52]

Two concerns stem from that scenario, however – that one needs to have a great enough interest to invest the time in searching for news, and that accountability is lost. Very few people search online for international news, and even those who do are likely to look only for topics that they are predisposed to care about.[53] News organizations are trying to branch out into social media to make their international coverage easier to find and more appealing. In December 2009, for example, the AP and other agencies created a Facebook page for their coverage of the UN climate conference in Copenhagen. New research, however, is finding that the role of social media in promoting awareness of public affairs news among younger adults is minimal, even though it does help exposure.[54] Niche publications and sites that can monetize on audiences interested in specialized foreign news have been flourishing, from Bloomberg to the online-only, mostly freelance international news Web site Global Post. Several nonprofit upstarts, such as the Pulitzer Center on Crisis Reporting and the

49 For a series of journalistic perspectives on the future of foreign news, see "Reporting from Faraway Places: Who Does It and How?" *Nieman Reports* 64/3 (Fall 2010).

50 John Maxwell Hamilton, *Journalism's Roving Eye: A History of American Foreign Reporting* (Baton Rouge: Louisiana State University Press, 2009), 243.

51 David D. Perlmutter and John Maxwell Hamilton, eds. *From Pigeons to News Portals: Foreign Reporting and the Challenge of New Technology* (Baton Rouge: Louisiana State University Press, 2007).

52 Richard Sambrook, *Are Foreign Correspondents Redundant? The Changing Face of International News* (Oxford: Reuters Institute for the Study of Journalism, 2010), 34.

53 Sambrook, 40.

54 Wolfgang Donsbach, Mathias Rentsch and Cornelia Walter, "Everything but the News: Despite the Boom of Social Media, the Youth's Daily News Consumption Still Relies on Traditional News Sources" (paper presented at the annual meeting of the International Communication Association, Boston, May 29, 2011). Paper kindly provided by Dr. Donsbach.

International Reporting Project, give grants to journalists to pursue foreign stories and place them with national media outlets.[55] But none of them purport to routinely reach a mass audience, which is key to avoid the kind of information imbalance that has worrisome ramifications for political deliberations.

Also worrisome is that understanding complex events "takes skill, time, and experience, all of which are disappearing from the world of foreign reporting," in Sambrook's words, substituted by easy-in-and-out assignments and reliance on social media and non-professionals. Most have observed with dismay the rise in so-called parachute correspondents who, enabled by digital technology, can be efficiently dispatched wherever news breaks, but they tend to have very little knowledge of the country at hand.[56] The trend to parachute reporters goes up as foreign bureaus shut down, across not only newspapers but also broadcasters, including CNN but with the exception of National Public Radio, which is growing its international coverage on the air and online.[57] Whereas the ability of modern media organizations to react to news and to harness eyewitness accounts through social media is unparalleled, what risks being dangerously neglected is the expertise of journalists who have tried to understand a country *before* it became news, and therefore can explain it best when the crisis occurs.

People who want to communicate their opinion or bear witness to events from around the world do have an unprecedented ability to make their voice heard. It is undeniable, and encouraging, that non-professionals using social media are increasingly visible providers of hard-to-get information, as was evident in the 2011 uprisings across North Africa, known as the "Arab Spring."[58] From Tunisia to Syria, cell phone video and Facebook posts became such critical sources of news that mainstream media regularly relied on them. They are unlikely, however, to replace the mediator role of professional journalists who make it their job to tell a country's story – with sufficient financial, legal, copyediting, and distribution resources to ensure some standards. Across all forms of political news, professional journalists have drastically lost the ability to control the agenda. The inherent diffusion and breadth of voices portends well for democracy, but only if this new "media regime" retains some of the practices and values of the mainstream media, such as plurality, transparency and professionalism, as Williams and Delli Carpini argue.[59]

[55] Jodi Enda, "Retreating from the World," *American Journalism Review*, December/January 2011, 14–29.

[56] Sambrook, 18; Simon Cottle, "Journalism and Globalization," in *The Handbook of Journalism Studies*, ed. Karin Wahl-Jorgensen and Thomas Hanitzsch (New York: Routledge, 2009), 347.

[57] Lucinda Fleeson, "Bureau of Missing," *American Journalism Review*, October/November 2003, 32–39; Enda, 14–29.

[58] On the impact of social media on the "Arab Spring" and other protest movements, see the dedicated issue of *Journal of Communication* 6–2 (April 2012).

[59] Bruce A. Williams and Michael X. Delli Carpini, *After Broadcast News: Media Regimes, Democracy, and the New Information Environment* (Cambridge: Cambridge University Press, 2011).

Another growing and complex trend in foreign news is that local journalists working for U.S. media in their own countries are an increasingly large part of foreign staff at AP and elsewhere, because they have the advantage of local knowledge and access, in addition to cheaper costs. The expatriate American reporter, however, has the significant responsibility of bridging the discursive spaces of the foreign country and the home audience, as noted in Chapter 1, so an entirely local staff is unlikely to be the solution. The growing reliance on freelancers in conflict zones is also troubling, because they are less likely to have institutional protection and training, and can jeopardize not only their lives but also the work of all journalists trying to bear witness to dangerous situations.[60] When a freelancer is under arrest for accusations of spying, for example, the question of who is officially a "journalist" rings much more urgent than an academic debate.

The changing practices of foreign correspondence are having an impact on content, and changing content is likely to have a significant impact on policy formulation. In foreign correspondence, too, speed has become a dominant principle, forcing the fewer reporters out in the field to continuously produce breaking news updates, often at the expense of depth. The style also increasingly conforms to online content, with more vivid, personal accounts stronger in opinion than facts that can capture younger readers traditionally less interested in global political issues.[61] In foreign news as in all journalism in the digital age, editors and especially managers try to gauge public interest. The main problem in engaging the non-specialist public in foreign news is that crisis and disasters briefly fascinate, but ongoing issues are harder to follow.[62] In 2010, for example, the public was most interested in the devastating earthquake in Haiti, but the only other foreign story rounding up the top fifteen news of the year was the dramatic, live rescue of Chilean miners – both stories that required very little understanding of each country, both of which quickly disappeared from view.[63] A further irony is that dramatic news coverage, aimed at grabbing the public's attention, and shorn of contextual analysis, can also help alienate the audience from both the world and the media.[64]

A Pew study of Americans' news preferences from 1986 to 2007 found that "foreign news," defined as coverage of other countries, stayed consistently near the bottom of the nineteen separate categories of news, with an average of 17 percent of respondents following it "very closely," while "disaster" and

60 Shahan Mufti, "A World of Trouble: Who's a Journalist? In Today's War Zones, the Answer Matters," *Columbia Journalism Review*, July/August 2010, 14–16.

61 Sambrook, 31.

62 Sambrook, 62.

63 "Top Stories of 2010: Haiti Earthquake, Gulf Oil Spill," Pew Research Center for the People & the Press, December 21, 2010, retrieved from http://people-press.org.

64 Greg Philo, "The Mass Production of Ignorance: News Content and Audience Understanding," in *International News in the Twenty-First Century*, ed. Chris Paterson and Annabelle Sreberny (Hants: John Libbey, 2004), 222.

"money" news were at the top.[65] The survey might not tell the whole story, because it defined "foreign news" as stories not linked to the United States, but most foreign correspondence, as seen repeatedly in previous chapters, reveals precisely those links, and respondents did follow closely news from abroad that dealt with terrorism and wars, provided they involved Americans. Nevertheless, the author depressingly concluded, "Most of the important stories from abroad that lack an American connection go practically unnoticed."[66] The big exception in the entire period was the breakup of the Soviet Union in 1991, with nearly half of Americans following it closely – but interest in the former Soviet space plummeted immediately afterward. In an era of budget cuts and close attention to most-clicked patterns, scarce and fleeting public interest will likely continue to inform coverage choices.

Even today, when online content can be read by any audience in the world, not just in a particular news organization's home country, research suggests that most foreign news is reported with a target audience in mind, usually national, and that "global" perspectives are kept separate, as, for example, in the *New York Times*' online edition of the *International Herald Tribune*.[67] Furthermore, a handful of countries are still dominating information flows, generating imbalanced knowledge of the world among mass audiences.[68] A study of foreign desk editors' values in selecting stories from 1988 to 2008 found that their preference for "domesticated" news, with a clear U.S. angle, remained constant, while the importance attached to audience interest increased significantly.[69] Former CBS News Senior Foreign Correspondent Tom Fenton, in a scathing critique of what he called "junk news," tells of how his supervisors refused to send him and a producer to Afghanistan in 1997 to interview a local leader, believing he had nothing to say that would interest the audience. The leader was Osama bin Laden.[70] Fenton compares the episode with his efforts to get out of Dhaka in the 1970s, where another set of editors had sent him to see if indeed war would break out between Pakistan and India. After a few weeks and no war, Fenton sent a telex asking to come home that stated, "Even Jesus got a

65 Michael J. Robinson, "The News Interest Index, 1986–2007: Two Decades of American News Preferences," Pew Research Center for the People & the Press, retrieved from http://pewresearch.org.

66 Robinson, 31.

67 Bella Mody and Xun Liu, "The Influence of the Intended Audience on the Design of Foreign News" (paper presented at the annual conference for the International Communication Association, Boston, May 28, 2011). Paper kindly provided by Dr. Mody.

68 Itai Himelboim, Tsan-Kuo Chang and Stephen McCreery, "International Network of Foreign News Coverage: Old Global Hierarchies in a New Online World," *Journalism and Mass Communication Quarterly* 87–2 (Summer 2010): 297–314.

69 Tsan-Kuo Chang, Brian Southwell, Hyung-Min Lee and Yejin Hong, "A Changing World, Unchanging Perspectives: American Newspaper Editors and Enduring Values in Foreign News Reporting," *International Communication Gazette* 74–4 (June 2012): 367–384.

70 Tom Fenton, *Junk News: The Failure of the Media in the 21st Century* (Golden, CO: Fulcrum, 2009), 7.

reprieve after 40 days." "When you can walk on water, you can come home," the reply came, and Fenton covered the devastating conflict that erupted a few weeks later.[71] The result of such change in foreign correspondence, Fenton concluded, is more political spin, less understanding of foreign situations on which to debate policy initiatives, and shallower perceptions of how others see the United States. It might be what the majority of the public wants, but it certainly is not what it needs.

Professional journalists are not alone in worrying about the decimation of foreign correspondence. Activists and human rights workers have often lamented the lack of American media's interest in dire foreign situations of no immediate relevance to Washington. The senior-most UN official in Sudan in 2003–2004, for example, recently wrote that the delay in press coverage of atrocities in the Darfur region influenced Western powers to do too little, too late. Mukesh Kapila then speculated about the future of correspondence: "The key question is still whether the twenty-first century's technologically enhanced press can help prevent a future Darfur or whether it will just get ever more skilled in beautifully recording our failures."[72] Political scientists have also studied the change in foreign news for its relationship to public orientations toward specific or broad policy choices.

In exit polls from the midterm election in 2010, a meager 8 percent of voters said that a foreign policy issue mattered in their candidate choice, even though the United States was still waging two wars abroad, among many other relevant international issues.[73] Policymakers' assumptions that the American people pay little attention to, and have little knowledge of, foreign issues might lead them to reconsider their positions when the public turns out to actually care about something like an Ethiopian famine, research suggests.[74] The implication is that lack of coverage might impoverish not only public discourse but also the range of policy options, which is the problem at the heart of this book. Bringing the connection between changing news production and consumption to the White House, a study suggested that digital-age presidents might be reshaping their messages to appeal to specific, narrower audiences, further disengaging the mass public from momentous policies, including foreign ones.[75] In fact, the State Department under the Obama administration has taken to the microblogging service Twitter and other social media to bypass traditional media and bring its diplomacy straight to the public, tweeting U.S. positions

[71] Fenton, 29–30.

[72] Bella Mody, *The Geopolitics of Representation in Foreign News: Explaining Darfur* (Lanham, MD: Lexington Books, 2010), xi.

[73] Andrew Kohut, "Voting in Foreign-Policy Oblivion," *The National Interest*, November 30, 2010.

[74] Thomas Knecht, "A Pragmatic Response to an Unexpected Constraint: Problem Representation in a Complex Humanitarian Emergency," *Foreign Policy Analysis* 5–2 (2009): 141.

[75] Jeffrey E. Cohen, *The Presidency in the Era of 24-Hour News* (Princeton, NJ: Princeton University Press, 2008).

before calling in the press corps, in the latest version of a historical trend that worries proponents of accountability journalism.[76]

Just as in journalism in general, a perilous spiral seems to be at work in foreign correspondence in the twenty-first century. Desperate for cash and perceiving that foreign news is not popular enough to invest in, news organizations are producing less in-depth, hard-news foreign correspondence. Faced with less serendipitous exposure, the mass public further loses interest, which in turn reduces journalistic involvement and threatens a vital public "marketplace of ideas" precisely when international interconnectedness makes foreign news crucial to more people than ever before.

Despite such obstacles, leaders at the five U.S. news organizations interviewed for this chapter are soldiering on, keeping robust corps of foreign correspondents and proudly holding on to the belief that they best serve the American public by scouring and explaining the world. Some have suggested that these institutions might benefit from the retrenchment from hard national and international news in most other newspapers, but the editors argue that a world with less reporting is bad for all.[77] In such a world, these news organizations embody the challenges, but also the possible future, of foreign correspondence. They were chosen for this research, not as a representative sample of U.S. foreign newsgathering but, on the contrary, as uniquely insightful experiences because, as detailed in the last two chapters, they are the principal providers of professional foreign correspondence for the American press.[78] The next section details their logistical and normative strategies for international news in the digital era.

It's What We're Here For: U.S. News Leaders Protect Foreign Reporting

Although the AP and the four newspapers studied here have all experienced the financial crunch of the late 2000s, with its consequent retrenchment or at least frozen expansion, their numbers offer hope in the picture of gloom that dominates the industry. The papers have won Pulitzer Prizes for international reporting every year since 2001, each at least once; the AP has won the 2005 and 2007 Pulitzer Prizes in breaking news photography, in both cases from foreign countries. Their commitment to foreign reporting today is solid: The AP has correspondents in more than eighty countries, from Afghanistan to Zimbabwe. The *Wall Street Journal* relies on 450 reporters outside the United

[76] Matthew Lee, "US Diplomacy Embracing Twitter amid Global Crises," Associated Press, January 23, 2011.

[77] Paul Starr, "Goodbye to the Age of Newspapers (Hello to a New Era of Corruption)," in McChesney and Pickard, 36.

[78] For the use of qualitative, semi-structured interviews in communication research, see chapters 7–8 in David Silverman, ed. *Qualitative Research: Theory, Method and Practice* 2nd ed. (Thousand Oaks, CA: Sage, 2004).

States who work not only for its U.S. print and online editions but also for its regional Europe and Asia publications as well as other Dow Jones news units, according to Assistant Managing Editor Alan Anspaugh.[79] The *New York Times* has correspondents in two dozen foreign bureaus, from Caracas to Dakar, from Paris to Jakarta, in addition to journalists for its global edition, the *International Herald Tribune*. The *Washington Post* and the *Los Angeles Times* each has more than a dozen full-time correspondents across the world. Such an expensive commitment has not put them out of business but rather the contrary: The four newspapers were among the top eight circulations in the country. The *Wall Street Journal* dominated with more than 2.1 million readers of its combined print and digital editions, the *New York Times* closed in at more than 1.5 million, and the *Los Angeles Times* and *Washington Post* both had circulations of more than half a million, according to Audit Bureau of Circulations figures from March 2012.

Their editors consider robust foreign reporting essential to their brands, their profession, and their service to the American public. For all of them, the digital age has also meant adapting to new ways of doing international journalism – doing more with less, as several put it, and doing it faster across multiple platforms. In-person and phone interviews conducted between January 2009 and July 2011, however, reveal that their strategies for the future revolve around two core, enduring principles that have not changed since the first reporters went abroad in the nineteenth century. Solid understanding of the world cannot be simply reactive to breaking news, and that understanding is of enough value to enough readers that it amounts to "what we are here for," in the words of the *New York Times*'s Greg Winter, the foreign desk editor responsible for sub-Saharan Africa, Latin America and Mexico, the Caribbean, and the United Nations. That is why they are hanging on and betting that the public will follow.

Doing More with Less

In the late 2000s, the Associated Press revolutionized its foreign news operations in an effort to be more efficient and to become a less U.S.-centric organization. It got rid of the storied international desk, the New York-based clearinghouse of news from all over the world intended for U.S. media and most often the training ground for future foreign correspondents. Instead, it operates editing desks in London, Johannesburg, Cairo, Mexico City and Bangkok that handle all news from their respective regions, both for U.S. members and new regional wires. One effect was to end the gatekeeping role that New York editors had always had on foreign copy, said Larry Heinzerling, who started for AP as correspondent from West Africa in 1968 and retired in 2009 as deputy international editor. Another, more practical ramification at a time of tight budgets is that news reports are faster, more voluminous and more integrated

[79] Personal communication, July 1, 2011.

across text, video and photos. "We are able to do more with less," said John Daniszewski, the senior managing editor for international news and a former AP correspondent who was shot in the late 1980s in Romania while covering the rebellion against Nicolai Ceausescu.[80]

Newspaper foreign correspondents too are working on tighter schedules and are under increased competitive pressures to cover large parts of the world where the high-tech gadgets of American newsrooms are unheard of. "Reporting in the U.S. is hard enough . . . imagine taking that to a place like Zimbabwe where you have to dial one hundred times to get a line, with non-existent infrastructure and institutional chaos," Winter said. Today's nonstop demand for breaking news as well as analysis "doesn't seem sustainable in theory," he added, but there is no choice. "People work harder than they thought they could do. We can't complain because there is no going back. We don't want to become irrelevant." The fight against becoming irrelevant in the onslaught of online, nonjournalistic information is a challenge but also an opportunity – "it creates more pressure to find things out," said David E. Hoffman, who spent twenty-seven years at the *Washington Post*, most recently as foreign editor and assistant managing editor for foreign news from 2001 to 2009.

Citing Pulitzer Prize–winning stories from Iraq and Mexico under his tenure, however, Hoffman insisted that some major international stories still require correspondents to take weeks, even months to pursue them. That is an increasingly risky "gamble" in today's media environment, unlike in his early days as correspondent from the Middle East and Russia in the 1980s and 1990s, when he "could go for two–three months without hearing from a top editor," Hoffman added. Peter Osnos, who joined the *Washington Post* in 1966 in London, went on to Vietnam and Moscow and was foreign editor in the early 1980s, similarly recalled when communication was by terse telex cables and correspondents were very much on their own, "and that was a plus." Then, in the heyday of foreign correspondence, the *Post* and its competitors wanted to get everything, all the news that is fit to print and beyond – they were, in Hoffman's words, "a reporter's paper."

A Reporter's Paper, or What Readers Pay For

Even as the distance between correspondents and editors closes, and the line between professional journalists and Net-savvy users becomes increasingly fine, all leaders interviewed still believe that a reporter's, and a foreign correspondent's, paper is the ideal standard. "The best ideas come from people on the ground, who are absorbing a society, feeling its pulse," said Mark Porubcansky, the *Los Angeles Times* deputy foreign editor. "A big part of foreign correspondence is connecting and communicating in an understandable way" a foreign reality for readers, while still retaining some of the critical differences, said

[80] Reporters of the Associated Press, *Breaking News: How the Associated Press Has Covered War, Peace, and Everything Else* (New York: Princeton Architectural Press, 2007), 278.

AP forty-year veteran and Special Correspondent Charles Hanley, who won a Pulitzer Prize in 2000 for investigative reporting of how American soldiers in the Korean War killed hundreds of civilians in a single massacre.

Behind the correspondent is another layer of professionals, from managing to copy editors, who together strive for the balance, fairness and relevance of the stories. It is in that collective process, even more than in the individual skills of a reporter, that some see the value of professional journalism as opposed to information freely shared online and in social media. "The difference is not in the person but in the organization, there is just no comparison," Hanley said. John Bussey, a *Wall Street Journal* columnist who in his nearly thirty-year career at the paper also ran the foreign desk and the Asian edition, echoed him by arguing that with "two bucks," readers buy not only news and analysis but also "all editing, all layers of approval, the ethics editor for columns." Winter, like Bussey, believes that "people will pay for quality journalism" – another gamble that seems to be rewarding both of their papers, which charge for most online content. The AP's Dan Perry, who ran the Europe and Africa desk in London for six years before returning to Jerusalem as chief of bureau in 2010, put the difference in news value even more succinctly: "A professional journalist is like a professional basketball player. I don't pay to watch my neighbors play."

All editors interviewed agreed that two main values in professional correspondence were the opportunity and the ability to make a sizable mass of people care about the world, and to be there before, when and after breaking news happens. Put another way, they stake their claims to serving the public with professional news judgment and continued coverage from all corners of the world.

Some Spinach on Your Plate (and, OK, Royal Weddings)

"We have always done stories that are important, not sexy," Winter said. "We have never really approached news as what people want to read." Of course, the *New York Times* and all other organizations are not immune from the pressures of audience interest, nor from tensions with other sections of the paper that clamor for Page One and with panic-stricken marketing strategies aimed at getting the most eyeballs. All editors interviewed, however, defended the prerogatives of professional news judgment as essential to serving their audiences.

Porubcansky, for example, said that the *Los Angeles Times* foreign desk "wasn't terribly interested" in the royal wedding of Prince William and Kate Middleton in April 2011 in London, which turned out to be a global media spectacle, because the paper tends "to be more hard-news oriented." The wedding fell into the category of stories "we do from time to time, even though we don't think they have tremendous news value," because there is a readership for them, Porubcansky said. A healthy debate ensued on how much coverage would be appropriate, ranging from the London correspondent's story and blog postings to the paper's fashion critic take, and Porubcansky argued that even though the coverage exceeded what the foreign desk had originally thought sufficient, it still did not amount to "succumbing to the hype."

Wedding candy, in essence, does not mean delegating story selection to popular tastes: "We do a story on Pakistan because we think at least a few readers want it, and it's important and it's good for you, and there is going to be some spinach on your plate on any given day," he added. Even as the *Los Angeles Times* created an "umbrella blog" for foreign news, the biggest quandary was "how to ensure it was not captured by 'soft' material – that it remained true to what we do," Porubcansky said. Bussey also dismissed the notion that giving readers what they allegedly want is the way forward. "We are not looking at the world and saying, that's going to move the needle on [online] comments," he said. At the AP – which now has a "steering desk" in New York that monitors what is trending online to be more aware of the audience that should not be "force-fed medicine it doesn't want," in Daniszewski's words – parochial editing is out. "I tell people to edit stories not as a U.S. story, but for the whole world," Daniszewski said. Indeed, most editors noted that migration to the United States and the Internet have brought to newspapers a global readership that has a default interest in a wider variety of stories and is much harder to gauge than formerly national or metropolitan markets.

The paradox of the digital age is that "it's going to be harder for people to get things they don't want," in Hoffman's words – but what we do not want and therefore do not search for is often what we need, and what all editors considered essential to continue to provide. "We are story-tellers and discoverers, like ants going out exploring," Hoffman said. "Every society needs them." Sometimes a story will seem pure "spinach," with little built-in audience interest – and the mark of great foreign correspondence is that readers will see it and decide they want to read it. "The measure of the best correspondence is that you don't have to read it, but you want to, it takes you some place you didn't know to go," Osnos said. Put another way, the test for a foreign correspondent in the old "time-to-spare days was to go into a country where nothing seemed to be happening and produce three stories – a reporter's notebook feature, a profile of some fascinating character, and an analysis," said Alvin Shuster, foreign editor for the *Los Angeles Times* from 1983 to 1995 and chief of bureau in Saigon, London and Rome for the *New York Times* in the 1970s. As long as foreign correspondents see their substantial stories on the front page and have a chance of triggering that kind of interest, they will not care that the most emailed story on the Web site is about making bread at home rather than "events of importance to humanity," Winter said. And foreign stories will continue to break on Page One as long as correspondents are reliably and patiently working away at translating the world for their readers.

The Importance of Being There, or, Whatever Happened to Fukushima?

The most crucial and unique service that professional foreign correspondence provides to the public is to be there to cover the world before and after the big story breaks. "You don't want readers to wake up and wonder whatever happened to Japan, as I did this morning," Shuster said. Japan had been on front pages across the world when an earthquake and tsunami devastated it in March 2011, triggering a massive radioactive leak from the crippled Fukushima nuclear power plant. Less than three months later, when I interviewed Shuster, Japan had indeed disappeared from the news. "Who knows what we are missing," Shuster said. Despite reduced time and money, all leaders interviewed said that their goal is to have correspondents start digging before the crisis comes, and keep at it after the parachutes and the Twitterers have moved on. That holds true in remote corners as well as for some of the most critical players in world politics today, like China. Charles Hutzler, the AP's chief of bureau in Beijing, said foreign correspondents are particularly important there because Chinese media are state-controlled and foreign news organizations cannot hire Chinese nationals as reporters, although all of them, including the AP, hire them under other titles while still relying on their talents.

Long-term exposure to the country is pivotal in China, Hutzler added, because of the "never-ending battle to get sources," who clam up to foreigners the higher up in government bureaucracy they move. Even though many business and specialized publications have dispatched plenty of reporters to Beijing, Hutzler concluded, a generalist journalist who knows the whole country remains more essential than ever. "When you get to the day that it matters, you need to have people in place, especially in a place like China where it takes several years to figure out the system," he said. Also using China as an example, Bussey echoed him: "The citizen journalist is not dependable – will they be in Shenzhen the day I need them?"

Asked about the value of professional correspondents, Porubcansky cited the *Los Angeles Times*'s chief of bureau in Cairo, who was close to being moved to an opening in sub-Saharan Africa when revolt erupted in Egypt and across North Africa and the Middle East in early 2011. "It did not surprise him, because he was there. We did not have someone parachuting in; it's not the same as being on the ground. That's essential," Porubcansky said. Needless to say, the chief of bureau stayed in Egypt to tell that story, even though the "Arab Spring" also witnessed a flourishing of user-generated online information exchange. The kind of hard-earned expertise on the ground is what made newspapers in the golden age of foreign correspondence "like universities," in Osnos's words. Today, it continues to be the deeper stories that address major news issues in distinctive ways that ultimately are remembered by people and strengthen the journalistic brand, Perry said. In the middle of the AP's vast changes to be more "customer-facing," Daniszewski said, the news cooperative's overarching "sense of mission . . . will not change."

Ultimately, the editors agreed, being there – before, during and after – is what makes foreign correspondence relevant to a democracy. It helps readers understand what is happening abroad in ways that other sources of information do not duplicate, which is the central claim this book makes to the importance of the U.S. news media's continued involvement in foreign affairs. "Providing readers with context through which to see the world, that's our job," Bussey said. And when the news media do not keep it up, the consequences can be dire for policy. Hanley told me of a put-down among journalists years ago over what were considered "obscure pieces" from parts of the world where everyone assumed nothing important was happening or was ever likely to – the writer of such pieces was said to have succumbed to "afghanistanism." In continuing to operate under "afghanistanism" from across the globe despite internal tensions and debatable mass demand, the news leaders interviewed might be the exceptions to the crisis climate in American journalism, but their goals and strategies resonate with those of leading and emerging foreign news organizations, which are the subject of the next section.

"Pretty Bloody Crucial": International Correspondence Strategies Abroad

While American media dominated the global scene for much of the twentieth century, the crisis in journalism of the twenty-first century has hit them harder than most. In Europe, except for the United Kingdom, and in China, the problems of declining readership and revenue are far less acute than in the United States, because of a more faithful readership base and government support that blunts the losses in advertising, according to a 2011 survey.[81] Foreign organizations are jumping in the fray to compete over the hearts and minds of an increasingly borderless audience worldwide. The world continues to be more interested in the United States than vice versa, and U.S. organizations such as the AP and the *New York Times* remain mandatory first reading in newsrooms across the world, but the media are no longer American, as Jeremy Tunstall put it.[82]

In fact, since 2001, American readers have increasingly used foreign media with prominent presence online – from the BBC to Al Jazeera to a variety of foreign-language newspapers.[83] Late in 2007, for example, the British newspaper the *Guardian* launched "Guardian America," a U.S.-based Web site

[81] Laura Houston Santhanam and Tom Rosenstiel, "The State of the News Media 2011: Why U.S. Newspapers Suffer More Than Others," Pew Research Center's Project for Excellence in Journalism, retrieved from http://stateofthemedia.org/.

[82] Jeremy Tunstall, *The Media Were American: U.S. Mass Media in Decline* (New York: Oxford University Press, 2008).

[83] Samuel J. Best, Brian Chmielewski and Brian S. Krueger, "Selective Exposure to Online Foreign News during the Conflict with Iraq," *The Harvard International Journal of Press Politics* 10/4 (2005): 53.

tailored to U.S. readers; about a third of the paper's overall online readers are from the United States. Whether those sources will complement U.S. media for a better democratic dialogue or further fragment the audience as people scour foreign sites for information congruent with their existing perspectives remains to be seen, but international news organizations are a growing part of the twenty-first-century mix of information sources for Americans and, therefore, for policymakers who want to engage them.[84]

Based on in-person and telephone interviews with news leaders for British, Chinese, French and Middle Eastern media from November 2008 to November 2011, this section highlights how foreign organizations – selected for their impact, reach and diversity – envision correspondence in the twenty-first century.[85] Markedly different models exist in Europe, Asia and the Middle East across newspapers, broadcasting and news agency services, but all leaders interviewed for this section agree that maintaining a network of engaged foreign correspondents is, to quote former BBC World Assignment Editor Malcolm Downing, "pretty bloody crucial."

United Kingdom: The BBC, the Guardian *and Public Service*

I interviewed Downing, one of a small team of editors responsible for all foreign bureaus, foreign planning and UK foreign policy coverage, at the BBC's London headquarters the day after Michael Jackson died in June 2009. Just as Porubcansky in Los Angeles would later deal with covering a London royal celebrity event, Downing was struggling with how many staffers the paragon of global broadcasting should convey to California for the controversial pop star's demise. When I left his office, the total was already up to eighteen from across the world – and Downing was using this coverage as an example of the compromises mandated by perceived readers' interests with the public service that he considered paramount for the BBC to offer.

84 Elizabeth Hanson, *The Information Revolution and World Politics* (Lanham, MD: Rowman and Littlefield, 2008), 230. For a call to journalism studies to engage cross-national practices, see Martin Löffelholz and David Weaver, eds. *Global Journalism Research: Theories, Methods, Findings, Future* (Malden, MA: Blackwell Publishing, 2008).

85 Interviews were conducted with Patrick Jarreau, news editor (retired 2009), *Le Monde*, in Paris, November 21, 2008; Alain Frachon, managing editor, *Le Monde*, in Paris, November 21, 2008; Harriet Sherwood, former foreign editor (until June 2010) and Jerusalem staff correspondent, the *Guardian*, in London, January 12, 2009; Malcolm Downing, world assignment editor (retired late 2009), BBC, in London, June 26, 2009; Chen Weihua, deputy editor, *China Daily USA*, in New York, March 14, 2011; Paul Eedle, director of programmes, Al Jazeera English, via phone from Doha, Qatar, November 15, 2011; Heather Allan, head-newsgathering, Al Jazeera English, via phone from Doha, Qatar, November 16, 2011. All quotes from these journalists in this chapter are from these interviews; interviews with Jarreau and Frachon were conducted in French and the translation is the author's. The author is most grateful to all of them for taking time out of exceptionally busy schedules for interviews that lasted an average of sixty minutes.

Many judge the BBC, including its World Service that broadcasts in more than two dozen languages across the world, the most influential broadcasting organization globally, and there have been recent calls for the United States to start a similar service.[86] The BBC maintains half a dozen major regional hubs and a vast network of correspondents, both for its English-language programs and its foreign ones, all funded principally by license fees and, in the case of World Service broadcasting, by some resources from the British Foreign and Commonwealth Office. As that revenue shrank, particularly for non-entertainment programs, Downing said, the BBC was increasingly relying on local correspondents and freelancers rather than expatriate correspondents, like the AP. Still, the organization tried to keep "at least a stringer" virtually everywhere because "places pop up" – and when they do, flying somebody in will not always cut it, Downing said. A correspondent, on the contrary, will have a foundation of knowledge and numerous contacts that might never show until the moment when news breaks and they become essential. "What we are doing is a public service," he added, calling bringing the world to their audience the "whole argument" for taxpayers' funding an organization like the BBC.

Editors at the *Guardian* also have an ambitious definition of their role for the British polity. The newspaper, since the 1960s the voice of the British liberal Left, has about two dozens full-time correspondents to both explain the world to readers and to provide editorial urging to UK policymakers. The latter came out strongly when I sat in the morning meeting of the newspaper's top management and section editors, which on that date in January 2009 was dominated by discussion of Israeli attacks in the Gaza Strip. Israeli-Palestinian conflict is a hot topic for the *Guardian*, which received much criticism for being perceived as anti-Israeli, according to Siobhain Butterworth, then the readers' editor. Nevertheless, many editors debated at the meeting whether the *Guardian* should take a stronger editorial position, perhaps agitate for a boycott against Israel, in its capacity as what one editor called "the world's leading liberal voice."

In foreign correspondence, however, the advocacy role was subsumed to the main goal, which Foreign Editor Harriet Sherwood defined as providing the kind of analysis and context that only on-the-ground reporters can offer. "We are after an audience that wants to understand," Sherwood said. "The mission of the newspaper is to explain. Analysis can be hard work for readers, but the newspaper's job is to provide it." Even though the economic recession in 2008 briefly put on pause the paper's global expansion, Sherwood said, foreign news

[86] Chris Westcott and Jaideep Mukherjee, "New Media at the BBC World Service," in *International News in the Twenty-First Century*, ed. Chris Paterson and Annabelle Sreberny (Hants: John Libbey, 2004), 79; Lee C. Bollinger, "News for the World: A Proposal for a Globalized Era: An American World Service," *Columbia Journalism Review*, July–August 2011, 29–33.

would become an increasingly central part of the future, especially because the *Guardian*, like some of its U.S. counterparts, is also aiming for an international audience.

France: Le Monde *and the Value of News*

Across the English Channel in France, editors at *Le Monde*, widely considered the country's most influential newspaper and fielding about three dozen foreign correspondents, also said that international news was key to their survival in a market saturated by newspapers freely distributed on public transportation. "The condition for success for a newspaper is to be able to have an international article on Egypt or Colombia without any breaking news," said Alain Frachon, the paper's managing editor who also worked as foreign correspondent for Agence France-Presse for ten years. "That is the added value in paying for a newspaper." With all sections of the paper clamoring for global perspectives, Frachon said, the correspondents were busier and more needed than ever to produce analysis beyond the breaking news already circulating in free publications, on the radio and online. "If we want to preserve readers, we can't sell them just news," Frachon said.

Rather, the journalist's job is a "civic duty," a work of fact-checking, holding governments accountable, and making the public care about global affairs. The best journalism is "something that needs to be read, articles to make people think," Frachon said. *Le Monde*'s then-news editor and former Washington bureau chief, Patrick Jarreau, also talked about the "responsibility of media" in directing the public's attention outward to the world. "The responsibility of a newspaper is to select and present, otherwise it is just a catalogue," Jarreau said. The best foreign correspondence translates a foreign reality for its own people, and in so doing, he added, it is performing an "irreplaceable function" of mediator – exactly what this book argues the press has been and should continue to be.

China: China Daily *and News as Power*

State-sponsored news organizations from China, including the country's oldest national English-language paper, *China Daily*, and premier news service, Xinhua News Agency, are expanding in the world far faster and with more resources than the Western news media discussed thus far. For somewhat different reasons, *China Daily*'s deputy editor too said he envisioned their role as mediators – between China and the Western powers that, many Chinese feel, misrepresent and underrepresent their country. Chen Weihua, the deputy editor of *China Daily*'s U.S. edition, founded in 2009, recalled coverage of Chinese President Hu Jintao's early 2011 visit to the White House on CNN. The video showed President Barack Obama speaking and then cut to an anchor discussing China without quotes from Hu, Chen said. "[Hu] represents one fourth of humanity, be patient for thirty seconds even if you don't like him," Chen urged. "That is what you call democracy."

The Chinese government is investing heavily on a multiyear plan to enhance its soft power and raise its national profile through media such as *China Daily* and Xinhua, both of which are significantly expanding their U.S. offices and their English-language content.[87] Although these news organizations receive government subsidies and serve an ideological function, their potential impact seems poised to go beyond simple propaganda for China as a global power.[88] Therefore, even as the lack of press freedom remains a dominant problem, with limited government control over content, some of Chen's concerns echo those of his Western counterparts, starting with what he called "interpreting the world the Chinese way" – politically different, certainly, but still the same goal of "mediation" shared throughout this chapter.

Chen said he and his colleagues envisioned their journalism as based on facts and even in a watchdog role, despite party interference and the risks that criticisms or "sensitive" political subjects entail. He was also quick to criticize two trends that he saw as international – excessive partisanship, which he found in plenty of Western media, and commercialization with its inherent privileging of soft news, which he feared was rapidly transforming Chinese news organizations, making them a little "too capitalistic." Few would argue that party-controlled media are a desirable alternative to the revenue crisis plaguing Western media, but concern for caving in to commercial pressures by giving up hard news content resonated with all editors interviewed in this chapter.

Qatar: Al Jazeera English and Journalism Unbound

The major news organization least concerned about budget pressures and related content constraints is, arguably, Al Jazeera English, the Doha, Qatar-based broadcasting channel funded by what its head of newsgathering, Heather Allan, calls the "state of Qatar's extraordinarily deep pockets." It was started in 2006 as an editorially independent offshoot of the Arabic-language broadcaster Al Jazeera, which has been hailed as a new global voice for Arab peoples and a thorn in the side of authoritarian regimes, and it was also reviled by the U.S. government as a mouthpiece of anti-Western sentiments.[89] The English

[87] Hu Zhengrong, "China's Rise and Global Communication: Problems and Prospects" (paper presented at the annual meeting of the International Communication Association, Boston, May 27, 2011).

[88] John Jirik, "China's News Media and the Case of CCTV-9," in *International News in the Twenty-First Century*, ed. Chris Paterson and Annabelle Sreberny (Hants: John Libbey, 2004), 127.

[89] Mohamed Zayani, "The Changing Face of Arab News Media," in *The Rise of 24-Hour News Television: Global Perspectives*, ed. Stephen Cushion and Justin Lewis (New York: Peter Lang, 2010), 187; Leon Barkho, *News from the BBC, CNN, and Al-Jazeera: How the Three Broadcasters Cover the Middle East* (Cresskill, NJ: Hampton Press, 2010), 128–132. For Al Jazeera's impact on world politics, see Philip Seib, *The Al Jazeera Effect: How the New Global Media are Reshaping World Politics* (Washington: Potomac Books, 2008).

channel is exponentially expanding its global audience, reaching some 250 million households, even though it is still unavailable to most U.S. cable and satellite subscribers.[90] Five years after its inception, with six regional planning desks, major broadcasting centers in London and Washington, nearly three dozen bureaus across the world staffed by both local hires and foreign journalists, and "expansion still in full swing," according to Allan, Al Jazeera English competed daily with Western stalwarts such as the BBC. In fact, as American and European news organizations shrank their international coverage, "we see ourselves expanding into that gap," said Paul Eedle, who directs the organization's long-form video content programming.

Both Eedle and Allan are veterans of Western media, with long careers at Reuters and NBC News, respectively, before joining Al Jazeera English, which they consider as vastly different both structurally and editorially. The broadcasting channel focuses on the "emerging world," questioning "centers of power," and trying to avoid following "the agenda set by the rich and powerful" as many competitors do, Eedle said. "Reliable, accurate, fair information empowers people – that's what we're interested in," he added. "All journalists are, but in the West they might not always be conscious of the agenda of their parts of the world." That diverse perspective, Allan argued, drives newsgathering decisions, ranging from the big political news of the day to "stories about people making a difference," like Filipinos reusing Coke bottles as light fixtures. "We are constantly looking for stories about little people," Allan said, adding that, whereas Al Jazeera English competes on the top stories all major media cover, "below, our global spread is different."

Allan mourns the overall trends that shrivel many media's power to cover the world – "I light a candle every time a news organization closes down," she said – but she relishes the nearly unchecked freedom to pursue stories big and small that Qatar money guarantees Al Jazeera English. Liberated from concerns about ratings and advertisers, Allan can send reporters chasing any story across the world if it is compelling as news. And what of the dreaded preoccupation, looming above the decisions of so many of her U.S. counterparts, with the audience's likes and dislikes? "We really don't care," Allan said, echoing the assertion of journalistic independence repeated throughout this chapter.

Conclusions

In the end, what kind of journalism we will develop in the twenty-first century depends, as it always has in history, on what kind of governance we will have and what kind of society we will form. This chapter has examined the status of foreign correspondence in the U.S. press today, why it raises concerns for its ability to serve as an irreplaceable mediator, and what strategies a few crucial

90 Philip Seib, ed. *Al Jazeera English: Global News in a Changing World* (New York: Palgrave Macmillan, 2012), 30.

leaders in the United States and abroad are gambling on to preserve what they consider a critical public service. The urgent point is that concern over the crisis in print journalism is not an old-fashioned nostalgia for ink-stained wretches. I share these editors' position that, whereas social media and the rise in user-generated content can help broaden the marketplace of ideas, they cannot replace the newsgathering and distribution functions of professional journalism, for two major reasons. First, "old" media, especially newspapers and wire services, provide the vast majority of content surfed online, so while they are losing on the distribution and revenue-generating end, they dominate the production of news. Secondly, the online environment favors freewheeling choice, and very few people actively seek out foreign news, raising the specter of a vast digital divide in political awareness and knowledge that cannot benefit a democratic system of government.

Whether the news media market will be able to sustain the "marketplace of ideas" that newspapers have long provided is a question beyond the scope of this book. That such a public sphere needs to continue to exist and be informed for the necessary public debate over policies, however, is a crucial premise. In that light, the five U.S. news organizations whose editors were interviewed for this chapter provide a glimmer of hope in a time of crisis, and the resonance of their values with those of major foreign news outlets suggests agreement on the way ahead for the profession. They win Pulitzer Prizes, they win over large audiences and, in some cases, they even manage to get people to pay for hard-news products that some call "spinach." All the editors wrestle with the question of how to reconcile the public interest, which they feel is their responsibility to serve, with what the public is interested in. They agonize over marathon coverage of Michael Jackson and William & Kate, but in the end, they hold on to their news values as what gives news a value in the free-for-all of the Internet. "What we're trying to do is maintain our values while more of what we do migrates to the Web," in Porubcansky's words.

For these twenty-first-century international news leaders, foreign correspondence remains mostly about two pivotal goals – being there and making people care. The best foreign news story is from a place where there is no "news" but a correspondent has dug up information so relevant and interesting that readers will still want to read it, provided they can come across it. And when news breaks, that same correspondent will be uniquely capable of translating its meaning for the home audience and even, increasingly, the global audience. "Journalists relate to the rest of us those things to which we should pay attention, but to which we do not otherwise have access," argued the authors of a survey of journalism in ten countries, echoing the *New York Tribune*'s 1900 editorial about the Boxer siege.[91]

[91] Pamela J. Shoemaker and Akiba A. Cohen, *News around the World: Content, Practitioners, and the Public* (New York: Routledge, 2006), 3.

As the following chapter will conclude, that "pay attention!" function is indeed irreplaceable when it comes to international relations, which at the most fundamental level pivot around some understanding of the rest of the world and our place in it. At a time when every click is counted, and a million different snippets of content compete with foreign news for those two seconds of index-finger action on a mouse or tablet, it is a courageous and hopeful stand to continue to defend the "afghanistanism" of foreign correspondence. Indeed, countries will continue to pop up unexpectedly on the world's radar, and having professionals there remains "pretty bloody crucial" to the nuanced discourses of the world that provide the milieus for constructive policy debate.

7

Conclusion

Reaffirming Journalism's Role in World Affairs

> I make a distinction between public opinion and the media.... The media became extremely hostile and increasingly hostile and bought into the proposition that an evil government in both the Johnson Administration and then in the Nixon Administration was lying, tricking because it had some commitment to warlike policies. And that made it extremely difficult to conduct a policy... But the role of the media, on the whole, was, of course, destructive.
>
> Henry A. Kissinger, 2010

> While we assumed we had little or no ability to influence what WikiLeaks did, let alone what would happen once this material was loosed in the echo chamber of the blogosphere, that did not free us from the need to exercise care in our own journalism.... Your obligation, as an independent news organization, is to verify the material, to supply context, to exercise responsible judgment about what to publish and what not to publish and to make sense of it. That is what we did.
>
> Bill Keller, 2011

At a fall 2010 State Department conference on U.S. policies in Southeast Asia, I asked Henry Kissinger, one of the most influential foreign policymakers in U.S. history, what he believed that "the role of the media as informers and perhaps shapers of public opinion" had been in the Vietnam War era.[1] His trenchant answer – that it had been "destructive," as quoted at the beginning of this chapter – encapsulates the watchdog function performed by the press at the height of its investigative power as well as the prominence it held among foreign policy deliberations. Less than two months after that exchange, a tangle between the administration and the American press glaringly showed the continuities but also the crucial differences in the role of the media in foreign affairs in the digital age.

[1] Henry A. Kissinger, Q&A following address to "The American Experience in Southeast Asia, 1946–1975" conference, U.S. Department of State, Washington, September 29, 2010.

The *New York Times* and other news organizations published articles based on thousands of cables, some classified secret, between the State Department and diplomatic posts around the world that had been obtained by the online organization WikiLeaks. As Executive Editor Bill Keller later explained in the article quoted at the beginning of this chapter, the *Times* considered WikiLeaks a source, not a partner, and, in its effort to perform "responsible" journalism, had painstakingly gone over the cables to find the newsworthy material, verify it through its own journalists across the world, and eliminate information that would damage national security.[2] It consulted the Obama administration, followed some of its recommendations for more redactions, and urged WikiLeaks to take those concerns into account before posting the documents on its site. In a new era of proliferating, unverified information online, the *Times* seemed to define its journalistic role as vetting, analyzing and contextualizing the news – exercising responsible judgment while giving the American public information that would help it understand the world and Washington's role in it.

The fundamental premise of this book is also its urgent call for the future – a democracy has a critical need for its press to engage foreign affairs because the news media represent a pivotal discursive space where opinions about the world are molded and foreign policy parameters shaped. The most crucial aspect of that engagement is foreign correspondence, as it has always been in the nearly 200 years of American press history analyzed in the previous chapters, because it serves as a unique locus for the negotiation of meanings about foreign realities that inevitably form the environment within which decisions are taken and actions are formulated. Strategic interests, political considerations, miscalculations and manipulations all play a role in the way nations interact, and the relevance of particular areas of the world to Americans – citizens and policymakers alike – has very often been a driving factor in the quantity and quality of news media foreign coverage. This book's contribution, however, is to bring into the discussion as an essential explicative tool the images that nations form of one another, largely through the news media, and the consequent expectations that they bring to their relations.

The proposed theoretical model, supported by findings from twenty historical cases from 1848 to 2008, argues that media discourse functions as the public arena where meanings for things literally foreign become understandable realities that, in turn, serve as the basis for policy and action. It is in that broad sense, in their function of translating the meanings of national identities, and intentions, across national and cultural boundaries, and not in the narrower role of influencing particular policy decisions, that the news media serve as irreplaceable mediators between Americans and the world. And in order to fulfill that role, the news media need to continue to invest in foreign correspondence, because journalists with extensive experience of foreign realities

[2] Bill Keller, "The Boy Who Kicked the Hornet's Nest," *New York Times*, January 30, 2011, MM32. See also "A Note to Readers: The Decision to Publish Diplomatic Documents," *New York Times*, November 29, 2010, A10.

are uniquely positioned to enrich the discursive space with perspectives that are nearly impossible to find in domestic mass discussion.

This model serves as a theoretical and evidentiary causal exploration, therefore, of the range of policy formulations that decision makers act within, and the range of palatable options that ordinary citizens understand and support. It is borne out by the analysis of more than 2,000 news articles in the context of the history of both American journalism as a profession and the major driving trends of American foreign policy from Washington to Obama. In the nineteenth, twentieth and twenty-first centuries – in France as in Japan, in Mexico as in India – foreign correspondence constructed images of the world and, just as importantly, of the United States' role in it. Those discourses helped define the box within which Americans, including policymakers, thought about the world, and sometimes provided the chance to think outside of it. The great and necessary power and responsibility of the news media in foreign affairs stem from that subtler, more pervasive understanding of media effects on policymaking.

As noted in Chapter 1, most scholarship has failed to find direct and systemic causal links between the news media, public opinion and foreign policymakers. This book makes the case for a different kind of effect – that no one, ordinary citizen or policymaker, can conceive and then pursue a course of action toward a foreign country that does not fit existing discourses about that country and the United States' global role. For citizens especially, who do not have access to more specialized and restricted sources of knowledge such as intelligence, those discourses are formed and sustained through various channels, ranging from movies to travel, but most significantly and broadly through general-audience, wide-circulation news media. Policymakers too are imbued in such understandings, and, even if they were capable of seeing them as constructions, in a democratic regime they would still need to consider them so as not to lose popular support.

To oversimplify, this book does not suggest that the president reads about Mexico in the *New York Times* and suddenly decides how the administration will act toward it, nor does it argue that the *Washington Post* gobbles up a State Department press release about China and reprints it for general circulation. Rather, the argument put forth here is that the widely circulated images of Mexico and China and the rest of the world in the general interest news media help shape the public perception of what those countries are. In turn, those perceptions, combined with pervasive and enduring understandings of what the United States is and therefore should do, act as constraints on the range of policies that are widely considered possible. Therefore, the news media have a crucial responsibility to provide complex and nuanced understandings of the world, and their only chance of doing it is, quite simply, by going there.

This concluding chapter reviews the theoretical premises and implications of this model before summarizing the analytical findings to the two guiding questions: What narratives of the world outside the United States – and, by default, of the United States – have the American news media helped create over time? How have those discourses in news coverage interacted with U.S. foreign policy? A final section turns to the proposed answers to two more normative questions: What should the American press do to better cover the world? What might the future hold for American foreign correspondence?

The Discursive Role of Media in International Relations

This book has relied on insights from mass communication and international relations theories to conceptualize a new model of the role and the influence of the news media, particularly foreign correspondence, in international affairs. Three crucial assumptions about international politics, communication and journalism have been central to the research: Identities and interests cannot be taken for granted as material facts; rather, collective frameworks determine their meanings. Those same frameworks provide boundaries of interpretation for decision makers and for public opinion alike. Second, communication is a necessary locus for the negotiation of those meanings within widely accepted, historically and culturally specific understandings. Finally, despite mounting criticisms and many obvious failures, the news media do contribute to the public sphere with a sustained space for debate that is not blindly beholden to corporate and governmental interests, but their ability to continue to do so is gravely endangered.

Constructed Identities and the Policy Range

Constructivist approaches to international relations have long held that while power, interests and institutions matter, they need to be understood as constituted by ideas that exist within their specific cultural and historical times. That is not to relegate agency to some random structural formations, but rather to assume that it is co-constitutive, that our identities are shaped by social context but we have some freedom to respond to it.[3] Therein lies the power of discourse – once it is constituted and accepted as commonsensical, it provides the framework within which we act and the parameters within which policy can be both formulated and operationalized, and it requires major paradigm shifts to change its general orientations. Analyzing discourse to better comprehend foreign policy, therefore, means to uncover the intersubjectively constructed, historically situated ways of understanding and taking for granted certain characteristics of international affairs – the discourses that form the ecology within which meanings are formulated, communicated, and become the basis for actions.

Together with the consideration of systemic factors and individual-level representations and perceptions, a constructivist approach can complement a realist one to better explicate why a certain policy was undertaken in a certain

[3] J. Samuel Barkin, *Realist Constructivism: Rethinking International Relations Theory* (Cambridge: Cambridge University Press, 2010), 116.

society at a certain time. As many have noted, such a constructivist analysis is harder to apply to predictions of policy outcomes – it cannot foresee precise foreign policy actions or their support by the public, but understandings of foreign realities and America's position in the world are powerfully indicative of the range of policies that can be implemented.[4] The reason for looking for such discourses about national and international identities in the media, instead of in political deliberations, rests on the conceptualization of mass communication as the "marketplace of ideas," an essential site for the formation of meaning about aspects of social life that fall outside the purview of general experience for the majority of the public. Not only are policymakers part of that public too – if, at the highest levels, privy to more information than is generally available to all citizens – but also, in democracies, the success and failure of policies owe something to their resonance with the public. At the most basic level, a foreign policy can only exist within the same values and perceptions about the "self" and the "other" that mass media discourse creates and reflects. Elite and mass discourses are also co-constitutive, a point that enhances the overall power of discursive constructions to delimit ways of thinking and therefore, by default, of acting in foreign affairs. That is why it is ultimately unnecessary for the argument put forth here to tease out whether media discourses impact policymakers directly or through perceived public opinion. Policymakers and citizens belong to the same broad discursive environment, which is facilitated by the news media; and even if the actual foreign affairs knowledge of a State Department official varies enormously from that of an ordinary citizen, the parameters of thinkable actions are restricted by the understandings prevalent at that time.

Too often, the study of discourse, just like the study of media and policy in general, focuses on manipulation and persuasion at the hands of powerful interests, with language as a weapon and a carrier. Discourse, however, is most powerful not because it is used as a tool by political actors but rather because it becomes so widely associated with common sense that it defies questioning and explanation. Politically and ethically, the most troubling aspect of discursive practices is that they make it virtually impossible to think outside of them, eliminating other possible meanings and restricting change to rationalizations within those constructions. A discursively endorsed common sense is a most insidious straightjacket within which to create effective policy. Think of some of the most blatant generalizations found in this research – that post-apartheid South Africa risked becoming an "African" country, that Mexico despite regime change would still be "Mexico," and that Israelis and "Arabs" have hated each other since the dawn of time. No explanation was required, because readers presumably all knew what Mexico, a typical African country, and the conflict in the Middle East were. Those "commonsensical" understandings, so widely shared that they are taken for granted even for mass circulation,

[4] Barkin, 166–173.

and further constructed as immutable, cannot but severely impoverish debate toward the countries and regions in question.

A New Model of Media Effects

The influence of the richness or poverty of discourse on the range of policy options and deliberations is the media effects model proposed here. Shrinking news holes, increased reliance on infotainment programs, and the technology-enabled trend to choose only congruent sources are leading to a reevaluation of the effects of mainstream news media on political behavior and to a questioning of the media's continued function as a distinct political institution.[5] The inability of most existing models to establish causality and directionality between the media, public opinion and foreign policy seems to support that skepticism. And yet, Kissinger found the media destructive in the Vietnam War, and Keller positioned the *New York Times* as the responsible intermediary between WikiLeaks, the State Department and the American public. Throughout history, policymakers have resented the news media's portrayal of foreign realities that did not resonate with the official line, arguing the media should be on the "team." Journalists, on the other hand, often prided in doing just that, and they have increasingly worried about their diminishing ability to tell stories without losing relevance in the public's eye to both PR practitioners and non-professionals.

To both policy and journalism practitioners, the effects are real. I argue that the press has a meaningful influence on policies – both in their creation and their public reception – because it is largely through the ecology of discourses created, circulated and maintained through the press that foreign realities enter the public sphere. To paraphrase Walter Lippmann, when it comes to realities outside our experience – as foreign realities are to the vast majority of Americans – our feelings and actions are shaped by our mental images, by what we think we know. And to paraphrase the former *New York Times* foreign correspondent and *Los Angeles Times* foreign editor quoted in Chapter 6, without foreign correspondence we do not even know what we do not know.

Knowing our understanding of foreign cultures is especially relevant in the twenty-first century, which is characterized by the information and communication revolution as well as a historically rare long peace between dominant nation-states. The balance of power is especially susceptible to the distribution of ideas, and power struggles are increasingly sustained not only on geopolitical and economic battlefields but also on the sites where actors dispute whose

[5] R. Lance Holbert, R. Kelly Garrett and Laurel S. Gleason, "A New Era of Minimal Effects? A Response to Bennett and Iyengar," *Journal of Communication* 60/1 (March 2010): 15–34; W. Lance Bennett and Shanto Iyengar, "The Shifting Foundations of Political Communication: Responding to a Defense of the Media Effects Paradigm," *Journal of Communication* 60/1 (March 2010): 35–39; Timothy E. Cook, "The News Media as a Political Institution: Looking Backward and Looking Forward," *Political Communication* 23 (2006): 159–171.

definitions of reality become socially accepted as fact. In the future, power will reside in the combination of arsenals of tanks and dollars (or renminbi) and soft power resources, meaning the winning stories a country will be able to tell about itself and its role in the world to attract others to do what it wants them to, as Joseph Nye has argued.[6] In order to be effective, as always but especially so in this environment, U.S. foreign policymakers will need to be extremely attuned to how foreign interlocutors perceive themselves and the United States.[7] To do so they will need, simply, to know foreign cultures better, another essential link between policy and foreign correspondence.

The discursive uniqueness and the understanding potential of foreign correspondence lie in its ability to function as mediator between different national discourses. By being exposed for extended periods of time to foreign realities and by translating some of a foreign culture's way of seeing itself for the American audience, foreign correspondents provide a unique merging of meanings that enriches the public space for informed construction of identities. As all editors interviewed for this book put it, their role is not to shape public opinion on foreign policy matters. Rather, it is to provide the ordinary reader with an opportunity to engage the world and to do so with relevant context. Despite the many failings of the news media and the grave crisis of American journalism, this function is still unmatched, even in the era of social media and blurred lines between producers and users of content.

Of all the media organizations that exist today, I argue that newspapers and the general interest wire services that serve them still fulfill a unique – and uniquely threatened – role. The printed product is irrelevant. What matters is that newspapers as organizations have demonstrated the ability to invest substantially in reporting and to possess the institutional checks and balances to produce generally accurate, relatively fair information about what is happening in the world. Furthermore, they have had incentives to reach large audiences, bringing that random exposure beyond immediate personal interest that is essential to a public agenda. Perhaps the most worrisome development in the future of foreign correspondence is the possibility of a fragmentation of the American public into a minority with enough interest and resources, financial and educational, to search out quality journalism and a much larger mass lacking both whose news diet is relegated to talk shows and Facebook.

Foreign Correspondence and Democracy

It is critical not to underestimate the consequences of such a scenario for democracy. History certainly shows that professional journalism is a relatively new phenomenon associated with a specific polity and economic system, and therefore it might change as we enter a new era. But democracy, in its modern,

[6] Joseph S. Nye, Jr., *The Future of Power* (New York: Public Affairs Books, 2011).

[7] Inderjeet Parmar and Michael Cox, eds. *Soft Power and U.S. Foreign Policy: Theoretical, Historical and Contemporary Perspectives* (London: Routledge, 2010).

egalitarian and equalizing model, is also a recent experiment, one that is inextricably connected to the ideal of an informed citizenry. The implications of the impossibility of the latter are dire to contemplate for the continued existence of self-government. If the U.S. public is to be engaged in informed, rational debate over matters of public interest, the media need to continue to provide what the public apparently is not interested in. As Delli Carpini and Keeter put it at the dawn of the Internet era, political knowledge depends on the information environment we live in, not just on individual engagement.[8] Writing about recently democratizing countries, Snyder and Ballentine argued that a free marketplace of ideas will not prevent dangerously nationalistic "mythmaking" unless it contains "media access, the training of journalists in the verification of sources and the separation of fact from opinion, and the development of expert evaluative institutions whose prestige depends on maintaining a reputation for objectivity."[9] Might not the same qualification be applied to the United States' current media environment?

For the public sphere to function, Americans must have more access to information and the information already readily available must be of better quality. This is particularly vital in the realm of foreign policy, where the stakes are often literally life or death, and therefore in foreign correspondence. A study of public opinion and U.S. military interventions across the world from the 1950s to the 2000s argued that the media tended to follow the White House line, with one exception: "The determining variable seems to be whether or not the media has a significant presence of correspondents with regional and language training in the field."[10] The more the media "leave" the world, the author concluded, the easier it will be for policymakers to carry along public opinion and perhaps even lose a useful additional perspective for themselves. Similarly, research on the influence of news media on U.S. foreign policy in the late 2000s also suggests that explanatory journalism is a key to accountability in policymaking.[11] To quote what Herbert Matthews, one of the most widely known *New York Times* foreign correspondents in the twentieth century, wrote in the 1940s: "True journalism, like true historiography, is not mere chronology . . . but placing the event in its proper category as a moral act and judging it as such. It is too glib to say of newspapermen that they are writing history. Those of us with our noses to the daily grindstone are not

[8] Michael X. Delli Carpini and Scott Keeter, *What Americans Know about Politics and Why It Matters* (New Haven, CT: Yale University Press, 1996), 272–274.

[9] Jack Snyder and Karen Ballentine, "Nationalism and the Marketplace of Ideas," *International Security* 21–2 (Fall 1996): 22.

[10] Jon Western, *Selling Intervention and War: The Presidency, the Media, and the American Public* (Baltimore: Johns Hopkins University Press, 2005), 19.

[11] Robert M. Entman, Steven Livingston, Sean Aday and Jennie Kim, "Condemned to Repeat: The Media and the Accountability Gap in Iraq War Policy," in *Public Policy and Mass Media: The Interplay of Mass Communication and Political Decision Making*, ed. Sigrid Koch-Baumgarten and Katrin Voltmer (London: Routledge, 2010), 194–214.

writing history when we describe the events we see or hear; we are merely providing the material for history."[12]

This book argues that the continued engagement of the news media in foreign coverage is necessary for the diffusion among the broadest possible public of information and context that make rational debate feasible. Independent professional journalism is also a necessary counterweight to the ability of political actors to control what narratives about the world dominate public discussion. Foreign correspondence, then, is doubly relevant in the nexus between foreign policy and news media: It is an essential site of discursive constructions of foreign realities that delimits the range of policy options, and it can provide discursive openings into other cultures that are rarely available elsewhere for the majority of Americans. Less coverage means restricted understanding on which to base reduced policy choices that might provoke uninformed actions. Discourse might not predict policy, but an impoverished discourse environment is bound to lead to less democratic debate and possibly an unnecessarily restricted policy range.

Evolving Media Discourses of the World

The analysis of the commonsensical, widely shared, self-sustaining understandings of foreign countries in press foreign correspondence at critical policy history junctures, from the 1840s through the 2000s, supports this theoretical conceptualization. Such discursive milieus encompassed a generalized construction of the "other," the accompanying discourse of the United States and its role, and discourses about the specific identity of a particular country or region. They were analyzed together with relevant social, political, and institutional practices to answer the following questions: What discourses of the world have emerged in foreign news in the American press? How do those images compare with U.S. foreign policies contemporary to them? Crucially, do both media coverage and actual policies belong to the same general frameworks of understanding of the world, specific countries, and regions and the United States' role in them? What can the narratives of the world created in the media tell us about the role of the press in international affairs?

The cases detailed in the previous chapters spotlight both press accomplishments as well as failures, times when the media provided nuanced analysis of the world and others when their constructions were absurdly minimal. In both cases, they corresponded to general policy orientations, supporting the argument that they mattered to their formulations. Therefore, the historical evidence also supports this book's normative prescription for the future – professional foreign correspondence matters.

[12] Herbert L. Matthews, *The Education of a Correspondent* (New York: Harcourt, Brace and Company, 1946), 11.

Throughout the nineteenth century, American correspondence from overseas principally shaped the discourse of the United States, not of the world. The overarching preoccupation was to define foreign realities as unlike America, arguably a natural development for a country and a profession that were still new and finding their legs. A few constructions established in this period, however, continued to influence foreign correspondence into the twenty-first century. The focus on whether France in 1848 would be able to establish a republican government "on the model" of that of the United States was nearly identical to the questioning of whether Vicente Fox, elected in Mexico in 2000, would establish a "U.S.-style" regime and a justice system on the American model. In both cases, the implicit understanding is that there is only one right way to govern, the American way, and that foreigners might not be capable of implementing it but should – the kind of assumptions that underlie the morality, almost the necessity, of regime-change and nation-building interventions. Even though the vast majority of nineteenth-century correspondence similarly buttressed perceptions of American uniqueness and superiority, journalists also allowed themselves, on occasion, to be surprised by encounters that defied their expectations. Bayard Taylor, sailing to Japan in 1853, found "a much higher civilization" than he had expected, as quoted in Chapter 2, a very condescending remark and yet one that points to an opening toward understanding foreign cultures that is an essential unique contribution provided by foreign correspondents.

In the first half of the twentieth century, the United States graduated into global power status and, despite some of its most isolationist periods, intervened in conflicts and disputes of all sizes around the world. The press also expanded its presence, sending growing numbers of foreign correspondents to analyze the vast sociopolitical changes that were occurring from St. Petersburg to Madrid, from Mexico City to Shanghai. The changes between the correspondence from Mexico in 1911 and from Madrid in 1937 are striking. Covering the early stages of the Mexican Revolution, the correspondence continued to focus on its possible repercussions on the United States, giving almost no space to considerations of how it would affect the Mexican people. The dominant discourses constructed the revolutionaries as "brigands" and Mexico as incapable of carrying on democratic reform – much like the discourses about the 1917 revolution in Russia. Much more widely covered, the Bolshevik takeover in St. Petersburg was portrayed in ominous if incredulous terms; understanding Marxism was a major challenge, for its ideology was perceived as utterly antithetical to American principles. In both cases, the press constructed major social movements as chaos and anarchy, which likely inhibited understanding of their causes and their enduring consequences.

When witnessing horrifying attacks on civilians in the 1930s in Shanghai and Madrid, American journalists constructed objectivity not as detachment but as passionate, firsthand observation of atrocities. For the first time in coverage studied in this book, journalists focused on vivid, graphic personal accounts of tragedy that implicitly questioned the neutrality that Americans were trying to hold on to. It is hard to imagine readers unmoved by a story from Madrid describing how "the machine-gunner turned his deadly spray of bullets straight into a long line of women who had stood patiently for hours, as Madrid women have to these days, waiting their turn to enter a butcher shop."[13] Constructions of Spanish suffering lacked the condescension that had characterized similar reports about Chinese civilians under the Japanese bombing of Shanghai. American intervention was not explicitly mentioned in either case, but the correspondents' identification with locals, particularly in the Spanish Civil War, suggests that Americans felt they had a role to play in global affairs.

In Cold War–era correspondence, American global leadership was largely taken for granted within the frame of zero-sum Soviet competition. There is, however, a critical difference between countries at the U.S. "doorstep," as Cuba was described, and those further removed. In the case of Cuba in 1959, the dominant construction was of a lush, sun-blessed, luxuriant pseudo-colonial terrain for American investment, which must have made Castro's radical turn to the Soviets almost unfathomable to the American public. In the Middle East, where reporters flocked in 1967 to witness the war between Israel and a coalition of Arab countries, the dominant construction of U.S. involvement was as necessary but likely futile. In increasingly similar articles that speak of the incipient homogenization of news as well as of strict news management on the part of governments, the constructions clearly differentiated between righteous Israel and a mass of undistinguishable, uncivilized "Arabs." Their atavistic hatred, rooted in history and religion, generated an unsolvable conflict, but still the United States had to try to do something lest the Soviets get the upper hand.

When relations normalized between the United States and China in 1979, journalists scoured the country and perceptively reported on many of its contradictions, especially the two very different tracks between economic laissez-faire and political repression. Interestingly, the correspondence focused on Chinese business, a rather reductive but recurrent discourse of foreign countries. The most obvious Cold War imprint dominated the coverage of the Soviet withdrawal from Afghanistan in 1988, where correspondents mostly discussed the Soviet Union and its "taste of military failure," rather than concentrating on a mystifying country. When the correspondence did discuss Afghanistan, however, it constructed a complex picture of divergent and incompatible sociopolitical trends, particularly Islamism, which sat uneasily with Washington's gung-ho backing of the mujahideen. In covering the collapse of the Soviet Union in late 1991, the correspondence created the most complex, rich discourses found in this book. The repeated mentions of nuclear arsenals and communism were

[13] Herbert L. Matthews, "100 Killed, 200 Hurt in Madrid Air Raid," *New York Times*, January 5, 1937, 5.

almost secondary to a discourse that engaged the troubled present and even more worrisome future of the disintegrating giant. The end of the Cold War was constructed not as a U.S. victory but as the portent of further, possibly worse threats in the future for America.

The construction of apathetic Russian citizens who cared more about sausages than about the shattering of an empire fit the rather ethnocentric and omnipresent media discourse that foreign people might not be able to handle democratic government. In a few cases, however, correspondents questioned their ability to perceive such a dramatic change as did the people who were living it. One anecdote in a *New York Times* story constructs the gulf between perceived American eagerness and Soviet apathy, but it also reveals, perhaps unwittingly, the discursive incommunicability between foreign journalists and locals. The article recounts how an American reporter turned down a Russian's invitation to have dinner, claiming to be too busy working because "your country is falling apart." The Russian imperturbably retorted, "How about tomorrow?" Despite those difficulties and the predominant Cold War frame, correspondence in this period did try to shed some light on specific questions for the countries covered – the rise of Islamism in Afghanistan, the ethnic tensions in Russia, and the contrasting trends in China – that helpfully allowed local realities to become part of the discourse.

In the post–Cold War era, correspondence constructed the world as cruelly falling apart – or, astonishingly, failing to, on a few rare occasions. Journalists in the former Yugoslavia in 1993 portrayed the Balkans as a Middle East without Israel – a relentless, hopeless, barbaric hellhole where everybody had hated everyone else since the beginning of history and would prove it to the point of inhumanity. No American declinism here – the United States was clearly and repeatedly identified as the only possible chance to stem the violence. The 1993 discourse of U.S. indispensability as humanity's last best hope was the strongest found in this research. A U.S. role, on the contrary, was conspicuously absent from stories from South Africa in 1994. The discourse reflected the localized version of a constant foreign policy preoccupation – how do you pursue human rights without messing with economic interests? In this case, the discourses celebrated Nelson Mandela's peaceful election, signaling the end of apartheid, but left open to question whether black rule might endanger that rare African economic success story. As one writer put it, white South Africa resembled Europe but black Africa was, well, Africa – enough said. The fact that the name of a continent could be journalistic shorthand for the antithesis of progress, order and civilization is revealing of how restrictive correspondence could be from the least-prioritized region in U.S. foreign policy.

Much closer to home, the majority of the correspondence from Mexico during the historic election of 2000 focused, again, on economic repercussions for the United States. It was, in a way, the globalization version of the colonial attention to natural resources that had been so noticeable in correspondence about Japan in 1853. Mexicans might have shown a "surprising" political "maturity," as some editors argued, but whether that would be enough to change the corruption-ridden country was debatable. Mexico is Mexico, one *Los Angeles Times* correspondent wrote, again implying that readers would know what was meant. The insistence on American models in discourse also harked back to some nineteenth-century correspondence, as noted earlier, with "gringos" the model for all traits of modernity. Fox was always the former Coca-Cola executive, and one correspondent even spotlighted one of his supporters as selling Chevrolets and eating at McDonald's – the best new hope for change in Mexico, such formulas imply, was to approximate as best it could the United States.

The constant comparison with the United States dominated discourse about the European Union during the introduction of its common currency at the beginning of 2002. The correspondence constructed European countries that, yes, had not plunged into utter chaos as might have been expected, but whose ghosts of bloodied history still stalked peoples reluctant to unite. They were in no shape to pose a serious threat to the dominance and global leadership of "another wealthy transcontinental power, the United States," as one writer put it. There would be nothing particularly noteworthy in such insistence on the world's inability to measure up to the United States were it not for the fact that in virtually all analyzed correspondence in the twentieth century, it had hardly rated an explicit mention. The renewed insistence on U.S. superiority could be attributed to the souring post-9/11 transatlantic relation or to journalists pressed for time who resorted to readily available tropes, but it might also be indicative of America's unsettling doubts about its power and vulnerability in the new millennium.

The construction of America's role in the world that transpired in correspondence from Mumbai during the 2008 terrorist attacks, the last case studied here, was also much more restrictive than that found in the Bosnian reports, the first case for the post–Cold War era. In trying to prevent another set of inveterate rivals, India and Pakistan, from going at each other in yet another historical and religious conflict – albeit one in the shadow of nuclear weapons – the United States was portrayed as acting to further its own interests in the "war on terror," not some larger free-world agenda. As to India itself, the correspondence was rather miserly in nuances – India was largely depicted as a country with nukes that attracted a lot of Muslim terrorists even as it pushed for global economic powerhouse status.

Throughout its history, then, U.S. foreign correspondence has always constructed both an image for the United States as well as for other countries. The relative dominance of the two constructions is likely to have shaped understanding of foreign realities, and signs that twenty-first century texts are privileging American discourses over foreign ones could indicate renewed uncertainties about the United States' global role. A few recurrent discourses of the generalized "other" included the difficulty of democratic institutions to flourish in foreign soil, the mismatch between bountiful resources and apathetic peoples, and the weight of history. The individual discourses about countries, which were not always present, gave a subtler picture. It is in presenting those constructions, ranging from Chinese determination to Russian nationalism, that correspondence helped enrich the picture of the world beyond recurrent stereotypes. In its essence, and aside from those cases, media coverage belonged to the same general frameworks of understanding of the world, and of the United States, that guided U.S. foreign policy.

Evolving Foreign Policy Paradigms

From the very beginning, the dominant belief that the U.S. republican form of government was uniquely positioned as a beacon of freedom produced the two major contradictory trends that have guided American foreign policy. On the one hand, there is a constant reluctance to get entangled in the affairs of an inferior world; balancing that reluctance is the certainty that intervention would be missionary, would benefit other peoples even more than the United States itself. Even when they intervened to provoke or prevent regime change, an apparent contradiction for a nation born of the people's revolution that fought ferociously for its independence, U.S. administrations firmly believed that what they were doing was unique and intrinsically different from anything history had seen before or elsewhere.[14] Throughout the nineteenth century, as Washington first took control of the continent and then tested the waters of overseas possession, its trust in the superiority of American ways and the reflexive disdain for all foreign countries were constant. That made American exceptionalism and expansionistic policies really unique, for, unlike European imperialism, they encompassed all non-American cultures, with little distinction in condescension for the French and the Japanese, to name but two. Foreign correspondence, focused as it was on images of the United States, did little to challenge these discourses.

The real test came when the United States entered the Great Power realm at the turn of the twentieth century. Two dominant figures in foreign policy between 1900 and 1945 were Wilson and Roosevelt, and they both shared a fundamental sense that the United States needed to use its power to expand the benefits of capitalism and democracy to a world convulsed by total wars. In order to do that, by the end of the Second World War, Washington gave up its preference for unilateralism and entered a series of enduring security alliances across the world that would make it a de facto power everywhere. One important ideological push in the direction of global leadership was the 1917 Russian Revolution. After a few botched attempts to encourage the Russians to get rid of the Bolsheviks, the United States had to reconcile itself with a nearly

[14] For a similar point on the importance of socially constructed U.S. identity in the formulation of foreign policy, see Karl K. Schonberg, *Constructing 21st Century U.S. Foreign Policy: Identity, Ideology, and America's World Role in a New Era* (New York: Palgrave Macmillan, 2009).

incomprehensible fact – that a communist government would be a great power to contend with.

Partially because of that incomprehension, the 1917 revolution essentially started an ideological confrontation that would last for more than seventy years and come to dominate U.S. foreign policy for the majority of the twentieth century. Washington, much like U.S. foreign correspondents, understood Russia as intent on hurting the West from the very first days when Lenin announced the Soviets would pull the country out of the First World War. Violence, however, was erupting everywhere in the 1930s, from China to Spain, and the graphic discourses of appalling acts of cruelty in correspondence from Asia and Europe fit the paradoxical U.S. paradigms for involvement. Aghast at the horrors that the world presented, Americans would naturally have wanted to stay as far removed as possible, and, in between the two world wars, many have seen vestiges of isolationism. When the threats became acute and the outrage rampant, however, Washington slipped easily into global leadership on behalf of the free world. Discursively, there was nobody else available.

Intervention in the Western Hemisphere, for example, in revolution-torn Mexico, was supported by the fact that Americans had long assumed their right to protect their interests in their "backyard." Intervention to shape world events so that democracy and capitalism would reign, however, brought policy to a different level. At the end of the Second World War, the United States was committed – ideologically, economically and strategically – to a global role. Forged by the double threats of fascist and communist totalitarianism, American resolve was also likely steeled by the images of helpless, ravaged countries that correspondents had been fervently producing. Washington had to be more than a beacon on the hill – interests and ideology made global commitment seem inevitable, and it would remain so until the Soviet threat imploded nearly fifty years later.

Containing that threat was the default political and strategic factor in nearly all policy decisions made from the late 1940s to the early 1990s. In those years, be it in Cuba, the Middle East, or Afghanistan, local realities mattered less than the grand scheme of American versus Soviet influence. In Cuba, still believing in a special hemispheric influence and with extraordinarily little understanding that benevolent American interest might be perceived as suffocating exploitation, Washington was so caught off guard by Castro's Soviet turn that the period's worst nuclear crisis nearly happened there. In the Middle East, pro-Soviet placement further alienated Americans from Arabs, leading to tighter ties with Israel that rendered repeated peace-mediating efforts there usually futile and dragged Washington into a draining problem that remained as dangerous and urgent in 2012 as it had been in 1967. Perhaps the most striking example of the no-questions-asked approach to world politics at the height of containment was the millions of dollars spent in arming Islamic rebels in Afghanistan against the Soviets. The originally covert aid was such a prominent part of the media discourse about Afghanistan that it can only make sense within a larger framework of opposing the Soviet Union everywhere, at all costs, even in the late 1980s as détente was already peaking.

The turning point into a new era was what some called the anticlimactic demise of the Soviet Union. Washington's profound pessimism as the Soviet Union disintegrated in 1991 fits the existing discourse that foreign people could not be trusted with democratic self-government, but it also foreshadowed the difficulties that the lone superpower would have in facing the quagmires that the Cold War had kept, paradoxically, under control. The United States had preponderantly dominated the political, economic, military and media scene of the second half of the twentieth century. Suddenly deprived of an immediate security threat, Washington tried to refocus inward, but it kept finding itself, almost reluctantly, involved in all manners of new, destabilizing conflicts. Its initial aloofness and then sudden burst of military action, exemplified by the Bosnian War – the poster child of ethnic conflict – cemented doubts about both the triumph of freedom and the ability of America to lead in the post–Cold War era. As globalization spread, Washington in the 1990s found itself pursuing its economic self-interest across the world, continuing an entangling trend parallel to the skepticism about political and military commitments. That skepticism toward the missionary role that marked U.S. global involvement mirrored public disillusionment with American values and institutions, and they fed on each other.

As discourses about foreign countries' needs and worth shifted in the post–Cold War era, they affected not so much the concepts of American uniqueness and its global role, but how they should be carried over in policies. The terrorist attacks on 9/11 resurrected the powerful and enduring strain of unilateralism that had lingered underneath the multiple commitments of the twentieth century, reaffirming that, hated for its unique essence, America had a right to defend itself anywhere, anytime and against anybody. That unilateral strain, of course, is encouraged by the common discourse of all other countries as inferior, as incapable of dealing with freedom even when they are dealt it, as so stubbornly stuck in their gory pasts (like European nations and India) that they cannot mount real challenges to Washington. But the prolonged conflicts in Iraq and Afghanistan have called into question whether U.S. national interests are best served by the kind of extensive global intervention that had marked the twentieth century.

As the country entered the second decade of the twenty-first century, questions about America's role in the world remained unsettled. The preemptive doctrine that had accompanied forced democratization seemed largely discredited. The overriding economic expansion motive faltered in front of the rise of the "rest." A polarized and wallet-conscious public seemed to have lost the desire to remake the world in the image of an America it increasingly found faulty. Once again, media discourses have shifted to discuss more the United States than foreign realities, impoverishing the debate when it is most needed to evaluate the future role of American power.

The guiding principles of U.S. foreign policy as thus briefly detailed fit within the box of media discourses about the rest of the world, and America's place in it, as found in the foreign correspondence examined. The inward discursive turn of the latter in the 2000s, therefore, is troubling for the ability and willingness of Washington to engage the world more than in self-interested forays that do little to promote a more equitable international system. If the history traced in this book can be used as a guide, more media engagement with foreign affairs is needed for Washington to also reengage the world in a productive leadership position, even though American political disengagement itself makes foreign media coverage less likely. It should be stated clearly that this does not mean an interventionist press clamoring for specific policies, but rather journalists covering the world with sufficient depth that the debate over policies can be broadened. In fact, most foreign correspondence studied in this book has shied from prescribing explicit policy actions, even those espoused by the editorial pages. Correspondents have, however, left an illuminating record of how they perceived their job and the news media in general affecting world affairs, as discussed in the next section.

Foreign Correspondence and World Affairs

Splashing on the front page a cable directly from a Chinese official with news of the Boxer siege in Beijing, the editors of the *New York Tribune* in 1900 smugly affirmed that the paper was "the most authoritative medium" to reach the "thoughtful and intelligent masses of the American people." Throughout the correspondence studied here, however, reporters made extremely infrequent explicit mentions of the impact the news might have on the American public, even as they increasingly recognized journalists were being played by political actors for maximum visibility, as noted later in this section. Rather than as opinion shapers, correspondents appear to have written as eyewitnesses and recorders – roles they cherished and explained to their readers in impassionate detail.

The Eyewitness

Writing from Paris in 1848 for the *New York Herald*, an unidentified correspondent offered his readers this basic guideline for all foreign news reporting: Correspondents made a difference because they were there when news happened, eyewitnesses to history, intent in giving not only the most accurate and vivid accounts of events abroad, but also in-depth analysis of how other cultures understood their world. Across the years, the importance of being there has remained a constant of journalism's crucial involvement in world affairs. For the vast majority of the American press, which rarely could afford its own eyewitness, the Associated Press has covered the globe, making it a vastly understudied influence in America's relation to the world. One of the contributions of this book is to analyze AP dispatches in addition to standard scholarly sources like the *New York Times*, making the findings of this research reflect images of the world not only in the most influential newspapers in large metropolises, but in the small-town papers read across the country.

By virtue of their eyewitness performances, correspondents have also affirmed and cherished independence from their newspapers' editorial lines, again suggesting that correspondence provides a unique source of images that is less susceptible to domestic manipulation. Whereas this research focused on correspondence, not on editorials, many examples of the latter suggested that they tended to provide a very limited construction of foreign countries. A *Washington Post* editorial in 2000 that praised Mexicans for having "shown a remarkable democratic vocation and political maturity," for example, appears to belong to a patronizing discourse of foreign people's childish inability to self-govern that is especially questionable in the twenty-first century.

Hints of correspondents' independence, already visible in reportage from the French Revolution of 1848, became blatant when provoked by atrocities, as in Shanghai. Editorials discussing the Japanese attack on the Chinese population there had been strongly against American intervention and disparagingly dismissive of Chinese suffering. Not many readers, however, could have failed to perceive the seething outrage at U.S. aloofness that transpired from descriptions of the bombing such as this one by a *Chicago Daily News* correspondent: "Surrounded by marines from California, Texas and Virginia, I watched the Japanese bomb the defenseless city.... Hundreds of Chinese jammed their faces against the huge steel gates leading into the American quarter, hoping to enter the lines of exit from the Chinese city, but they were not allowed to do so."[15] In the Bosnian War, when first-person reporting had become rare and U.S. journalists tended to minimize their own voice, correspondents channeled their outrage through gripping quotes from civilians. *Washington Post* readers, for example, heard from a cook in a besieged Mostar public kitchen, where snipers had just killed a man as he made his way for breakfast, saying, "We want the Americans to save us and send us parachutes of food."[16]

Pride at being present at the making of history is something that transpires from all correspondence across the years. There is a palpable sense that only by being there could one really appreciate what happened. Most editors today would probably feel like those at the *Chicago Daily News* who thus enthused about Louis Edgar Browne's coverage of the 1917 Soviet coup: "His picture of the congress of soviets – the delegates wearing fur overcoats and fur caps in a superheated room blue with tobacco smoke, workmen and common soldiers laboriously deciding upon a policy for the vastest nation on earth amid the clatter of hobnailed boots on the wooden floor – deserves to live as a classic bit

15 Reginald Sweetland, "Daily News Man Witnesses Slaughter in Chinese City; Tells of Death from Air," *Chicago Daily News*, January 29, 1932, 1.

16 John Pomfret, "'Maybe It's Better to Die by Shelling Than of Hunger,'" *Washington Post*, August 23, 1993, A11.

of reporting."[17] Much as U.S. correspondence has been criticized for its analytical faults, journalists covering those historical events in November 1917 did provide an unprecedented number of eyewitness accounts that vividly showed readers what it meant to be in St. Petersburg during the revolution.

To many correspondents through the years, being present was necessary but not sufficient – the key difference was their extended experience of the country, which allowed them to give readers the kind of context "parachuting" journalists and occasional visitors could not provide. Whereas the tendency to send out journalists to cover global happenings from a domestic base is increasing in the 2000s, foreign correspondents made fun of it throughout the history covered in this book. An AP correspondent in Rome at the time of Mussolini's historic speech in 1925, for example, had this snide remark for his drop-in colleagues: "Despite the lull in the political situation, a flock of foreign newspaper correspondents, including many from the United States and England who poured into Rome from other European capitals to watch the fireworks this week, refused to be convinced that the 'shooting' is over, and they are still trying with might and main to interview Mussolini."[18] In Johannesburg during Mandela's election, a correspondent for the *Washington Post* blasted a visiting American political figure for being so ignorant of the situation on the ground he could not even pronounce the name of the place: "'Where are you going to watch the voting?' [the Reverend Al] Sharpton was asked. 'So-weee-to,' he replied. 'You mean So-weh-to?' the journalist inquired. 'That's right,' Sharpton said."[19]

The Player

While correspondents defended their ability to act as independent and knowledgeable observers, they sometimes became part of the story, too. Another enduring aspect of foreign correspondence is how often it served as semiofficial diplomatic conduit, making it overtly relevant to policy deliberations. Already in Cuba in 1895, both Spanish and insurgent leaders addressed Washington through American foreign correspondents. In Israel in 1967, one reporter similarly aimed at the White House by ending an article by saying, "There is hope here that Washington and other capitals will remember that the Arabs were trying to liquidate Israel, not merely bring about border changes."[20] In that Middle East war, correspondents also remarked on overt news management by the Israeli government, which might have been related to a certain homogenization of news (the same stories from Bethlehem and the same plane ride over the Sinai, for example) that became evident then.

17 "Great Story from Petrograd," *Chicago Daily News*, November 12, 1917, 8.
18 "Mussolini Asserts No Elections Will Be Held This Year," *Baltimore Sun*, January 11, 1925, 11.
19 Paul Taylor, "The Election Onlookers, Ogling as History Happens," *Washington Post*, April 26, 1994, E1.
20 Sydney Gruson, "Cabinet Confers," *New York Times*, June 12, 1967, 18.

Trying to capture the attention of American reporters seems to have been a constant in all countries, both outside and within governments. The *New York Times* correspondent in Shanghai after the normalization of relations in 1979 wrote that a group of young Chinese men wanting to get permission to return to the city from their distant farm jobs "tried to publicize their cause by using an event attended not only by local notables but also by American reporters."[21] Similarly, the AP bureau chief wrote that Nelson Mandela in 1994 had picked reporters "with special attention to those from industrialized countries that can help with South Africa's development"[22] for his postelection press conference.

In a subtle Cold War irony, U.S. intelligence satellites watching the Soviet-Afghan border in 1988 had alerted "reporters that the Soviets were planning something out of the ordinary" – which turned out to be the media-ready, welcome-home event for Soviet soldiers withdrawing from Afghanistan. Notes of media manipulation for PR purposes were a constant reference in stories from the post–Cold War era, a telling revelation of both global media's reach and the sophisticated attempts of political actors to use them. In Bosnia, reporters noted the evacuation of a handful of children from Sarajevo under television's glare. In South Africa, Mandela's inauguration was a red-carpet event. In Mexico, president-elect Fox was called "telegenic," a quality that, beamed to the remotest villages, was considered essential to his victory. In the Mumbai attacks in 2008, the press also reported on the then-new power of Internet tools like blogs and photo-sharing services to allow ordinary citizens to spread information about the events as they unfolded and often before the mass media could deploy.

In the face of such growing recognition of the importance of publicity, correspondents continued to defend the necessity of their eyewitness role as a check against rumor mills and official cover-ups. Reporters in the Spanish Civil War and the Cuban Revolution had pointedly revealed direct observations that contradicted official sources. When Castro's government refused to confirm news of mass executions of Batista supporters, for example, an AP correspondent had gone to the scene and reported, without comment, that he had seen "a big mound of fresh earth" there. Interviews with today's news leaders at some of America's top circulation newspapers and the AP showed that having foreign correspondents in place was considered vital to getting the story right, to check against misleading statements from officials and from unverified information online, and to give breaking news the necessary context and analysis. Across time, editors and correspondents who felt a civic duty, as one put it, to do all of that for their public also wondered about whether that public would care and how to make it do so.

[21] Harold C. Schonberg, "Shanghai Youths Use Boston Symphony Visit for Protest," *New York Times*, March 16, 1979, A11.

[22] John Daniszewski, "All-but-President Mandela Meets the Press," Associated Press, April 29, 1994.

The Lookout

Two overarching values for professional foreign correspondence stood out from the analysis of stories as well as interviews: to bring eyewitness testimony to all parts of the world before, during and after they found themselves in the media glare, and, in so doing, to make a sizable mass of people care about the world. As Greg Winter of the *New York Times* foreign desk told me, "We have always done stories that are important, not sexy. We have never really approached news as what people want to read." While painfully aware that foreign news is not often of pressing interest to the vast majority of the American public, correspondents and editors believed their public service was to make more Americans, if not all, better equipped to understand the world. In 1920, European correspondent Paul Scott Mowrer of the *Chicago Daily News* wrote a letter with "suggestions for reorganizing the foreign service."[23] In it, describing what the basic aim of the service should be, Mowrer argued,

> The Daily News will perhaps interest only such readers as are public spirited; but these are perhaps more numerous than is generally imagined. It is, I believe, an illusion to hope that any foreign service can reach *everybody*. It is better to give a first-class service to those who can appreciate it than to aim to please all, and succeed in pleasing none. Nevertheless, the prestige which would be gradually acquired by a fine service would doubtless suffice to win many supplementary readers who are content to follow the leadership of others.

More than ninety years later, it is easy to imagine correspondents and editors making the same arguments to newly penny-pinching, most-emailed-sensitive media managers. In interviews, they spoke of their function as news gatherers and interpreters of the world as a crucial public service that transcended fleeting trends. Foreign correspondence certainly changed significantly from 1900 to today, but the note that *New York Tribune* editors inserted on a summary of the Boxer Rebellion in Beijing points to a core that has remained constant: "[The events] are here briefly reviewed for the benefit of those readers of The Tribune who *did not pay that attention* to them which they would have done *had they appreciated* the grave historical importance which now attaches to them."[24] Write it and they will come – solid foreign correspondence will always have an audience, and its contribution to the public discourse is to offer up the world even when people fail to pay the attention they should.

Conclusion: The Irreplaceable Mediator in Danger

The essential eyewitness, mediator role of the American media in world affairs is the core conclusion and normative position of this book. That is not to cast

[23] The letter is reprinted in Jaci Cole and John Maxwell Hamilton, eds. *Journalism of the Highest Realm: The Memoir of Edward Price Bell, Pioneering Foreign Correspondent for the* Chicago Daily News (Baton Rouge: Louisiana State University Press, 2007), 327–329.

[24] "Story of China's Crime," *New York Tribune*, July 20, 1900; emphasis added.

the news media as without sin – rather, it is to point out as suggestive that where media discourses have been particularly reductive, as in the Middle East or Cuba cases analyzed in previous chapters, policies have also been stalemated or worse. Examples of correspondence expanding the policy parameters for positive outcomes are harder to isolate, although one might point to the impassionate pleas against carnage in Shanghai, Madrid and Mostar as conducive to effective leadership, and the 1991 pessimism as aligned with a more realistic assessment of the post–Cold War than "the end of history." Direction of causality is beside the point – the central argument is that the news media contribute to the American polity's understanding of the world, and lack thereof, with consequences for U.S. global engagement.

With few exceptions, such as the organizations studied here, U.S. news media in the twenty-first century are disengaging from the world and from news in general, scrambling to try any seemingly popular trend that will make stockholders happier. Despite the unprecedented availability of information online for those with the interest, time and resources to search for it, the dwindling of hard news in general distribution media is hurting the richness of the "marketplace of ideas." The history presented here shows glaring failures by the press to give readers sufficiently nuanced discourses of the world to sustain public debate on how the United States should act. But it also shows that those failures were occasionally mitigated and overcome when foreign correspondents engaged foreign countries, let themselves be "surprised" by how they did not fit their preconceived discourses, and wrote texts that incorporated local realities instead of merely reflecting constructions of the United States.

At a time when instantaneous communication has shrunk the world but not bridged cultural and ideological divides, the necessity for professional foreign correspondence to provide a rich public arena for the formation of meanings about foreign realities is more critical than ever. A democratic self-government cannot endure with a misinformed citizenry – as James Madison eloquently summed it up in the 1820s, "A popular government without popular information, or the means of acquiring it, is but a prologue to a farce or a tragedy; or perhaps both."[25] Foreign correspondents are a critical link between foreign meanings and the American public's opportunity to form some understanding of them. In that capacity, they are also essential to international relations, because the discursive environment about foreign realities that they help shape provides the parameters within which the range of foreign policies toward other countries can be understood and American diplomatic strategies can be envisioned and implemented. If there is one clear prescription that emerges from this book's historical analysis, it is that "afghanistanism" is a good malady for journalists to succumb to.

25 Quoted in Mitchell Stephens, *A History of News* 3rd ed. (New York: Oxford University Press, 2007), 181.

Today, however, the belt-tightening insularity of the American press is making it more difficult to get substantive foreign news in the United States. Some observers have argued that it is wrong and elitist to "make people care" about wars and famine by extensive reporting from across the world when the people have spoken and they want Kate Middleton and recipes to make bread. On the contrary, did people not fault the press for not digging deeper into the Bush administration's reasons for war in Iraq and for not alerting Americans of the looming menace of al-Qaeda before the 9/11 attacks, two events that have defined America's foreign policy at the beginning of the twenty-first century? If not the press, who will provide the necessary information citizens need to make the right decisions in a democracy that still has a leadership position in an ever-more interdependent world?

Even beyond the record-keeping, fact-finding missions of the news media are the pivotal functions they serve as "investigator, explainer and . . . arbiter of our national conversations," in the words of the managing editor of the *Columbia Journalism Review*.[26] Making processes and events that were in the background available for "collective notice" and understanding is one of the ways in which journalism serves democracy, the book aptly titled "Why Democracies Need an Unlovable Press" argues.[27] "Witnessing, deciphering, interpreting" – those are the combined characteristics that foreign correspondence in the twenty-first century should not abandon, according to Timothy Garton Ash.[28]

One of the main lessons from the history presented in this book is that journalism has long been a fundamental way for Americans to form images about the rest of world and themselves, and consequently to act in it. Newspapers remain a vital, but vitally endangered, part of the journalistic mixture, not because of the *paper* part but because of their still unparalleled investment in *news* reporting.[29] This is the time for the press to reaffirm its responsibility of giving people worldwide more quality information on which to base momentous decisions. It might be hard for cash-strapped media to continue to provide international news – it has always been expensive, whether carried by pigeons or satellites – but misinformation about one another is precisely what the citizens of the twenty-first century world cannot afford.

For better or for worse, foreign correspondence in the American press has been an irreplaceable mediator between the public and a complicated globe in which America has been a driving presence for more than a hundred years. Today is a time of unprecedented challenge for the American press to embrace

[26] Brent Cunningham, "Take a Stand: How Journalism Can Regain Its Relevance," *Columbia Journalism Review*, September/October 2009, 32.

[27] Michael Schudson, *Why Democracies Need an Unlovable Press* (Cambridge: Polity Press, 2008), 17.

[28] Timothy Garton Ash, "The Foreign Correspondent Is Dead. Long Live the Foreign Correspondent," *Guardian*, December 9, 2010, 37.

[29] Alex S. Jones, *Losing the News: The Future of the News That Feeds Democracy* (Oxford: Oxford University Press, 2009), 198.

its role as translator of international meanings to better serve the public interest, by which I mean not one country's global predominance but the ability of countries to work together in a just international system. Better understanding, fostered by a broader opportunity to form more profound images of one another, will be the first step in more constructive interactions between the United States and the world.

Bibliography

Aday, Sean. "Chasing the Bad News: An Analysis of 2005 Iraq and Afghanistan War Coverage on NBC and Fox News Channel." *Journal of Communication* 60–1 (March 2010): 144–164.

Aday, Sean. "Leading the Charge: Media, Elites, and the Use of Emotion in Stimulating Rally Effects in Wartime." *Journal of Communication* 60–3 (September 2010): 440–465.

Adler, Emanuel. "Constructivism and International Relations." In *Handbook of International Relations*, edited by Walter Carlsnaes, Thomas Risse and Beth A. Simmons, 95–118. London: SAGE, 2002.

Aguayo, Sergio. *Myths and [Mis]Perceptions: Changing U.S. Elite Visions of Mexico*. La Jolla: Center for U.S.-Mexican Studies, University of California, San Diego, 1998.

Alesina, Alberto, and Francesco Giavazzi, eds. *Europe and the Euro*. Chicago: University of Chicago Press, 2010.

Allison, William. *American Diplomats in Russia: Case Studies in Orphan Diplomacy, 1916–1919*. Westport, CT: Praeger, 1997.

Almond, Gabriel A. *The American People and Foreign Policy*. Westport, CT: Greenwood Press, 1960.

Anderson, Benedict. *Imagined Communities*. London: Verso, 1991.

Anft, Michael. "The World, in Eight Weeks." *Johns Hopkins Magazine*, February 2009, 33.

Arnett, Peter. "Goodbye, World." *American Journalism Review*, November 1998, 50–67.

The Associated Press. *Lightning out of Israel: The Six-Day War in the Middle East*. New York: Associated Press, 1967.

Avery, Donald R. "American over European Community? Newspaper Content Changes, 1808–1812." *Journalism Quarterly* 63–2 (Summer 1986): 311–314.

Baldasty, Gerald J. *The Commercialization of News in the Nineteenth Century*. Madison: University of Wisconsin Press, 1992.

Barkho, Leon. *News from the BBC, CNN, and Al-Jazeera: How the Three Broadcasters Cover the Middle East*. Cresskill, NJ: Hampton Press, 2010.

Barkin, J. Samuel. *Realist Constructivism: Rethinking International Relations Theory.* Cambridge: Cambridge University Press, 2010.

Baum, Matthew A. *Soft News Goes to War: Public Opinion and American Foreign Policy in the New Media Age.* Princeton, NJ: Princeton University Press, 2003.

Baum, Matthew A., and Philip B.K. Potter. "The Relationships between Mass Media, Public Opinion, and Foreign Policy: Toward a Theoretical Synthesis." *Annual Review of Political Science* 11 (2008): 39–65.

Bennett, Andrew. *Condemned to Repetition? The Rise, Fall, and Reprise of Soviet-Russian Military Interventionism, 1973–1996.* Cambridge, MA: MIT Press, 1999.

Bennett, W. Lance. "Toward a Theory of Press-State Relations in the United States." *Journal of Communication* 40–2 (Spring 1990): 103–125.

Bennett, W. Lance, and Robert M. Entman, eds. *Mediated Politics: Communication in the Future of Democracy.* Cambridge: Cambridge University Press, 2001.

Bennett, W. Lance, and Shanto Iyengar. "The Shifting Foundations of Political Communication: Responding to a Defense of the Media Effects Paradigm." *Journal of Communication* 60–1 (March 2010): 35–39.

Bennett, W. Lance, Regina G. Lawrence and Steven Livingston. *When the Press Fails: Political Power and the News Media from Iraq to Katrina.* Chicago: University of Chicago Press, 2007.

Bennett, W. Lance, and David L. Paletz, eds. *Taken by Storm: The Media, Public Opinion, and U.S. Foreign Policy in the Gulf War.* Chicago: University of Chicago Press, 1994.

Berg, Eiki, and Piret Ehin, eds. *Identity and Foreign Policy: Baltic-Russian Relations and European Integration.* Farnham: Ashgate, 2009.

Berger, Peter L., and Thomas Luckmann. *The Social Construction of Reality: A Treatise in the Sociology of Knowledge.* Garden City, NY: Doubleday, 1966.

Berinsky, Adam J. *In Time of War: Understanding Public Opinion from World War II to Iraq.* Chicago: University of Chicago Press, 2009.

Berry, Nicholas O. *Foreign Policy and the Press: An Analysis of* The New York Times' *Coverage of U.S. Foreign Policy.* New York: Greenwood Press, 1990.

Best, Samuel J., Brian Chmielewski and Brian S. Krueger. "Selective Exposure to Online Foreign News during the Conflict with Iraq." *The Harvard International Journal of Press/Politics* 10/4 (2005): 52–70.

Bickers, Robert, and R.G. Tiedemann, eds. *The Boxers, China, and the World.* Lanham, MD: Rowman & Littlefield, 2007.

Blanchard, Margaret A. *Revolutionary Sparks: Freedom of Expression in Modern America.* New York: Oxford University Press, 1992.

Blankson, Isaac A., and Patrick D. Murphy, eds. *Negotiating Democracy: Media Transformations in Emerging Democracies.* Albany: State University of New York Press, 2007.

Bleyer, Willard Grosvenor. *Main Currents in the History of American Journalism.* Boston: Houghton Mifflin Company, 1927.

Blitz, Brad, ed. *War and Change in the Balkans: Nationalism, Conflict and Cooperation.* Cambridge: Cambridge University Press, 2006.

Bloch-Elkon, Yaeli. "Studying the Media, Public Opinion, and Foreign Policy in International Crises: The United States and the Bosnian Crisis, 1992–1995." *The Harvard International Journal of Press/Politics* 12/4 (2007): 20–51.

Blondheim, Menahem. *News over the Wires: The Telegraph and the Flow of Public Information in America, 1844–1897*. Cambridge, MA: Harvard University Press, 1994.

Boczkowski, Pablo J. *News at Work: Imitation in an Age of Information Abundance*. Chicago: University of Chicago Press, 2010.

Boehmer, Elleke. *Nelson Mandela: A Very Short Introduction*. Oxford: Oxford University Press, 2008.

Bollinger, Lee C. "News for the World: A Proposal for a Globalized Era: An American World Service." *Columbia Journalism Review*, July–August 2011, 29–33.

Borg, Dorothy, and Shumpei Okamoto, eds. *Pearl Harbor as History: Japanese-American Relations, 1931–1941*. New York: Columbia University Press, 1973.

Boulding, K.E. "National Images and International Systems." *The Journal of Conflict Resolution* 3–2 (June 1959): 120–131.

Bozeman, Adda B. *Politics & Culture in International History: From the Ancient Near East to the Opening of the Modern Age*. 2nd ed. New Brunswick, NJ: Transaction Publishers, 1994.

Bradsher, Henry S. *Afghan Communism and Soviet Intervention*. Oxford: Oxford University Press, 1999.

Braumoeller, Bear F. "The Myth of American Isolationism." *Foreign Policy Analysis* 6 (2010): 349–371.

Brewer, Stewart. *Borders and Bridges: A History of U.S.-Latin American Relations*. Westport, CT: Praeger Security International, 2006.

Britton, John A. *Revolution and Ideology: Images of the Mexican Revolution in the United States*. Lexington: University Press of Kentucky, 1995.

Brown, Richard D. *Knowledge Is Power: The Diffusion of Information in Early America, 1700–1865*. New York: Oxford University Press, 1989.

Brown, Richard D. *The Strength of a People: The Idea of an Informed Citizenry in America, 1650–1870*. Chapel Hill: University of North Carolina Press, 1996.

Brzezinski, Zbigniew, and Brent Scowcroft. *America and the World: Conversations on the Future of American Foreign Policy*. New York: Basic Books, 2008.

Buchanan, William, and Hadley Cantril. *How Nations See Each Other*. Urbana: University of Illinois Press, 1953.

Bulla, David W., and Gregory A. Borchard. *Journalism in the Civil War Era*. New York: Peter Lang, 2010.

Burg, Steven L., and Paul S. Shoup. *The War in Bosnia-Herzegovina: Ethnic Conflict and International Intervention*. Armonk, NY: M.E. Sharpe, 1999.

Burstein, Paul. "The Impact of Public Opinion on Public Policy: A Review and an Agenda." *Political Research Quarterly* 56–1 (March 2003): 29–40.

Carey, James W. *Communication as Culture: Essays on Media and Society*. New York: Routledge, 1992.

Carlsnaes, Walter, Thomas Risse and Beth A. Simmons, eds. *Handbook of International Relations*. London: SAGE, 2002.

Carruthers, Susan L. *The Media at War: Communication and Conflict in the Twentieth Century*. New York: St. Martin's Press, 2000.

Carter, John Booth. "American Reactions to Italian Fascism, 1919–1933." PhD diss., Columbia University, 1954.

Chamberlin, Wilbur J. *Ordered to China*. New York: Frederick A. Stokes, 1903.

Chang, Tsan-Kuo. "All Countries Not Created Equal to Be News." *Communication Research* 25–5 (1998): 528–563.

Chang, Tsan-Kuo. *The Press and China Policy: The Illusion of Sino-American Relations, 1950–1984*. Norwood, NJ: Ablex Publishing, 1993.

Chang, Tsan-Kuo, Brian Southwell, Hyung-Min Lee and Yejin Hong. "A Changing World, Unchanging Perspectives: American Newspaper Editors and Enduring Values in Foreign News Reporting." *International Communication Gazette* 74–4 (June 2012): 367–384.

Checkel, Jeffrey T. "The Constructivist Turn in International Relations Theory." *World Politics* 50–2 (1998): 324–348.

Cohen, Jeffrey E. *The Presidency in the Era of 24-Hour News*. Princeton, NJ: Princeton University Press, 2008.

Cohen, Warren I. *America's Response to China: A History of Sino-American Relations*. 5th ed. New York: Columbia University Press, 2010.

Cole, Jaci, and John Maxwell Hamilton. "The History of a Surviving Species: Defining Eras in the Evolution of Foreign Correspondence." In *The Future of Newspapers*, edited by Bob Franklin, 169–183. London: Routledge, 2010.

Cole, Jaci, and John Maxwell Hamilton, eds. *Journalism of the Highest Realm: The Memoir of Edward Price Bell, Pioneering Foreign Correspondent for the* Chicago Daily News. Baton Rouge: Louisiana State University Press, 2007.

Combs, Jerald A. *The History of American Foreign Policy: Volume I, To 1920*. 3rd ed. Armonk, NY: M.E. Sharpe, 2008.

Combs, Jerald A. *The History of American Foreign Policy: Volume II, From 1895*. 3rd ed. Armonk, NY: M.E. Sharpe, 2008.

Cook, Timothy E. "The News Media as a Political Institution: Looking Backward and Looking Forward." *Political Communication* 23 (2006): 159–171.

Copeland, Fayette. *Kendall of the Picayune*. Norman: University of Oklahoma Press, 1943.

Cottam, Martha L. *Images and Intervention: U.S. Policies in Latin America*. Pittsburgh, PA: University of Pittsburgh Press, 1994.

Cotter, Colleen. *News Talk: Investigating the Language of Journalism*. Cambridge: Cambridge University Press, 2010.

Cottle, Simon. "Journalism and Globalization." In *The Handbook of Journalism Studies*, edited by Karin Wahl-Jorgensen and Thomas Hanitzsch, 341–356. New York: Routledge, 2009.

Cox, Michael, and Doug Stokes, eds. *US Foreign Policy*. Oxford: Oxford University Press, 2008.

Crack, Angela M. *Global Communication and Transnational Public Spheres*. New York: Palgrave Macmillan, 2008.

Crofts Wiley, Stephen B. "Rethinking Nationality in the Context of Globalization." *Communication Theory* 14–1 (2004): 78–96.

Crouthamel, James L. *Bennett's New York Herald and the Rise of the Popular Press*. Syracuse, NY: Syracuse University Press, 1989.

Cunningham, Brent. "Take a Stand: How Journalism Can Regain Its Relevance." *Columbia Journalism Review*, September/October 2009, 32–39.

Cushion, Stephen, and Justin Lewis, eds. *The Rise of 24-Hour News Television: Global Perspectives*. New York: Peter Lang, 2010.

Dabney, Thomas Ewing. *One Hundred Great Years: The Story of the* Times-Picayune *from Its Founding to 1940*. Baton Rouge: Louisiana State University Press, 1944.

Daly, Christopher B. *Covering America: A Narrative History of a Nation's Journalism*. Amherst: University of Massachusetts Press, 2012.

Davies, David R. *The Postwar Decline of American Newspapers, 1945–1965*. Westport, CT: Praeger, 2006.

Davis, Donald E., and Eugene P. Trani. *The First Cold War: The Legacy of Woodrow Wilson in U.S.-Soviet Relations*. Columbia: University of Missouri Press, 2002.

Davis, Elmer. *History of the* New York Times, *1851–1921*. New York: The New York Times, 1921.

De Beer, Arnold S., and John C. Merrill. *Global Journalism: Topical Issues and Media Systems*. 4th ed. Boston: Pearson, 2004.

De Cillia, Rudolf, Martin Reisigl and Ruth Wodak. "The Discursive Construction of National Identities." *Discourse & Society* 10–2 (1999): 149–174.

Deibert, Ronald J. *Parchment, Printing, and Hypermedia: Communication in World Order Transformation*. New York: Columbia University Press, 1997.

Delli Carpini, Michael X., and Scott Keeter. *What Americans Know about Politics and Why It Matters*. New Haven, CT: Yale University Press, 1996.

Dell'Orto, Giovanna. *Giving Meanings to the World: The First U.S. Foreign Correspondents, 1838–1859*. Westport, CT: Greenwood Publishing Group, 2002.

Dell'Orto, Giovanna. *The Hidden Power of the American Dream: Why Europe's Shaken Confidence in the United States Threatens the Future of U.S. Influence*. Westport, CT: Praeger Security International, 2008.

Desmond, Robert. *The Press and World Affairs*. New York: D. Appleton-Century Co., 1937.

Deutsch, Karl W., and Richard L. Merritt. "Effects of Events on National and International Images." In *International Behavior: A Social-Psychological Analysis*, edited by Herbert C. Kelman, 132–184. New York: Holt, Rinehart and Winston, 1985.

Dicken-Garcia, Hazel. *Journalistic Standards in Nineteenth-Century America*. Madison: University of Wisconsin Press, 1989.

Dicken-Garcia, Hazel, and K. Viswanath. "An Idea Whose Time Has Come: International Communication History." *Mass Communication & Society* 5–1 (2002): 1–6.

Diggins, John P. *Mussolini and Fascism: The View from America*. Princeton, NJ: Princeton University Press, 1972.

Domínguez, Jorge I., and Rafael Fernández de Castro. *The United States and Mexico: Between Partnership and Conflict*. 2nd ed. New York: Routledge, 2009.

Domínguez, Jorge I., and Chappell Lawson, eds. *Mexico's Pivotal Democratic Election: Candidates, Voters, and the Presidential Campaign of 2000*. Stanford, CA: Stanford University Press, 2004.

Domínguez, Jorge I., and Alejandro Poiré, eds. *Toward Mexico's Democratization: Parties, Campaigns, Elections, and Public Opinion*. New York: Routledge, 1999.

Dorman, William A., and Mansour Farhang. *The U.S. Press and Iran: Foreign Policy and the Journalism of Deference*. Berkeley: University of California Press, 1987.

Dorronsoro, Gilles. *Revolution Unending: Afghanistan: 1979 to the Present*. New York: Columbia University Press, 2005.

Dougherty, Patricia. *American Diplomats and the Franco-Prussian War: Perceptions from Paris and Berlin*. Washington: Georgetown University, 1980.

Douglas, George H. *The Golden Age of the Newspaper*. Westport, CT: Greenwood Press, 1999.

Downie, Leonard Jr., and Michael Schudson. "The Reconstruction of American Journalism." *Columbia Journalism Review*, November/December 2009, 28–51.

Drury, A. Cooper, Mary Caprioli, Axel Huelsemeyer, Erin K. Jenne, Sara McLaughlin Mitchell and James M. Scott. "Note from the Editors." *Foreign Policy Analysis* 3–3 (July 2010): 187–190.

Duncan, Bingham. *Whitelaw Reid: Journalist, Politician, Diplomat*. Athens: University of Georgia Press, 1975.

Edmonds-Poli, Emily, and David A. Shirk. *Contemporary Mexican Politics*. Lanham, MD: Rowman & Littlefield, 2009.

Edwards, David, and David Cromwell. *Newspeak in the 21st Century*. London: Pluto Press, 2009.

Elman, Colin, and Miriam Fendius Elman, "The Role of History in International Relations." *Millennium – Journal of International Studies* 37–2 (2008): 357–364.

Emadi, Hafizullah. *Dynamics of Political Development in Afghanistan: The British, Russian, and American Invasions*. New York: Palgrave Macmillan, 2010.

Emery, Michael. *On the Front Lines: Following America's Foreign Correspondents Across the Twentieth Century*. Washington: American University Press, 1995.

Emery, Michael, Edwin Emery and Nancy Roberts. *The Press and America: An Interpretive History of the Mass Media*. 9th ed. Boston: Allyn and Bacon, 2000.

Enda, Jodi. "Retreating from the World." *American Journalism Review*, December/January 2011, 14–29.

Entman, Robert M. "Framing U.S. Coverage of International News." *Journal of Communication* 41–4 (1991): 6–27.

Entman, Robert M. *Projections of Power: Framing News, Public Opinion, and U.S. Foreign Policy*. Chicago: University of Chicago Press, 2004.

Epstein, Charlotte. *The Power of Words in International Relations: Birth of an Anti-Whaling Discourse*. Cambridge, MA: MIT Press, 2008.

"Escape the Silos." *Columbia Journalism Review*, November/December 2010, 4.

Fairclough, Norman. *Media Discourse*. New York: Edward Arnold, 1995.

Farber, Samuel. *The Origins of the Cuban Revolution Reconsidered*. Chapel Hill: University of North Carolina Press, 2006.

Feifer, George. *Breaking Open Japan: Commodore Perry, Lord Abe, and American Imperialism in 1853*. New York: HarperCollins, 2006.

Fenby, Jonathan. *The International News Services*. New York: Schocken Books, 1986.

Fenton, Tom. *Junk News: The Failure of the Media in the 21st Century*. Golden, CO: Fulcrum, 2009.

Finkelstein, Norman G. *Image and Reality of the Israel-Palestine Conflict*. London: Verso, 2001.

Finnemore, Martha, and Kathryn Sikkink. "Taking Stock: The Constructivist Research Program in International Relations and Comparative Politics." *Annual Review of Political Science* 4 (2001): 391–416.

Fitzgerald, Richard, and William Housley, eds. *Media, Policy and Interaction*. Farnham: Ashgate, 2009.

Foglesong, David S. *America's Secret War against Bolshevism*. Chapel Hill: University of North Carolina Press, 1995.

Foltz, Charles, Jr. *The Masquerade in Spain*. Boston: Houghton Mifflin, 1948.

Fortner, Robert S. *International Communication: History, Conflict, and Control of the Global Metropolis*. Belmont, CA: Wadsworth Publishing, 1993.

Foucault, Michel. *The Archaeology of Knowledge*. New York: Pantheon Books, 1972.

Foucault, Michel. "The Order of Discourse." In *Untying the Text*, edited by Robert Young, 48–78. Boston: Routledge & Kegan Paul, 1981.

Frederick, Howard H. *Global Communication & International Relations*. Belmont, CA: Wadsworth Publishing, 1993.

Friel, Howard, and Richard Falk. *The Record of the Paper: How the* New York Times *Misreports US Foreign Policy*. London: Verso, 2004.

Fuller, Jack. *What Is Happening to News: The Information Explosion and the Crisis of Journalism*. Chicago: University of Chicago Press, 2010.

Gaddis, John Lewis. *The United States and the End of the Cold War: Implications, Reconsiderations, Provocations*. New York: Oxford University Press, 1992.

Gamson, William A., and Andre Modigliani. "Media Discourse and Public Opinion on Nuclear Power: A Constructionist Approach." *American Journal of Sociology* 95–1 (July 1989): 1–37.

Ganguly, Sumit, Brian Shoup and Andrew Scobell, eds. *US-Indian Strategic Cooperation into the 21st Century: More Than Words*. London: Routledge, 2006.

Gans, Herbert J. *Deciding What's News: A Study of* CBS Evening News, NBC Nightly News, Newsweek *and* Time. New York: Random House, 1979.

Gardner, Lloyd C. *Safe for Democracy: The Anglo-American Response to Revolution, 1913–1923*. New York: Oxford University Press, 1984.

Garrison, Jean A. *Making China Policy: From Nixon to G. W. Bush*. Boulder, CO: Lynne Rienner, 2005.

Garton Ash, Timothy. "The Foreign Correspondent Is Dead. Long Live the Foreign Correspondent." *Guardian*, December 9, 2010.

Garton Ash, Timothy. "We Are Getting Less Foreign News at the Very Moment When We Need More." *Guardian*, April 16, 2009.

George, Jim. *Discourses of Global Politics: A Critical (Re)Introduction to International Relations*. Boulder, CO: Lynne Rienner, 1994.

Giddings, T.H. "Rushing the Transatlantic News in the 1830s and 1840s." *The New York Historical Society Quarterly* 42–1 (1958): 50–51.

Gienow-Hecht, Jessica C.E. *Transmission Impossible: American Journalism as Cultural Diplomacy in Postwar Germany, 1945–1955*. Baton Rouge: Louisiana State University Press, 1999.

Gilboa, Eytan. "Media-Broker Diplomacy: When Journalists Become Mediators." *Critical Studies in Media Communication* 22–2 (June 2005): 99–120.

Gilboa, Eytan, ed. *Media and Conflict: Framing Issues, Making Policy, Shaping Opinions*. Ardsley, NY: Transnational Publishers, 2002.

Glenn, John. "Realism versus Strategic Culture: Competition and Collaboration?" *International Studies Review* 11–3 (September 2009): 523–551.

Goldstein, Judith, and Robert O. Keohane, eds. *Ideas and Foreign Policy: Beliefs, Institutions, and Political Change*. Ithaca, NY: Cornell University Press, 1993.

Gould, Harold A. *The South Asia Story: The First Sixty Years of U.S. Relations with India and Pakistan*. Los Angeles: SAGE, 2010.

Graber, Doris A., Denis McQuail and Pippa Norris, eds. *The Politics of News, the News of Politics*. 2nd ed. Washington: CQ Press, 2008.

Graebner, Norman A. *Foundations of American Foreign Policy: A Realist Appraisal from Franklin to McKinley*. Wilmington, DE: Scholarly Resources, 1985.

Graham, Helen. *The Spanish Republic at War: 1936–1939*. Cambridge: Cambridge University Press, 2002.

Greenberg, Bradley S. and Walter Gantz, eds. *Desert Storm and the Mass Media*. Cresskill, NJ: Hampton Press, 1993.

Gregg, Heather S. "Crafting a Better US Grand Strategy in the Post-September 11 World: Lessons from the Early Years of the Cold War." *Foreign Policy Analysis* 6–3 (2010): 237–255.

Grenville, J.A.S. *Europe Reshaped: 1848–1878*. 2nd ed. Oxford: Blackwell, 2000.

Grunwald, Henry A. "The Post-Cold War Press: A New World Needs a New Journalism." *Foreign Affairs*, Summer 1993, 12–16.

Gunther, Albert C. "The Persuasive Press Inference." *Communication Research* 25–5 (1998): 486–504.

Gunther, Albert C., and J. Douglas Storey. "The Influence of Presumed Influence." *Journal of Communication* 53–2 (June 2003): 199–215.

Gutman, Roy. *How We Missed the Story: Osama bin Laden, the Taliban, and the Hijacking of Afghanistan*. Washington: United States Institutes of Peace, 2008.

Hachten, William A., and James F. Scotton. *The World News Prism: Global Media in an Era of Terrorism*. 6th ed. Ames: Iowa State Press, 2002.

Hall, Stuart. "The Rediscovery of 'Ideology': Return of the Oppressed in Media Studies." In *Culture, Society and the Media*, edited by Michael Gurevitch, Tony Bennett, James Curran and Janet Woollacott, 56–90. London: Methuen, 1982.

Hall, Stuart, and Paul du Gay, eds. *Questions of Cultural Identity*. London: SAGE, 1996.

Hallin, Daniel C. "Hegemony: The American News Media from Vietnam to El Salvador, A Study of Ideological Change and Its Limits." In *Political Communication Research*, edited by David Paletz, 3–25. Norwood, NJ: Ablex, 1987.

Hallin, Daniel C. *The "Uncensored" War: The Media and Vietnam*. New York: Oxford University Press, 1986.

Hamilton, James T. *All the News That's Fit to Sell: How the Market Transforms Information into News*. Princeton, NJ: Princeton University Press, 2004.

Hamilton, John Maxwell. *Journalism's Roving Eye: A History of American Foreign Reporting*. Baton Rouge: Louisiana State University Press, 2009.

Hamilton, John Maxwell, and Regina G. Lawrence. "Bridging Past and Future: Using History and Practice to Inform Social Scientific Study of Foreign Newsgathering." *Journalism Studies* 11–5 (2010): 683–699.

Hammond, Philip. *Framing Post–Cold War Conflicts: The Media and International Intervention*. Manchester: Manchester University Press, 2007.

Hansen, Lene. *Security as Practice: Discourse Analysis and the Bosnian War*. London: Routledge, 2006.

Hanson, Elizabeth. *The Information Revolution and World Politics*. Lanham, MD: Rowman and Littlefield, 2008.

Harvey, Robert. *The Fall of Apartheid: The Inside Story from Smuts to Mbeki*. Basingstoke: Palgrave, 2001.

Heald, Morrell. *Transatlantic Vistas: American Journalists in Europe, 1900–1940*. Kent, OH: Kent State University Press, 1988.

Hearder, Harry. *Italy: A Short History*. Cambridge: Cambridge University Press, 1990.

Hendler, Clint. "Message Control: Is Obama's White House Tighter Than Bush's?" *Columbia Journalism Review*, July/August 2010, 19–20.

Henriksen, Thomas H. *American Power after the Berlin Wall*. New York: Palgrave Macmillan, 2007.

Herman, Edward S. "The Media's Role in U.S. Foreign Policy." *Journal of International Affairs* 47–1 (Summer 1993): 23–45.

Herman, Edward S., and Noam Chomsky. *Manufacturing Consent: The Political Economy of the Mass Media*. New York: Pantheon Books, 1988.

Herman, Edward S., and Robert W. McChesney. *The Global Media: The New Missionaries of Global Capitalism*. London: Cassell, 1997.

Herring, George C. *From Colony to Superpower: U.S. Foreign Relations since 1776*. Oxford: Oxford University Press, 2008.

Hess, Stephen. *International News & Foreign Correspondents*. Washington: Brookings Institution, 1996.

Hester, Al, Susan Parker Humes and Christopher Bickers. "Foreign News in Colonial North American Newspapers, 1764–1775." *Journalism Quarterly* 57–1 (Spring 1980): 18–22, 44.

Hills, Jill. *Telecommunications and Empire*. Urbana: University of Illinois Press, 2007.

Himelboim, Itai, Tsan-Kuo Chang and Stephen McCreery. "International Network of Foreign News Coverage: Old Global Hierarchies in a New Online World." *Journalism and Mass Communication Quarterly* 87–2 (Summer 2010): 297–314.

Hoffmann, Matthew J. "Is Constructivist Ethics an Oxymoron?" *International Studies Review* 11–2 (June 2009): 231–252.

Hohenberg, John. *Foreign Correspondence: The Great Reporters and Their Times*. 2nd ed. Syracuse, NY: Syracuse University Press, 1995.

Holbert, R. Lance, R. Kelly Garrett and Laurel S. Gleason. "A New Era of Minimal Effects? A Response to Bennett and Iyengar." *Journal of Communication* 60–1 (March 2010): 15–34.

Holquist, Peter. *Making War, Forging Revolution: Russia's Continuum of Crisis, 1914–1921*. Cambridge, MA: Harvard University Press, 2002.

Holsti, K.J. "National Role Conceptions in the Study of Foreign Policy." *International Studies Quarterly* 14–3 (1970): 233–309.

Holsti, Ole. R. "The Belief System and National Images: A Case Study." *The Journal of Conflict Resolution* 6–3 (September 1962): 244–252.

Holsti, Ole R. *Public Opinion and American Foreign Policy*. Revised edition. Ann Arbor: University of Michigan Press, 2004.

Hosli, Madeleine O. *The Euro: A Concise Introduction to European Monetary Integration*. Boulder, CO: Lynne Rienner, 2005.

Howard, Peter. "Triangulating Debates within the Field: Teaching International Relations Methodology." *International Studies Perspectives* 11–4 (November 2010): 393–408.

Jamieson, Kathleen Hall, and Paul Waldman. *The Press Effect: Politicians, Journalists, and the Stories That Shape the Political World*. Oxford: Oxford University Press, 2003.

Jervis, Robert. *The Logic of Images in International Relations*. Princeton, NJ: Princeton University Press, 1970.

Jones, Alex S. *Losing the News: The Future of the News That Feeds Democracy*. Oxford: Oxford University Press, 2009.

Kamalipour, Yahya R., ed. *Images of the U.S. around the World*. Albany: State University of New York Press, 1999.

Kaplan, Richard L. *Politics and the American Press: The Rise of Objectivity, 1865–1920*. Cambridge: Cambridge University Press, 2002.

Katz, Friedrich. *The Secret War in Mexico: Europe, the United States and the Mexican Revolution*. Chicago: University of Chicago Press, 1981.

Katzenstein, Peter J., ed. *The Culture of National Security: Norms and Identity in World Politics*. New York: Columbia University Press, 1996.

Katzenstein, Peter J., and Robert O. Keohane, eds. *Anti-Americanisms in World Politics*. Ithaca, NY: Cornell University Press, 2007.

Kavoori, Anandam. *The Logics of Globalization: Studies in International Communication*. Lanham, MD: Rowman & Littlefield, 2009.

Keller, Bill. "The Boy Who Kicked the Hornet's Nest." *New York Times*, January 30, 2011.

Kelman, Herbert, ed. *International Behavior*. New York: Holt, Rinehart and Winston, 1966.

Kennedy, David M. *Freedom from Fear: The American People in Depression and War, 1929–1945*. Oxford: Oxford University Press, 1999.

King, Elliot. *Free for All: The Internet's Transformation of Journalism*. Evanston, IL: Northwestern University Press, 2010.

King, Gary, Robert O. Keohane and Sidney Verba. *Designing Social Inquiry: Scientific Inference in Qualitative Research*. Princeton, NJ: Princeton University Press, 1994.

Kinsley, Philip. *The Chicago Tribune: Its First Hundred Years*. Vol. 1. New York: Alfred Knopf, 1943.

Kirby, William C., Robert S. Ross and Gong Li, eds. *Normalization of U.S.-China Relations: An International History*. Cambridge, MA: Harvard University Press, 2003.

Kluger, Richard. *The Paper: The Life and Death of the* New York Herald Tribune. New York: Alfred Knopf, 1986.

Knecht, Thomas. "A Pragmatic Response to an Unexpected Constraint: Problem Representation in a Complex Humanitarian Emergency." *Foreign Policy Analysis* 5–2 (2009): 135–168.

Knightley, Phillip. *The First Casualty: The War Correspondent as Hero and Myth-Maker from the Crimea to Iraq*. Baltimore: Johns Hopkins University Press, 2004.

Knudson, Jerry W. "John Reed: A Reporter in Revolutionary Mexico." *Journalism History* 29/2 (Summer 2003): 59–68.

Koch-Baumgarten, Sigrid, and Katrin Voltmer, eds. *Public Policy and Mass Media: The Interplay of Mass Communication and Political Decision Making*. London: Routledge, 2010.

Kolstø, Pål, ed. *Media Discourse and the Yugoslav Conflicts: Representations of Self and Other*. Farnham: Ashgate, 2009.

Krabill, Ron. *Starring Mandela and Cosby: Media and the End(s) of Apartheid*. Chicago: University of Chicago Press, 2010.

Kress, Gunther. "Ideological Structures in Discourse." In *Handbook of Discourse Analysis: Discourse Analysis in Society*, vol. 4, edited by Teun van Dijk, 27–42. London: Academic Press, 1985.

Krishnaiah, Jothik, Nancy Signorielli and Douglas M. McLeod. "The Evil Empire Revisited: *New York Times* Coverage of the Soviet Intervention in and Withdrawal from Afghanistan." *Journalism Quarterly* 70–3 (Autumn 1993): 647–655.

Kull, Steven, and Clay Ramsay. "U.S. Public Opinion on Intervention in Bosnia." In *International Public Opinion and the Bosnia Crisis*, edited by Richard Sobel and Eric Shiraev, 69–106. Lanham, MD: Lexington Books, 2003.

Kull, Steven, Clay Ramsay and Evan Lewis. "Misperceptions, the Media, and the Iraq War." *Political Science Quarterly* 118/4 (2003–2004): 569–598.

Kumar, Krishna. *Promoting Independent Media: Strategies for Democracy Assistance*. Boulder, CO: Lynne Rienner, 2006.

Laffey, Mark, and Jutta Weldes. "Beyond Belief: Ideas and Symbolic Technologies in the Study of International Relations." *European Journal of International Relations* 3–2 (June 1997): 193–237.

Lake, David A. *Entangling Relations: American Foreign Policy in Its Century*. Princeton, NJ: Princeton University Press, 1999.

Langford, Paul. "British Correspondence in the Colonial Press, 1763–1775: A Study in Anglo-American Misunderstanding before the American Revolution." In *The Press and the American Revolution*, edited by Bernard Bailyn and John B. Hench, 273–313. Boston: Northeastern University Press, 1980.

Larres, Klaus, ed. *The US Secretaries of State and Transatlantic Relations*. London: Routledge, 2010.

Larsen, Henrik. *Foreign Policy and Discourse Analysis: France, Britain and Europe*. London: Routledge, 1997.

Latham, Michael E. *The Right Kind of Revolution: Modernization, Development, and U.S. Foreign Policy from the Cold War to the Present*. Ithaca, NY: Cornell University Press, 2011.

Layne, Christopher. "This Time It's Real: The End of Unipolarity and the Pax Americana." *International Studies Quarterly* 56–1 (March 2012): 203–213.

Lee, Chin-Chuan. "Established Pluralism: US Elite Media Discourse about China Policy." *Journalism Studies* 3–3 (2002): 343–357.

Lee, James Melvin. *History of American Journalism*. Boston: Houghton Mifflin, 1923.

Leonard, Thomas C. *News for All: America's Coming-of-Age with the Press*. New York: Oxford University Press, 1995.

Leonard, Thomas M. *Castro and the Cuban Revolution*. Westport, CT: Greenwood Press, 1999.

Lippmann, Walter. *Public Opinion*. New York: Free Press, 1922.

Little, Douglas. *Malevolent Neutrality: The United States, Great Britain, and the Origins of the Spanish Civil War*. Ithaca, NY: Cornell University Press, 1985.

Löffelholz, Martin, and David Weaver, eds. *Global Journalism Research: Theories, Methods, Findings, Future*. Malden, MA: Blackwell Publishing, 2008.

Luther, Catherine. "National Identities, Structure, and Press Images of Nations: The Case of Japan and the United States," *Mass Communication & Society* 5–1 (2002): 57–85.

Luther, Catherine A. *Press Images, National Identity, and Foreign Policy: A Case Study of U.S.-Japan Relations from 1955–1995*. New York: Routledge, 2001.

Lyttelton, Adrian. *The Seizure of Power: Fascism in Italy, 1919–1929*. 2nd ed. Princeton, NJ: Princeton University Press, 1987.

MacKinnon, Stephen R., and Oris Friesen. *China Reporting: An Oral History of American Journalism in the 1930s and 1940s*. Berkeley: University of California Press, 1987.

MacMillan, Margaret. *Nixon and Mao: The Week That Changed the World*. New York: Random House, 2007.

Mandelbaum, Michael. "Demography and American Foreign Policy," *SAISPHERE*, 2010–2011, 8–11.

Manners, Ia, and Richard G. Whitman. "The 'Difference Engine': Constructing and Representing the International Identity of the European Union." *Journal of European Public Policy* 10–3 (2003): 380–404.

Marshall, Jon. *Watergate's Legacy and the Press: The Investigative Impulse*. Evanston, IL: Northwestern University Press, 2011.

Mathews, Joseph J. *George W. Smalley: Forty Years a Foreign Correspondent*. Chapel Hill: University of North Carolina Press, 1973.

Matthews, Herbert L. *The Education of a Correspondent*. New York: Harcourt, Brace and Company, 1946.

May, Ernest. *American Imperialism*. New York: Atheneum, 1968.

McChesney, Robert W., and Victor Pickard, eds. *Will the Last Reporter Please Turn Out the Lights: The Collapse of Journalism and What Can Be Done to Fix It*. New York: The New Press, 2011.

McDougal, Dennis. *Privileged Son: Otis Chandler and the Rise and Fall of the* L.A. Times *Dynasty*. Cambridge, MA: Perseus Publishing, 2001.

McLaughlin, Greg, and Stephen Baker. *The Propaganda of Peace: The Role of Media and Culture in the Northern Ireland Peace Process*. Chicago: Intellect, 2010.

McPhail, Thomas L. *Global Communication: Theories, Stakeholders and Trends*. Boston: Allyn & Bacon, 2002.

McPherson, James Brian. *Journalism at the End of the American Century, 1965–Present*. Westport, CT: Praeger, 2006.

Meadows, Bryan. "Distancing and Showing Solidarity via Metaphor and Metonymy in Political Discourse: A Critical Study of American Statements on Iraq during the Years 2004–2005." *Critical Approaches to Discourse Analysis across Disciplines* 1–2 (2007): 1–17.

Mendelson, Sarah E. *Changing Course: Ideas, Politics, and the Soviet Withdrawal from Afghanistan*. Princeton, NJ: Princeton University Press, 1998.

Merk, Frederick. *Manifest Destiny and Mission in American History*. Cambridge, MA: Harvard University Press, 1995.

Mermin, Jonathan. *Debating War and Peace: Media Coverage of U.S. Intervention in the Post-Vietnam Era*. Princeton, NJ: Princeton University Press, 1999.

Merrill, John C., Peter J. Gade and Frederick R. Blevens. *Twilight of Press Freedom: The Rise of People's Journalism*. Mahwah, NJ: Lawrence Erlbaum Associates, 2001.

Mersey, Rachel Davis. *Can Journalism Be Saved? Rediscovering America's Appetite for News*. Santa Barbara, CA: Praeger, 2010.

Meyer, Michael C., and William H. Beezley, eds. *The Oxford History of Mexico.* Oxford: Oxford University Press, 2000.

Meyer, Philip. *The Vanishing Newspaper: Saving Journalism in the Information Age.* Columbia: University of Missouri Press, 2004.

Migone, Gian Giacomo. *Gli Stati Uniti e il Fascismo: Alle origini dell'egemonia americana in Italia.* Milan: Feltrinelli, 1980.

Miller, Derek B. *Media Pressure on Foreign Policy: The Evolving Theoretical Framework.* New York: Palgrave Macmillan, 2007.

Mills, Sara. *Discourse.* London: Routledge, 2004.

Milton, Joyce. *The Yellow Kids: Foreign Correspondents in the Heyday of Yellow Journalism.* New York: Harper & Row, 1989.

Mindich, David T.Z. *Just the Facts.* New York: New York University Press, 1998.

Mindich, David T.Z. *Tuned Out: Why Americans under 40 Don't Follow the News.* New York: Oxford University Press, 2005.

Mody, Bella. *The Geopolitics of Representation in Foreign News: Explaining Darfur.* Lanham, MD: Lexington Books, 2010.

Moorcraft, Paul L., and Philip M. Taylor. *Shooting the Messenger: The Political Impact of War Reporting.* Washington: Potomac Books, 2008.

Mott, Frank Luther. *American Journalism: A History of Newspapers in the United States through 260 Years: 1690 to 1950.* New York: Macmillan, 1950.

Mufti, Shahan. "A World of Trouble: Who's a Journalist? In Today's War Zones, the Answer Matters." *Columbia Journalism Review*, July/August 2010, 14–16.

Nabers, Dirk. "Filling the Void of Meaning: Identity Construction in U.S. Foreign Policy After September 11, 2001." *Foreign Policy Analysis* 5–2 (2009): 191–214.

Nacos, Brigitte L., Robert Y. Shapiro and Pierangelo Isernia, eds. *Decisionmaking in a Glass House: Mass Media, Public Opinion, and American and European Foreign Policy in the 21st Century.* Lanham, MD: Rowman & Littlefield, 2000.

Nayak, Meghana V. and Christopher Malone. "American Orientalism and American Exceptionalism: A Critical Rethinking of US Hegemony." *International Studies Review* 11–2 (2009): 253–276.

Neumann, William L. *America Encounters Japan: From Perry to MacArthur.* Baltimore: Johns Hopkins University Press, 1963.

Nikolaev, Alexander G., and Ernest A. Hakanen, eds. *Leading to the 2003 Iraq War: The Global Media Debate.* New York: Palgrave Macmillan, 2006.

Norris, Pippa, and Ronald Inglehart. *Cosmopolitan Communications: Cultural Diversity in a Globalized World.* Cambridge: Cambridge University Press, 2009.

Nye, Joseph S. Jr. *The Future of Power.* New York: Public Affairs Books, 2011.

Nye, Joseph S. Jr. "Public Diplomacy and Soft Power." *Annals of the American Academy of Political and Social Science* 616 (March 2008): 94–109.

Nye, Joseph S. Jr. "The Twenty-First Century Will Not Be a 'Post-American' World." *International Studies Quarterly* 56–1 (March 2012): 215–217.

Oberdofer, Don. *From the Cold War to a New Era: The United States and the Soviet Union, 1983–1991.* Baltimore: Johns Hopkins University Press, 1998.

Offner, John L. *An Unwanted War: The Diplomacy of the United States and Spain Over Cuba, 1895–1898.* Chapel Hill: University of North Carolina Press, 1992.

Oren, Michael B. *Six Days of War: June 1967 and the Making of the Modern Middle East.* Oxford: Oxford University Press, 2002.

Osgood, Kenneth, and Andrew K. Frank, eds. *Selling War in a Media Age: The Presidency and Public Opinion in the American Century*. Gainesville: University Press of Florida, 2010.

Owen, John, and Heather Purdey, eds. *International News Reporting: Frontlines and Deadlines*. Chichester: Wiley-Blackwell, 2009.

Park, Hong-Won. "The Press, the State and Hegemony: A Theoretical Exploration." PhD diss., University of Minnesota, 1999.

Parker, Richard B. *The Six-Day War: A Retrospective*. Gainesville: University Press of Florida, 1996.

Parmar, Inderjeet, and Michael Cox, eds. *Soft Power and U.S. Foreign Policy: Theoretical, Historical and Contemporary Perspectives*. London: Routledge, 2010.

Pastor, Robert A., ed. *A Century's Journey: How the Great Powers Shape the World*. New York: Basic Books, 1999.

Paterson, Chris, and Annabelle Sreberny, eds. *International News in the Twenty-First Century*. Hants: John Libbey, 2004.

Paterson, Thomas G. *Contesting Castro: The United States and the Triumph of the Cuban Revolution*. New York: Oxford University Press, 1994.

Paul, T.V., James J. Wirtz and Michel Fortmann, eds. *Balance of Power: Theory and Practice in the 21st Century*. Stanford, CA: Stanford University Press, 2004.

Payne, Stanley G. *Fascism in Spain, 1923–1977*. Madison: University of Wisconsin Press, 1999.

Pearlstein, Edward W. *Revolution in Russia! As Reported by the New York Tribune and the New York Herald, 1894–1921*. New York: Viking Press, 1967.

Pedelty, Mark. *War Stories: The Culture of Foreign Correspondents*. New York: Routledge, 1995.

Perkins, Bradford. *The Cambridge History of American Foreign Relations: Volume I, The Creation of a Republican Empire, 1776–1865*. Cambridge: Cambridge University Press, 1993.

Perlmutter, David D., and John Maxwell Hamilton, eds. *From Pigeons to News Portals: Foreign Reporting and the Challenge of New Technology*. Baton Rouge: Louisiana State University Press, 2007.

Perry, David K. "The Image Gap: How International News Affects Perceptions of Nations." *Journalism Quarterly* 64 (1987): 416–433.

Phillips, Louise, and Marianne W. Jørgensen. *Discourse Analysis as Theory and Method*. London: SAGE, 2002.

Phillips, Nelson, and Cynthia Hardy. *Discourse Analysis: Investigating Processes of Social Construction*. Thousand Oaks, CA: SAGE, 2002.

Price, Monroe E. *Media and Sovereignty: The Global Information Revolution and Its Challenge to State Power*. Cambridge, MA: MIT Press, 2002.

Price, Richard, and Christian Reus-Smit. "Dangerous Liaisons? Critical International Theory and Constructivism." *European Journal of International Relations* 4–3 (1998): 259–294.

Price, Vincent, and Edward J. Czilli. "Modeling Patterns of News Recognition and Recall." *Journal of Communication* 46–2 (Spring 1996): 55–78.

Pugliese, Stanislao, ed. *Fascism, Anti-Fascism and the Resistance in Italy: 1919 to the Present*. Lanham, MD: Rowman & Littlefield, 2004.

Puniyani, Ram, and Shabnam Hashmi, eds. *Mumbai Post 26/11: An Alternate Perspective*. Los Angeles: SAGE, 2010.

Putnis, Peter. "Overseas News in the Australian Press in 1870 and the Colonial Experience of the Franco-Prussian War." *History Australia* 4/1 (2007): 1–18.

Ramprasad, Jyotika, and Daniel Riffe. "Effect of U.S.-India Relations on New York *Times* Coverage." *Journalism Quarterly* 64–2/3 (Summer/Fall 1987): 537–543, 663.

Renan, Ernest. "What Is a Nation?" In *Nation and Narration*, edited by Homi Bhabha, 8–22. London: Routledge, 1990.

Reporters of the Associated Press. *Breaking News: How the Associated Press Has Covered War, Peace, and Everything Else*. New York: Princeton Architectural Press, 2007.

"Reporting from Faraway Places: Who Does It and How?" *Nieman Reports*, 64–3 (Fall 2010).

Roberts, Chalmers M. *The* Washington Post*: The First 100 Years*. Boston: Houghton Mifflin, 1977.

Robinson, John, and Mark Levy. *The Main Source: Learning from Television News*. Beverly Hills, CA: Sage Publications, 1986.

Robinson, Piers. *The CNN Effect: The Myth of News, Foreign Policy and Intervention*. London: Routledge, 2002.

Robinson, Piers, Peter Goddard, Katy Parry and Craig Murray. "Testing Models of Media Performance in Wartime: U.K. TV News and the 2003 Invasion of Iraq." *Journal of Communication* 59–3 (September 2009): 534–563.

Roeder, George H., Jr. *The Censored War: American Visual Experience during World War Two*. New Haven, CT: Yale University Press, 1993.

Rosenblum, Mort. *Coups and Earthquakes: Reporting the World for America*. New York: Harper & Row, 1979.

Rosenblum, Mort. *Who Stole the News?* New York: J. Wiley, 1993.

Rosewater, Victor. *History of Cooperative News-Gathering in the United States*. New York: D. Appleton and Co., 1930.

Said, Edward W. *Covering Islam: How the Media and the Experts Determine How We See the Rest of the World*. New York: Pantheon Books, 1981.

Sambrook, Richard. *Are Foreign Correspondents Redundant? The Changing Face of International News*. Oxford: Reuters Institute for the Study of Journalism, 2010.

Saul, Norman E. *War and Revolution: The United States and Russia, 1914–1921*. Lawrence: University Press of Kansas, 2001.

Schanberg, Sydney. *Beyond the Killing Fields: War Writings*. Washington: Potomac Books, 2010.

Schiller, Dan. "An Historical Approach to Objectivity and Professionalism in American News Reporting." *Journal of Communication* 29 (1979): 46–51.

Schlesinger, Arthur M. *Prelude to Independence: The Newspaper War on Britain, 1764–1776*. New York: Alfred Knopf, 1958.

Schonberg, Karl K. *Constructing 21st Century U.S. Foreign Policy: Identity, Ideology, and America's World Role in a New Era*. New York: Palgrave Macmillan, 2009.

Schudson, Michael. "Culture and the Integration of National Societies." In *The Sociology of Culture*, edited by Diana Crane, 21–44. Cambridge, MA: Blackwell Publishers, 1994.

Schudson, Michael. *Discovering the News*. New York: Basic Books, 1978.

Schudson, Michael. *Why Democracies Need an Unlovable Press*. Cambridge: Polity Press, 2008.

Seaver, Brenda M. "The Public Dimension of Foreign Policy." *International Journal of Press/Politics* 3–1 (1998): 65–91.

Seib, Philip. *Headline Diplomacy: How News Coverage Affects Foreign Policy*. Westport, CT: Praeger, 1997.

Seib, Philip. *The Al Jazeera Effect: How the Global Media Are Reshaping World Politics*. Washington: Potomac Books, 2008.

Seib, Philip, ed. *Al Jazeera English: Global News in a Changing World*. New York: Palgrave Macmillan, 2012.

Seib, Philip, ed. *Media and Conflict in the Twenty-First Century*. New York: Palgrave Macmillan, 2005.

Seib, Philip, ed. *New Media and the New Middle East*. New York: Palgrave Macmillan, 2007.

Semati, Mehdi, ed. *New Frontiers in International Communication Theory*. Lanham, MD: Rowman & Littlefield, 2004.

Serfaty, Simon, ed. *The Media and Foreign Policy*. New York: St. Martin's Press, 1991.

Shanor, Donald R. "CDN: What We'll Miss about the *Chicago Daily News*." *Columbia Journalism Review*, May/June 1978: 35–37.

Shaw, Donald L. "At the Crossroads: Change and Continuity in American Press News, 1820–1860," *Journalism History* 8–2 (1981): 38–50.

Shoemaker, Pamela J., and Akiba A. Cohen. *News around the World: Content, Practitioners, and the Public*. New York: Routledge, 2006.

Silverblatt, Art, and Nikolai Zlobin. *International Communications: A Media Literacy Approach*. Armonk, NY: M.E. Sharpe, 2004.

Skidmore, David. "The Obama Presidency and US Foreign Policy: Where's the Multilateralism?" *International Studies Perspectives* 13–1 (February 2012): 43–64.

Skidmore, Thomas E., Peter H. Smith and James N. Green. *Modern Latin America*. 7th ed. New York: Oxford University Press, 2010.

Smith, Anthony. *The Geopolitics of Information: How Western Culture Dominates the World*. New York: Oxford University Press, 1980.

Snyder, Jack, and Karen Ballentine. "Nationalism and the Marketplace of Ideas." *International Security* 21–2 (Autumn 1996): 5–40.

So, Alvin. *Social Change and Development*. Newbury Park, CA: SAGE, 1990.

Sobel, Richard, Peter Furia and Bethany Barratt, eds. *Public Opinion and International Intervention: Lessons from the Iraq War*. Dulles, VA: Potomac Books, 2012.

Sosale, Sujatha. *Communication, Development and Democracy: Mapping a Discourse*. Cresskill, NJ: Hampton Press, 2008.

Southworth, Herbert Rutledge. *Guernica! Guernica! A Study of Journalism, Diplomacy, Propaganda, and History*. Berkeley: University of California Press, 1977.

Sparrow, Bartholomew H. *Uncertain Guardians: The News Media as a Political Institution*. Baltimore: Johns Hopkins University Press, 1999.

Sperber, Jonathan. *The European Revolutions, 1848–1851*. 2nd ed. Cambridge: Cambridge University Press, 2005.

Spiegel, Steven L. *The Other Arab-Israeli Conflict: Making America's Middle East Policy, from Truman to Reagan*. Chicago: University of Chicago Press, 1985.

Spurr, David. *The Rhetoric of Empire: Colonial Discourse in Journalism, Travel Writing, and Imperial Administration*. Durham, NC: Duke University Press, 1993.

Sremac, Danielle S. *War of Words: Washington Tackles the Yugoslav Conflict*. Westport, CT: Praeger, 1999.

Starr, Paul. *The Creation of the Media: Political Origins of Modern Communications*. New York: Basic Books, 2004.

Stephens, Mitchell. *A History of News*. 3rd ed. New York: Oxford University Press, 2007.

Stevenson, Robert L. *Global Communication in the Twenty-First Century*. New York: Longman, 1994.

Strobel, Warren P. *Late-Breaking Foreign Policy: The News Media's Influence on Peace Operations*. Washington: United States Institute of Peace Press, 1997.

Sweeney, Michael S. *The Military and the Press: An Uneasy Truce*. Evanston, IL: Northwestern University Press, 2006.

Tarling, Nicholas. *Southeast Asia and the Great Powers*. London: Routledge, 2010.

Taylor, Bayard. *A Visit to India, China, and Japan, in the Year* 1853. New York: G.P. Putnam, 1855.

Taylor, Philip M. *Global Communication, International Affairs and the Media since 1945*. London: Routledge, 1997.

Teel, Leonard Ray. *The Public Press, 1900–1945: The History of American Journalism*. Westport, CT: Praeger, 2006.

Tehranian, Majid. *Global Communication and World Politics: Domination, Development, and Discourse*. Boulder, CO: Lynne Rienner, 1999.

Thomson, Alex. *U.S. Foreign Policy towards Apartheid South Africa, 1948–1994*. New York: Palgrave Macmillan, 2008.

Thorne, Christopher. *The Limits of Foreign Policy: The West, the League and the Far Eastern Crisis of 1931–1933*. New York: G.P. Putnam's Sons, 1972.

Thussu, Daya Kishan. *International Communication: Continuity and Change*. 2nd ed. New York: Oxford University Press, 2008.

Thussu, Daya Kishan, ed. *Internationalizing Media Studies*. New York: Routledge, 2009.

Tierney, Dominic. *FDR and the Spanish Civil War: Neutrality and Commitment in the Struggle That Divided America*. Durham, NC: Duke University Press, 2007.

Tuchinsky, Adam. *Horace Greeley's New-York Tribune: Civil War–Era Socialism and the Crisis of Free Labor*. Ithaca, NY: Cornell University Press, 2009.

Tuchman, Gaye. *Making News: A Study in the Construction of Reality*. New York: Macmillan, 1978.

Tunstall, Jeremy. "Are the Media Still American?" *Media Studies Journal* 9–4 (Fall 1995): 7–16.

Tunstall, Jeremy. *The Media Are American*. New York: Columbia University Press, 1977.

Tunstall, Jeremy. *The Media Were American: U.S. Mass Media in Decline*. New York: Oxford University Press, 2008.

2012 *State of the News Media Report*. Project for Excellence in Journalism. www.stateofthemedia.org, accessed in May 2012.

Van Belle, Douglas A. "Bureaucratic Responsiveness to the News Media: Comparing the Influence of the *New York Times* and Network Television News Coverage on US Foreign Aid Allocations." *Political Communication* 20–3 (2003): 263–285.

Van Ginneken, Jaap. *Understanding Global News*. London: SAGE, 1998.

Vevier, Charles. "American Continentalism: An Idea of Expansion, 1845–1910." *American Historical Review* 65–2 (1960): 323–335.

Walsh, Maurice. *The News from Ireland: Foreign Correspondents and the Irish Revolution.* London: I.B. Tauris, 2008.

Wanta, Wayne, Guy Golan and Cheolhan Lee. "Agenda Setting and International News: Media Influence on Public Perceptions of Foreign Nations." *Journalism and Mass Communication Quarterly* 81–2 (Summer 2004): 364–377.

Wasburn, Philo C. *The Social Construction of International News: We're Talking about Them, They're Talking about Us.* Westport, CT: Praeger, 2002.

Weaver, David H., ed. *The Global Journalist: News People around the World.* Cresskill, NJ: Hampton Press, 1998.

Weaver, David H., and Lars Willnat, eds. *The Global Journalist in the 21st Century.* New York: Routledge, 2012.

Weiss, Gilbert, and Ruth Wodak, eds. *Critical Discourse Analysis: Theory and Interdisciplinarity.* New York: Palgrave Macmillan, 2003.

Weldon, Michele. *Everyman News: The Changing American Front Page.* Columbia: University of Missouri Press, 2008.

Welter, Rush, *The Mind of America: 1820–1860.* New York: Columbia University Press, 1975.

Wendt, Alexander. "Anarchy Is What States Make of It: The Social Construction of Power Politics." *International Organization* 46–2 (1992): 391–425.

Wendt, Alexander. *Social Theory of International Politics.* Cambridge: Cambridge University Press, 1999.

Wendt, Lloyd. Chicago Tribune*: The Rise of a Great American Newspaper.* Chicago: Rand McNally, 1979.

Wendt, Lloyd. *The* Wall Street Journal*: The Story of Dow Jones and the Nation's Business Newspaper.* Chicago: Rand McNally, 1982.

Western, Jon. *Selling Intervention and War: The Presidency, the Media, and the American Public.* Baltimore: Johns Hopkins University Press, 2005.

Whitcomb, Roger S. *The American Approach to Foreign Affairs.* Westport, CT: Praeger, 1998.

White, Paul W. *News on the Air.* New York: Harcourt, Brace and Co., 1947.

Williams, Bruce A., and Michael X. Delli Carpini. *After Broadcast News: Media Regimes, Democracy, and the New Information Environment.* Cambridge: Cambridge University Press, 2011.

Williams, Harold A. *The* Baltimore Sun, *1837–1987.* Baltimore: Johns Hopkins University Press, 1987.

Williams, Walter, and Frank L. Martin. *The Practice of Journalism: A Treatise on Newspaper Making.* Columbia, MO: E.W. Stephens Publishing, 1911.

Winseck, Dwayne R., and Robert M. Pike. *Communication and Empire: Media, Markets, and Globalization, 1860–1930.* Durham, NC: Duke University Press, 2007.

Wisan, Joseph E. *The Cuban Crisis as Reflected in the New York Press (1895–1898).* New York: Columbia University Press, 1934.

Wodak, Ruth, and Michael Meyer, eds. *Methods of Critical Discourse Analysis.* 2nd ed. Los Angeles: SAGE, 2009.

Wohlforth, William C. "How Not to Evaluate Theories." *International Studies Quarterly* 56–1 (March 2012): 519–522.

Woodward, Julian Laurence. *Foreign News in American Morning Newspapers: A Study in Public Opinion*. New York: Columbia University Press, 1930.

Yetiv, Steve. "History, International Relations, and Integrated Approaches: Thinking about Greater Interdisciplinarity." *International Studies Perspectives* 12–2 (May 2011): 94–118.

Young, Louise. *Japan's Total Empire: Manchuria and the Culture of Wartime Imperialism*. Berkeley: University of California Press, 1998.

Index

9/11, 17, 140, 158, 161, 163, 166–167, 169, 187, 191–192, 196, 201–202, 247, 250, 257
Abend, Hallett, 95, 99–100
advertising, 21, 37, 110, 112, 159–160, 208, 211, 214–215, 227, 232
Afghanistan, 198, 219, 221, 227, 234, 249, 256
  Soviet withdrawal, 109–110, 139–145, 155–156, 167, 245, 254
    correspondence discourses, 139, 141–145, 246
    editorials about, 144
  U.S. war, 17, 32, 109, 158, 165, 167–169, 191, 203, 220, 250
Al Jazeera, 227, 231–232
All the President's Men, 113, 215
Allan, Heather, 228, 231–232
Allen, Larry, 124, 126
American revolutionary era, 10, 22, 35–38, 48, 70, 146, 207, 248
Anderson, Benedict, 8
apartheid. *See* Mandela, Nelson; South Africa
Arab Spring, 217, 226
Associated Press, 19
  coverage by, 68, 78, 80, 84–86, 91–94, 97, 99, 102, 104, 106, 110, 121, 123-124, 126–128, 131–132, 139–140, 142–145, 149–151, 158, 171, 173–176, 183–184, 190, 193–194, 196–197, 199, 251–254
  history of, 35, 38–39, 55, 58, 62, 73–74, 115–116, 135, 162, 179, 205–206, 209–211, 213, 216, 218, 221–227, 229
Baltimore Sun, 72–73, 78, 82, 87, 91–94, 96, 104–105
Batista, Fulgencio, 119, 122–125, 254
Beijing, 60, 62–63, 65, 120, 134–136, 156, 226, 251, 255
  see also China, Boxer rebellion
Bell, Edward Price, 71, 73, 74, 91
Bennett, James Gordon, 35, 39, 48
Boczkowski, Pablo, 211–212
Bolshevism. *See* Russia, revolution
Bosnian War, 158, 166–167, 171–177, 191, 202, 250
  correspondence discourses, 171, 173–177, 246–247, 252
  editorials about, 171–173
Broadcast journalism, 28, 106, 110, 116, 159, 164, 183, 204, 209, 217, 219, 229, 231
  radio, 69–70, 72, 97, 101, 112, 129, 183, 217, 230
  television, 13, 24, 28, 110, 112–113, 120, 123, 135, 145, 156, 157, 173, 178, 180, 186, 197, 202, 206–207, 254
  see also BBC; CNN
Browne, Louis Edgar, 82, 84, 86–88, 252
British Broadcasting Corporation (BBC), 208, 216, 227–229, 232
Bush, George H.W., 120, 146, 167, 178
Bush, George W., 33, 160, 167–169, 187, 192, 199, 257
Bussey, John, 205, 224–227

CNN, 2, 112, 145, 160, 217, 230
  CNN effect, 14–15, 162–163

Campos, Arsenio Martínez de, 57–60
capitalism, 71, 75, 96, 107, 113–114, 117, 123, 133–134, 147, 151, 155, 166, 231, 248–249
Carey, James, 10
Carter, Jimmy, 120, 135, 140, 178
Castro, Fidel, 110, 119, 121–127, 153, 155, 178, 245, 249, 254
citizen journalism, 20–21, 157, 159–160, 197, 201, 208–209, 211, 216–217, 223, 226, 233, 254
Chang, Tsan-Kuo, 23–24, 29, 135, 162, 219
Chen, Weihua, 228, 230–231
Chicago Daily News, 71–74, 78, 82, 84–85, 91, 93, 96–98, 104, 252, 255
Chicago Tribune, 34, 40, 44, 49, 54–55, 58, 60–63, 124–125, 161
China, 35, 43, 48, 50, 60–61, 63, 66, 75, 77, 79, 107–108, 116, 118, 120, 134, 168, 226–227, 230–231, 237, 246, 248–249
  Boxer Rebellion, 35–36, 60–65, 97, 149, 233, 251, 255
    correspondence discourses, 60–64
    editorials about, 61–62
  reopening of relations with U.S., 110, 133–139, 155–156, 245, 254
    correspondence discourses, 133–139
    editorials about, 136
  Shanghai attack, 61–62, 68, 95–100, 106–107, 244–245, 256
    correspondence discourses, 95–100, 252
    editorials about, 96
  see also Beijing
China Daily, 230–231
Churchill, Winston, 57
civil rights, 45, 59, 61, 110, 116, 139
Clinton, Bill, 160, 166–167, 172, 178
Coca-Cola, 136, 156, 175, 188, 190, 232, 247
Cold War, 28, 31, 68, 75, 77, 83, 89, 94, 108, 158, 168, 177, 186, 191, 196
  end of. *See* Soviet Union
  journalism and, 2, 109, 113–157, 245–246, 254
colonialism, 40-41, 51, 118, 119, 126, 136, 166, 179, 181, 184, 185, 190, 195, 245–246
Columbia Journalism Review, 21, 112, 160, 208, 213, 218, 229, 257
communism, 94, 107, 113–115, 118–121, 146, 163, 166, 168, 171, 175, 178–179, 249
  anti-communism, 89, 95, 117, 139, 145
  in Afghanistan, 143–144, 155
  in China, 96, 100, 118, 133–134, 137–139, 155
  in Cuba, 119, 122–123, 125–127
  in Russia/Soviet Union, 75–76, 147–150, 244–245, 249
  in Spain, 101
  in United States, 70, 83, 93
Congress (U.S.), 2, 17–18, 41, 42, 56, 60, 120, 178
constructivism,
  in communication theory, 3, 9–19, 33, 238
  in foreign policy, 3, 6–10, 13, 30, 33, 238–240
  in IR theory, 3–9, 13, 33, 238–240
  social construction of reality, 10–12, 238
  see also discourse
Corneau, Grace, 60, 63–64
Cuba, 61, 66, 75, 119, 133, 249, 256
  1890s revolution, 2, 31, 35, 37, 56–60, 64–65, 122, 245, 253
    correspondence discourses, 58–60
    editorials about, 57–58
  1950s revolution, 110, 121–127, 153–155, 254
    correspondence discourses, 121–127
    editorials about, 124–125

Daniszewski, John, 183, 205, 223, 225–226, 254
Delli Carpini, Michael, 22, 113, 207, 217, 242
democracy,
  abroad, 45, 47–48, 65, 75, 77, 83, 89, 107–108, 122, 124–125, 147–148, 155, 166–168, 170–171, 177, 179, 187, 189–190, 195, 198, 200, 248
    pessimism about, 10, 80–82, 108, 146, 150–151, 153–155, 177, 182, 185, 202–203, 244, 246–247, 250, 252
  in United States, 10, 45, 47–48, 65, 94, 113–114, 155, 183, 230
  and informed citizenry, 22, 33, 55, 71, 115, 203, 207, 215, 217, 233, 241–243, 256–257
  role of journalism in, 14–15, 18, 20–22, 29, 33, 37, 48, 65, 159–161, 206–207, 209, 213–215, 217, 227, 233, 236, 241–243, 256–257
Department of State, 17, 40, 83, 103, 166, 220, 235–237, 239–240

diplomacy (and diplomats), 15, 23, 34, 42, 48, 49, 53, 55, 58, 61–63, 65, 75, 83, 84, 97, 101, 120, 135, 147, 166–168, 196, 220, 236, 256
  see also foreign policy
discourse,
  in communication theory, 3, 9–19
  discursive environment, 3, 6, 9, 18, 22, 33, 107, 205, 213, 216, 234, 236–238, 240, 243, 256
  about foreign countries, 18–20, 25–26, 28, 31, 35, 44–66, 68, 77–108, 121–156, 170–203, 218, 236–248, 256
  see also specific countries
  and foreign policy, 3, 6–10, 13, 18, 22–23, 26, 33, 107, 169, 202, 205, 220, 236, 243, 256
  and framing, 13, 16, 18, 136, 148, 170, 179
  about history, 89, 125, 129, 131, 133, 153–154, 171, 177, 190–191, 194–195, 202, 245–248, 250
  in IR theory, 3, 5, 9, 238–240, 243
  oversimplification, 27, 182, 184–185, 190, 198, 201–203, 239, 243, 246–247, 256
  about United States, 5, 10, 19, 27–28, 46–47, 65–66, 78, 184–185, 187, 189–190, 200, 202–203, 239, 243–244, 247, 250, 256
discourse analysis, 2, 6, 9, 18, 25–30, 44, 78, 121, 170, 237, 243
  critical discourse analysis, 7, 11, 239
Downing, Malcolm, 228–229

economic crisis, 32, 45, 68, 76, 146, 161, 166, 168, 229
economic development, 15, 24, 79, 118, 131, 134, 137–138, 158, 165–167, 170, 178, 182, 190, 196, 199, 247
Eedle, Paul, 228, 232
Eisenhower, Dwight, 123
entertainment media, 113, 159, 163–164, 178, 198, 237
Entman, Robert, 13, 16, 208, 242
ethnic identity, 8, 90, 152, 156, 163, 165–166, 171–172, 175–176, 179, 202, 246, 250
European 1848 revolutions, 28, 35, 44–48, 64–65, 125, 244, 252
  correspondence discourses, 44–48
  editorials about, 45
European Union, 5, 31, 47, 201, 250
  euro changeover, 28, 158, 190–195, 202
    correspondence discourses, 190–191, 193–195, 247
    editorials about, 192
exceptionalism, 41–43, 65, 107, 154, 165, 169, 195, 203, 244, 247–248, 250

Fairclough, Norman, 12, 27
Fascism, 89–94, 101–102, 105, 108, 249
  see also Mussolini; Franco
Federal Communications Commission, 21, 208
foreign correspondence (and correspondents), 24–25, 216
  as diplomatic conduit, 1, 56–57, 59–60, 64, 66, 138, 183, 253–254
  as eyewitness, 19, 34, 44, 46, 51, 60, 62, 64, 66, 74, 82, 85, 98, 100, 103, 124, 174, 184, 224, 226, 229, 233, 251–255
  crisis of, 19–23, 31–33, 117, 141, 158, 161–162, 165, 201, 205–206, 215–221, 256–257
  domestication, 24, 28, 29, 36, 46, 62, 114, 126, 185, 219, 225
  future of, 1, 3, 31, 203–206, 212, 215–227, 236, 238, 243
  interest in, 21–22, 29, 48–50, 52, 58, 64, 91, 101, 120, 162–163, 165, 173–174, 188, 197, 204, 206–207, 213, 216, 218–219, 221, 224–225, 228, 233, 255
  language skills, 22, 55, 62, 98, 124, 180, 184, 242
  as lookout, 64, 66, 100, 108, 121, 155, 205, 224, 230, 233–234, 355, 157
  in non-U.S. media, 205, 227–232
  relationship with editors, 46, 61, 64, 84, 114, 124, 162, 223, 252
  responsibility of, 19, 23, 26, 32–33, 64, 71, 205, 107, 214, 218, 221–222, 224–225, 229–230, 235, 237, 257
  unique value of, 3, 19–20, 22, 32–33, 51, 64, 66, 83, 100, 106, 108, 115, 138–139, 154–156, 216, 222, 225–226, 230, 237, 241, 244, 257–258
foreign correspondence history,
  in 19th century, 31, 34–35, 38–40, 237, 244
  in 20th century, 24, 31, 68, 70–74, 113–117, 161–163, 237, 244–246
  in 21st century, 31, 162–165, 205–206, 215–227, 232, 237, 246–248

foreign policy,
containment, 75, 118, 134, 140, 142, 147, 155–156, 166, 191, 249
economic interests, 9, 24–25, 40, 42, 43, 61, 65, 75–76, 78, 80, 107, 117, 118, 126, 135, 137, 155, 158, 163, 166, 185, 188, 202, 245–246, 250
expansionism, 29, 40–42, 65, 248, 250
global leadership, 17, 31–32, 35, 38, 42–43, 57, 65–67, 74, 77, 106, 108, 110, 145, 147, 154–155, 167, 169–170, 173, 176, 191–192, 196, 203, 244–249, 256–257
doubts about, 82, 114, 117, 120, 158, 165–166, 171, 177, 184–185, 195, 201–202, 247, 250
imperialism, 40–43, 49, 50, 61, 66, 74, 137, 154, 248
interventionism, 10, 42–43, 48, 54, 60–61, 68–69, 95–96, 100, 106–108, 125, 128, 155, 166–167, 171, 197, 244, 248–250
military intervention, 15, 17, 68, 75–77, 79, 83, 114–115, 118–120, 163, 164, 167, 172, 242, 244, 250
nonintervention, 102, 105, 164, 166, 169, 248
isolationism, 17, 43, 66, 68, 73, 74, 76, 166, 244, 249
neutrality, 40, 42, 53, 54, 65, 76, 107, 129, 245
and perceptions, 6-7, 12, 16, 135, 164, 166–169, 186–188, 191, 220, 230, 237–238
trade, 17, 40, 42, 43, 48–51, 61, 65, 75, 79, 126, 135, 178, 190, 216
unilateralism, 17, 76, 118, 164–165, 167, 169, 248, 250
"war on terror," 158, 163, 165, 167–169, 196–198, 200–202, 247
see also constructivism, in foreign policy; journalism, and foreign policy; public opinion, and foreign policy
foreign policy history,
in 19th century, 40–43, 248
in 20th century, 74–77, 90, 117–121, 165–167, 248–250
in 21st century, 165–170, 250–251
Foucault, Michel, 5, 8, 10–12
Fox, Vicente, 158, 185–187, 189–190, 244, 247, 254
see also Mexico, elections
Frachon, Alain, 228, 230
France, 6, 40, 45, 47, 53–54, 94, 102, 168, 173, 194–195, 228, 230, 237, 248
see also European Revolutions; Franco-Prussian War
Franco, Francisco, 100–102, 104–105
Franco-Prussian War, 34–35, 52–56, 64
correspondence discourses, 54–56
editorials about, 52–54
freedom of the press, 17–18, 21, 37, 70–71, 111, 135, 160, 207, 214–215, 231
censorship, 51, 52, 54–55, 58–59, 70, 72, 84–85, 94, 102, 107, 110, 123, 132
suppression, 37, 70–71, 90, 93, 110, 114, 144
Supreme Court, 70–71, 111, 159, 160, 214

Garton Ash, Timothy, 19, 21, 257
Germany, 34, 46, 53–54, 65, 76–77, 83, 87–89, 101–102, 117, 118, 120, 146, 168, 189, 191, 193–195
see also Franco-Prussian War
globalization, 8, 16, 24, 136, 158, 166, 168, 185, 189, 193, 201, 250
Gómez, Máximo, 56–57, 59
Google, 206
Gorbachev, Mikhail, 2, 120, 141, 145–149, 152
Great Britain, 4, 6, 32, 40–43, 53, 76, 102, 168, 176, 192, 196
British journalism, 36, 38, 40, 44, 57, 62–63, 73, 74, 227, 253
US journalism in London, 34, 39, 45, 46, 52, 62–63, 72, 84, 91, 105, 116, 222–225, 228
Greeley, Horace, 39, 45, 54
Guardian (London), 227–230

Haiti, 204, 218
Hall, Stuart, 10, 12
Hamilton, John Maxwell, 2, 21, 22, 24, 71–74, 91, 113–114, 161, 165, 216, 255
Hanley, Charles, 205, 224, 227
Havana, 57–59, 65, 122–126
see also Cuba
Heinzerling, Larry, 205, 222
Hoffman, David E., 205, 223, 225
Holsti, Ole, 6, 16–17

human rights, 135, 138, 154, 155, 163, 165–166, 171–172, 177, 191, 220, 246
Hutzler, Charles, 205, 226

ideology,
in international affairs, 15, 75–76, 89, 95, 102, 105–108, 117–118, 121, 134–135, 145, 169, 249, 256
and media, 8, 11–12, 106, 212, 231
and public opinion, 17, 42, 79, 143, 153–155, 244
immigration, 32, 61, 76, 90–91, 186–188, 190, 198–199, 203, 208, 216, 225
India, 168–169, 219, 237, 250
Mumbai 2008 attacks, 157–158, 195–202, 254
correspondence discourses, 196–201, 247
editorials about, 197–198
information flow, 2, 23–24, 74, 118, 219
infotainment, 71, 112, 156, 158, 161, 163, 198, 107, 211–214, 216, 225, 228, 240, 257
international communication, 5, 8, 15, 20, 23–24, 27, 114, 256
International Herald Tribune, 204, 219, 222
international relations, 8, 31–32, 170
agency, 5, 238
constructivism, 3–9, 238–240
and journalism, 1, 2, 5, 10, 20, 25, 32, 70, 215, 234, 238, 256
realism, 4, 7, 11, 29, 77, 108, 238
see also foreign policy
Iraq wars, 33, 114, 119, 158, 159, 162, 164–165, 167–169, 187, 191, 220, 223, 250, 257
Islam, 109, 129, 140–141, 143, 145, 167, 170, 196, 201, 245–246, 249
see also Afghanistan; India
Israel, 119, 127–133, 229, 245–246, 249, 253
see also Middle East
Italy, 40, 101–102, 107, 192, 193, 225
Mussolini takeover, 68, 89–95, 106
correspondence discourses, 89–95
editorials about, 92
see also Mussolini

James, Edwin, 89, 94
Japan, 40, 48, 61, 65–66, 68, 76, 77, 95–96, 100, 108, 117, 195, 226, 237, 248
opening of trade, 28, 35, 48–51, 64–65, 137, 244
correspondence discourses, 48–51, 246
editorials about, 49–50
attack on Shanghai. *See* China
Jarreau, Patrick, 228, 230
Jervis, Robert, 6–7
Jerusalem, 128, 131–133, 154, 224
see also Middle East
Johnson, Lyndon, 119, 128, 235
journalism (and journalists),
accountability, 21, 112, 160, 213, 216, 221, 230, 242
analytical, 39, 55–56, 65, 67, 70, 73–74, 78, 81–82, 94–95, 100, 105, 108, 112, 115, 126, 133, 141, 161, 163, 170, 173, 177, 185, 207–208, 215, 218, 223, 229–230, 251
audience influence on, 114, 160–161, 211–213, 219, 224, 232
audience interest in, 3, 17, 21, 36, 38, 64, 71, 113, 160–161, 210–212, 214, 233, 241–242
crisis of, 21, 32, 158, 206–215, 227, 233, 238, 241
criticism of, 3, 23–25, 29, 33, 71, 111, 158, 164, 209, 219, 229, 257
and diversity, 39, 70, 111, 178, 232
education, 2, 29, 67, 69, 97, 112, 208
ethics, 2, 69, 78, 103, 112, 212, 214, 224, 239
and foreign policy, 1, 13–16, 20, 65, 70, 114, 133, 149, 154–156, 162–163, 170, 172, 214, 218, 227, 235, 242, 248–251, 256
freelance, 206, 216, 218, 229
future of, 206–215
investigative, 68, 111, 113, 160, 162, 201, 207–209, 211–213, 224, 235
nonprofit, 74, 208, 216–217
online, 21, 32, 157, 159–160, 163–165, 197, 202, 206–207, 209–219, 222–230, 233–236, 254–256
as profession, 2, 29, 34–38, 47, 67–69, 71, 102, 106, 112, 153, 158–161, 207–208, 210, 212, 215, 217–218, 220, 223–224, 233–234, 240–241, 243
and public interest, 18–19, 33, 67–68, 72, 78, 106, 111, 159, 207, 209, 228, 233, 254–255, 258
and public trust, 111–112, 154, 159, 161, 163, 213–214
responsibility of, 21, 111, 212–213, 236–237

journalism (and journalists) (*cont.*)
  and technology, 8, 13–15, 20, 39, 56, 106, 158–159, 162, 197, 212, 217, 223, 240, 257
  see also democracy; news media
journalism history, 206–207, 209
  19th century, 34–40
  20th century, 68–71, 110–113, 159–160
  21st century, 160–161

Katzenstein, Peter, 4
Keller, Bill, 27, 180–184, 235–236, 240
Keen, Victor, 97–98
Kendall, George Wilkins, 39, 45–47
Kennedy, John F., 112, 177
Kerensky, Alexander, 85
Kissinger, Henry, 119, 135, 235, 240
Klerk, F.W. de, 178–180

Larsen, Henrik, 3, 4, 6, 8–9
Lawson, Victor, 72–74
Le Monde, 230
Lenin, Vladimir, 83, 85, 87–88, 93, 107, 149, 151, 249
Lippmann, Walter, 18, 71, 82, 161, 240
Los Angeles Times, 112, 116, 121, 123–125, 129, 131–134, 138, 141, 143–144, 147, 149, 161–162, 171, 173, 175, 177, 185, 188, 197, 205, 208, 222–226, 240, 247

Madero, Francisco, 79–80, 82
Madrid, 68, 101–107, 130, 244–245, 256
  see also Spain
Mandela, Nelson, 158, 177–183, 246, 253–254
marketplace of ideas, 18, 22, 24–25, 71, 206, 214, 221, 233, 239, 242, 256
Mathews, Linda, 134–138
Matthews, Herbert, 100–106, 122, 125, 242, 245
McKinley, William, 43, 56, 60–61
media effects, 11–16, 18, 163, 220
  and causality, 14, 18, 30, 163, 237, 240, 256
  on international relations, new model, 1, 3, 9–11, 13, 18–19, 28, 30, 65, 78, 121, 158, 205, 236–241, 256
Medill, Joseph, 40
Mexico, 38, 39, 41, 45, 75, 107, 161, 167–168, 201–202, 223, 237, 239, 249
  2000 elections, 158, 185–190, 193, 244, 246–247, 254
    correspondence discourses, 185–190
    editorials about, 187, 252
  revolution, 28, 68, 75, 78–82, 106–108, 125, 186, 203, 244
    correspondence discourses, 78–82
    editorials about, 81–82
Middle East, 31, 117, 119, 167, 223, 228, 231, 239, 246, 249, 256
  1967 war, 110, 116, 119, 127–133, 144, 154, 156, 167, 245, 253
    correspondence discourses, 127–133
    editorials about, 129
Miller, Derek, 13, 18
Minifie, James, 102–105
Moderwell, Hiram Kelly, 93–94
Moscow, 86, 123, 127, 140–141, 145, 150–151, 153, 168, 223
  see also Russia; Soviet Union
Mostar, 171–176, 252, 256
  see also Bosnian War
Mowrer, Paul Scott, 71, 255
Mowrer, Richard, 103–105
Mussolini, Benito, 68, 89–94, 107, 253
  see also Italy

nation-state, 8, 14, 157, 240
national identity, 2, 7–9, 14, 19, 25–26, 30, 192, 194, 236
  in IR, 4–5, 169, 238–239, 241
  media and, 3, 11, 38, 236, 241
national interest, 3, 9, 14, 33, 77, 87, 108, 166, 238, 250
New Orleans Picayune, 39, 44–45, 47, 50, 54–55, 58, 59, 61, 63
New York Herald, 35, 39, 44, 46–50, 54–59, 61, 63, 73, 78, 80–81, 85, 87–88, 251
New York Herald Tribune, 67, 72–74, 78, 91–92, 96–97, 100, 102, 116
New York Times,
  coverage by, 2, 27, 44, 49–50, 52–56, 58–60, 62–63, 78, 80–83, 85–89, 92–97, 100, 104, 121–125, 127–133, 138, 141–143, 147, 149–151, 153, 171, 175, 183–184, 187–188, 192, 194, 197, 199, 201, 246, 252, 254–255
  history of, 39–40, 72–73, 111, 114–116, 161–163, 204–206, 210, 212, 214, 219, 222, 224–225, 227, 236–237, 240, 242

New York Tribune, 39, 44–49, 51–54, 56, 58, 61–64, 73, 78, 80–81, 85–86, 233, 251, 255
news homogenization, 112, 128, 131–133, 148, 156, 161, 170, 201, 211, 245, 253
news language, 3, 8, 11–12, 29, 62–63, 126, 142, 148, 149, 173, 179, 187, 212, 239
news media,
as business, 15, 20–21, 26, 35, 67–69, 71, 106, 112–113, 158–161, 205–206, 208–210, 212–215, 224, 226, 230, 255, 257
and government, 14–15, 18, 26, 70, 110–111, 114, 159, 186, 208, 211, 220, 227, 229, 232, 235–236
news management by, 12, 74, 128, 132, 156, 158, 160, 231, 243, 245, 251, 253–254
manipulation of, 3, 9–10, 12–13, 23, 26, 43, 110, 133, 144, 164, 170, 173, 183, 188, 209, 215, 220, 236, 239, 252
as mediators, 2, 19, 21, 33, 60, 66, 69, 107, 160, 170, 201, 203, 205, 217, 227, 230–232, 236, 241, 255, 257
and military, 15, 36, 51–52, 54–55, 66, 111, 114–115, 164
and partisanship, 34, 36–37, 54, 69, 159, 161, 164, 207–208, 213–214, 231
power of, 2, 19, 26, 36, 67, 70, 107, 145, 155, 202, 211, 235, 254
watchdog function, 14, 70, 109–111, 121, 158, 214, 231, 235
news values, 29, 113–114, 177, 208, 212–213, 217, 219, 224, 233
Nixon, Richard, 111, 119–120, 134–135, 235
North American Free Trade Agreement, 166–167, 186
North Atlantic Treaty Organization, 118, 167–168, 172, 191
nuclear weapons, 4, 118, 119, 122, 123, 127, 145–148, 152–153, 166, 196–198, 200–202, 245, 247, 249
Nye, Joseph, 32, 168, 170, 241

Obama, Barack, 160, 168–169, 220, 230, 236–237
objectivity, 10, 20, 29, 32, 37, 54, 67–70, 73, 95, 103, 106, 110, 131, 152, 161, 212, 214, 242, 244
Ochs, Adolph, 72
Osnos, Peter, 205, 223, 225–226

Pakistan, 109, 140, 143, 196–197, 200, 202, 219, 225, 247
see also India
parachute journalism, 21, 32, 91, 162, 165, 202, 216–217, 226, 229, 253
Paris, 44–47, 52–53, 55–56, 65, 86, 222, 251
see also European Revolutions; France; Franco-Prussian War
Perry, Dan, 205, 224, 226
Perry, Matthew, 48–51, 61, 137, 155
Pew Research Center, 21, 162, 170, 207–213, 215, 218–219, 227
picturesqueness, 51, 55–56, 65, 91, 93–94, 99, 107, 123, 125, 126, 136–137, 153, 175
political knowledge, 3, 22, 28, 113, 163–164, 184, 204, 207, 211, 219–220, 233, 242
Porubcansky, Mark, 205, 223–226, 228, 233
primitiveness, 50, 59, 63, 81, 129, 132–133, 150, 180, 182, 189, 195
print journalism, 21, 28, 67, 112–113, 157, 159–161, 206–217, 233, 241, 257
see also journalism (and journalists); news media
propaganda, 70, 72, 74, 102, 118, 119, 164, 209, 231
public opinion, 16–19, 22
and media, 14–16, 37, 57–58, 60, 65, 71, 101, 114, 164, 235, 237, 241
and foreign policy, 14, 16–17, 43, 54, 56, 58, 60, 65, 71, 76, 114, 144, 164, 166–168, 172, 218, 220, 237, 239, 242
polls, 16, 76, 101, 113, 118, 120, 135, 164, 168–170, 186, 220
public relations, 17, 71, 110–112, 145, 156, 173, 180, 209, 240, 254
public sphere, 3, 10, 16, 37, 66, 71, 160, 207–208, 214–215, 233, 238, 240, 242
Pulitzer Prize, 113, 116, 159, 162, 221, 223, 224, 233

race, 41, 75, 85, 97, 177–185, 202
Raymond, Henry, 40
Reagan, Ronald, 112, 120–121, 139–140, 146, 178
religion, 37, 60, 62, 109, 125, 129, 131–133, 143, 146, 154, 157, 163, 165, 171–173, 196–197, 199, 204, 245, 247
reporting practices, 21, 27, 29–30, 32, 36, 50, 52–53, 58, 69–70, 91, 112, 131, 153, 174, 210–213, 217–218, 222–223, 227

reporting practices (*cont.*)
enterprise, 34, 36, 40, 52–53, 57–58, 63–65, 85, 89, 124
interview, 2, 19, 56, 59, 80, 85, 90–91, 98, 102, 105, 122–124, 148, 219, 253
personal storytelling, 85, 95, 97, 100–103, 106, 130, 161, 213, 218, 244, 252
speed, 35, 36, 38, 53, 56, 62, 64, 161, 162, 201, 211, 214, 218, 222–223
Reuters, 39, 211, 232
Roosevelt, Franklin Delano, 76–77, 96, 102, 108, 248
Rosenblum, Mort, 115, 194
Russia, 19–20, 96
1917 Revolution, 68, 70, 75–76, 79, 82–89, 91, 92, 102, 106–108, 149, 151, 244, 248–249, 253
correspondence discourses, 82, 84–89
editorials about, 84, 87–89, 252

Sambrook, Richard, 216–218
Sarajevo, 162, 173–175, 202, 254
see also Bosnian War
Schudson, Michael, 8, 36, 208–209, 257
Scovel, Sylvester, 57, 58
sensationalism, 37, 57, 59, 63, 71, 73, 80
Sharpton, Al, 184, 253
Sherwood, Harriet, 228–229
Shuster, Alvin, 205, 225–226
Serbia. *See* Bosnian War
socialism, 45, 53, 83, 87–89, 107, 142
social media, 157, 160, 197, 207, 212, 215–217, 220, 224, 226, 233, 241
soft power, 5, 32, 169, 231, 240–241
South Africa, 27, 201–202, 239
1994 elections, 28, 158, 166, 177–185, 188, 193, 246, 253–254
correspondence discourses, 177, 179–185
editorials about, 179
Soviet Union, 76–77, 101, 109, 117, 119, 127–129, 223, 245, 248, 250
end of, 2, 14, 28, 109–110, 117, 120, 145–154, 157, 163, 165, 177, 201, 219, 250, 256
correspondence discourses, 145, 148–153, 245-246
editorials about, 146–147
withdrawal from Afghanistan. *See* Afghanistan
Spain, 40, 57–60, 95, 108, 195, 249
Civil War, 68, 76, 90, 96, 100–108, 122, 124, 130, 245, 254
correspondence discourses, 100, 102–106
editorials about, 105
see also Cuba; Spanish-American War
Spanish-American War, 2, 35, 43, 56–57, 61, 66, 67, 74
Stephens, Mitchell, 36, 69, 113, 159, 205, 207, 256
stereotypes, 6, 33, 56, 59, 127, 129, 136, 139, 185, 248
Sweetland, Reginald, 97–98, 252

Taylor, Bayard, 39, 48, 51, 65, 244
terrorism, 15, 97, 101, 139, 147, 157–158, 166–167, 169–170, 178–179, 194, 196–201, 219, 247
see also 9/11; Afghanistan; India, 2008 attacks
Times (London), 40, 62
Tocqueville, Alexis de, 37–38
tourism, 126, 133, 136, 197–198, 215, 237
Truman, Harry S., 118

United Nations, 77, 128–129, 171–176, 178, 216, 220, 222

Vietnam War, 17, 110–111, 114, 118–121, 129, 134, 140–142, 162, 172, 223, 225, 235, 240

Wall Street Journal, 109, 116, 121, 123–126, 129, 131, 147, 162, 171, 173–174, 183, 187–188, 192, 194–195, 198, 200, 205, 210, 214, 221–222, 224
war reporting, 17–18, 25, 28, 38, 52–53, 59, 66, 72, 113, 130, 133, 159, 164–165, 174, 218
see also foreign correspondence
Washington Post, 111, 113, 116, 121, 123, 125, 129, 131, 133, 135, 138, 142, 146–147, 157, 162, 171, 173–175, 180, 183–184, 187, 191, 194, 198, 200, 205, 222–223, 237, 252–253
Washington press corps, 48, 50, 56, 78, 83, 112, 115, 139, 221, 230, 232
Wendt, Alexander, 3–5, 26
Wikileaks, 215, 235–236, 240
Will the Last Reporter Please Turn Out the Lights, 208–209, 215, 221
Williams, Bruce, 207, 217

Williams, Harold, 73, 86–89
Wilson, Woodrow, 69, 75–76, 79–80, 83, 248
Winter, Greg, 205, 222–225, 255
World War I, 53, 68, 70–72, 75–77, 83, 87–90, 95, 107, 194–195, 201, 249
World War II, 17, 49, 53, 68, 70, 72, 76–77, 80, 89, 94–95, 109, 114, 119, 129, 154, 170, 191, 194–195, 201, 248–249

Zapata, Emiliano, 79–81, 186
see also Mexico

Made in the USA
San Bernardino, CA
29 July 2015